1타 강사의 속성 과외!

토익 950+ 벼락치기

10일 완성 LC+RC

토익 950+ 벼락치기 10일 완성 LC+RC

초판 1쇄 인쇄 2022년 3월 2일
초판 1쇄 발행 2022년 3월 10일
초판 4쇄 발행 2024년 1월 8일

지 은 이 | 라수진
펴 낸 이 | 박경실
펴 낸 곳 | **PAGODA Books** 파고다북스
출판등록 | 2005년 5월 27일 제 300-2005-90호
주 소 | 06614 서울특별시 서초구 강남대로 419, 19층(서초동, 파고다타워)
전 화 | (02) 6940-4070
팩 스 | (02) 536-0660
홈페이지 | www.pagodabook.com

ISBN 978-89-6281-884-0 (13740)

파고다북스 www.pagodabook.com
파고다 어학원 www.pagoda21.com
파고다 인강 www.pagodastar.com
테스트 클리닉 www.testclinic.com

▎낙장 및 파본은 구매처에서 교환해 드립니다.

1타 강사의 속성 과외!

토익 950+ 벼락치기

10일 완성 LC+RC

PAGODA Books

목차

표현 중심 LC

전략 중심 RC

실전 모의고사

해설은 파고다북스 홈페이지(www.pagodabook.com)에서 다운로드하실 수 있습니다.

이 책의 구성과 특징

표현 중심 LC

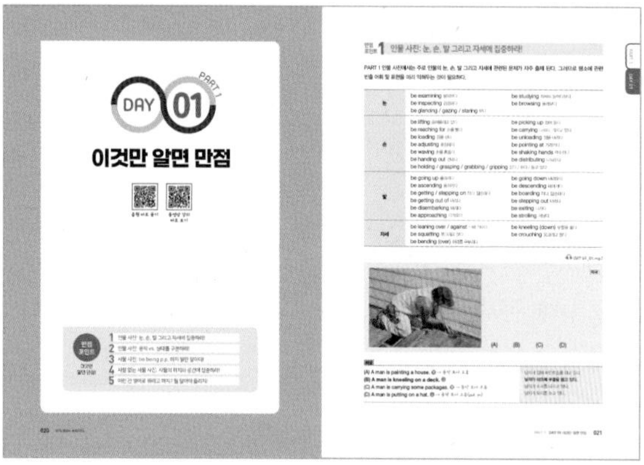
DAY 01
이것만 알면 만점

핵심 유형과 전략 소개

1타 강사가 소개하는 반드시 출제되는
빈출 고난도 문제 유형과 핵심 전략 학습 단계

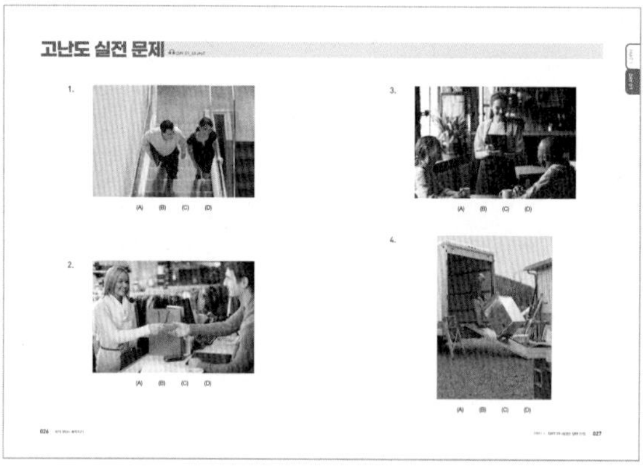
고난도 실전 문제

고난도 실전 문제

앞서 학습한 전략을 토대로 1타 강사가 선별한
적중율 100%의 실전 문제를 풀어보는 단계

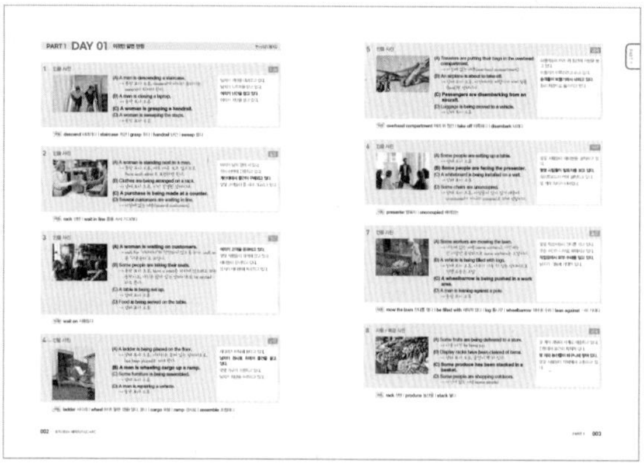
PART 1 DAY 01

고난도 실전 문제 해설

왜 정답인지 또는 오답인지를 명쾌하게
짚고 넘어가는 단계

전략 중심 RC

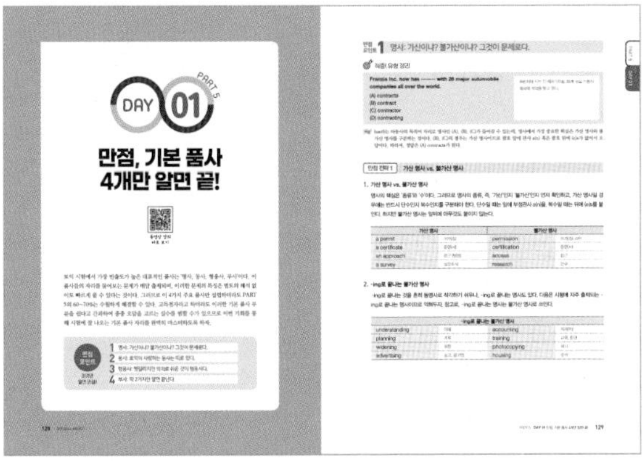

핵심 유형과 전략 소개

1타 강사가 소개하는 반드시 출제되는
빈출 고난도 문제 유형과 핵심 전략 학습 단계

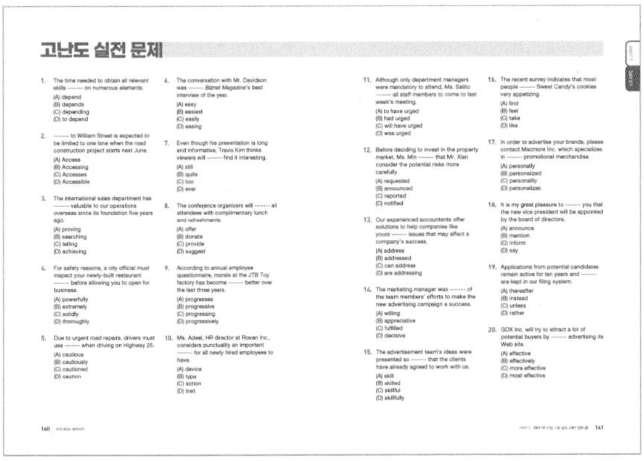

고난도 실전 문제

앞서 학습한 전략을 토대로 1타 강사가 선별한
적중율 100%의 실전 문제를 풀어보는 단계

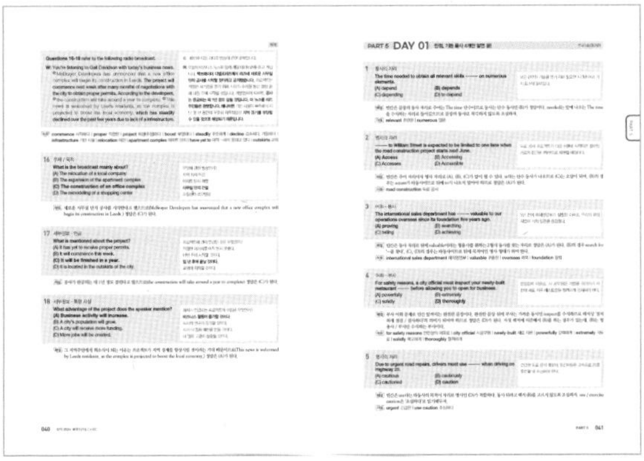

고난도 실전 문제 해설

왜 정답인지 또는 오답인지를 명쾌하게
짚고 넘어가는 단계

★ 시험 전 총정리를 위한 **실전 모의고사 3회** 제공
해설지 및 MP3 파일 무료 다운로드: www.pagodabook.com(QR코드 스캔)

효율적인 10일 벼락치기로 목표 점수 달성

저자 직강 무료 동영상 강의
큐알코드를 스캔해서 볼 수 있습니다.

이제 혼자 공부하지 마세요! 교재를 열심히 공부하고, 문제까지 다 풀었다면! 그런데 해설지를 봐도 알쏭달쏭한 문제들이 있다면, 저자 직강의 무료 동영상 강의로 모든 궁금증을 해결하세요!

토익 모의고사 추가 2회분 무료 다운로드
cafe.naver.com/pagodatoeicbooks 〈파고다 토익 – 공용자료실 → 온라인 실전 모의고사〉

토익 전문가들이 만든 실제 시험과 유사한 토익 모의고사 2회분을 무료로 다운로드 받을 수 있습니다. 문제지, 해설지, 무료 동영상 강의까지! 토익 시험 전 마무리 모의고사 놓치지 마세요!

LC/RC 파트별, 유형별 문제 무료 다운로드
cafe.naver.com/pagodatoeicbooks
〈파고다 토익 – 공용자료실 → LC 자료실 / RC 자료실〉

토익 어휘만 공부하실 건가요! 토익 시험의 파트별 연습 문제를 무료로 다운로드 받아 연습해 보세요. 토익 전문가들이 파트별 문제 유형을 분석하여 만든 엄청난 양의 문제를 다운로드 받으세요.

토익에 관한 모든 질문! 파고다 토익 카페
cafe.naver.com/pagodatoeicbooks

혼자 공부하는 혼공족들! 더 이상 외로운 혼공족이 아닙니다! 모르는 게 있어도, 해설지를 봐도 도저히 이해가 안가는 경우, 누구한테 질문할 수 있을까요? 파고다 토익 카페에 오시면 현직 토익 강사와 R&D 전문가들의 실시간 답변을 들을 수 있습니다.

단어 시험지 자동 생성기
www.pagodabook.com 〈각 교재별 단어 시험지 자동 생성기〉

단어를 외우기만 할 건가요? 외우고 나서 테스트를 해봐야죠. 「토익 950+ 벼락치기 10일 완성 LC+RC」의 단어 시험지 자동 생성기로 시험지를 만들어 테스트 해 보세요. 그룹 스터디 하는 학생들도 유용하게 활용할 수 있답니다.

다양한 토익 무료 컨텐츠
유튜브에서 〈Pagoda Books〉를 검색하세요.

파고다 어학원의 1타 선생님들의 다양한 토익 강의가 무료로 제공됩니다. 높은 품질의 수업을 무료로 수강하면서 목표 점수를 향해 매진하세요!

1타 강사의 10일 벼락치기 권장 학습 스케줄

반드시 교재 내용을 철저히 학습하고
문제를 다 푼 다음, 채점까지 하고
왜 틀렸는지 다시 한번 리뷰를 한 후
동영상 강의를 봐주세요.

★ **단어 시험지 자동 생성기: www.pagodabook.com**

DAY 01	• **LC** DAY 01 • **RC** DAY 01	**DAY 06**	• **LC** DAY 06 • **RC** DAY 06
DAY 02	• **LC** DAY 02 • **RC** DAY 02	**DAY 07**	• **LC** DAY 07 • **RC** DAY 07
DAY 03	• **LC** DAY 03 • **RC** DAY 03	**DAY 08**	실전 모의고사 1회
DAY 04	• **LC** DAY 04 • **RC** DAY 04	**DAY 09**	실전 모의고사 2회
DAY 05	• **LC** DAY 05 • **RC** DAY 05	**DAY 10**	실전 모의고사 3회

★ **보충 학습(파고다 토익 카페에서 다운로드 cafe.naver.com/pagodatoeicbooks)**

- PART 1 & 2 추가 문제 풀이
- PART 5 & 6 빈출 문제 공략
- PART 5 & 6 실전 문제 공략
- PART 7 독해 기초 공략 문제풀이
- PART 7 이중 지문 공략 문제풀이
- 추가 실전 모의고사 2회분

토익 파트별 벼락치기 전략

PART 1

1 벼락치기 전략

– 파트 1에 자주 출제되는 사진의 상황별 빈출 표현들을 정리하여 암기한다.
– 파트 1에서는 정답을 찾기보다 오답을 소거해야 한다. 오답 소거 연습을 반복하여 훈련한다.

2 오답 소거법

❶ 혼동되는 상태 동사와 동작 동사를 이용한 오답

(A) He is **wearing** glasses. 남자는 안경을 착용한 상태이다. ⓞ
(B) He is **putting on** glasses. 남자는 안경을 착용하고 있는 중이다. ⓧ

★ wear와 put on은 한국어로는 둘 다 '입다, 착용하다'로 해석이 되지만 wear는 착용한 상태를 나타내고 put on은 착용하는 동작을 나타내므로 주의해야 한다.

❷ 사진에 없는 사람, 사물, 동작을 연상시키는 오답

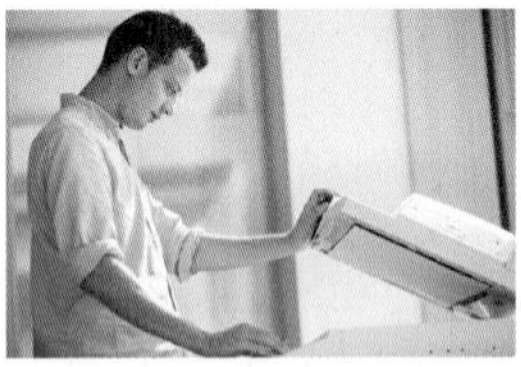

(A) He is **holding a lid** of a machine. 남자는 기계의 덮개를 손으로 잡고 있다. ⓞ
(B) He is **putting some papers on a machine**.
남자는 기계 위에 서류를 놓고 있다. ⓧ

★ 복사하기 위해서는 복사기 위에 서류를 놓아야 한다는 것을 연상해 (B)를 답으로 고를 수 있지만, 사진에 papers(서류)가 없기 때문에 답이 될 수 없다.

❸ 혼동되는 유사 발음의 단어를 이용한 오답

(A) She is **riding** bicycles. 여자는 자전거를 타고 있다. ⓞ
(B) She is **writing** on a notepad. 여자는 메모장에 무언가를 쓰고 있다. ⓧ

★ 맞는 표현은 is riding bicycles(자전거를 타고 있다)이지만 riding과 유사한 발음의 writing을 이용하여 전혀 다른 내용의 함정이 나온다.

❹ 여러 가지 의미가 있는 다의어를 이용한 오답

(A) The man is **pushing a stroller**. 남자가 유모차를 밀고 있다. ⓞ
(B) They are walking toward the **car park**. 사람들이 주차장 쪽으로 걸어가고 있다. ⓧ

★ park라는 단어만 듣고 사진의 공원을 연상해서 (B)를 답으로 고를 수 있는데, park의 다른 의미를 이용한 함정 문제이다. park는 주차와 관련된 의미로도 많이 출제된다.

PART 2

1 벼락치기 전략

– 질문의 앞 세 단어를 집중적으로 듣는 연습을 한다. 앞 세 단어에 정답 힌트가 다 들어 있다.
– 가장 까다로운 파트인 파트 2 역시 질문의 키워드에 어울리지 않는 오답을 소거하는 연습이 필요하다.
– 집중력이 가장 필요한 파트이다. 집중해서 25문제를 끝까지 푸는 연습을 해야 하고, 앞 문제에 신경 쓰느라 다음 문제를 놓치는 실수를 하지 않도록 훈련한다.
– "잘 모르겠습니다"류의 답을 암기해 두자.

2 오답 소거법

❶ 의문사 의문문에 Yes / No 등으로 답하는 오답

Q **When will Mr. Kim return from the conference?** Mr. Kim은 언제 콘퍼런스에서 돌아오나요?
(A) He was in the meeting this morning. 아침에 회의에 있었는데요. ⓞ
(B) **Yes**, he will participate in the **conference**. 네, 그는 콘퍼런스에 참가할 거예요. ⓧ

★ conference가 반복되어 (B)가 정답처럼 들리지만, 의문사로 시작하는 의문문에는 Yes나 No로 답할 수 없다.

❷ 똑같은 발음 또는 유사한 발음을 이용한 오답

Q **Have you reviewed the report?** 보고서를 검토했나요?
(A) I just got back from my vacation. 휴가에서 막 돌아왔어요. (그래서 아직 검토하지 못했다) ⓞ
(B) It has a nice **view**. 전망이 참 좋네요. ⓧ

★ (B)는 내용상 전혀 상관없는 오답이지만 질문의 review와 발음이 비슷한 view를 이용한 함정이다. 똑같은 발음 또는 유사한 발음이 들리면 왠지 정답처럼 들리지만, 오답 함정인 경우가 대부분이므로 주의해야 한다.

❸ 연상되는 어휘를 이용한 오답

Q **Where is the museum?** 박물관은 어디에 있나요?
(A) It is on 5th Avenue. 5번가에 있어요. ⓞ
(B) It was a great **exhibit**. 아주 멋진 전시회였어요. ⓧ

★ (B)는 질문과는 상관없는 오답이지만 질문의 museum(박물관)을 듣고 연상되는 exhibit(전시회)를 이용한 함정이다. 의미상 관련이 있는 어휘가 보기에서 들리면 왠지 정답처럼 들리지만, 오답 함정인 경우가 많으므로 주의해야 한다.

❹ 질문과 응답의 주어 불일치 오답

Q **How did you enjoy your stay at our hotel?** 저희 호텔에서의 숙박은 어떠셨나요?
(A) It was great. 아주 좋았어요. ⓞ
(B) **He** stayed late. 그는 늦게까지 있었어요. ⓧ

★ stay라는 같은 단어가 반복되어 (B)가 정답처럼 들리지만, 질문에서의 주어가 you였기 때문에 답은 I로 나와야 한다. (B)는 주어가 He라서 답이 될 수 없다. 질문은 you(2인칭)에 대해 묻고 있지만, He(3인칭)로 대답한 오답이다.

PART 3

1 벼락치기 전략

- 내용어 위주로 들으면서 답을 바로바로 골라내는 연습을 해야 한다.
- 패러프레이징 문제가 반 이상이 출제되므로 문제를 풀면서 패러프레이징 된 표현들의 짝을 정리하여 외워 둔다. 파트 4도 마찬가지이다.
- 화자 의도 파악 문제는 화자가 말한 문장의 문자적인 해석이 아니라 대화의 전반적인 흐름 이해가 필요하다. 평소 단순 듣기에서 벗어나 대화의 전반적 흐름을 이해하는 훈련이 필요하다. 하지만 난이도가 가장 높은 문제이기 때문에 잘 모르겠으면 빨리 포기하고 다음 문제에 집중하는 것도 전략 중 하나이다. 파트 4도 마찬가지이다.

2 공략법

❶ 대화를 듣기 전에 문제를 먼저 읽는다. 문제를 미리 읽으면서 키워드에 표시해둔다. 이는 파트 3와 파트 4 공통이다.

- **What** are the speakers mainly **discussing**? 화자들은 주로 무엇을 논의하고 있는가?
  ➲ 주제를 찾는 문제임을 미리 파악한다.
- **What** is **special** about the **product**? 그 제품에 대해 특별한 점은 무엇인가?
  ➲ 어떤 제품에 대해 특별한 점을 들을 준비를 한다.

❷ 문제의 순서와 문제에 대한 힌트가 나오는 순서는 대개 일치하므로 대화를 들으면서 세 문제에 대한 힌트 표현들을 바로바로 포착하여 차례대로 답을 체크해 나가야 한다. 마찬가지로 파트 3와 파트 4 공통이다.

대화 전반부
↓
대화 중반부
↓
대화 후반부

세 문제를 읽어주고
정답 고를 시간을 준다.
(각 문제 간격 8초)

▶▶

첫 번째 문제 힌트
(보기를 보고 있다가 힌트가 들리면 바로 정답 체크!)
↓
두 번째 문제 힌트
(보기를 보고 있다가 힌트가 들리면 바로 정답 체크!)
↓
마지막 문제 힌트
(보기를 보고 있다가 힌트가 들리면 바로 정답 체크!)

★ 대화가 끝남과 동시에 정답 체크를 끝내고,
남는 약 24초 동안 다음 문제를 미리 읽기 시작한다.

PART 4

1 벼락치기 전략

- 문제로 출제되는 담화의 종류는 정해져 있다. 방송, 광고, 연설 등 각 담화의 종류별로 정해져 있는 화제 전개 방식을 익혀 두면 앞으로 나올 내용을 쉽게 예측할 수 있다.
- 각 글의 종류별로 정답 힌트가 나오는 시그널 표현들이 있으므로 그 시그널 표현을 반드시 익혀 둔다.

2 공략법

❶ 각 담화의 종류별로 정해져 있는 화제 전개 방식을 익혀 둔다.

- **Questions 71-73 refer to the following announcement.** 71번-73번은 다음 안내 방송을 참조하시오.
  ➲ 디렉션에서 announcement(안내 방송)라는 담화의 종류를 파악하자마자 안내 방송의 전형적인 화제 전개 방식을 떠올린다. 안내 방송은 장소에 따라 세부적인 내용에는 차이가 있지만, 전반적인 전개 방식은 화자의 자기소개, 청자나 장소에 대한 정보, 안내 방송의 주제 언급 후, 관련 세부 사항 당부나 요청 사항 전달 순으로 전개된다.

❷ 각 문제별로 정답 힌트가 나오는 시그널 표현들은 익혀 두었다가 나오면 바로 정답을 고를 준비를 한다.

- **Where is the announcement taking place?** 안내 방송이 어디에서 이루어지고 있는가? (장소 문제)
  장소를 묻는 문제가 나오면

  Welcome to 장소. 장소에 오신 것을 환영합니다.
  Thank you for coming to [join / attend] 장소. 장소에 와 주셔서[함께해 주셔서 / 참석해 주셔서] 감사합니다.

  와 같은 표현들이 정답 힌트가 나오는 시그널 표현이다.

- **Who is the speaker?** 화자는 누구인가? (화자의 정체 문제)
  화자가 누구인지를 묻는 문제가 나오면

  I'm/My name is 이름. 저는/제 이름은 이름입니다.
  I'm a 직업 / 직책. 저는 직업 / 직책입니다.
  As 직업 / 직책, I ~. 직업/직책으로서, 저는 ~.

  와 같은 표현들이 정답 힌트가 나오는 시그널 표현이다.

- **What are listeners instructed to do?** 청자들은 무엇을 하도록 지시 받는가? (요청, 지시 사항 문제)
  요청, 지시 사항을 묻는 문제가 나오면

  Please ~. ~해 주세요.
  I would like you to ~. 당신이 ~해 주셨으면 합니다.

  와 같은 표현들이 정답 힌트가 나오는 시그널 표현이다.

PART 5

1 벼락치기 전략

– 무조건 해석부터 하지 말고 선택지를 보고 [문법 문제 / 어휘 문제 / 접속사, 전치사 문제] 중 어떤 문제인지부터 파악한다. 문법 문제는 해석 없이도 답이 나오는 문제가 대부분이므로 최대한 시간을 절약할 수 있는 방법으로 풀어 나가야 한다.
– 고득점을 얻기 위해서는 한 단어를 외우더라도 품사, 파생어, 용법을 함께 암기해야 한다. 예를 들어, announce와 notify를 똑같이 '알리다'라고 외워 두면 두 단어가 같이 선택지로 나오는 어휘 문제는 풀 수 없다. notify 뒤에는 사람만이 목적어로 나온다는 사실을 꼭 알아 두어야 한다.

2 공략법

❶ 문법 문제

한 단어의 네 가지 형태가 선택지로 나오는 문제들이다. 문법 문제는 빈칸이 [주어, 동사, 목적어, 보어, 수식어] 중에 어떤 자리인지를 파악해서 선택지 중 알맞은 품사나 형태를 고르는 문제이다.

- **Billy's Auto Repair has ------- with 15 different parts suppliers.**
  (A) contracting (B) contracts (C) contractor (D) contract

  ➲ 빈칸은 목적어 자리로 명사가 들어가야 하는데 보기에 명사가 세 개나 나와 있다. 이런 문제들은 자리만 찾는 것으로 끝나지 않고 한 단계 더 나아가 명사의 특성을 알고 있어야 풀 수 있는 문제이다. 한정사 없이 가산 단수 명사는 쓸 수 없으므로 복수 명사 (B)가 답이 되는 문제이다.

❷ 어휘 문제

같은 품사의 네 가지 다른 단어가 선택지로 나오는 문제이다. 어휘 문제는 해석을 해야만 풀 수 있고, 어려운 문제의 경우에는 가산/불가산 명사의 구분, 자/타동사의 구분과 같은 문법 사항까지 같이 포함되어 출제되기도 한다.

- **I have enclosed a copy of my résumé for your ------- and look forward to hearing from you soon.**
  (A) explanation (B) participation (C) reference (D) consideration

  ➲ 빈칸은 전치사 for의 목적어 자리에 어떤 명사 어휘를 넣을지 고르는 문제인데 '당신의 고려를 위해 제 이력서를 첨부합니다' 정도는 해석해야만 정답 (D)를 고를 수 있는 문제로 어형 문제보다는 훨씬 난이도가 높다.

❸ 접속사 / 전치사 문제

종속접속사, 등위접속사, 전치사, 부사 등이 선택지에 같이 나오는 문제를 문법 문제라고 한다. 접속사/전치사 문제는 그 문장의 구조를 파악하여 구와 절을 구분하고 절이라면 어떤 절인지를 파악해야 하는 어려운 문제들로 대부분 해석까지도 필요하다.

- **We need more employees on the production line ------- production has increased by 60 percent.**
  (A) although (B) since (C) because of (D) so

  ➲ 빈칸은 두 개의 절을 연결하는 접속사 자리이다. 전치사인 (C)는 답이 될 수 없고, 접속사 (A), (B), (D) 중에서 '생산이 증가했기 때문에 추가 직원을 고용해야 한다'라는 의미에 맞는 (B)를 답으로 고르는 문제이다.

PART 6

1 벼락치기 전략

- 파트 5처럼 단순히 문장 구조나 문법을 묻는 문제도 출제되지만, 전체적인 내용이나 앞뒤 문장 내용과 연결되는 어휘나 시제, 접속부사를 묻는 문제들이 주로 출제된다는 것에 유의한다.
- 접속부사가 적어도 두 문제는 꼭 출제되므로 접속부사 리스트를 완전히 외워 두어야 한다.
- 문맥상 적절한 문장 고르기 문제는 빈칸 앞뒤 문장의 대명사나 연결어 등을 확인하고 상관 관계를 파악한다.
- 지문의 길이가 짧기 때문에 전체 내용을 파악하는 데 많은 시간이 걸리지 않으므로 정독해서 읽으면 오히려 더 쉽게 해결할 수 있다.

2 공략법

❶ 어휘 문제

파트 5 어휘 문제와는 달리 그 한 문장만 봐서는 여러 개가 답이 될 수 있을 것 같은 선택지들이 나온다. 따라서 파트 6의 어휘 문제는 앞뒤 문맥을 정확히 파악하여 답을 골라야 한다. 파트 6에서는 특히 어휘 문제가 어려우므로 전체 맥락을 파악하여 신중히 답을 고른다.

❷ 문법 문제

한 단어의 네 가지 형태가 선택지로 나오는 문제가 문법 문제이다. 파트 5와 마찬가지 방법으로 풀면 되지만, 동사 시제 문제는 문맥을 파악하는 까다로운 문제로 출제된다.

❸ 문장 고르기 문제

파트 6에서 가장 어려운 문제로 전체적인 문맥을 파악하고, 접속부사나 시제 등을 종합적으로 봐야 답을 고를 수 있다.

❹ 접속사/전치사 문제

접속사/전치사 문제는 파트 5와 같이 보통 문장의 구조를 파악하여 구와 절을 구분하는 문제로 출제된다. 평소에 전치사와 접속사, 접속부사의 품사를 철저하게 외워 두어야 한다. 같은 접속사들끼리 선택지에 나와 고르는 문제들은 어휘 문제가 되므로 역시 해석이 필요한 문제들이다.

PART 7

1 벼락치기 전략

- 파트 7은 RC에서 반 이상을 차지하는 중요한 파트이므로 빠르고 정확한 독해력이 필요하다. 어휘력을 쌓고 문장의 구조를 파악하는 훈련을 통해 독해력을 뒷받침하는 기본기를 다져야 한다.
- 문자 메시지나 온라인 채팅은 난이도가 비교적 높지 않다. 그러나 구어체적 표현이 많이 나오고 문자 그대로의 사전적인 의미가 아닌 문맥상 그 안에 담겨 있는 숨은 뜻을 찾는 화자 의도 파악 문제가 꼭 출제되기 때문에 평소 구어체 표현을 숙지하고 대화의 흐름을 파악하는 연습을 한다.
- 질문의 키워드를 찾고 질문이 요구하는 핵심 정보를 본문에서 신속하게 찾아내는 연습이 필요하다.
- 본문에서 찾아낸 정답 정보는 선택지에서 다른 표현으로 제시되므로 같은 의미를 여러 가지 다른 표현들(paraphrased expressions)로 전달하는 연습이 필요하다.

2 공략법

❶ 지문 순서대로 풀지 말자.

파트 7은 처음부터 또는 마지막부터 순서대로 풀지 않아도 된다. 15개의 지문 중에서 당연히 쉬운 것부터 먼저 풀고 어려운 문제는 시간이 남으면 푼다는 마음으로 풀어야 한다. 다음과 같은 순서로 문제를 풀어 보도록 한다.

- **난이도 하:** 광고, 온라인 채팅, 양식(청구서, 주문서, 초대장 등), 웹페이지
- **난이도 중:** 이메일, 편지, 회람, 공지, 첫 번째 이중 지문, 첫 번째 삼중 지문
- **난이도 상:** 기사, 두 번째 이중 지문, 나머지 삼중 지문

❷ 패러프레이징 된 정답을 찾는 것이 핵심이다.

같은 어휘는 절대 반복되지 않는다. 정답은 지문에 나온 표현을 다른 말로 바꿔 나온다. 문제를 풀면서 패러프레이징 된 표현들의 짝을 정리하여 외워 둔다.

❸ 지문 내용에 기반하여 정답을 찾는다.

정답은 반드시 지문 내용에 기반하여 사실인 것만 고른다. 절대 '그럴 것 같다, 그렇겠지'라고 상상하여 답을 고르면 안 된다. 파트 7 문제 유형 중에는 추론해야 하는 문제들이 많이 나오기는 하지만 아무리 추론 문제이더라도 지문에 있는 근거 문장을 패러프레이징한 보기를 찾는 문제일 뿐이다. 추론 이상의 상상은 금물이다.

1타 강사의 시험 당일 20분 벼락치기 꿀팁!

토익 시험은 오전 시험과 오후 시험에 따라 아래와 같이 진행된다.

오전시험	9:30~9:45	9:45~9:50	9:50~10:05	10:05~10:10	10:10~10:55	10:55~12:10
오후시험	2:30~2:45	2:45~2:50	2:50~3:05	3:05~3:10	3:10~3:55	3:55~5:10
	15분	5분	15분	5분	45분	75분
	답안지 작성 Orientation	수험자 휴식 시간	신분증 확인 (감독교사)	문제지 배부, 파본 확인	듣기 평가(LC)	읽기 평가(RC) 2차 신분확인

오전 9시 30분부터 9시 50분 까지(오후 시험일 경우는 오후 2시 30분부터 2시 50분까지) 20분간은 답안지 작성에 대한 오리엔테이션과 휴식시간이다. 이 시간에 처음으로 시험을 보는 학생이 아니라면 오리엔테이션 내용을 귀담아 들을 필요는 없다. 처음 시험을 보는 학생들도 OMR 카드 작성은 그렇게 어려운 일은 아니다. 이 시간에 충분한 벼락치기가 가능하다! 이 시간에는 LC 보다는 RC 내용을 정리하면서 벼락치기 하는 것이 효율적이다.

1. 접속사, 전치사, 접속부사 표를 다시 한 번 보면서 정리한다.
2. 가산 명사와 불가산 명사 표를 보면서 다시 한 번 정리한다.
3. 자동사 + 전치사 표를 보면서 특정 전치사가 붙는 자동사들을 다시 한 번 외운다.
4. 빈출 접속부사 표를 외워 둔다.
5. 가장 시험에 많이 출제되는 전치사 리스트를 보고 다신 외운다.

PART 1

LC PART 1은 총 6문제로 구성되어 있다. 문항수도 적은 편이고 비교적 난이도가 쉬운 문제로 구성이 되어 다른 PART에 비해 부담이 적은 편이다. 또한, 고득점자의 경우 PART 1은 거의 다 만점을 맞는 부분이기도 하다. 하지만, 간혹 전혀 모르는 단어나 표현이 나올 경우 실수를 하게 된다면 토익 시험의 첫 파트인 만큼 전체 시험 페이스에 영향을 줄 수가 있으므로 너무 안일하게 생각하지 않아야 할 파트이기도 하다. 설사 잘 안 들리거나 모르는 어휘나 표현이 나와 정답을 잘 못 듣더라도 걱정할 필요가 전혀 없다. 오답 버리기 전략과 PART 1 만점 전략을 잘 숙지한다면, 정확하게 보기를 못 들었다 하더라도 충분히 정답을 찾을 수가 있기 때문이다. 그렇다면, 어떤 전략들이 있는지 살펴보자.

DAY 01

LC	DAY 01	DAY 02	DAY 03	DAY 04	DAY 05	DAY 06	DAY 07
RC	DAY 01	DAY 02	DAY 03	DAY 04	DAY 05	DAY 06	DAY 07

PART 1 만점 핵심 공략

1. 6문제, 한 문제도 놓치지 마라!
2. 정답을 찾지 말고, 오답을 버려라!
3. 사진에 없는 단어면 과감히 버려라!
4. 사진에 나와있지도 않은 것을 확대 해석하여 상상하지 마라!
5. 토익은 포괄적이고 집합적인 개념을 좋아한다.

   예 fork lift 지게차, crane 크레인 → heavy machinery 중장비
   wipe 닦다, sweep 빗자루로 쓸다, mop 대걸레질하다 → clean 청소하다

PART 1

DAY 01

이것만 알면 만점

음원 바로 듣기

동영상 강의 바로 보기

만점 포인트

이것만 알면 만점!

1 인물 사진: 눈, 손, 발 그리고 자세에 집중하라!
2 인물 사진: 동작 vs. 상태를 구분하라!
3 사물 사진: be being p.p. 하지 말란 말이야!
4 사람 없는 사물 사진: 사물의 위치와 공간에 집중하라!
5 이런 건 영어로 뭐라고 하지? 뭘 알아야 들리지!

만점 포인트 1 인물 사진: 눈, 손, 발 그리고 자세에 집중하라!

PART 1 인물 사진에서는 주로 인물의 눈, 손, 발 그리고 자세에 관련된 문제가 자주 출제 된다. 그러므로 평소에 관련 빈출 어휘 및 표현을 미리 익혀두는 것이 필요하다.

눈	be examining 살펴보다 be inspecting 점검하다 be glancing / gazing / staring 보다	be studying 자세히 들여다보다 be browsing 둘러보다
손	be lifting 들어올리고 있다 be reaching for 손을 뻗다 be loading 짐을 싣다 be adjusting 조정하다 be waving 손을 흔들다 be handing out 건네다 be holding / grasping / grabbing / gripping 잡다 / 쥐다 / 들고 있다	be picking up 집어 들다 be carrying 나르다, 가지고 있다 be unloading 짐을 내리다 be pointing at 가리키다 be shaking hands 악수하다 be distributing 나눠주다
발	be going up 올라가다 be ascending 올라가다 be getting / stepping on 타다, 탑승하다 be getting out of 내리다 be disembarking 내리다 be approaching 다가오다	be going down 내려오다 be descending 내려가다 be boarding 타다, 탑승하다 be stepping out 내리다 be exiting 나가다 be strolling 거닐다
자세	be leaning over / against ~에 기대다 be squatting 쪼그리고 앉다 be bending (over) 허리를 구부리다	be kneeling (down) 무릎을 꿇다 be crouching 웅크리고 앉다

DAY 01_01.mp3

미국

(A) (B) (C) (D)

해설

(A) A man is painting a house. ⊗ ··· 동작 묘사 오류
(B) A man is kneeling on a deck. ⓞ
(C) A man is carrying some packages. ⊗ ··· 동작 묘사 오류
(D) A man is putting on a hat. ⊗ ··· 동작 묘사 오류(put on)

남자가 집에 페인트칠을 하고 있다.
남자가 데크에 무릎을 꿇고 있다.
남자가 소포를 나르고 있다.
남자가 모자를 쓰고 있다.

인물 사진에서는 '동작'인지 '상태'인지를 반드시 구분해야 한다.

만점 포인트 2 인물 사진: 동작 vs. 상태를 구분하라!

동작과 상태의 대표적인 예로는 모자를 쓰고 있을 때, '동작'일 경우 put on a hat, '상태'일 경우 wear a hat으로 쓴다.

동작		상태
put on 입다 try on 입어보다 tie 묶다 / 매다	take off 벗다 adjust 조정하다 fasten 매다	wear 입다
pick up 집다	lift 들어 올리다	hold, grab, grasp, grip 잡다
get on / in 타다 get off / out of 내리다 enter 들어가다	board, embark 탑승하다 disembark 내리다 exit 나오다	ride 타다

DAY 01_02.mp3

영국

(A) (B) (C) (D)

해설

(A) Display racks are being refilled. ⊗ ···› 상태 묘사 오류
(B) The man is lifting a basket. ⊗ ···› 동작 묘사 오류, lift는 들어 올리는 동작
(C) Merchandise is being arranged. ⊗ ···› 상태 묘사 오류
(D) The man is studying an item. ⓞ

진열대가 채워지고 있는 중이다.
남자가 바구니를 들어 올리고 있다.
물건이 배열되고 있는 중이다.
남자가 물건을 자세히 살펴보고 있다.

만점 포인트 3 사물 사진: be being p.p. 하지 말란 말이야!

진행 수동 「be + being + p.p.」는 사물의 입장에서 봤을 때 누군가에 의해서 행해지고 있을 때 사용한다. 따라서, 사람이 없는 사진이라면 진행 수동은 오답이 될 수밖에 없다. 하지만, 사람이 없어도 진행 수동 「be + being + p.p.」를 쓸 수 있는 다음 예외의 경우(display, cast, grow)를 조심하자.

be being p.p. 예외

Some items **are being displayed** on the shelf. 상품들이 선반에 진열되어 있다.
Shadows **are being cast**. 그림자들이 드리워져 있다.
Some plants **are being grown**. 식물들이 자라고 있다.

DAY 01_03.mp3

미국

(A) (B) (C) (D)

해설

(A) Desserts are being served on a table. ⓧ ···› 사물 사진 be being p.p. — 디저트가 테이블에 내어지고 있다.
(B) Cakes are being cut into pieces. ⓧ ···› 사물 사진 be being p.p. — 케익이 조각으로 잘려지고 있다.
(C) Shelves are being stocked with baked goods. ⓧ ···› 사물 사진 be being p.p. — 선반이 제빵으로 채워지고 있다.
(D) A variety of cakes are on display. ⓞ — **다양한 케익이 진열되어 있다.**

만점 포인트 4 사람 없는 사물 사진: 사물의 위치와 공간에 집중하라!

PART 1에서 인물이 등장하지 않는 사물 사진에서는 '사물의 위치 묘사'와 그 '공간의 사용 여부'에 대해서 물어보는 문제가 반드시 출제된다. 그러므로 평소에 사물의 위치를 의미하는 어휘와 표현을 익혀두는 것이 필요하다.

사물의 위치 및 상태	be placed / positioned / put / set 놓여 있다 be stacked / piled 쌓여 있다 be mounted 고정되어 있다 be scattered 흩어져 있다 overlook 내려다보다 be stocked / filled with ~로 채워져 있다 lead to ~로 이어지다 be deserted 비어 있다	be arranged / organized 정리되어 있다 be propped against ~에 받쳐 있다 be erected 세워져 있다 span 가로지르다 cast a shadow 그림자를 드리우다 be reflected in / on ~에 비치다 be unattended, left unattended 방치된 채 있다
공간 사용 여부	be taken / occupied 차지하다 / 사용하다 be unoccupied / vacant / empty 비어 있다	

DAY 01_04.mp3

호주

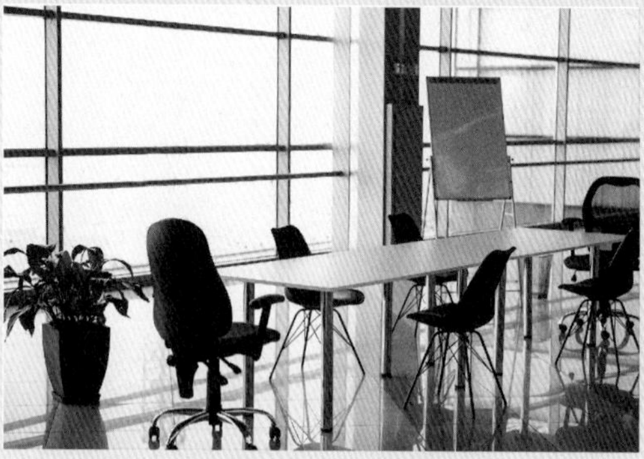

(A) (B) (C) (D)

해설

(A) Potted plants are being placed on a table. ⓧ
···› 사물 사진 be being p.p.

(B) The chairs have been stacked on top of each other. ⓧ
···› 사물 상태 오류

(C) The seats are all unoccupied. ⓞ

(D) Light fixtures are hanging from the ceiling. ⓧ
···› 사진에 없는 내용(light fixtures)

화분이 테이블 위에 놓여지고 있다.
의자가 겹겹이 쌓여져 있다.
좌석이 비어 있다.
조명이 천장에 매달려 있다.

만점 포인트 5 이런 건 영어로 뭐라고 하지? 뭘 알아야 들리지!

PART 1 만점을 위해서 알아두어야 하는 어휘이다. 모르는 어휘가 나왔을 때 당황하지 않기 위해 꼭 알아두자.

wheelbarrow	외바퀴 손수레	utensil	주방기구, 요리기구
rack	선반, 옷걸이, 거치대	garment, apparel	옷, 의류
crate, carton	상자	patio, terrace	파티오, 테라스
canopy	천막	awning	차양
ledge	창문 아래 선반	windowsill	창문턱
stool	등받이 없는 의자	stall	가판대
partition	칸막이	pottery	도자기류
broom, broomstick	빗자루	spoke	바큇살
outlet	콘센트	paddle, oar	노
pier, dock	부두	lamppost	가로등
curb	연석, 턱	fountain	분수대
ramp	경사로	overhead compartment	머리 위 짐칸
scaffolding	(공사장의) 비계	railing, handrail	난간
column, pillar	기둥	pavilion	가건물, 경기장
light fixture	조명	light bulb	전구
podium	연단	electrical wire	전선
forklift	지게차	rake	갈고리(갈퀴)
body of water	수역	scale	저울
fishing pole / rod	낚싯대	rug	깔개
potted plant	화분	bucket	양동이
(door) knob, handle	손잡이	lid	뚜껑

DAY 01_05.mp3

호주

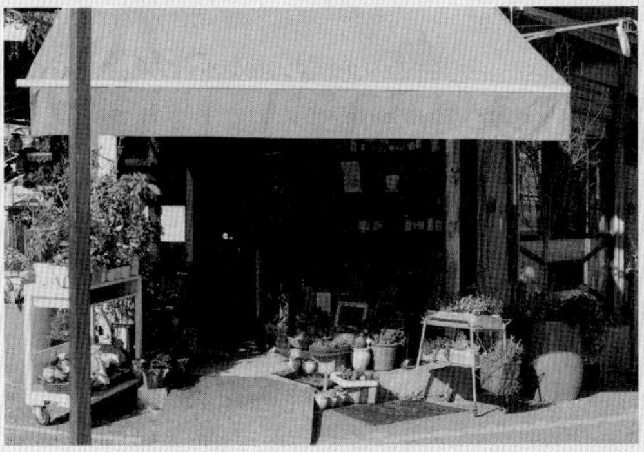

(A) (B) (C) (D)

해설

(A) A shop owner is setting up a canopy. ✗ ···› 사진에 없는 내용(a shop owner)
(B) Customers are shopping outside. ✗ ···› 사진에 없는 내용(customers)
(C) Potted plants are being delivered to a store. ✗ ···› 사물 사진 be being p.p.
(D) Some merchandise is shaded by an awning. O

한 상인이 천막을 설치하고 있다.
고객들이 야외에서 쇼핑을 하고 있다.
화분들이 가게로 배달되고 있다.
차양이 상품 위에 그늘을 만들고 있다.

고난도 실전 문제

DAY 01_06.mp3

1.

(A) (B) (C) (D)

2.

(A) (B) (C) (D)

3.

(A) (B) (C) (D)

4.

(A) (B) (C) (D)

고난도 실전 문제

5.

(A) (B) (C) (D)

6.

(A) (B) (C) (D)

7.

(A) (B) (C) (D)

8.

(A) (B) (C) (D)

9.

(A) (B) (C) (D)

10.

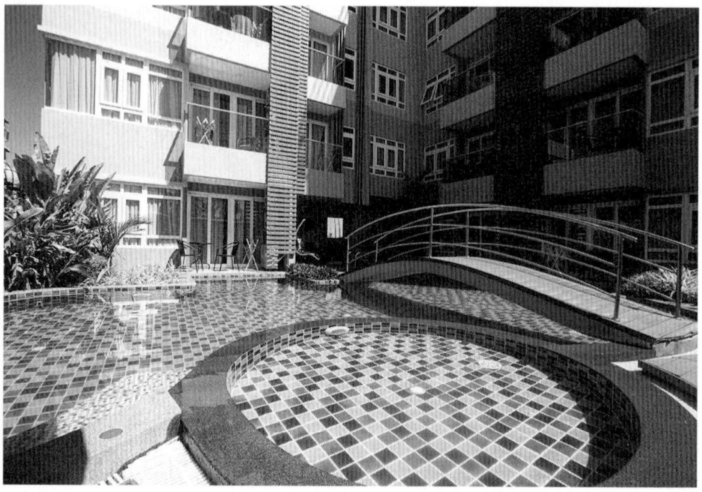

(A) (B) (C) (D)

11.

(A) (B) (C) (D)

12.

(A) (B) (C) (D)

고난도 실전 문제

13.

(A) (B) (C) (D)

14.

(A) (B) (C) (D)

15.

(A) (B) (C) (D)

PART 2

최근 들어, PART별 난이도가 PART 2 〉 PART 4 〉 PART 3 〉 PART 1으로 PART 2의 난이도가 점점 높아지고 있어 고득점자들이 만점을 받기가 힘들어졌다. 단순하게 질문에 대한 응답을 하는 것으로 그치지 않고, 우회적으로 표현을 하거나 예상치 못한 답변이 정답으로 출제가 되므로 그 어느 파트보다 순발력과 집중력을 요하는 파트가 되었다. 하지만 PART 2 역시 다른 파트와 마찬가지로 시험에 자주 출제되는 정답 패턴이 있으므로 이를 익힌다면 난이도와 상관없이 정답을 쉽게 찾을 수 있다.

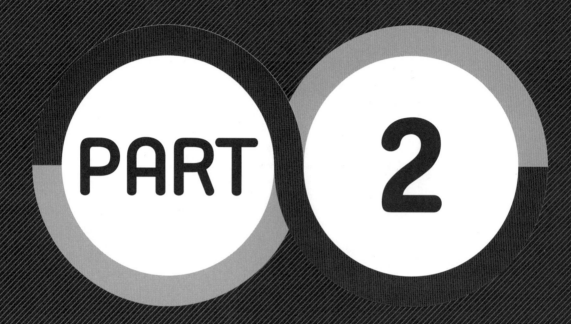

DAY 02-03

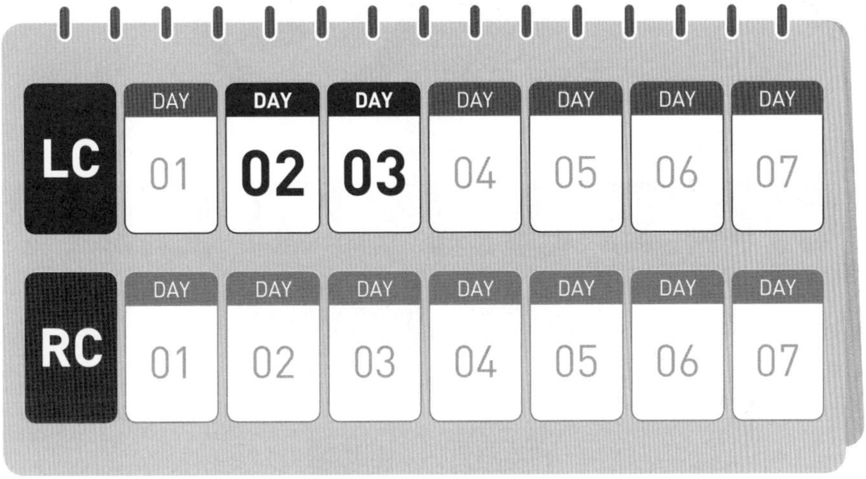

PART 2 만점 핵심 공략

- 최근 들어 어려워지고 있는 PART 2는 '순발력'과 '집중력'이 생명이다.
- PART 2 '오답 5계명'을 명심하여 정답을 찾기보다는 오답을 버리자!
- 출제 빈도가 높은 '의문사 의문문'부터 확실하게 해 두자.
- 토익이 좋아하는 PART 2 정답 패턴을 익히자.
- 토익은 진화하고 있다. PART 2의 정답 패턴을 최대한 활용하자.

PART 2

DAY 02

아직도 정답 찾고 있니? 오답 버려!

음원 바로 듣기

동영상 강의 바로 보기

만점 포인트

이것만 알면 만점!

1 오답 5계명을 명심하자!

2 출제 빈도가 높은 의문사 의문문을 확실하게 익히자!

3 일반 / 부정 / 부가 의문문

4 기타 의문문 (평서문, 선택 의문문)

만점 포인트 1 오답 5계명을 명심하자!

최근에 난이도가 높아지고 있는 PART 2의 경우, 예전처럼 질문에 곧이곧대로 응답을 하는 경우보다는 우회적으로 표현하거나 예상치 못한 답변을 하는 경우가 종종 있어 정답을 찾는 데 어려움을 겪고 있다. 이런 경우에는 정답을 찾으려 애쓰기보다는 오답을 하나씩 지워나가는 '소거법'을 이용하는 것이 효과적이다. 그러므로 다음에 나오는 오답 5계명만 잘 익혀두면 PART 2는 쉽게 고득점을 얻을 수 있다.

1. 의문사로 시작하는 질문에 Yes, No, Of course, Sure, OK가 나오면 버려라!

Q **When** does Mr. Kim leave for Hong Kong? 김 씨는 언제 홍콩으로 떠나나요?

A (A) **No**, he didn't leave. ✗ 아니요, 그는 떠나지 않았어요.

(B) Sometime in March. O 3월쯤에요.

2. 동문서답하지 마라! 질문과 응답의 '주어 불일치'는 버려라!

Q Have **you** received the sales report? 당신은 판매 보고서를 받았나요?

A (A) **He** works in the Accounting Department. ✗ 그는 회계부서에서 일합니다.

(B) I just returned today from a business trip. O 저는 오늘 출장에서 막 돌아왔어요.

3. 동문서답하지 마라! 질문과 응답의 '시제 불일치'는 버려라!

Q Isn't there a meeting for new employees **this Friday**? 이번 주 금요일에는 신입사원 모임이 없나요?

A (A) Where **was** it held? ✗ 어디서 열렸어요?

(B) Let me find out for you. O 제가 알아봐 드릴게요.

4. 상상하지 마라! '연상 어휘'는 버려라!

Q When should I **print out** the documents? 서류를 언제 출력해야 하나요?

A (A) **Double-sided**, please. ✗ 양면으로 해주세요.

(B) The meeting has been canceled. O 회의가 취소되었습니다.

5. 단어에 집착하지 마라! '똑같은 발음' 혹은 '유사 발음'은 버려라!

Q Who's leading the employee **training** session? 직원 연수회는 누가 진행하나요?

A (A) My **train** departs in 30 minutes. ✗ 제 기차는 30분 후에 떠납니다.

(B) I'm assigning that task to Ms. Tina. O 그 일은 티나 씨에게 맡길게요.

DAY 02_01.mp3

1.	Mark your answer on your answer sheet.	(A)	(B)	(C)
2.	Mark your answer on your answer sheet.	(A)	(B)	(C)
3.	Mark your answer on your answer sheet.	(A)	(B)	(C)
4.	Mark your answer on your answer sheet.	(A)	(B)	(C)
5.	Mark your answer on your answer sheet.	(A)	(B)	(C)

해설

1. **Why hasn't Tara signed the document yet?**

영국 | 미국

(A) We already signed up for a class. ···› 주어 불일치, sign 어휘 반복
(B) Yes, I totally agree with you. ···› 의문사 의문문에 Yes로 대답
(C) It's still being reviewed.

타라는 왜 아직 서류에 서명을 하지 않았나요?
우리는 벌써 수업에 등록했어요.
네, 전적으로 동의합니다.
아직 검토 중이에요.

2. **Are you available on Saturday the 5th?**

미국 | 미국

(A) Yes, on the fifth floor. ···› fifth 어휘 반복
(B) I should be free later in the afternoon.
(C) No, he will be out of the office all week. ···› 주어 불일치

5일 토요일에 시간 되세요?
네, 5층에서요.
오후에는 시간이 괜찮을 것 같아요.
아니요, 그는 일주일 내내 사무실에 없을 거예요.

3. **Do I have to pay the subscription fee monthly or yearly?**

호주 | 미국

(A) On the first of every month. ···› 매달의 우회적 표현
(B) No, a weekly magazine. ···› subscription의 연상 어휘
(C) We only accept credit cards. ···› pay의 연상 어휘

정기구독료를 매달 지불해야 하나요? 매년 지불해야 하나요?
매달 첫날입니다.
아니요, 주간 잡지책이에요.
저희는 신용카드만 받습니다.

4. **Which television program should we promote our new products in?**

영국 | 호주

(A) After a 30-second commercial. ···› promote의 연상 어휘
(B) Sure, I heard it on the radio station. ···› 의문사 의문문에 Sure로 대답
(C) What about *The Weekend Evening Show*? ···› 되묻기 / 반문

어느 텔레비전 프로그램에 우리 신제품을 홍보해야 할까요?
30초 광고 이후에요.
물론이죠, 라디오 방송국에서 그것을 들었어요.
〈The Weekend Evening Show〉는 어때요?

5. **What are we going to discuss at tomorrow's weekly meeting?**

미국 | 호주

(A) He already talked about the weekly magazine.
···› 주어 불일치, 시제 불일치
(B) Let's figure it out after lunch.
(C) No, Dylan is the manager. ···› 의문사 의문문에 No로 대답

내일 주간 회의에서 무엇에 관해 논의할 것인가요?
그는 벌써 주간 잡지에 대해서 이야기했어요.
점심 먹고 생각하죠.
아니요, 딜런이 매니저에요.

만점 포인트 2 출제 빈도가 높은 의문사 의문문을 확실하게 익히자!

PART 2의 가장 많은 부분을 차지 하고 있는 '의문사 의문문'은 총 27문제 중에서 1/3 정도의 비중으로 출제되고 있다. Who, When, Where, Why, How, What, Which 의문사에 대한 대답을 찾는 문제로 시험에 자주 출제되는 정답 패턴이 정해져 있으므로 미리 암기해 둔다면 별 어려움 없이 정답을 고를 수가 있다. 설사 예상치 못한 답변이 나올지라도 만점 포인트 1에서 학습한 '오답 소거법'을 통해서 정답을 효과적으로 찾으면 된다.

1. Who 의문문에서는 일반적으로 '부정대명사'가 정답이다.

Q **Who** sent the contract to the CEO? 누가 CEO에게 계약서를 보냈나요?

A **Someone** from Human Resources. 인사부에 누군가가요.

2. Who 의문문에 대한 예외적인 답변은 Where 의문문에 대한 답변처럼 '회사 / 부서명 / 장소 / 위치'로 대답이 가능하다.

Q **Who** has the list of participants for the workshop? 누가 워크숍 참석자 명단을 갖고 있나요?

A It should be in **the top drawer**. 제일 위 서랍에 있어요.

3. Where 의문문은 주로 '~해봐라 / ~가봐라' 등 Try를 좋아한다.

Q **Where** can I find a membership application form? 어디서 회원 신청서를 찾을 수 있나요?

A **Try** the company Web site. 회사 웹사이트를 보세요.

4. When과 How long을 헷갈리지 마라! When의 정답으로 not ~ until, not for가 나오면 찍어라!

– When 대답: 시점 표현(not ~ until, not for, no later than, once, as soon as, ago, soon)
– How long 대답: for + 기간 명사, since + 시간 표현, about + 시간 표현

Q **When** do I need to submit the sales report? 언제 영업보고서를 제출할 필요가 있나요?

A **Not until** next Monday. 다음 주 월요일이요.
No later than next Monday. 늦어도 다음 주 월요일이요.
Not for another week. 일주일 후에요.

5. Why 의문사라고 무조건 because를 찍지 마라!

주로 because, because of, since, so that, in order to, to부정사로 '목적 / 이유'가 정답이 된다.
부정적인 것(변명, 고장, 바빠서, 문제가 있어서 등)을 정답으로 골라라.

Q **Why** is Mr. Kim coming to the workshop? 김 씨가 워크숍에 왜 참석하나요?

A **To meet** the new employees. 신입직원들을 만나기 위해서요.

6. Why와 Why don't(권유 / 요청)는 다르다.

Q **Why don't** you come to the party? 파티에 참석하시는 게 어떤가요?

A **Sure!** That would be great! 물론이요! 좋아요!

7. How 의문문이라면 by -ing 혹은 through가 나오면 찍어라!

Q **How** can I join the upcoming anniversary event? 다가오는 기념회에 어떻게 참석할 수 있나요?

A **By calling** Mr. Lee in the marketing department. 마케팅 부서의 이 씨에게 연락하셔서요.

Throughout our Web site. 웹사이트를 통해서요.

8. How라고 해서 다 '방법'이 아니다.

How do you like ~? ~ 어떤가요?

How is it going? 어떻게 되어 가나요?

How come ~ 왜 그런가요?

How about ~ ~는 어때요?

DAY 02_02.mp3

1.	Mark your answer on your answer sheet.	(A)	(B)	(C)
2.	Mark your answer on your answer sheet.	(A)	(B)	(C)
3.	Mark your answer on your answer sheet.	(A)	(B)	(C)
4.	Mark your answer on your answer sheet.	(A)	(B)	(C)
5.	Mark your answer on your answer sheet.	(A)	(B)	(C)

해설

1. Where can I get an extra key card made for my office?

미국 | 미국

(A) I found it on the desk. ···› '키카드가 어디에 있냐'로 착각하지 말자!

(B) Ask the security office.

(C) The office is located on the second floor. ···› office 어휘 반복

사무실 여분의 키카드를 어디서 얻을 수 있죠?
책상에서 찾았어요.
경비실에 문의해보세요.
사무실은 2층에 위치해 있어요.

2. When is your orientation meeting with new employees?

영국 | 호주

(A) No, that's not what I heard. ···› 의문사 의문문에 No로 대답

(B) Not for another month.

(C) Approximately three months. ···› How long에 대한 대답

신입직원들을 위한 오리엔테이션 미팅이 언제인가요?
아니에요, 제가 들은 것은 그게 아니에요.
한 달 후에요.
대략 3개월요.

3. Who's seen the latest survey results?

호주 | 미국

(A) Have you checked the group folder? ···› 되묻기 / 반문

(B) Yes, Dave did it last night. ···› 의문사 의문문에 Yes로 대답

(C) Almost 500 responses. ···› survey의 연상 어휘

최근 설문조사 결과를 누가 봤나요?
그룹 폴더를 확인해 보셨어요?
네, 데이브는 어젯밤에 그것을 했어요.
거의 500개의 응답요.

4. Why didn't you take any pictures at the museum?

영국 | 미국

(A) Because it is a famous art gallery. ···› Why에 대한 대답

(B) It was prohibited.

(C) The photo was taken a few years ago. ···› picture의 연상 어휘: photo

박물관에서 왜 사진을 찍지 않으셨어요?
유명한 아트 갤러리여서요.
금지였어요.
몇 년 전에 찍은 사진이에요.

5. How did the representative from Harrington Inc. like the project proposal?

미국 | 미국

(A) Through our company Web site. ···› How에 대한 대답

(B) He talked to Linda about it.

(C) The monthly sales projection. ···› project의 유사 발음: projection

해링턴 사의 대표는 프로젝트 제안서를 어떻게 생각하던가요?
우리 회사 웹사이트를 통해서요.
그는 그것에 대해 린다에게 이야기했어요.
월 판매 예상액이요.

만점 포인트 3 일반 / 부정 / 부가 의문문

처음에 나오는 의문사만 잘 들으면 되는 '의문사 의문문'과는 달리 be / do / have / will / should 등의 조동사로 시작하는 의문문의 경우는 아무리 긴 문장이 나온다고 하더라도 당황하지 말고 '동사 + 주어 + 목적어' 혹은 '동사 + 주어'만 잘 듣더라도 충분히 답을 찾을 수가 있다.

주어와 동사 시제 일치!

1. 일반 의문문에 대한 대답은 '동사 + 주어 + 목적어' 혹은 '동사 + 주어'만이라도 잘 듣자!

Q Has Mr. Diaz confirmed the dates of his business trip? 디아즈 씨가 출장 날짜를 확인했나요?

A Yes, he has booked the flight for June 13. 네, 그는 6월 13일 비행기로 예약했습니다.

2. 부정 / 부가 의문문의 핵심은 이것! Yes면 Yes! No면 No!

아무것도 신경쓰지 말고, 긍정이면 yes, 부정이면 no를 하면 된다.

Q Weren't the clients satisfied with the brochure? 고객들이 브로슈어에 만족했나요?

A No, they had some complaints. 아니요, 그들은 몇 가지에 대해 불만이 있었어요.

3. Would you mind ~?로 물어보면 정답은 무조건 No?

Would you mind ~?나 Do you mind ~?의 대답은 주로 no, not at all, of course not이 일반적이다.

Q Would you mind opening a window? 창문 열면 안 될까요?

A No, I don't mind at all. 아니요, 전혀 상관 없어요.

DAY 02_03.mp3

1.	Mark your answer on your answer sheet.	(A)	(B)	(C)
2.	Mark your answer on your answer sheet.	(A)	(B)	(C)
3.	Mark your answer on your answer sheet.	(A)	(B)	(C)
4.	Mark your answer on your answer sheet.	(A)	(B)	(C)
5.	Mark your answer on your answer sheet.	(A)	(B)	(C)

해설

1. Would you mind coming to the restaurant this weekend?

호주 | 영국

(A) No, she can come next weekend. ··· weekend 어휘 반복, 주어 불일치

(B) I had an enjoyable meal. ··· restaurant의 연상 어휘

(C) Do you want me on both days? ··· 되묻기 / 반문

이번 주말에 레스토랑에 안 오시겠어요?
아니요, 그녀는 다음 주말에 올 수 있어요.
저는 즐거운 식사를 했어요.
이틀 동안 제가 필요하세요?

2. Has the new personnel manager been named yet?

미국 | 호주

(A) About the recruitment process. ··· personnel의 연상 어휘

(B) He was named the Employee of the Year. ··· name 어휘 반복

(C) I think it's going to be Mr. Park.

아직 새 인사부장이 안 정해졌나요?
채용 절차에 관해서요.
그는 올해의 직원으로 명명되었어요.
제 생각에는 박 씨가 될 거예요.

3. Wasn't the printer on the 5th floor just recently fixed?

미국 | 미국

(A) No, the photocopier is on the second floor. ···› floor 어휘 반복
(B) Is it not working again? ···› 되묻기 / 반문
(C) Print in color, please. ···› printer의 유사 발음: print

5층에 있는 프린터가 최근에 수리되지 않았나요?
아니요, 복사기는 2층에 있어요.
또 작동이 안 되나요?
컬러로 출력해 주세요.

4. Mr. Leonard knows the clients will be visiting our new office today, doesn't he?

영국 | 미국

(A) I'll visit you later. ···› visit 어휘 반복
(B) I think he has been informed.
(C) Yes, new office supplies. ···› office 어휘 반복

레너드 씨가 고객들이 새 사무실에 방문할 거라는 것을 알고 있죠, 그렇죠?
제가 나중에 방문할게요.
제 생각에는 그는 알고 있어요.
네, 새로운 사무용품이요.

5. Shouldn't we inform the guests about the updated policy?

미국 | 호주

(A) Please update the application form. ···› inform의 유사 발음: form
(B) Janet said she will do it. ···› 제3자 / 책임 전가
(C) Sure, I'll reserve it. ···› 동문서답

우리는 손님들에게 업데이트된 정책에 대해서 알려드려야 하지 않을까요?
신청서를 업데이트해 주세요.
자넷이 본인이 할 것이라고 했어요.
물론이죠, 제가 예약할게요.

만점 포인트 4 기타 의문문 (평서문, 선택 의문문)

기타 의문문 문제는 다른 의문사 유형에 비해서 출제 빈도수가 낮은 편이긴 하지만 간과할 수 없는 부분이다. 평서문의 경우는 어떤 대답이 나올지 몰라 굉장히 까다롭고 난이도가 높은 유형에 속한다. 하지만 평서문에 대한 단골 정답 패턴이 있으므로 미리 익히도록 하자.

1. 평서문의 단골 정답 '공감형 인간'이 되어라!

보기에 이런 것이 나오면 무조건 평서문의 정답이다.

– 동조와 맞장구

– 해결책 제시 / 제안

– 되묻기

– 자세한 설명과 정보 제공

Q The air conditioner won't turn on. 에어컨이 안 켜져요.

A Yes, I noticed as well. 네, 저도 확인했어요. **동조와 맞장구**

Why don't you move to another conference room then? 그러면 다른 회의실로 옮기는 건 어때요? **해결책 제시 / 제안**

Have you contacted the Maintenance Department? 유지보수팀에 연락하셨어요? **되묻기**

I heard it has not been working since last week. 지난주부터 작동이 안 되었다고 들었어요. **자세한 설명**

2. 선택 의문문의 정답은 '우유부단'과 '선택 장애'가 대세이다.

하지만, 요즘의 PART 2의 정답 패턴으로 자기 의견을 당당하게 피력하기도 한다.

» 선택 의문문의 단골 정답

예를 들어, 짜장면 먹을래요? 짬뽕 먹을래요?

❶ 우유부단: 둘 중에 어느거나 괜찮아요.

❷ 짜장면 / 짬뽕: 둘 중에 하나를 확실히 언급

❸ 제3안을 제시: 탕수육은 없나요?

❹ 우회적 표현: 국물 있는 것으로 주세요. (즉, 짬뽕)

Q Would you like to have a hamburger or sandwich for lunch?
점심으로 버거를 드시겠어요, 샌드위치를 드시겠어요?

A Either is fine. 둘 중에 어느 것이든 좋습니다. **우유부단**

Whichever is fine. 어느 것이든 좋아요. **우유부단**

It doesn't matter. 상관없어요. **우유부단**

I don't care. 상관없어요. **우유부단**

A How about pasta? 파스타는 없나요? **제3안을 제시**

Do you have anything else? 다른 것은 없나요? **제3안을 제시**

I prefer pasta. 저는 파스타를 더 선호합니다. **제3안을 제시**

1.	Mark your answer on your answer sheet.	(A)	(B)	(C)
2.	Mark your answer on your answer sheet.	(A)	(B)	(C)
3.	Mark your answer on your answer sheet.	(A)	(B)	(C)
4.	Mark your answer on your answer sheet.	(A)	(B)	(C)
5.	Mark your answer on your answer sheet.	(A)	(B)	(C)

해설

1. The internet connection is not working again.
영국 – 호주
(A) By visiting the Web site. ···› internet의 연상 어휘: web site
(B) Ok, I will have someone assist you. ···› 해결책 제시
(C) It was connected to the subway station. ···› connection의 유사 발음

인터넷 연결이 또 안 되네요.
웹사이트를 방문함으로써요.
네, 제가 누군가 도와줄 사람에게 부탁할게요.
지하철역에 연결되었습니다.

2. Do you prefer to fill out the digital form or a paper application?
미국 – 호주
(A) The deadline is next Friday. ···› application의 연상 어휘: deadline
(B) Either is fine.
(C) I feel pretty good. ···› fill의 유사 발음: feel

디지털 형태로 신청하시겠어요? 아니면 종이 신청서로 하시겠어요?
마감 날짜가 다음 주 금요일입니다.
어느거나 괜찮습니다.
기분 좋습니다.

3. I think we were supposed to replace the desks in the office this week.
미국 – 미국
(A) Yes, we ordered office supplies. ···› office의 어휘 반복
(B) Didn't you check the notice on the board? ···› 되묻기 / 반문
(C) Put the chairs on the desks. ···› desk 어휘 반복

제 생각에 이번 주에 사무실의 책상을 교체하기로 되어있었는데요.
네, 우리는 사무용품을 주문했어요.
게시판에 공지사항 확인 못 하셨어요?
책상 위에 의자를 두세요.

4. Should we take the subway or drive?
영국 – 미국
(A) Sure, I will take you to the station.
···› 선택 의문문에 sure로 대답, 그리고 subway의 연상 어휘: station
(B) It depends on the traffic.
(C) It will take five minutes. ···› 얼마나 오래 걸릴 것이냐에 대한 대답

우리 지하철을 타고 가야 할까요, 아니면 운전해서 갈까요?
물론이죠, 제가 역까지 모셔다드릴게요.
교통 상황에 따라 다르죠.
5분 소요될 것입니다.

5. The Marketing Department hired more employees this month.
호주 – 영국
(A) Didn't Jason get a higher salary? ···› hire의 유사 발음: higher
(B) They don't need to work overtime then.
(C) He is a famous marketing expert. ···› marketing 어휘 반복

마케팅 부서에서 이번 달에 더 많은 직원들을 고용했어요.
제이슨이 더 높은 연봉을 받지 않았나요?
그러면 초과 근무할 필요가 없네요.
그는 유명한 마케팅 전문가예요.

고난도 실전 문제

DAY 02_05.mp3

1. Mark your answer on your answer sheet. (A) (B) (C)
2. Mark your answer on your answer sheet. (A) (B) (C)
3. Mark your answer on your answer sheet. (A) (B) (C)
4. Mark your answer on your answer sheet. (A) (B) (C)
5. Mark your answer on your answer sheet. (A) (B) (C)
6. Mark your answer on your answer sheet. (A) (B) (C)
7. Mark your answer on your answer sheet. (A) (B) (C)
8. Mark your answer on your answer sheet. (A) (B) (C)
9. Mark your answer on your answer sheet. (A) (B) (C)
10. Mark your answer on your answer sheet. (A) (B) (C)
11. Mark your answer on your answer sheet. (A) (B) (C)
12. Mark your answer on your answer sheet. (A) (B) (C)
13. Mark your answer on your answer sheet. (A) (B) (C)
14. Mark your answer on your answer sheet. (A) (B) (C)
15. Mark your answer on your answer sheet. (A) (B) (C)
16. Mark your answer on your answer sheet. (A) (B) (C)
17. Mark your answer on your answer sheet. (A) (B) (C)
18. Mark your answer on your answer sheet. (A) (B) (C)
19. Mark your answer on your answer sheet. (A) (B) (C)
20. Mark your answer on your answer sheet. (A) (B) (C)
21. Mark your answer on your answer sheet. (A) (B) (C)
22. Mark your answer on your answer sheet. (A) (B) (C)
23. Mark your answer on your answer sheet. (A) (B) (C)
24. Mark your answer on your answer sheet. (A) (B) (C)
25. Mark your answer on your answer sheet. (A) (B) (C)
26. Mark your answer on your answer sheet. (A) (B) (C)
27. Mark your answer on your answer sheet. (A) (B) (C)

PART 2

DAY 03

이게 요즘의 정답 대세, 무조건 찍어라!

음원 바로 듣기

동영상 강의 바로 보기

최근 들어 토익 시험의 난이도와 유형이 점차 어렵게 진화하고 있다. 특히 고득점을 위해서 반드시 기본이 되어야 하는 PART 2에서 예전보다 높아진 난이도로 고득점의 발목을 잡기도 하는데, 그 이유 중에 하나는 단순하게 질문에 대한 응답을 찾기보다는 우회적으로 표현하거나 예상치 못한 고난도 답변에 익숙해지지 못해서이다. 그러므로, 고난도 정답 패턴과 출제 경향이 무엇인지를 미리 익힌다면 쉽게 답을 찾을 수 있다.

만점 포인트

이것만 알면 만점!

1 이것이 요즘 PART 2 정답 대세다.

되묻기 / 반문, 우회적 표현, 불친절, 책임 전가, 선택 장애 / 우유부단

2 회피성 답을 찍어라(모른다 / 확인해 볼게요)!

3 부정적인 내용이나 변명을 좋아한다.

취소, 지연, 변경, actually / well / already / still 정답을 좋아한다.

만점 포인트 1 이것이 요즘 PART 2 정답 대세다.

PART 2가 갈수록 어려워지는 이유는 질문에 대해 예상과는 전혀 다른 답변이 정답으로 출제되기 때문이다. 물론 오답 소거법을 통해서 정답을 찾을 수가 있지만, 이와 같은 고난도 답변도 분석해보면 매달 자주 출제되는 패턴이 있다. 그러므로 평소에 출제 패턴을 익혀둔다면 쉽게 정답을 찾을 수가 있다.

1. 되묻기 / 반문

Q Do you know where I can find the financial report? 어디서 재무 보고서를 찾을 수 있는지 아시나요?

A **Didn't you check your e-mail yet?** 이메일 확인을 안 하셨어요?

2. 우회적 표현(직접적인 정답을 피한다), 돌려 말하기

Q Have you ordered new uniforms for our staff? 우리 직원들을 위해 새 유니폼을 주문하셨나요?

A **We can't afford that.** 우린 그럴 여유가 없습니다.

3. 불친절하게 혹은 참고 / 참조를 하라

Q Where is the monthly meeting taking place? 월례 미팅이 어디서 열리나요?

A **It should say on the document.** 문서에 나와 있습니다.

4. 책임 전가 또는 제 3자를 끌어들이기

Q I have no idea when the proposal deadline is. 제안서 마감일이 언제인지 잘 모르겠습니다.

A **Check with Mr. Cramer.** 크래머 씨에게 확인해보세요.

5. 선택 장애 / 우유부단

Q Do you prefer to work in a team or independently?
팀으로 일하는 것을 선호하세요? 아니면 독립적으로 일하는 것을 선호하세요?

A **Either is fine. / Whichever is fine.** 둘 중에 어느 것이든 좋습니다. / 어느 것이든 좋습니다.

DAY 03_01.mp3

1. Mark your answer on your answer sheet. (A) (B) (C)
2. Mark your answer on your answer sheet. (A) (B) (C)
3. Mark your answer on your answer sheet. (A) (B) (C)
4. Mark your answer on your answer sheet. (A) (B) (C)
5. Mark your answer on your answer sheet. (A) (B) (C)

해설

1. **Do you know how to install this software?**

호주 | 미국

(A) Of course, she knew it. ···› 주어 불일치
(B) Have you asked Mr. Joe? ···› 되묻기 / 반문, 제3자 언급
(C) For almost three hours. ···› how long에 대한 대답

이 소프트웨어 어떻게 설치하시는지 아시나요?
물론이죠, 그녀는 알았습니다.
조 씨에게 물어보셨나요?
거의 3년 동안이요.

2. **Is tomorrow's meeting going to be held on the 2nd floor or 3rd floor?**

미국 | 미국

(A) It will start at 3 P.M. ···› 숫자 3의 반복
(B) I think it's been canceled. ···› 취소되었다는 우회적 표현
(C) Video conference equipment. ···› meeting의 연상 어휘

내일 미팅이 2층에서 열리나요? 3층에서 열리나요?
오후 3시에 시작될 예정입니다.
취소되었어요.
화상회의 장비요.

3. **Who should I talk to about getting the projector fixed?**

영국 | 호주

(A) 3:30 in the afternoon. ···› When에 대한 대답
(B) The phone number is on your desk.
···› 불친절하게 혹은 참고 / 참조
(C) In conference room B. ···› projector의 연상 어휘

프로젝터를 수리하려면 누구에게 이야기해야 하나요?
오후 3시 30분이요.
전화번호가 책상 위에 있어요.
회의실 B요.

4. **When will the construction of the office be completed?**

미국 | 영국

(A) Around 5 months. ···› how long에 대한 대답
(B) Mr. Yamamoto might know. ···› 제3자 언급
(C) Complete the application form. ···› complete 어휘 반복

사무실 공사가 언제 끝나나요?
거의 5개월이요.
야마모토 씨가 알 거예요.
신청서를 작성해 주세요.

5. **Would you like to go directly to the head office or visit the factory first?**

미국 | 미국

(A) No, she already visited the factory.
···› 선택 의문문에 No로 대답, visit the factory 반복
(B) Either is fine. ···› 선택 장애
(C) On the second floor. ···› first의 연상 어휘

바로 본사로 가시겠습니까? 공장에 먼저 들리시겠습니까?
아닙니다, 그녀는 벌써 공장을 방문했어요.
어느 것이든 좋습니다.
2층에요.

만점 포인트 2 회피성 답을 찍어라(모른다 / 확인해 볼게요)!

PART 2의 고난도 답변으로 회피성 정답이 자주 출제된다. 예를 들어, '모른다' 혹은 '확인해 보겠다', '제3자에게 확인하거나 물어봐라' 등의 책임 회피성 대답이나 이유나 변명을 설명하는 경우가 출제된다. 평소에 그러한 표현으로 어떤 것이 있는지 확실히 익혀두도록 하자.

모른다.	Not that I know of ~ ~에 관해 아는 바 없는데요. Not to my knowledge ~ 내가 아는 바로는 없어요. I have no idea. 저는 모르겠어요.
결정되지 않았어요.	It hasn't been decided (yet). 아직 결정되지 않았어요. I haven't made a decision (yet). 아직 결정되지 않았어요. I haven't been told / informed / notified ~ 아직 알려지지 않았어요.
담당자가 아니에요. 다른 사람한테 물어보세요.	I am not in charge. 제 소관이 아니에요. Ask someone else. 다른 사람한테 물어보세요. Why don't you ask James? 제임스에게 물어보는 게 어때요? Check the price list. 가격 리스트를 확인하세요. You can find it on our Web site. 저희 웹사이트에서 확인하실 수 있습니다.
확인해 볼게요.	I'll check. 확인해 볼게요. Let me check. 확인해 볼게요. Would you like me to check? 제가 확인해 드릴까요? Check your calendar. 일정을 확인해보세요. Refer to the manual. 매뉴얼을 참조하세요. Consult the manual. 매뉴얼을 참고하세요.

DAY 03_02.mp3

1. Mark your answer on your answer sheet. (A) (B) (C)
2. Mark your answer on your answer sheet. (A) (B) (C)
3. Mark your answer on your answer sheet. (A) (B) (C)
4. Mark your answer on your answer sheet. (A) (B) (C)
5. Mark your answer on your answer sheet. (A) (B) (C)

해설

1. Who got promoted to senior marketing director?

영국 – 미국

(A) Okay. I'll think about it. ···› 의문사 의문문에 Okay로 대답
(B) It hasn't been decided yet. ···› 모른다
(C) Seminar on marketing strategy. ···› marketing 어휘 반복

누가 시니어 마케팅부장으로 승진했나요?
좋아요. 생각해 볼게요.
아직 결정된 바 없습니다.
마케팅 전략에 관한 세미나요.

2. When will the company unveil the new software product?

미국 – 미국

(A) Why don't you ask Sato? ···› 되묻기 / 확인, 제3자 언급
(B) Yes, it's about five kilometers from here. ···› 의문사 의문문(When)에 Yes로 대답
(C) Last year's convention in Vancouver. ···› Where에 대한 대답

회사가 새로운 소프트웨어 제품을 언제 출시하나요?
사토에게 물어보는 게 어떨까요?
여기서부터 약 5킬로미터입니다.
밴쿠버의 작년 컨벤션에서요.

3. Would you like me to send a copy of the contract or the original one?

영국 - 미국

(A) No, it was a long-term contract.
…→ 선택 의문문에 No로 대답, contract 어휘 반복

(B) Let me check with James. …→ 확인, 제3자 언급

(C) To the potential clients …→ send의 연상 어휘

제가 계약서 사본을 보내기를 원하세요? 원본을 원하세요?
아니에요. 장기계약이에요.
제임스와 확인해 볼게요.
잠재적 고객들에게요.

4. Have you ordered safety goggles for the laboratory employees?

미국 - 미국

(A) I already cancelled it. …→ order의 연상 어휘

(B) Here is the safety manual. …→ safety 어휘 반복

(C) We haven't finished taking inventory yet.

실험실 직원들을 위해서 안전 고글을 주문하셨나요?
벌써 취소했어요.
여기에 안전 매뉴얼이 있어요.
아직 재고 조사를 못 마쳤어요.

5. I'd like to discuss the salary negotiation sometime next week.

호주 - 영국

(A) Yes, that was a good deal. …→ negotiation의 연상 어휘: deal

(B) The CEO is out of the office all next week.

(C) Almost 50,000 dollars a year. …→ salary의 연상 어휘

저는 다음 주쯤 연봉 협상에 대해 논의하고 싶습니다.
네, 좋은 거래였어요.
CEO가 다음 주 내내 사무실에 안 계세요.
거의 일 년에 5만 달러요.

만점 포인트 3 부정적인 내용이나 변명을 좋아한다.

PART 2의 또 다른 빈출 정답으로 취소, 지연, 변경 등의 부정적인 내용이나 변명이 있다. 또한 actually, well, already, still과 같은 단어들이 나오면 거의 정답일 가능성이 높다.

1. 취소, 지연, 변경 등의 부정적인 내용이나 변명

Q Weren't you supposed to be at the seminar this morning? 오늘 아침에 세미나에 참석하지 않았나요?

A My train was delayed. 열차가 지연되었어요.

2. actually, well, already, still이 나오면 정답일 가능성이 높다.

Q Who does this document belong to? 이 문서 누구 것인가요?

A **Actually**, it's mine. 실은, 제 것입니다.

Q When did the award ceremony take place? 시상식은 언제 개최되었나요?

A **Well**, it was cancelled. 음, 그게 취소되었습니다.

Q When are you going to place an order for this model? 이 모델 언제 주문할 예정이신가요?

A I **already** did it this morning. 제가 오늘 아침에 벌써 주문했어요.

A It **still** needs a supervisor's approval. 그것은 여전히 상사의 승인이 필요해요.

DAY 03_03.mp3

1. Mark your answer on your answer sheet. (A) (B) (C)
2. Mark your answer on your answer sheet. (A) (B) (C)
3. Mark your answer on your answer sheet. (A) (B) (C)
4. Mark your answer on your answer sheet. (A) (B) (C)
5. Mark your answer on your answer sheet. (A) (B) (C)

해설

1. How long does it take to train new employees?

미국 – 미국

(A) At 9 A.M. in conference room A. ···› When / Where에 대한 대답
(B) We've just changed the schedule. ···› 변경에 관련된 내용
(C) Nearly 50 staff members. ···› employees의 연상 어휘

신입 직원을 교육하는 데 얼마나 오래 걸리나요?
회의실 A에서 오전 9시에요.
스케줄을 변경했습니다.
거의 50명의 직원들이요.

2. When are we going to update the office layout?

영국 – 미국

(A) Probably on the internet. ···› How에 대한 대답
(B) Ms. Jones already took care of it. ···› already가 들어간 정답
(C) The office is more spacious than before. ···› office 어휘 반복

언제 사무실 배치를 업데이트할 예정이신가요?
아마도 인터넷에서요.
존스 씨가 벌써 해결했어요.
사무실이 이전보다 넓습니다.

3. You went to see the doctor this morning, didn't you? 영국 – 호주 (A) Can you pick up my prescription? ···› doctor의 연상 어휘 (B) Bring your medical records. ···› doctor의 연상 어휘 **(C) Actually, I had to run some other errands.** ···› actually가 들어간 정답	오늘 아침에 병원에 가셨죠, 그렇지요? 처방전을 가지고 오실 수 있나요? 의료 기록을 가지고 오세요. **실은 다른 볼일이 있었습니다.**
4. The company is launching the new Web site next Monday, right? 미국 – 미국 **(A) There have been some delays.** ···› 부정적인 내용이나 변명(지연) (B) Yes, it was last Friday. ···› next Monday의 연상 어휘 (C) The newest mobile application. ···› Web site의 연상 어휘	다음 주 월요일에 회사에서 새로운 웹사이트를 개시하죠, 그렇지요? **지체가 있었습니다.** 네, 지난주 금요일이었어요. 최신 모바일 어플이요.
5. Why wasn't the annual sales report sent out this week? 호주 – 미국 (A) The last Monday of every month. ···› this week의 연상 어휘 **(B) We had some mechanical issues.** ···› 부정적인 내용이나 변명 (C) Okay, that's great news. ···› 의문사 의문문에 Okay로 대답	이번 주에 연간 판매 보고서를 왜 보내지지 않았나요? 매달 마지막 월요일이요. **기계적 문제가 있었습니다.** 좋아요, 좋은 소식이에요.

고난도 실전 문제

DAY 03_04.mp3

1. Mark your answer on your answer sheet. (A) (B) (C)
2. Mark your answer on your answer sheet. (A) (B) (C)
3. Mark your answer on your answer sheet. (A) (B) (C)
4. Mark your answer on your answer sheet. (A) (B) (C)
5. Mark your answer on your answer sheet. (A) (B) (C)
6. Mark your answer on your answer sheet. (A) (B) (C)
7. Mark your answer on your answer sheet. (A) (B) (C)
8. Mark your answer on your answer sheet. (A) (B) (C)
9. Mark your answer on your answer sheet. (A) (B) (C)
10. Mark your answer on your answer sheet. (A) (B) (C)
11. Mark your answer on your answer sheet. (A) (B) (C)
12. Mark your answer on your answer sheet. (A) (B) (C)
13. Mark your answer on your answer sheet. (A) (B) (C)
14. Mark your answer on your answer sheet. (A) (B) (C)
15. Mark your answer on your answer sheet. (A) (B) (C)
16. Mark your answer on your answer sheet. (A) (B) (C)
17. Mark your answer on your answer sheet. (A) (B) (C)
18. Mark your answer on your answer sheet. (A) (B) (C)
19. Mark your answer on your answer sheet. (A) (B) (C)
20. Mark your answer on your answer sheet. (A) (B) (C)
21. Mark your answer on your answer sheet. (A) (B) (C)
22. Mark your answer on your answer sheet. (A) (B) (C)
23. Mark your answer on your answer sheet. (A) (B) (C)
24. Mark your answer on your answer sheet. (A) (B) (C)
25. Mark your answer on your answer sheet. (A) (B) (C)
26. Mark your answer on your answer sheet. (A) (B) (C)
27. Mark your answer on your answer sheet. (A) (B) (C)

PART 3&4

PART 3 &4의 고득점을 위해 반드시 뒷받침되어야 하는 것은 '패러프레이징(paraphrasing)' 즉, 말 바꾸기다. 많은 어휘를 아는 것도 중요하지만, 스크립트에 나왔던 어휘가 패러프레이징 되어서 보기에 어떻게 표현되는지를 구분하는 것이 중요하다. 난이도가 낮은 문제라면 단순하게 들리는 단어를 보기에서 찾으면 되겠지만, 오히려 들리는 대로 답을 했다가 낭패를 볼 수 있다. 따라서 PART 3 & 4의 경우는 '청취력'뿐만 아니라 들으면서 동시에 '패러프레이징'이 된 문장을 읽어내려 갈 수 있는 '독해력'까지 수반되는 멀티테스킹을 요구하는 어려운 파트이다. 그러므로, 평소에 자주 나오는 단골 지문 유형과 문제를 파악하고 빈출 패러프레이징 표현을 많이 익혀두는 것이 좋다.

DAY 04-07

LC	DAY 01	DAY 02	DAY 03	**DAY 04**	**DAY 05**	**DAY 06**	**DAY 07**
RC	DAY 01	DAY 02	DAY 03	DAY 04	DAY 05	DAY 06	DAY 07

PART 3&4 만점 핵심 공략

1. 주어진 문제를 미리 읽고 '키워드'를 잡는다.
   - 키워드는 주로 '고유명사(사람, 지명, 회사 이름, 시간, 날짜, 요일)'이다.
2. 여유가 된다면 보기를 먼저 읽는 것도 좋다.
   - 많은 문제를 풀어본 고득점자의 경우, 보기만 읽어보고도 대강의 내용과 답을 유추할 수 있는 경우도 종종 있다. 토익에 빈출되는 스토리 유형이 있기 때문에 평소에 그 유형에 익숙하게 공부를 했다면 충분히 그럴 수 있기 때문이다.
3. 눈과 귀를 바쁘게 움직인다.
   - '청취력'과 동시에 '독해력'도 뒷받침되어야 한다.
4. 이제 순차적으로 들으면서 문제를 푼다.
   - 보통 스크립트의 내용과 질문이 순차적이나, 순서 파괴적인 문제도 종종 등장하니 긴장하자.
   - 들은 단어에 무작정 의존하기보다는 패러프레이징 표현에 유의하자.

PART 3&4

DAY 04

매달 단골로 나오는 문제는 이것이다!

음원 바로 듣기

동영상 강의 바로 보기

만점 포인트

이것만 알면 만점!

1. '주제'나 '목적'은 첫 두 문장이 결정한다!
2. '문제점'이나 '걱정거리'는 화자의 입에서 나온다!
3. '장소 / 직업 / 정체' 정답은 초반부를 주목하라!
4. 반전에 주목하라!
5. 요청 / 제안 / 미래의 일은 '후반부'에 집중하라!

만점 포인트 1 '주제'나 '목적'은 첫 두 문장이 결정한다!

주제나 목적을 묻는 문제의 경우 초반 1-2줄에서 판가름이 난다. PART 3의 경우 보통 첫 번째 화자가 대화의 주제나 목적을 말하는 경우가 대부분이지만, 두 번째 화자가 나와서야 비로소 주제나 목적이 좀 더 분명해지는 경우가 있으므로 성급하게 답을 고르지 않도록 주의해야 한다.

1. PART 3의 문제 유형

What are the speakers **mainly discussing**? 화자들이 주로 논의하는 것은 무엇인가?
What are the speakers **talking about**? 화자들은 무엇에 대해 이야기하고 있는가?
What is the **conversation mainly about**? 주로 무엇에 대한 대화인가?
Why is the man / woman **calling**? 남자 / 여자가 전화한 이유는 무엇인가?

2. PART 4의 문제 유형

What is the **purpose** of the talk? 이 강연의 목적은 무엇인가?
What is the **main purpose** of the announcement? 이 발표의 주된 목적은 무엇인가?
What is the broadcast **mainly about**? 그 방송은 주로 무엇에 관한 것인가?
What is **being advertised**? 무엇을 광고하고 있는가?

* 전체 지문의 목적과 지문 내에 언급된 '특정 연설 / 행사의 목적'을 묻는 문제는 다른 문제 유형이다. 예를 들어, What is the topic of the seminar?는 전체 지문의 목적을 묻는 게 아니라 지문에 등장하는 seminar의 목적을 물어보는 문제이다.

DAY 04_01.mp3

PART 3

1. Why is the woman calling?
(A) To follow up on a job offer
(B) To file a complaint about an employee
(C) To change a travel itinerary
(D) To discuss the terms of a contract

2. What did the man recently do?
(A) He closed a company merger.
(B) He planned a charity event.
(C) He gave a keynote speech.
(D) He returned from a vacation.

3. What will happen in the third week of June?
(A) A conference will take place.
(B) A job posting will be updated.
(C) Some clients will visit.
(D) Some letters will be sent.

PART 4

4. What is the main topic of the announcement?
(A) Reimbursing workers for wellness programs
(B) Permitting employees to go on paid vacations
(C) Allowing staff to work remotely from home
(D) Offering a more stable retirement plan

5. According to the speaker, why is a change being made?
(A) To encourage better communication
(B) To satisfy some employees
(C) To improve staff retention
(D) To increase productivity

6. What are the listeners told to do?
(A) Attend management seminars
(B) Inform team members of a change
(C) Update their employee ID badges
(D) Receive an online certification

Questions 1-3 refer to the following conversation.

W: Hi, Mr. Gomez. I'm Abigail Cabot. ❶ I got offered a position with your company as an in-house interpreter, but you didn't send me a confirmation letter yet.

M: Oh, I apologize for the confusion, Ms. Cabot. ❷ I was out of the office on holiday, and I got back this morning. I asked my colleagues to reach out to you, but they must have forgotten about it.

W: Ah, I see. Well, last time you contacted me, you wanted me to start working for your company in June. Does that offer still stand?

M: Of course. I'll draft your contract right away. ❸ We have an international meeting in the third week of June, so we need you on board before that.

1-3번은 다음 대화에 관한 문제입니다.

여: 안녕하세요, 고메즈 씨. 저는 아비가일 카봇입니다. **저는 귀사의 내부 통역자 일자리 제의를 받았는데, 아직 확인서를 받지 못했습니다.**

남: 오, 카봇 씨, 혼동을 드려서 죄송합니다. **휴일로 사무실에 없었고, 오늘 아침에 돌아왔습니다.** 제가 동료들에게 연락을 드리라고 했는데, 아마 잊어버렸나 봅니다.

여: 아, 네 그렇군요. 지난번에 저에게 연락 주셨을 때, 6월에 일을 시작하기를 원하셨는데요. 여전히 그 제안이 유효한가요?

남: 물론이죠. 지금 계약서 초안을 작성하겠습니다. **6월 셋째 주에 국제회의가 있으므로, 그 전에 합류해 주시기를 바랍니다.**

어휘 offer a position 일자리를 제안하다 | in-house 내부의 | confirmation letter 확인서 | out of the office 부재중인 | draft 초안 | file a complaint 항의를 제기하다 | travel itinerary 여행 일정표 | terms of a contract 계약 조건 | company merger 회사 합병 | charity event 자선 행사 | keynote speech 기조연설

1. Why is the woman calling?

(A) To follow up on a job offer
(B) To file a complaint about an employee
(C) To change a travel itinerary
(D) To discuss the terms of a contract

여자가 전화를 건 목적은?

일자리 제공에 대한 후속 조치를 취하기 위해서
직원에 대한 불만을 제기하기 위해서
여행 일정표를 변경하기 위해서
계약 조건을 논의하기 위해서

해설 여자가 회사의 내부 통역자 일자리 제의를 받았지만, 아직 확인서를 못 받았다고 했으므로(I got offered a position with your company as an in-house interpreter, but you didn't send me a confirmation letter yet.) 이전에 이야기 했던 것에 대한 후속 조치를 취한다는 (A)가 정답이다.

2. What did the man recently do?

(A) He closed a company merger.
(B) He planned a charity event.
(C) He gave a keynote speech.
(D) He returned from a vacation.

남자가 최근에 했던 것은?

그는 회사 합병을 마무리 지었다.
그는 자선행사를 계획했다.
그는 기조연설을 했다.
그는 휴가에서 돌아왔다.

해설 남자가 휴일로 사무실에 없었고 오늘 아침에 돌아왔다고 했으므로(I was out of the office on holiday, and I got back this morning.) 정답은 (D)가 된다.

3. What will happen in the third week of June?

(A) A conference will take place.
(B) A job posting will be updated.
(C) Some clients will visit.
(D) Some letters will be sent.

6월 셋째 주에 무슨 일이 일어날 것인가?

회의가 열릴 것이다.
일자리 공지가 업데이트될 것이다.
몇몇 고객들이 방문할 것이다.
몇 개의 편지들이 보내어질 것이다.

해설 문제의 핵심 키워드는 6월 셋째 주이며, 6월 셋째 주에 국제회의가 있다고 했으므로(We have an international meeting in the third week of June, so we need you on board before that.) 정답은 회의가 열릴 것이라는 (A)가 된다.

Questions 4-6 refer to the following announcement.

M: This morning, ❹ I'd like to make an announcement about an update to our employee health benefits program. For decades, our company has been providing our employees with top-notch medical and dental insurance. But we would like to suggest a more preventive measure to help employees stay healthy. Some of our employees fell ill over the last few years, leaving a void in our resources. ❹ ❺ In hopes of increasing workplace productivity, we decided to provide financial compensation for employees who sign up for gym memberships. All employees are eligible for this program as long as they provide proper documentation. All they need to do is fill out a form and submit it with their receipt. ❻ Please make sure to tell your team about this update and help them reap the benefits from this new program.

4-6번은 다음 공지사항에 관한 문제입니다.

남: 오늘 아침 **저는 직원 건강복지 프로그램 업데이트에 관한 공지를 하려고 합니다.** 수십 년 동안, 우리 회사는 직원들에게 최고의 의료와 치과 보험을 제공해왔습니다. 하지만 직원들의 건강을 돕기 위해서 더 나은 예방조치를 제안하고 싶습니다. 지난 몇 해 동안에 우리 직원들 중 몇몇이 아파서 우리 인력에 공백이 생겼습니다. **생산성을 증대시키기 위해, 우리는 체육관 회원으로 등록하시는 직원들에게 재정적으로 보상을 제공하기로 결정했습니다.** 적합한 서류를 제공한다면 모든 직원들이 이 프로그램에 자격이 됩니다. 필요한 것은 신청서를 작성하는 것과 영수증을 제출하는 것입니다. **바뀐 내용을 반드시 팀에 이야기해 주고** 이 새로운 프로그램의 혜택을 이용할 수 있도록 해주세요.

어휘 employee health benefits program 직원 건강복지 프로그램 | decade 10년 | top-notch 최고의 | preventive measure 예방책 | workplace productivity 직장 생산성 | financial compensation 재정적 보상 | eligible for ~에 자격이 있는 | remotely 멀리서, 원격으로 | stable 안정적인 | retirement plan 은퇴 계획

4. What is the main topic of the announcement?

(A) Reimbursing workers for wellness programs
(B) Permitting employees to go on paid vacations
(C) Allowing staff to work remotely from home
(D) Offering a more stable retirement plan

공지사항의 주제는 무엇인가?

건강 프로그램에 대해 직원들에게 보상하는 것
직원들이 유급휴가를 사용하는 것을 허락하는 것
직원들이 재택근무하는 것을 허용하는 것
좀 더 안정적인 은퇴 계획을 제공하는 것

해설 건강복지 프로그램에 대한 업데이트를 한다고 했고(I'd like to make an announcement about an update to our employee health benefits program.) 재정적 보상을 해준다고 했으므로(In hopes of increasing workplace productivity, we decided to provide financial compensation for employees who sign up for gym memberships.) 정답은 (A)가 된다.

5. According to the speaker, why is a change being made?

(A) To encourage better communication
(B) To satisfy some employees
(C) To improve staff retention
(D) To increase productivity

화자에 따르면, 왜 변화가 생겼는가?

더 나은 의사소통을 권장하기 위해서
몇몇 직원들을 만족시키기 위해서
직원 유지(이직 방지)를 개선하기 위해서
생산성을 증대시키기 위해서

해설 생산성을 증대시키기 위해서라는 말이 언급되어 있으므로(In hopes of increasing workplace productivity, we decided to provide financial compensation for employees who sign up for gym memberships.) 정답은 (D)가 된다. Why에 대한 정답은 because가 일반적이기는 하나 '~하기 위해서'라는 목적으로 대답하는 'in order to부정사'를 주의해서 듣도록 하자.

6. What are the listeners told to do?

(A) Attend management seminars
(B) Inform team members of a change
(C) Update their employee ID badges
(D) Receive an online certification

청자는 무엇을 하라고 요청받았는가?

경영 세미나에 참석한다
팀멤버들에게 변경사항에 대해서 알려준다
직원 ID 배지를 바꾼다
온라인 증명서를 받는다

해설 요청받는 내용은 주로 지문의 후반부에 위치하며 명령문에 초점을 둔다. 바뀐 내용을 팀원에게 말하라고 했으므로(Please make sure to tell your team about this update) 정답은 (B)가 된다.

만점 포인트 2 '문제점'이나 '걱정거리'는 화자의 입에서 나온다!

문제점이나 걱정거리에 관련된 단서는 주로 초반부에 나온다. PART 3의 경우는 worried / concerned (걱정하는), trouble / problem (문제점)과 같은 단어를 사용하여 화자가 직접 말하는 경우가 있으므로 미리 문제를 읽어두고 남자 / 여자를 구분하여 잘 듣도록 한다. 그리고 but / however / unfortunately 등과 같은 분위기의 반전을 나타내는 단어 다음에 문제점이나 걱정거리가 제시되는 경우가 대부분이므로 이러한 단어가 나오면 주의해서 듣도록 하자.

1. 문제점 / 걱정거리 문제 유형

What is the man / woman's **problem**? 남자 / 여자의 문제는 무엇인가?
What is the man / woman **concerned about**? 남자 / 여자가 걱정하는 것은?
What **problem** does the man / woman mention? 남자 / 여자는 어떤 문제를 언급하고 있는가?

2. 문제점 / 걱정거리 표현

- I am **concerned** / **worried** about ~ 저는 ~가 걱정됩니다.
- I have **trouble** / **problem** / **difficulty** ~ 저는 ~에 문제가 있어요.
- **But** / **However** / **Unfortunately** / **Actually** / I'm **afraid** ~
  하지만 / 하지만 / 유감스럽게도 / 사실 / 저는 ~가 우려됩니다.
- The **problem** is ~ 문제는 ~입니다.

DAY 04_02.mp3

PART 3

1. Who most likely is the man?
(A) An auto repairperson
(B) A restaurant manager
(C) An Internet technician
(D) A construction worker

2. What is the man's problem?
(A) He needs more supplies.
(B) He is late for an appointment.
(C) He has a family emergency.
(D) He cannot complete a job on time.

3. What does the woman suggest?
(A) Checking traffic updates
(B) Modifying a design plan
(C) Taking an alternative route
(D) Finishing a job tomorrow

PART 4

4. Where does the listener most likely work?
(A) At a manufacturing plant
(B) At a market research firm
(C) At a retail store
(D) At an auto repair shop

5. What is the speaker's supervisor worried about?
(A) A pricing change
(B) A contract term
(C) A price quote
(D) A specification error

6. What does the speaker imply when she says, "Mr. Reid is quite anxious about this"?
(A) A response should be sent quickly.
(B) A document has not been sent.
(C) She is unable to proceed with a request.
(D) Her manager may be busy later.

해설

Questions 1-3 refer to the following conversation.

W: Jonathan, ❶ how's the Internet cable installation going?
M: Not too bad, Ms. Segal. I'll be done setting up the cables in your restaurant within an hour or two, but I came across a minor problem.
W: Really? What is it?
M: ❷ I'm afraid I don't have enough cables to cover your kitchen. I'll need to head down to Hampton's on Delaware Street to pick up some more.
W: Well, I just came from that area. ❸ There was an accident on Delaware Street. You should probably go around and take Prospect Road instead.
M: Thanks for telling me.

1-3번은 다음 대화에 관한 문제입니다.

여: 조나단, **인터넷 케이블 설치 어떻게 되어 가요?**
남: 나쁘지는 않아요. 시갈 씨. 1시간 혹은 2시간 내로 당신의 레스토랑 케이블 설치가 다 끝날 것 같아요. 하지만 사소한 문제들이 있었어요.
여: 정말요? 무슨 문제인가요?
남: **부엌에 필요한 케이블이 충분하지 않아요.** 케이블이 좀 더 필요해서 델라웨어 가에 있는 햄프턴에 가야 할 것 같아요.
여: 음, 방금 그쪽에서 왔는데요. **델라웨어 가에 사고가 있었어요. 대신에 프로스펙트 도로로 우회해서 가셔야 해요.**
남: 알려줘서 감사해요.

어휘 installation 설치 | accident 사고 | repairperson 정비사 | emergency 긴급한 일 | on time 제시간에 | alternative route 우회도로

1. Who most likely is the man?
(A) An auto repairperson
(B) A restaurant manager
(C) An Internet technician
(D) A construction worker

남자는 누구겠는가?
자동차 정비사
레스토랑 매니저
인터넷 기사
건설 노동자

해설 인터넷 케이블 설치가 어떻게 되어 가고 있는지 물어보고 있어서(how's the Internet cable installation going?) 남자는 인터넷을 설치하는 기사인 (C)가 정답이다. 남자 / 여자 직업을 헷갈리지 않도록 주의하자.

2. What is the man's problem?
(A) He needs more supplies.
(B) He is late for an appointment.
(C) He has a family emergency.
(D) He cannot complete a job on time.

남자가 갖고 있는 문제는?
그는 재료가 더 필요하다.
그는 약속에 늦었다.
그는 가족에게 긴급한 일이 있다.
그는 제 시간에 일을 마치지 못한다.

해설 케이블을 설치하는데, 충분한 케이블이 없다고 했으므로(I'm afraid I don't have enough cables to cover your kitchen.) 재료가 더 필요하다는 (A)가 정답이 된다.

3. What does the woman suggest?
(A) Checking traffic updates
(B) Modifying a design plan
(C) Taking an alternative route
(D) Finishing a job tomorrow

여자가 제안하는 것은 무엇인가?
교통 상황을 확인하는 것
디자인 계획을 수정하는 것
우회도로로 가는 것
내일 일을 끝마치는 것

해설 여자가 거기에서 오는 길인데, 사고가 있어서 프로스펙트 도로로 돌아가라고 했으므로(There was an accident on Delaware Street. You should probably go around and take Prospect Road instead.), 우회도로를 택하는 정답은 (C)가 된다.

해설 미국

Questions 4-6 refer to the following telephone message.

W: Hi there. ❹ It's Gemma Morales from Magic Motors. Thanks for sending the invoice for the new parts we ordered. Based on the inspections we did prior to ordering, we were all highly impressed with the quality of your products. We are hoping to secure some long-term arrangements in the future. ❺ However, my supervisor, Mr. Reid, is concerned about the total cost you quoted. ❻ Would you mind confirming a detailed pricing chart? Mr. Reid is quite anxious about this. Therefore, if you could handle this request at your earliest convenience, that'd be highly appreciated.

4-6번은 다음 전화 메시지에 관한 문제입니다.

여: 안녕하세요. **매직 모터스의 젬마 모럴입니다. 우리가 주문했던 새 부품에 대한 송장을 보내 주셔서 감사합니다.** 주문하기 전에 했던 검사를 봤을 때, 귀사의 제품 품질에 매우 감동했습니다. 향후에 장기간 계약을 맺고 싶습니다. **하지만, 제 상사인 레이드 씨는 견적을 내신 전체 금액에 대해서 우려하고 있습니다. 상세한 가격에 대해서 확인해 주실 수 있을까요? 레이드 씨는 이것에 대해 몹시 알고 싶어합니다. 그래서, 만약 가능한 한 빨리 이 요청을 다루실 수 있다면, 매우 감사하겠습니다.**

어휘 invoice 송장 | inspection 검사 | prior to 이번에 | quote 견적을 내다 | anxious 염려하는

4. Where does the listener most likely work?

(A) At a manufacturing plant
(B) At a market research firm
(C) At a retail store
(D) At an auto repair shop

청자가 일할 것 같은 장소는?

제조공장
마케팅 조사 회사
소매점
자동차 정비소

해설 화자가 매직 모터스에서 일한다고 해서 자동차가 들어가는 (D)를 고르지 않도록 주의하자. 화자가 아닌 청자를 물어보는 것이며, 화자가 새로운 부품을 주문했다고 했으므로(It's Gemma Morales from Magic Motors. Thanks for sending the invoice for the new parts we ordered.) 부품을 만드는 공장인 (A)가 답이 된다.

5. What is the speaker's supervisor worried about?

(A) A pricing change
(B) A contract term
(C) A price quote
(D) A specification error

화자의 상사가 걱정하는 것은 무엇인가?

가격 변동
계약조건
가격 견적서
사양 오류

해설 상사인 레이드 씨가 견적을 낸 비용에 대해서 우려한다고 나와 있으므로(However, my supervisor, Mr. Reid, is concerned about the total cost you quoted.) 정답은 가격 견적서인 (C)가 된다.

6. What does the speaker imply when she says, "Mr. Reid is quite anxious about this"?

(A) A response should be sent quickly.
(B) A document has not been sent.
(C) She is unable to proceed with a request.
(D) Her manager may be busy later.

화자가 "레이드 씨는 이것에 대해 몹시 알고 싶어합니다"라고 말할 때 그녀가 의미하는 것은?

응답을 빨리 받아야 한다.
서류가 아직 보내지지 않았다.
요청을 진행할 수 없다.
그녀의 상사가 나중에 바쁠 수도 있다.

해설 견적서를 상세하게 확인해 줄 수 있는지 물었고, 그 말을 한 뒤에 가능한 한 빨리 요청을 해결해 달라고 했으므로(Would you mind confirming a detailed pricing chart? Mr. Reid is quite anxious about this. Therefore, if you could handle this request at your earliest convenience, that'd be highly appreciated.) 정답은 (A)가 된다.

만점 포인트 3 '장소 / 직업 / 정체' 정답은 초반부를 주목하라!

장소 / 직업 / 정체에 관한 문제는 주로 초반부에 자기 소개와 함께 정답이 나온다. 혹은 처음 부분의 this / here / your / our과 같은 표현이 나오면 집중해서 들을 필요가 있다. 예를 들어, this department store, your marketing team 등으로 쓰여 보다 쉽게 답을 찾을 수 있는 경우가 있기 때문이다. 때로는 사람이나 회사 이름과 같은 고유명사 뒤에 동격으로 다시 말해 설명하는 경우도 있다. 하지만, 직접적으로 언급하지 않고 대화의 전반적인 내용을 통해서 유추해야 하는 고난도의 문제도 출제되므로 주의깊게 잘 들어야 한다.

1. 장소 / 직업 / 정체 문제 유형

Who most likely is the man / woman? 남자 / 여자는 누구일 가능성이 가장 높은가?

Who most likely are the speakers? 화자들은 누구일 가능성이 가장 높은가?

Where are the speakers? 화자들은 어디에 있나요?

Where does the conversation most likely take place? 대화가 이루어질 가능성이 가장 높은 장소는 어디인가?

2. 장소 / 직업 / 정체 정답 표현

This is Jeffrey Campbell, the manager of the IT Department. 저는 IT 부서의 매니저인 제프리 캠벨입니다.

I would like you to come by **here** at Hanlon Auto Shop. 당신이 이곳 핸론 오토샵으로 와주셨으면 합니다.

One of **your** inspectors visited **our** restaurant this morning.
당신의 검사관 중 한 명이 오늘 아침에 우리 식당을 방문했습니다.

Our department store is located near City Hall. 저희 백화점은 시청 근처에 있습니다.

My name is **Carrie Myers**, a reporter from the local newspaper.
저는 캐리 마이어스라고 하며, 지역 신문의 기자입니다.

DAY 04_03.mp3

PART 3

1. Where do the speakers most likely work?
(A) At a hotel
(B) At a bank
(C) At a marketing agency
(D) At an architecture firm

2. What does the woman mean when she says, "I don't know what to tell you"?
(A) She cannot commit to a project yet.
(B) She has made some mistakes.
(C) She lacks experience in the field.
(D) She thinks the information is confidential.

3. What does the man propose?
(A) Signing an agreement
(B) Joining a meeting
(C) Preparing a document
(D) Updating a travel plan

PART 4

4. What type of business is the speaker calling?
(A) A university
(B) A dining establishment
(C) A design firm
(D) A real estate agency

5. How did the speaker learn about the company?
(A) He viewed a sample of the company's work.
(B) He was recommended by an acquaintance.
(C) He watched a commercial on television.
(D) He knew the company's telephone number.

6. What is the speaker mostly concerned about?
(A) The location of a meeting
(B) The timeframe of a project
(C) The requirements of a business
(D) The cost of a service

Questions 1-3 refer to the following conversation.

M: Enid, ❶ I just got a chance to look at the blueprints you've made for Tate Hotel. You did an amazing job!

W: Oh, thank you. I had a lot of fun working on it.

M: Well, how would you like to join my team? Our client is Windham National Bank. We'll be designing their new branch in Vermont.

W: ❷ Wow, that would be a great opportunity. But as of now, I don't know what to tell you. I'll be meeting with my manager this afternoon, though.

M: OK. ❸ Then how about I drop by your meeting and discuss the project with you two? This way, I can explain the details to both you and your manager.

W: Sounds great. I'll be looking forward to it!

1-3번은 다음 대화에 관한 문제입니다.

남: 이너드, **테이트 호텔을 위해 만든 청사진을 방금 봤어요. 굉장히 잘하셨어요!**

여: 오, 감사합니다. 작업하면서 재미있었습니다.

남: 음, 우리 팀에 합류하는 게 어때요? 우리 고객이 윈덤 국제 은행이에요. 우리는 버몬트에 있는 새 지사를 디자인할 거예요.

여: **와우, 굉장히 좋은 기회네요. 하지만 지금으로써, 뭐라고 말씀드릴 수가 없네요.** 오늘 오후에 제가 매니저와 만나긴 할 거예요.

남: 좋아요. **그러면 제가 미팅에 들려서 당신과 매니저와 함께 프로젝트에 대해서 논의하는 것은 어떨까요?** 이렇게 하면 당신과 매니저 두 사람에게 상세한 설명을 할 수 있을 거예요.

여: 좋습니다. 기대하겠습니다!

어휘 blueprint 청사진 | commit 맡다 | confidential 기밀의

1. Where do the speakers most likely work?

(A) At a hotel
(B) At a bank
(C) At a marketing agency
(D) At an architecture firm

화자들은 어디서 근무하겠는가?

호텔에서
은행에서
마케팅 회사에서
건축 회사에서

해설 테이트 호텔이 나온다고 해서 (A)를 고르지 않도록 주의하자. 테이트 호텔의 청사진을 봤다고 했으므로(I just got a chance to look at the blueprints you've made for Tate Hotel. You did an amazing job!) 정답은 (D)가 된다.

2. What does the woman mean when she says, "I don't know what to tell you"?

(A) She cannot commit to a project yet.
(B) She has made some mistakes.
(C) She lacks experience in the field.
(D) She thinks the information is confidential.

여자가 "뭐라고 말씀드릴 수가 없네요"라고 말하는 의미는 무엇인가?

그녀는 프로젝트를 아직 맡을 수가 없다.
그녀는 몇몇 실수를 했다.
그녀는 그 분야에 대해서 경험이 부족하다.
그녀는 정보가 기밀이라고 생각한다.

해설 남자가 요청한 내용에 대해서 지금 당장은 말할 수 없다고 이야기 했으므로(Wow, that would be a great opportunity. But as of now,) 정답은 (A)가 된다.

3. What does the man propose?

(A) Signing an agreement
(B) Joining a meeting
(C) Preparing a document
(D) Updating a travel plan

남자가 제안하는 것은 무엇인가?

계약을 맺는 것
미팅에 참여하는 것
서류를 준비하는 것
여행 계획을 업데이트하는 것

해설 제안 / 요청일 때는 why don't / how about / what about ~이라는 표현에 주목하자. 미팅에 들른다고 했으므로 (Then how about I drop by your meeting and discuss the project with you two?) 미팅에 참여하는 정답은 (B)가 된다.

해설 미국

Questions 4-6 refer to the following telephone message.

M: Hi, my name is Mike Burns. You might have seen my restaurant called Burns Kitchen on Pembroke Fields. ❹ I'm calling to get some new menus designed. ❹❺ I saw a menu you designed at a local restaurant in the area, and I absolutely loved your work. I was wondering whether you could also design my menus in the same style. However, I do have to regrettably inform you that my restaurant has not been doing well. ❻ Therefore, I am worried your price point may be too high. I would like to discuss details such as the price and the timeframe expected, though. If you could give me a call at 555-1977, we can set up a meeting and go from there.

4-6번은 다음 전화 메시지에 관한 문제입니다.

남: 안녕하세요. 제 이름은 마이크 번즈입니다. 펨브룩 필드의 번즈 키친이라는 제 레스토랑을 보셨을 것입니다. **제가 전화를 건 이유는 새로운 메뉴를 디자인하기 위해서입니다. 저는 귀하께서 이 지역에 있는 레스토랑에 디자인한 메뉴를 보았고, 굉장히 마음에 들었습니다.** 똑같은 스타일로 저의 메뉴도 디자인 할 수 있을 지 궁금합니다. 하지만, 유감스럽게도 제 레스토랑 상황이 그렇게 좋지는 않습니다. **그러므로 제가 우려하는 부분은 가격이 너무 비싸지 않을까 걱정이 됩니다.** 가격과 예상 소요 시간에 관한 자세한 것을 논의하고 싶습니다. 555-1977로 연락 주신다면, 만나서 이야기 하고 싶습니다.

어휘 wonder 궁금해하다 | regrettably 유감스럽게도 | inform 알리다 | acquaintance 지인

4. **What type of business is the speaker calling?**

(A) A university
(B) A dining establishment
(C) A design firm
(D) A real estate agency

화자가 전화를 건 곳은 어떤 종류 사업체인가?

대학교
음식 도매업체
디자인 회사
부동산 중개소

해설 화자의 회사를 물어본 것이 아닌, 화자가 전화를 건 곳을 물어보는 문제이므로 헷갈리지 않도록 조심하자. 청자가 디자인한 메뉴를 보고 좋았다고 했으므로(I'm calling to get some new menus designed. I saw a menu you designed at a local restaurant in the area, and I absolutely loved your work.) 정답은 (C)가 된다.

5. **How did the speaker learn about the company?**

(A) He viewed a sample of the company's work.
(B) He was recommended by an acquaintance.
(C) He watched a commercial on television.
(D) He knew the company's telephone number.

화자는 그 회사를 어떻게 알게 되었는가?

회사가 작업한 샘플을 봤다.
지인에게 소개받았다.
TV 광고에서 봤다.
회사 전화번호를 알고 있었다.

해설 그 지역의 다른 레스토랑에서 한 메뉴를 보고 마음에 들었다고 했으므로(I saw a menu you designed at a local restaurant in the area, and I absolutely loved your work.) 정답은 (A)가 된다.

6. **What is the speaker mostly concerned about?**

(A) The location of a meeting
(B) The timeframe of a project
(C) The requirements of a business
(D) The cost of a service

화자가 우려하는 것은 무엇인가?

회의 장소
프로젝트의 기간
요구사항
서비스 비용

해설 concern을 worry로 표현한 부분에서 가격이 너무 비싸지 않을까 걱정된다고 했으므로(Therefore, I am worried your price point may be too high.) 정답은 (D)가 된다.

만점 포인트 4 반전에 주목하라!

'역접'이나 '화제 전환'을 하는 단어인 but, however, unfortunately, actually, in fact, I'm afraid, by the way가 나오면 전달하고자 하는 목적이나 문제를 제기하는 결정적인 이유를 알려주는 단서가 나오므로 집중해서 들어야 한다.

I'm pleased to accept the job offer, **but** I would have to move to Chicago.
일자리 제안을 받아들이게 되어 너무 기쁘지만, 제가 시카고로 이사를 갑니다.

I found the book I want. **Unfortunately**, I can't find my library card.
제가 찾던 책을 찾았습니다. 유감스럽게도, 도서관 카드를 못 찾겠습니다.

W: Mr. Kim is participating too, right? 김 씨도 참석하지요, 그렇죠?
M: Actually, Mr. Kim is meeting with an important client. 실은, 김 씨는 중요한 고객과 만나고 있어요.

M: Could you please let her know that I'm here? 그녀에게 제가 여기 있다고 알려주시겠어요?
W: Oh, **I'm afraid** her flight was canceled last night. 오, 죄송하지만 그녀의 비행기가 어젯밤에 취소되었어요.

DAY 04_04.mp3

PART 3

1. What problem does the woman mention?
(A) A staff member has been injured.
(B) A product is selling poorly.
(C) Some merchandise has been damaged.
(D) Some items are missing from the inventory.

2. Why does the woman say, "He hasn't done that before"?
(A) To comfort a customer
(B) To express concern
(C) To criticize a coworker
(D) To offer some assistance

3. What does the man say he will do?
(A) Negotiate a contract
(B) Submit an application
(C) Reserve a room
(D) Set up a meeting

PART 4

4. What event is the listener planning to attend?
(A) A sporting event
(B) An exposition
(C) A farmers market
(D) A film festival

5. Why does the speaker say, "They usually have a few employees who cancel the trip"?
(A) To change a detail
(B) To agree with an opinion
(C) To deny a request
(D) To suggest a remedy

6. What requires a supervisor's approval?
(A) Some materials
(B) Vacation requests
(C) Some contract terms
(D) Some product samples

해설 영국 - 미국

Questions 1-3 refer to the following conversation.

W: Our new intern Fred sent me his first quarterly sales report last night. I got a chance to review his data. ❶ Unfortunately, it turns out that our sportswear, specifically running shoes, is underperforming in all our stores.

M: Oh?

W: The report also suggested that we should still strongly advertise our sportswear because these products have the highest profit margin out of all of the items we carry.

M: That's a valid point. ❷ We should ask Fred to present his findings to the rest of the Sales Department.

W: He hasn't done that before. ❷ I could do the presentation instead.

M: No. I actually think Fred could learn a lot from this experience. ❸ Let me arrange a meeting with the Sales Department for next Friday.

1-3번은 다음 대화에 관한 문제입니다.

여: 새로운 인턴인 프레드가 지난밤에 1분기 영업 보고서를 저에게 보냈습니다. 그가 보낸 데이터를 검토할 기회가 있었는데요. **불행하게도, 스포츠웨어, 특히 운동화가 모든 점포에서 판매가 저조한 것으로 나타났습니다.**

남: 오?

여: 그 보고서에는 또한 우리가 갖고 있는 제품들 중에서 수익 마진이 가장 좋은 제품이기 때문에 여전히 스포츠웨어 광고를 많이 해야 할 것으로 제안했습니다.

남: 일리가 있네요. **우리는 프레드가 나머지 영업부에게 그가 조사한 것을 발표하라고 요청해야 합니다.**

여: **그는 전에 그것을 해본 적이 없는데요. 제가 대신에 발표를 하겠습니다.**

남: 아니에요. 제 생각에는 프레드도 이 경험을 통해서 많이 배울 수 있을 거예요. **다음 주 금요일에 영업부와의 미팅을 잡겠습니다.**

어휘 quarterly 분기별의 | turn out 판명되다 | profit 이익 | injure 부상을 입다 | merchandise 물건 | inventory 재고 | application 신청서

1. What problem does the woman mention?

(A) A staff member has been injured.
(B) A product is selling poorly.
(C) Some merchandise has been damaged.
(D) Some items are missing from the inventory.

여자가 언급하고 있는 문제는 무엇인가?

한 직원이 부상을 당했다.
제품의 판매가 저조하다.
몇 개의 물건이 손상되었다.
몇 개의 물건이 재고에서 사라졌다.

해설 보고서에 따르면 스포츠웨어 판매가 저조하다고 했으므로(Unfortunately, it turns out that our sportswear, specifically running shoes, is underperforming in all our stores.) 정답은 (B)가 된다. 앞에는 좋은 내용이 나오다가 반전을 이야기하는 unfortunately부터 잘 듣도록 하자.

2. Why does the woman say, "He hasn't done that before"?

(A) To comfort a customer
(B) To express concern
(C) To criticize a coworker
(D) To offer some assistance

여자가 왜 "그는 전에 그것을 해본 적이 없는데요"라고 말하는가?

고객을 안심시키기 위해서
우려를 표명하기 위해서
동료를 비난하기 위해서
도움을 제공하기 위해서

해설 프레드에게 조사한 것을 발표하도록 요청해야 한다는 말에 자기가 대신 한다고 했으므로(We should ask Fred to present his findings to the rest of the Sales Department., I could do the presentation instead.) 그 일을 맡기기에 우려를 표명하는 정답은 (B)가 된다.

3. What does the man say he will do?

(A) Negotiate a contract
(B) Submit an application
(C) Reserve a room
(D) Set up a meeting

남자가 이후에 무엇을 하겠다고 말하는가?

계약을 협상한다
신청서를 제출한다
방을 예약한다
미팅을 잡는다

해설 남자가 미팅을 잡는다고 했으므로(Let me arrange a meeting with the Sales Department for next Friday.) 정답은 (D)가 된다.

해설 영국

Questions 4-6 refer to the following telephone message.

W: Hi, Cedric. This is Anita. ❹ I'm calling you with regards to the trade show in Wadena next week. **Mr. Neill has made it clear that he would like two of our team members to join you there.** ❺ However, they don't seem to be selling any more passes. So, I'll ask some of the local businesses who are attending. **They usually have a few employees who cancel the trip. The two members will be meeting you at the event, and I've let them know where our booth is.** ❻ One more thing–remember that you will need to get authorization from your supervisor for approving your brochures before the trip. **Make sure you put in the request before you go.**

4-6번은 다음 전화 메시지에 관한 문제입니다.

여: 안녕하세요, 세드릭, 저는 애니타입니다. **제가 전화를 건 이유는 다음 주 와데나에서 하는 무역박람회에 관해서입니다.** 네일 씨가 팀원 중 2명이 합류해서 거기에 참석할 것이라고 확인해 줬습니다. **하지만, 더는 출입증을 판매하지 않는 것 같습니다. 그래서 참석하는 지역 업체에게 요청할 것입니다. 몇몇 직원들이 종종 취소하는 경우도 있습니다.** 2명의 직원이 그 행사에서 당신을 만나게 될 거고, 그들에게 우리 부스가 어디 있는지 알려줬어요. **한 가지 더 말씀드리면, 가시기 전에 브로슈어 승인을 위해서 상사의 허가 받는 것을 명심하세요.** 가시기 전에 요청서 제출하는 것도 잊지 마세요.

어휘 with regard to ~에 관해서 | authorization 승인 | exposition 박람회 | remedy 해결책

4. **What event is the listener planning to attend?**
(A) A sporting event
(B) An exposition
(C) A farmers market
(D) A film festival

청자가 참석할 행사는 무엇인가?
스포츠 경기
박람회
농산물 시장
영화 축제

해설 Trade show에 참석한다고 나와있으므로(I'm calling you with regards to the trade show in Wadena next week.) 정답은 (B)가 된다.

5. **Why does the speaker say, "They usually have a few employees who cancel the trip"?**
(A) To change a detail
(B) To agree with an opinion
(C) To deny a request
(D) To suggest a remedy

화자는 왜 "몇몇 직원들이 종종 취소하는 경우도 있습니다"라고 말하는가?
세부적인 사항을 변경하기 위해서
의견에 동의하기 위해서
요청을 거절하기 위해서
해결책을 제안하기 위해서

해설 앞에서 출입증을 더는 판매하지 않는다고 나왔고, 그 뒤에 종종 취소하는 직원들이 있어 다른 업체에게 물어보겠다고 했으므로(However, they don't seem to be selling any more passes. So, I'll ask some of the local businesses who are attending.) 통행증을 구할 수 있다는 의미가 내포되어 있는 정답은 (D)가 된다. 화자의 의도를 본격적으로 드러내는 반전을 나타내는 however 뒤를 잘 듣도록 하자.

6. **What requires a supervisor's approval?**
(A) Some materials
(B) Vacation requests
(C) Some contract terms
(D) Some product samples

상사의 승인이 필요한 것은 무엇인가?
자료
휴가 요청서
계약 조건
제품 샘플

해설 상사의 브로슈어 승인이 필요하다고 나와있으므로(One more thing–remember that you will need to get authorization from your supervisor for approving your brochures before the trip.) 정답은 (A)가 된다.

만점 포인트 5 요청 / 제안 / 미래의 일은 '후반부'에 집중하라!

요청 / 제안 / 미래의 일을 물어보는 문제는 정답이 주로 후반부에 나온다. 특히, 명령문이나 You를 언급한 문장을 주의해서 듣도록 하자. PART 4의 경우는 미래의 일어날 일에 대해서 후반부가 아닌 초반이나 중반부에 언급하는 순서 파괴적인 문제가 종종 출제되는 경우도 있으므로 전체의 내용을 모두 이해하고 소화할 수 있는 능력이 필요하다.

1. 요청 / 제안 / 미래의 일 문제 유형

What does the woman **request** the man to do? 여자가 남자에게 부탁하는 것은 무엇인가? 요청
What are listeners **asked** to do next? 청자들은 다음에 무엇을 하라고 요청받나요? 요청
What does the man / woman **recommend / suggest**? 남자 / 여자는 무엇을 추천/제안하나요? 제안
What will listeners **hear** about **next**? 청자들은 다음에 무엇을 들을 것인가요? 미래
What will **happen next**? 다음에 무슨 일이 일어날까요? 미래
What does the woman say **she will do**? 여자는 무엇을 할 것이라고 말하나요? 미래
What will the man most likely **do next**? 남자는 다음에 무엇을 할 것 같은가요? 미래

2. 요청 / 제안 / 미래의 일 정답 표현

- Please, Make sure, Be sure ~
- Why don't you ~?, How about ~?, What about ~?, Can you ~?, Could you ~?
- Do you mind ~?, I'd like you to ~, I want you to ~
- I recommend / suggest / propose ~
- You should ~, You have to ~, You can ~, You could ~, You might want to ~, You'd better ~
- Let's ~

DAY 04_05.mp3

PART 3

1. What project is the woman working on?
(A) Editing a video clip
(B) Designing a Web site
(C) Renovating an office
(D) Organizing a company dinner

2. What does the man suggest changing?
(A) Some images
(B) Some furniture
(C) An e-mail address
(D) A company logo

3. What does the woman say she will do?
(A) Reserve a conference room
(B) Contact a coworker
(C) Take more photographs
(D) Rent some equipment

PART 4

4. Where does the announcement most likely take place?
(A) On an airplane
(B) On a cruise ship
(C) On a bus
(D) On a train

5. What is the reason for the delay?
(A) Vehicle maintenance
(B) Heavy Traffic
(C) Some damaged machinery
(D) Inclement weather condition

6. What does the speaker say she expects will happen?
(A) The weather will not impact the travel time.
(B) The listeners will arrive at their destination later than anticipated.
(C) A different vehicle will have to be used.
(D) An alternative route may have to be taken.

Questions 1-3 refer to the following conversation.	1-3번은 다음 대화에 관한 문제입니다.
M: Hey, Chloe. ❶ Great job updating the company Web site! The new designs look much more professional than before.	**남:** 안녕하세요, 클로에. **회사 웹사이트 업데이트 너무 잘하셨던데요!** 새로운 디자인이 이전보다 훨씬 전문적으로 보여요.
W: Thanks! I agree. Should we launch it now?	**여:** 고맙습니다! 저도 그렇다고 생각해요. 지금 개시할까요?
M: We're just about ready. ❷ I think the photos of our office are a little old, though. We should replace them with more current ones since we renovated the office a few months ago.	**남:** 준비가 다 되었어요. **사무실 사진이 조금 오래돼 보이는데요. 몇 달 전에 사무실을 보수공사 했기 때문에 더 최근 사진으로 교체해야 해요.**
W: OK, that shouldn't be too hard. ❸ I'll email Tyler. I'm sure he has more recent photos since he was in charge of the renovation project.	**여:** 좋아요. 그건 어렵지 않아요. **제가 타일러에게 이메일을 보낼게요.** 보수공사 프로젝트를 그가 책임졌기 때문에 더 최근 사진을 갖고 있을 거예요.

어휘 professional 전문적인 | launch 개시하다 | replace 교체하다 | in charge of ~에 책임이 있다

1. What project is the woman working on? / 여자가 작업하고 있는 프로젝트는 무엇인가?

(A) Editing a video clip / 비디오 영상을 편집하는 것
(B) Designing a Web site / 웹사이트를 디자인하는 것
(C) Renovating an office / 사무실 보수 공사를 하는 것
(D) Organizing a company dinner / 회사 저녁을 주관하는 것

해설 남자가 여자에게 회사 웹사이트 업데이트를 너무 잘했다고 했으므로(Great job updating the company Web site!) 정답은 (B)가 된다.

2. What does the man suggest changing? / 남자가 바꾸라고 제안한 것은 무엇인가?

(A) Some images / 몇몇 사진들
(B) Some furniture / 몇몇 가구
(C) An e-mail address / 이메일 주소
(D) A company logo / 회사 로고

해설 사진이 오래되어 보여서, 최근 사진으로 교체하라고 했으므로(I think the photos of our office are a little old, though. We should replace them with more current ones since we renovated the office a few months ago.) 정답은 (A)가 된다.

3. What does the woman say she will do? / 여자가 무엇을 할 거라고 말하는가?

(A) Reserve a conference room / 회의실을 예약한다
(B) Contact a coworker / 동료에게 연락한다
(C) Take more photographs / 사진을 더 찍는다
(D) Rent some equipment / 장비를 대여한다

해설 이메일을 보낸다고 했으므로(I'll email Tyler.) 동료에게 연락한다고 하는 정답은 (B)가 된다. Contact를 전화한다는 의미로만 생각하지 말자.

해설 미국

Questions 4-6 refer to the following announcement.

W: Good evening, passengers. ❹ I'll be your pilot today for the 5:25 departure to Heath. ❺ I would first like to apologize for the unexpected delay caused by the blizzard last night. ❻ Our total travel time may be affected as a result. We thank you for your understanding.

4-6번은 다음 공지에 관한 문제입니다.

여: 안녕하세요, 승객 여러분. **저는 히스로 5시 25분에 출발하는 기장입니다. 우선 지난밤 눈보라로 인해 예상치 못한 지연에 사과를 드리고 싶습니다. 그래서 전체 비행 시간이 결과적으로 영향을 받을 것입니다.** 이해해 주셔서 감사합니다.

어휘 unexpected delay 예상치 못한 지연 | blizzard 눈보라 | maintenance 정비 | alternative route 우회도로

4. Where does the announcement most likely take place?

(A) On an airplane
(B) On a cruise ship
(C) On a bus
(D) On a train

공지가 일어나는 장소는 어디인가?

비행기
크루즈 배
버스
기차

해설 화자는 pilot이라고 자기 신분을 밝혔으므로(I'll be your pilot today for the 5:25 departure to Heath.) 정답은 (A)가 된다. 직업 / 직종을 묻는 질문에 대한 답변을 찾을 때 this / your / our / here에 주목하도록 하자.

5. What is the reason for the delay?

(A) Vehicle maintenance
(B) Heavy Traffic
(C) Some damaged machinery
(D) Inclement weather condition

지연의 이유는 무엇인가?

차량정비
교통 체증
손상된 기계
악천후

해설 눈보라로 인해 지체가 된다고 했으므로(I would first like to apologize for the unexpected delay caused by the blizzard last night.) 정답은 악천후인 (D)가 된다.

6. What does the speaker say she expects will happen?

(A) The weather will not impact the travel time.
(B) The listeners will arrive at their destination later than anticipated.
(C) A different vehicle will have to be used.
(D) An alternative route may have to be taken.

화자가 앞으로 일어날 것으로 예상하는 것은 무엇인가?

날씨가 여행 시간에 영향을 주지 않을 것이다.
청자들이 예상보다 목적지에 늦게 도착할 예정이다.
다른 차량이 사용되어야 할 것이다.
우회 도로를 선택해야 할지도 모른다.

해설 예상치 못한 지연으로 여행 시간에 영향을 준다고 했으므로(Our total travel time may be affected as a result.) 목적지에 늦게 도착한다는 정답은 (B)가 된다.

고난도 실전 문제

DAY 04_06.mp3

PART 3

1. What most likely is the woman's job?
   (A) Graphic designer
   (B) Editor
   (C) Bookkeeper
   (D) Sales representative

2. What do the men do at their company?
   (A) They coordinate orientation sessions.
   (B) They manage client accounts.
   (C) They make travel arrangements.
   (D) They review departmental budgets.

3. What does the woman inquire about?
   (A) A computer password
   (B) A salary figure
   (C) A parking permit
   (D) A dining area

---

4. Who will be visiting the company?
   (A) A CEO
   (B) A TV reporter
   (C) An overseas client
   (D) A local politician

5. Why does the man say, "I'm leading a training seminar all day Wednesday"?
   (A) He requests a list of seminar attendees.
   (B) He is unable to fulfill a request.
   (C) He needs help preparing for an event.
   (D) He is looking forward to completing a task.

6. According to the woman, what does the company hope to do by the end of the year?
   (A) Kick off a marketing campaign
   (B) Launch a new product line
   (C) Expand into a foreign market
   (D) Open a new location

---

7. What most likely is the woman's job?
   (A) Receptionist
   (B) Doctor
   (C) Lab researcher
   (D) Insurance agent

8. What does the woman want to change?
   (A) Payment information
   (B) The time of an appointment
   (C) The location of a hospital
   (D) A marketing strategy

9. What will the man do next?
   (A) Look for his medical records
   (B) Update a calendar
   (C) Call a credit card company
   (D) Complete a patient information form

PART 4

10. What is the broadcast about?
(A) The city's election results
(B) A performance review
(C) A new movie release
(D) A famous drama

11. According to the speaker, what did Marcella Richard do recently?
(A) She won a prestigious prize.
(B) She created a new organization.
(C) She returned from overseas.
(D) She participated in a play.

12. What will listeners most likely hear next?
(A) An advertisement
(B) An interview
(C) A traffic update
(D) A weather report

---

13. What type of event is taking place?
(A) A software convention
(B) A shareholder meeting
(C) A retirement party
(D) An awards ceremony

14. What product does the speaker highlight?
(A) An innovative device
(B) An eco-friendly automobile
(C) An adjustable desk
(D) A wireless keyboard

15. Who is Molly Underwood?
(A) A marketing director
(B) A human resources worker
(C) A corporate executive
(D) A product designer

---

16. Why does the speaker say, "it's only been two months"?
(A) To give an explanation
(B) To highlight a peculiarity
(C) To agree with an opinion
(D) To make a suggestion

17. What does the speaker show the listeners?
(A) A graph of monthly sales
(B) A study of some products
(C) A report on a new trend
(D) A list of some stores

18. What are the listeners expected to do by Friday?
(A) Sign up for a service
(B) Prepare a presentation
(C) Visit some stores
(D) Set up a meeting

PART 3&4

DAY 05

시각 정보 문제 두려워하지 마라!

음원 바로 듣기

동영상 강의 바로 보기

시각 정보 문제는 그래프, 지도, 리스트, 평면도 등 주어진 시각 정보를 보고 대화의 내용과 연결해서 정답을 찾는 유형의 문제로 자칫 어렵게 느껴질 수 있지만, 문제 자체의 난이도는 그렇게 높은 편이 아니다. 시각 정보 문제의 유형과 빈출 정답 패턴을 잘 숙지하고 문제를 푼다면 정답을 쉽게 찾을 수 있다.

만점 포인트

이것만 알면 만점!

1 시각 정보 문제의 보기는 절대로 똑같이 말해주지 않는다.
보기에 제시되지 않은 부분을 확인하라.

2 리스트, 목록, 일정표의 경우 변동 사항을 주목하라!
처음이 아니라 두 번째 세 번째 언급하는 것이 주로 정답이다.

3 지도, 좌석 배치도, 평면도 등의 문제는 '전치사'를 잘 이용하라!

4 막대 / 파이 / 선 그래프는 '수치'나 '최상급'을 주목하라!

5 쿠폰, 영수증, 탑승권, 청구서는 자료와 일치 또는 불일치를 확인하라!

만점 포인트 1 시각 정보 문제의 보기는 절대로 똑같이 말해주지 않는다.

시각 정보를 묻는 문제에서 나오는 보기는 녹음에서 절대로 똑같이 말해주지 않으므로, 보기에 제시되지 않은 부분을 예의주시하며 문제를 풀어야 한다. 만약 시각 자료만 보고 답이 나올 수 있는 문제라면 그건 거의 오답일 확률이 높다.

DAY 05_01.mp3

PART 3

www.openrestaurants.com / reviews	
Review of Fantasy Café	
Criteria	Rating (out of 5)
Taste	★★★★★
Ambience	★
Service	★
Value	★★★★

1. What is the woman worried about?
(A) Cost of ingredients
(B) Losing business
(C) Passing inspection
(D) Shortage of employees

2. Look at the graphic. Which area will be discussed at the next employee meeting?
(A) Taste
(B) Ambience
(C) Service
(D) Value

3. What does the man recommend doing?
(A) Providing a discount
(B) Hiring a consultant
(C) Purchasing new furniture
(D) Comparing vendor prices

PART 4

CEMA Convention Schedule		
Time	**Event**	**Speaker**
10:00	Best Electric Cars	Kelly Bernstein
11:00	Latest Navigation Systems	Sherman Brown
13:00	Improving Fuel Efficiency	Emily Hwang
14:00	Best Sports Cars	Jeremy Hopkins
15:00	Reception	CEMA President

4. What is the purpose of the call?
(A) To offer a job
(B) To check on an order
(C) To request product samples
(D) To make a reservation

5. Look at the graphic. Who is the speaker calling?
(A) Kelly Bernstein
(B) Sherman Brown
(C) Emily Hwang
(D) Jeremy Hopkins

6. What does the speaker ask the listener to do?
(A) Provide pricing information
(B) Visit a Web site
(C) Review a convention schedule
(D) Send a registration payment

Questions 1-3 refer to the following conversation and review.

M: Hey, Stacey. Come look at this Web site. Our restaurant received some negative reviews. Let me show you one.

W: Oh, no. Well, now we know which areas we could work on. Seeing this review, ❶ I'm concerned potential customers will choose our competitors' places instead.

M: Same here. At least we're renovating the dining hall. ❷ The dining environment will be more pleasant afterwards.

W: ❷ Yes, but let's make sure to discuss solutions for the other low rating at the next employee meeting.

M: Good idea. ❸ I actually think we should bring in a consultant for that. We can't have any more bad reviews.

1-3번은 다음 대화와 평가에 관한 문제입니다.

남: 안녕하세요, 스테이시. 와서 이 웹사이트 좀 보세요. 우리 레스토랑이 부정적인 평가를 몇 개 받았어요. 하나를 보여 드릴게요.

여: 오, 안 되는데. 음, 이제 우리가 어떤 분야에 좀 더 노력해야 할지 알겠네요. 이 평가를 보니, **우리 잠재 고객들이 경쟁업체를 대신 선택할까 봐 걱정이네요.**

남: 동감이에요. 적어도 우리는 식당을 보수공사하고 있어요. **분위기는 그 이후에 좋아질 거예요.**

여: **네, 하지만 낮은 점수를 받은 다른 부분에 대한 해결책에 대해 다음 직원회의에서 논의를 해봅시다.**

남: 좋은 생각이에요. **실은 저는 컨설턴트를 데리고 와야 한다고 봐요.** 더는 부정적인 평가를 받을 수는 없어요.

어휘 negative review 부정적인 평가 | work on 노력하다 | competitor 경쟁업체 | renovate 보수하다 | consultant 컨설턴트 | ingredient 재료 | inspection 통과 | shortage 부족 | ambience 분위기 | vendor 판매

1. **What is the woman worried about?**
(A) Cost of ingredients
(B) Losing business
(C) Passing inspection
(D) Shortage of employees

여자는 무엇을 우려하는가?
재료비
영업손실
검사 통과
직원 부족

해설 잠재 고객들이 다른 경쟁업체로 갈까 봐 우려한다고 말했으므로(I'm concerned potential customers will choose our competitors' places instead.) 정답은 (B)이다.

2. **Look at the graphic. Which area will be discussed at the next employee meeting?**
(A) Taste
(B) Ambience
(C) Service
(D) Value

시각 정보를 보시오. 어느 부분이 다음 직원회의에서 논의될 것인가?
맛
분위기
서비스
가치

해설 분위기는 괜찮아질 것이지만, 낮은 점수를 받은 다른 부분에 대해서 논의를 하자고 했으므로(The dining environment will be more pleasant afterwards., Yes, but let's make sure to discuss solutions for the other low rating at the next employee meeting.) 정답은 (C)가 된다.

3. **What does the man recommend doing?**
(A) Providing a discount
(B) Hiring a consultant
(C) Purchasing new furniture
(D) Comparing vendor prices

남자가 추천하는 것은 무엇인가?
할인을 제공하는 것
컨설턴트를 고용하는 것
새 가구를 구매하는 것
판매 가격을 비교하는 것

해설 컨설턴트를 데리고 오는 것이 좋다고 했으므로(I actually think we should bring in a consultant for that.) 정답은 (B)가 된다.

Questions 4-6 refer to the following telephone message and conference schedule.

W: Hello, it's Sooji Kim from HYD Motors. We spoke briefly at the CEMA Convention a month ago. I listened to your informative talk, and we discussed HYD's upcoming vehicle line for a moment afterwards. ❹❺ I'm contacting you because I want to hire you to advise us on how to make our cars more fuel-efficient. I know that this is your specialty, so I'd really like you to join us for this project. ❻ Would you mind sending a chart of your consulting fees to me here at blee@hydmotors.com? Thank you.

4-6번은 다음 전화 메시지와 회의 스케줄에 관한 문제입니다.

여: 안녕하세요, 저는 HYD 모터스의 수지 김입니다. 한 달 전에 CEMA 컨벤션에서 잠시 이야기를 나눈 적이 있죠. 제가 당신의 유익한 발표를 잘 들었고, 그 이후에 잠시 동안 HYD의 곧 출시될 차량 제품군에 대해서 논의했습니다. **저희 자동차의 연료 효율성을 좀 더 좋게 만들 방법에 관해 조언을 좀 해주십사 귀하를 채용하고 싶어서 연락을 드립니다.** 이 분야를 전문으로 하신다고 알고 있어서 이번 프로젝트에 꼭 참여해 주셨으면 좋겠습니다. **저에게 blee@hydmotors.com으로 상담료 표를 좀 보내주시겠습니까?** 감사합니다.

어휘 briefly 간단하게 | advise 조언하다 | efficient 효과적으로 | specialty 전공 분야 | registration payment 등록비

4. What is the purpose of the call?

(A) To offer a job
(B) To check on an order
(C) To request product samples
(D) To make a reservation

전화를 건 목적은 무엇인가?

일자리를 제공하기 위해서
주문을 확인하기 위해서
제품 샘플을 요청하기 위해서
예약을 하기 위해서

해설 전화를 건 목적이 고용하고 싶어서라고 나와 있으므로(I'm contacting you because I want to hire you to advise us on how to make our cars more fuel-efficient.) 정답은 (A)가 된다.

5. Look at the graphic. Who is the speaker calling?

(A) Kelly Bernstein
(B) Sherman Brown
(C) Emily Hwang
(D) Jeremy Hopkins

시각 정보를 보시오. 화자는 누구에게 전화하고 있는가?

켈리 번스타인
셔먼 브라운
에밀리 황
제레미 홉킨스

해설 연료 효율성에 대해서 언급하고 있으므로(I'm contacting you because I want to hire you to advise us on how to make our cars more fuele-fficient.) 도표에서 찾으면 정답은 (C)가 된다.

6. What does the speaker ask the listener to do?

(A) Provide pricing information
(B) Visit a Web site
(C) Review a convention schedule
(D) Send a registration payment

화자는 청자에게 무엇을 요구하는가?

가격 정보를 제공한다
웹사이트를 방문한다
컨벤션 일정을 검토한다
등록비를 송금한다

해설 요구 내용은 주로 후반부에 위치하며, 마지막에 상담료 표를 보내달라고 했으므로(Would you mind sending a chart of your consulting fees to me here at blee@hydmotors.com?) 정답은 (A)가 된다.

만점 포인트 2 리스트, 목록, 일정표의 경우 변동 사항을 주목하라!

리스트, 목록, 일정표와 같은 시각 정보 문제에서는 일반적으로 '취소'나 '변경' 혹은 '오류'로 인한 '변동 사항'을 언급하여 헷갈리게 만드는 경우가 있다. 따라서 보통 처음에 언급한 정보보다는 두 번째 혹은 세 번째 언급한 것이 주로 정답이 된다. 설문조사와 같은 시각 정보 문제는 제일 높게 평가된 항목뿐만 아니라 개선을 필요로 하는 낮게 평가된 것도 정답으로 종종 출제되므로 문제를 듣기 전에 정보를 미리 파악해 두는 것이 중요하다.

DAY 05_02.mp3

PART 3

Model	Price Per Square Foot
Synthetic – Acrylic	$10
Synthetic – Polyester	$15
Natural – Seagrass	$10
Natural – Wool Blend	$20

1. What does the client want?
(A) A discounted price
(B) A personalized design
(C) A faster delivery
(D) A different style

2. Look at the graphic. What will the client receive?
(A) Synthetic – Acrylic
(B) Synthetic – Polyester
(C) Natural – Seagrass
(D) Natural – Wool Blend

3. What will the woman most likely do next?
(A) Issue a coupon
(B) Visit another department
(C) Notify a colleague
(D) Ship a product

PART 4

Safety Inspection	
Name of Building: The Piercer	**Inspector:** David Nandigam
Safety Checklist: ☒ Earthquake safety measures ☒ Proper ventilation and heating ☒ Fire safety measures	**Notes:** No risks identified

4. Where does the speaker work?
(A) At a bank
(B) At an architecture firm
(C) At a real estate agency
(D) At a mechanic shop

5. Look at the graphic. Which section of the report does the speaker ask about?
(A) Name of Building
(B) Safety Checklist
(C) Inspector
(D) Notes

6. What does the speaker say he is worried about?
(A) Repairing some equipment
(B) Charging a client
(C) Finding a new tenant
(D) Fulfilling a service

해설 미국 - 영국

Questions 1-3 refer to the following conversation and bill.

M: Yoo-na, Ms. Moore contacted us last night. ❶ She told me that she'd like natural carpeting instead of the synthetic one she requested before. ❷ She also wants ones that are priced the same as the synthetic ones.

W: Thanks for letting me know. I'll take care of it

M: How long will it take?

W: Not long at all. I just need the name of the model the client requested initially so we can cancel the order right away.

M: Give me a second. I wrote it down somewhere... Here you go. ❷ She originally ordered acrylic.

W: Thank you. ❸ I just have to call the production team and let them know about the update. Then we'll need to issue a new invoice and send it to Ms. Moore.

1-3번은 다음 대화와 청구서에 관한 문제입니다.

남: 유나, 무어 씨가 지난밤에 연락했습니다. **그녀가 이전에 요청했던 합성제품 대신에 천연산 카펫으로 하고 싶다고 말했습니다. 또한 합성제품과 가격이 똑같은 것을 원합니다.**

여: 알려주셔서 감사합니다. 처리할게요.

남: 얼마나 걸릴까요?

여: 오래 걸리지 않을 거예요. 바로 취소할 수 있도록 맨 처음에 고객이 요청한 모델명이 필요합니다.

남: 잠시만요. 어딘가에 적어놨는데요… 여기 있네요. **맨 처음에 주문한 것은 아크릴로 만든 것이에요.**

여: 고맙습니다. **생산팀에 연락해서 바꿀 수 있도록 할게요.** 그러고 나서 새 송장을 만들어 무어 씨에게 보내야 해요.

어휘 contact 연락하다 | natural 천연의 | synthetic 합성의 | initially 처음에 | acrylic 아크릴의 | personalized 맞춤화된

1. What does the client want?

(A) A discounted price
(B) A personalized design
(C) A faster delivery
(D) A different style

고객이 원하는 것은 무엇인가?

할인된 가격
맞춤화된 디자인
빠른 배송
다른 스타일

해설 합성이 아닌 천연산을 원한다고 했으므로(She told me that she'd like natural carpeting instead of the synthetic one she requested before.) 정답은 (D)가 된다.

2. Look at the graphic. What will the client receive?

(A) Synthetic – Acrylic
(B) Synthetic – Polyester
(C) Natural – Seagrass
(D) Natural – Wool Blend

시각 정보를 보시오. 고객은 무엇을 받게 될 것인가?

합성 – 아크릴
합성 – 폴리에스테르
천연 – 해변 식물
천연 – 울 블랜드

해설 맨 처음에 주문한 아크릴과 가격이 같은 천연산을 찾아보면(She also wants ones that are priced the same as the synthetic ones., She originally ordered acrylic.) 정답은 (C)가 된다.

3. What will the woman most likely do next?

(A) Issue a coupon
(B) Visit another department
(C) Notify a colleague
(D) Ship a product

여자가 다음으로 무엇을 할 것 같은가?

쿠폰을 발행한다
다른 부서를 방문한다
동료에게 알려준다
제품을 배송한다

해설 생산팀에 전화를 한다고 했으므로(I just have to call the production team and let them know about the update.) 정답은 (C)가 된다.

해설 미국

Questions 4-6 refer to the following telephone message and inspection report.

M: ❹ Good morning. It's Eddie Drake from Keller Estates, the architects working on The Piercer. **You completed a building safety check on The Piercer, and I just received word that we failed the check.** ❺ I am confused by that because when the inspector was here, he did not mention any issues. I specifically showed the inspector where our fire extinguishers and smoke alarms are. **However, we weren't given any notes on why we failed that section.** ❻ It's extremely concerning because I have new tenants ready to move in. They have already signed their contracts and paid their deposits.

4-6번은 다음 전화 메시지와 검사 보고서에 관한 문제입니다.

남: 안녕하세요. 피어서를 작업하고 있는 켈러 에스테이트의 건축가 에디 드레이크입니다. 당신이 피어서의 건물 안전 검사를 끝내셨는데, 저희가 검사에서 통과되지 못했다는 말을 들었습니다. **검사관이 여기 왔을 때 어떠한 문제에 대해서도 언급하지 않았기 때문에, 그 이야기를 듣고 혼란스럽습니다. 저는 소화기와 연기 탐지기가 어디 있는지 검사관에게 특별히 보여줬습니다.** 하지만, 왜 우리가 그 부분에서 통과를 못했는지에 대해 어떠한 메모도 받지 못했습니다. **매우 걱정이 되는 부분은 곧 있으면 세입자가 이사 올 예정입니다. 그들은 벌써 계약서에 사인을 했고 보증금도 지불한 상태입니다.**

어휘 architect 건축가 | building safety check 건물 안전 검사 | inspector 검사자 | specifically 특별히 | fire extinguisher 소화기 | smoke alarm 연기 탐지기 | extremely 매우 | tenant 세입자 | deposit 계약금 | real estate agency 부동산 | mechanic shop 정비소

4. Where does the speaker work?

(A) At a bank
(B) At an architecture firm
(C) At a real estate agency
(D) At a mechanic shop

화자가 일하는 곳은 어디인가?

은행
건축 회사
부동산
정비소

해설 화자 본인이 건축가라고 밝혔으므로(Good morning. It's Eddie Drake from Keller Estates, the architects working on The Piercer.) 정답은 건축 회사인 (B)가 된다.

5. Look at the graphic. Which section of the report does the speaker ask about?

(A) Name of Building
(B) Safety Checklist
(C) Inspector
(D) Notes

시각 정보를 보시오. 보고서의 어느 부분을 화자가 요청하는가?

건물명
안전 점검 목록
검사관
메모

해설 화자가 검사원이 왔을 때 특별히 소화기와 연기 탐지기를 보여줬는데 그 부분이 왜 통과가 안 되었는지를 모르겠다고 했으므로(I am confused by that because when the inspector was here, he did not mention any issues. I specifically showed the inspector where our fire extinguishers and smoke alarms are.) 그 부분이 적혀 있는 정답은 (B)가 된다.

6. What does the speaker say he is worried about?

(A) Repairing some equipment
(B) Charging a client
(C) Finding a new tenant
(D) Fulfilling a service

화자가 말하기를 화자는 무엇을 우려하는가?

장비를 수리하는 것
고객에게 요금을 청구하는 것
새 세입자를 구하는 것
서비스를 이행하는 것

해설 새로운 세입자들이 곧 이사 올 예정이므로, 서비스를 이행할 수 없을까 봐 우려하고 있으므로(It's extremely concerning because I have new tenants ready to move in. They have already signed their contracts and paid their deposits.) 정답은 (D)가 된다.

만점 포인트 3 지도, 좌석 배치도, 평면도 등의 문제는 '전치사'를 잘 이용하라!

위치를 설명하는 유형의 시각 정보 문제에서 지도의 경우는 도로명을 먼저 파악하는 것이 중요하며, 좌석 배치도와 약도의 경우는 위치나 방향을 나타내는 전치사를(across from 건너편, opposite 맞은편, next to 옆, beside 옆, corner 모퉁이, in front of 앞, behind 뒤, window seat 창가 좌석, aisle seat 통로 좌석) 익혀두어야 한다.

DAY 05_03.mp3

PART 3

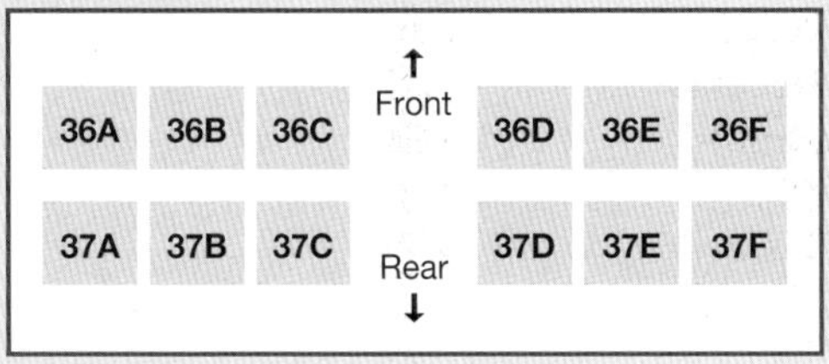

1. What is the purpose of the conversation?
(A) To negotiate a discount
(B) To resolve a conflict
(C) To explain a procedure
(D) To complain about a service

2. Look at the graphic. Which seat was the man originally assigned to?
(A) 36B
(B) 36C
(C) 37B
(D) 37C

3. What does the woman recommend doing?
(A) Issuing a new boarding pass
(B) Asking for a seat upgrade
(C) Notifying a crew member
(D) Requesting a voucher

PART 4

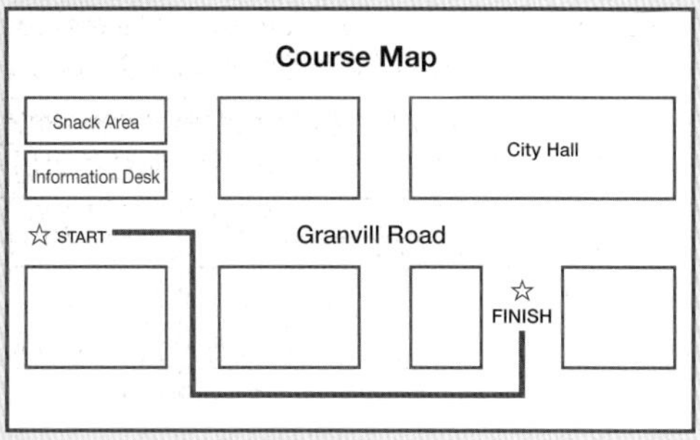

4. What event are the listeners probably attending?
(A) A street parade
(B) A charity event
(C) A sports competition
(D) A city tour

5. According to the speaker, what should the listeners pick up?
(A) A T-shirt
(B) A brochure
(C) A gift voucher
(D) A drink

6. Look at the graphic. Where will the listeners take a group photo?
(A) At the Information Desk
(B) At the Snack Area
(C) At the Finish Line
(D) At City Hall

해설 미국 - 미국

Questions 1-3 refer to the following conversation and seat map.

M: Excuse me. ❶ Sorry to bother you, but I think you're in my seat. My boarding pass says that I should be in seat C.

W: ❷ I'm quite sure I'm in 36C. Can I take a look at your boarding pass? See, here. Your seat is right behind mine.

M: Oh, thanks! Sorry for the confusion. But would you mind switching places with me? My colleague will be sitting in 36B, and we were hoping to finalize our presentation during the flight.

W: OK, no problem. I don't mind as long as I still get to sit in an aisle seat. ❸ We should probably tell the flight attendant about the change, though.

1-3번은 다음 대화와 좌석 배치도에 관한 문제입니다.

남: 실례합니다. **죄송한데, 제 생각에 제 자리에 앉으신 것 같아요. 제 탑승권에 제 자리가 C라고 되어 있거든요.**

여: 제 자리는 36C가 확실한데요. 탑승권 좀 볼 수 있을까요? 아, 여기 보세요. 당신 자리는 제 뒷자리입니다.

남: 오, 감사합니다! 혼동 드려서 죄송합니다. 그런데 저랑 자리 좀 바꿔 주실 수 있을까요? 제 동료가 36B에 앉는데, 비행하는 동안에 프레젠테이션을 같이 마무리하고 싶어서요.

여: 좋아요, 문제없어요. 복도 자리에만 앉는다면 괜찮습니다. **하지만 승무원에게 바꾸는 것에 대해 이야기해야 할 거예요.**

어휘 bother 괴롭히다 | boarding pass 탑승권 | confusion 혼란 | switch 바꾸다 | colleague 동료 | finalize 마무리하다 | flight attendant 승무원 | negotiate 협상하다 | resolve 해결하다 | conflict 갈등 | procedure 절차

1. What is the purpose of the conversation?

(A) To negotiate a discount
(B) To resolve a conflict
(C) To explain a procedure
(D) To complain about a service

대화의 목적은 무엇인가?

할인을 협상하기 위해서
문제를 해결하기 위해서
절차를 설명하기 위해서
서비스에 대해 불평하기 위해서

해설 자리가 바뀌었다는 대화이므로(Sorry to bother you, but I think you're in my seat. My boarding pass says that I should be in seat C.) 정답은 문제를 해결해 가는 (B)가 된다.

2. Look at the graphic. Which seat was the man originally assigned to?

(A) 36B
(B) 36C
(C) 37B
(D) 37C

시각 정보를 보시오. 어느 좌석이 남자가 맨 처음에 배정받았던 곳인가?

36B
36C
37B
37C

해설 남자가 배정받은 곳은 여자의 자리인 36C의 뒷자리이므로(I'm quite sure I'm in 36C. Can I take a look at your boarding pass? See, here. Your seat is right behind mine.) 정답은 (D)가 된다.

3. What does the woman recommend doing?

(A) Issuing a new boarding pass
(B) Asking for a seat upgrade
(C) Notifying a crew member
(D) Requesting a voucher

여자는 무엇을 추천하는가?

새 탑승권을 발권하는 것
좌석 업그레이드를 요청하는 것
승무원에게 알리는 것
바우처를 요청하는 것

해설 승무원에게 말해야 한다고 했으므로(We should probably tell the flight attendant about the change, though.) flight attendant를 crew member로 패러프레이징한 정답은 (C)가 된다.

Questions 4-6 refer to the following instruction and map.

W: ❹ I'd like to welcome all of you to our company's annual walk-a-thon. What a great turnout! ❺ This year, we're raising funds for Hunley Children's Hospital, so your attendance is greatly appreciated. All participants should start heading towards the information desk now. ❺ Please make sure to complete your registration and pick up a sports beverage there, compliments of our sponsors. Remember that you must stay on the course at all times. ❻ Once you're done with the course, please cross Granville Road. There we will take a group photograph. Don't worry. It will only take a few minutes.

4-6번은 다음 안내와 지도에 관한 문제입니다.

여: 회사 연례 워커톤에 오신 여러분들을 환영합니다. 참가자 수가 많네요! **올해는 헌리 어린이 병원을 위한 기금 마련을 합니다.** 그래서 여러분의 참석에 너무 감사드립니다. 모든 참석자들은 안내데스크로 지금 와주세요. **등록을 마쳐주시고 스폰서가 제공하는 스포츠음료를 가져가 주세요.** 항상 코스 선상에 있으셔야 함을 기억해주세요. **일단 코스가 끝나면, 그랑빌 로를 건너주세요. 거기에서 단체 사진을 찍겠습니다.** 걱정 마세요. 몇 분밖에 걸리지 않습니다.

어휘 annual 연례의 | fund 기금 | attendance 참석

4. What event are the listeners probably attending?
(A) A street parade
(B) A charity event
(C) A sports competition
(D) A city tour

청자들은 어떤 행사에 참석하는가?
거리 퍼레이드
자선행사
스포츠 경기
시티 투어

해설 헌리 어린이 병원을 위해 기금 마련을 한다고 했으므로(I'd like to welcome all of you to our company's annual walk-a-thon., This year, we're raising funds for Hunley Children's Hospital.) 정답은 (B)가 된다.

5. According to the speaker, what should the listeners pick up?
(A) A T-shirt
(B) A brochure
(C) A gift voucher
(D) A drink

화자에 따르면, 청자들은 무엇을 가져가야 하는가?
티셔츠
브로셔
상품권
음료수

해설 스포츠음료를 가지고 가라고 했으므로(Please make sure to complete your registration and pick up a sports beverage there.) 정답은 (D)가 된다.

6. Look at the graphic. Where will the listeners take a group photo?
(A) At the Information Desk
(B) At the Snack Area
(C) At the Finish Line
(D) At City Hall

시각 정보를 보시오. 청자들은 어디에서 단체 사진을 찍을 것인가?
안내데스크
스낵 구역
결승선
시청

해설 결승선에서 그랑빌 로를 가로지르라고 했으므로(Once you're done with the course, please cross Granville Road. There we will take a group photograph.) 정답은 시청인 (D)가 된다.

만점 포인트 4 막대 / 파이 / 선 그래프는 '수치'나 '최상급'에 주목하라!

판매량, 시장 점유율, 설문 조사 결과 등을 막대, 파이 그리고 선으로 나타낸 시각 정보 문제 유형에서는 '숫자 / 수치'에 집중하고, '최상급 표현'에 주목해야 한다. 빈출 정답으로는 가장 높거나(the highest), 가장 낮거나(the lowest), 두 번째로(the second most / the second highest) 높은 항목들이 있다. 그러므로 문제를 듣기 전에 미리 답을 추측해 보는 것도 좋은 방법이다.

DAY 05_04.mp3

PART 3

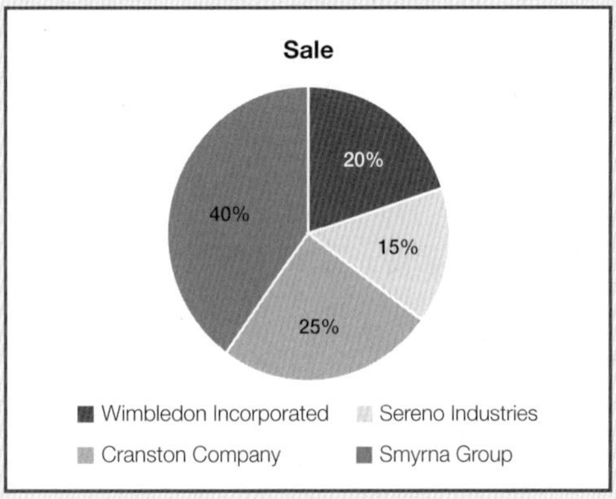

1. What are the speakers mainly discussing?
   (A) A marketing campaign
   (B) A corporate acquisition
   (C) An equipment purchase
   (D) An annual budget

2. Look at the graphic. Where do the speakers work?
   (A) At Wimbledon Incorporated
   (B) At Sereno Industries
   (C) At Cranston Company
   (D) At Smyrna Group

3. Why does the man say he is unsure?
   (A) He believes the price should be renegotiated.
   (B) He does not have much experience in the industry.
   (C) A company's profits have been declining.
   (D) Some figures are outdated.

PART 4

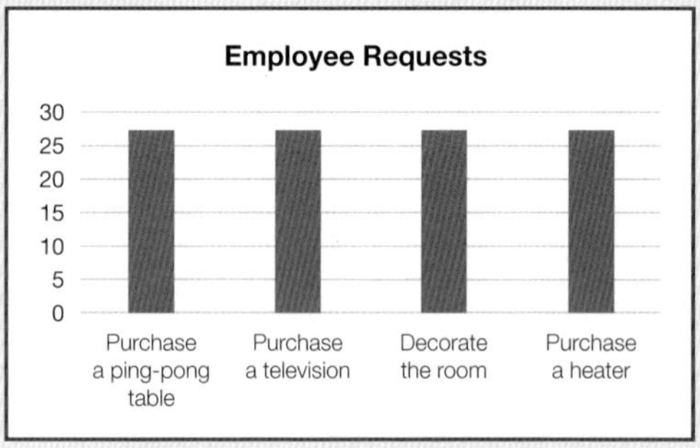

4. Where do the listeners most likely work?
   (A) At a library
   (B) At a gallery
   (C) At a restaurant
   (D) At an airline

5. Look at the graphic. Which request will the company start working on?
   (A) Purchase a ping-pong table
   (B) Purchase a television
   (C) Decorate the room
   (D) Purchase a heater

6. What will the employees receive for completing the survey?
   (A) A movie ticket
   (B) A vacation day
   (C) Notepads
   (D) Free beverages

Questions 1-3 refer to the following conversation and pie chart.

W: Tim, did you read the company-wide email? ❶ It looks like our company is planning to take over Sereno Industries.

M: I didn't get a chance to see it yet. Let me pull it up right now. Do you know when the purchase will take place?

W: That wasn't specified. But it will be beneficial for our company. The email shows how much market share the four major players have in our industry.

M: Oh, yeah. ❷ Acquiring Sereno Industries will mean that we'll own as much market share as Smyrna Group.

W: Yeah, it seems like a strategic move for our company.

M: I don't know. ❸ I'm not too sure about it. I recently read an article about how Sereno Industries has been losing profits for three consecutive years. I wonder if our company would reconsider.

1-3번은 다음 대화와 파이 차트에 관한 문제입니다.

여: 팀, 회사 전사 이메일을 읽어보셨어요? **우리 회사가 세레노 산업을 인수할 계획인 것 같아요.**

남: 아직 못 봤어요. 잠시만 기다려 주세요. 언제 인수하는지 아세요?

여: 구체적으로 명시되지는 않았어요. 하지만 우리 회사에는 좋을 거예요. 이메일에 보면 우리 업계에서 4개의 주요 회사가 시장을 얼마나 점유하고 있는지 나와 있어요.

남: 오, 그렇군요. **세레노 산업을 인수하게 되면 우리 회사가 서머나 그룹과 같은 시장 점유율을 가지겠네요.**

여: 네, 우리 회사에게 있어서 전략적인 결정인 것 같아요.

남: 잘 모르겠어요. **확실하지 않네요. 제가 최근에 읽어본 기사에는 세레노 산업이 3년 연속해서 적자라고 나와 있었어요.** 우리 회사가 다시 재고할 지 궁금하네요.

어휘 take over 인수하다 | take place 일어나다 | beneficial 이로운 | share 점유하다 | strategic 전략적인 | consecutive 연속의 | reconsider 다시 고려하다 | acquisition 인수 | outdated 오래된

1. What are the speakers mainly discussing?

(A) A marketing campaign
(B) A corporate acquisition
(C) An equipment purchase
(D) An annual budget

화자들은 주로 무엇에 관하여 이야기하고 있는가?

마케팅 캠페인
기업 인수
장비 구입
연간 예산

해설 Sereno Industries를 인수한다는 내용이 나오므로(It looks like our company is planning to take over Sereno Industries.) 정답은 (B)가 된다.

2. Look at the graphic. Where do the speakers work?

(A) At Wimbledon Incorporated
(B) At Sereno Industries
(C) At Cranston Company
(D) At Smyrna Group

시각 정보를 보시오. 화자들은 어디에서 일하는가?

윔블던 사에서
세레노 산업에서
크랜스턴 사에서
서머나 그룹에서

해설 우리 회사가 세네노 산업(15%)을 인수하게 되면, 40%인 서머나 그룹과 같다고 했으므로(Acquiring Sereno Industries will mean that we'll own as much market share as Smyrna Group.) 정답은 25%의 점유율을 가지고 있는 크랜스턴 사인 (C)가 된다.

3. Why does the man say he is unsure?

(A) He believes the price should be renegotiated.
(B) He does not have much experience in the industry.
(C) A company's profits have been declining.
(D) Some figures are outdated.

남자는 왜 그가 확신하지 못하다고 말하는가?

그는 가격이 다시 협상되어야 한다고 믿는다.
그는 업계에 많은 경험이 없다.
회사 수익이 떨어지고 있다.
몇몇 수치가 오래되었다.

해설 기사에서 3년 연속해서 적자인 것을 읽어봤다고 나오므로(I'm not too sure about it. I recently read an article about how Sereno Industries has been losing profits for three consecutive years.) 정답은 (C)가 된다.

Questions 4-6 refer to the following excerpt from a meeting and graph.

W: ❹ Let's discuss the recent survey results regarding our gallery's staff room. Most people are generally happy with it, but we also asked for specific requests. As you can see, our most popular requests revolve around buying more things for the staff room. A ping-pong table has been consistently talked about for months, and I will do my best to secure us the funding for one. ❺ However, I want us to focus on the only item that isn't about buying something, as that is something we have control of. As a reminder: ❻ all employees who participate in the survey are eligible to receive a free movie ticket.

4-6번은 다음 회의 발췌록과 그래프에 관한 문제입니다.

여: **갤러리 직원 휴게실에 관한 최근 설문조사 결과에 대해 논의합시다.** 대부분의 사람들은 만족하지만, 우리는 특별한 요청사항에 대해 또한 물어봤습니다. 보시다시피, 가장 많은 요청은 직원 휴게실에 더 많은 물건들을 구매해야 한다는 것입니다. 탁구대는 몇 달 동안 끊임없이 이야기되었으며, 저는 그것에 대해 자금을 확보하기 위해 최선을 다할 것입니다. **하지만 저는 무언가를 구매하는 것에 관한 것이 아닌, 우리가 컨트롤할 수 있는 유일한 항목에 초점을 두고 싶습니다.** 상기시켜드리오니, **모든 설문조사에 참석한 직원들은 무료 영화 티켓을 받을 자격을 가지게 됩니다.**

어휘 generally 일반적으로 | specific request 특별한 요청사항 | be eligible to ~할 자격이 있는

4. Where do the listeners most likely work?
(A) At a library
(B) At a gallery
(C) At a restaurant
(D) At an airline

청자들은 어디에서 일할 것 같은가?
도서관에서
갤러리에서
레스토랑에서
비행기에서

해설 갤러리 직원 휴게실에 대한 이야기이므로(Let's discuss the recent survey results regarding our gallery's staff room.) 정답은 (B)가 된다.

5. Look at the graphic. Which request will the company start working on?
(A) Purchase a ping-pong table
(B) Purchase a television
(C) Decorate the room
(D) Purchase a heater

시각 정보를 보시오. 회사가 어떤 요청 사항을 착수하기 시작할 것인가?
탁구대를 구매한다
텔레비전을 구매한다
방을 꾸민다
난방기를 구매한다

해설 구매에 관한 것 말고 우리가 컨트롤 할 수 있는 유일한 하나에 중점을 두고 싶다고 했으므로(However, I want us to focus on the only item that isn't about buying something, as that is something we have control of.) 제시된 시각 정보에서 유일하게 구매하는 것이 아닌 (C)가 정답이 된다.

6. What will the employees receive for completing the survey?
(A) A movie ticket
(B) A vacation day
(C) Notepads
(D) Free beverages

설문조사를 완성한 직원들은 무엇을 받게 되는가?
영화 티켓
휴가
노트패드
무료 음료

해설 설문조사에 응한 직원들에게는 무료 영화 티켓을 받을 자격이 주어 진다고 나와 있으므로(all employees who participate in the survey are eligible to receive a free movie ticket.) 정답은 (A)가 된다.

만점 포인트 5 쿠폰, 영수증, 탑승권, 청구서는 자료와 일치 또는 불일치를 확인하라!

쿠폰, 영수증, 탑승권, 청구서 등과 같은 시각 정보 유형에서는 주어진 자료와 '일치 또는 불일치'를 물어보는 경우가 많다. 특히, 쿠폰의 경우는 '유효기간'과 '할인'에 대한 정답이 단골로 출제된다.

DAY 05_05.mp3

PART 3

Discount Voucher

Order for 10 uniforms	5% off
Order for 15 uniforms	15% off
Order for 25 uniforms	20% off
Order for 50 uniforms	30% off

1. Why is the woman calling?
(A) To change a delivery address
(B) To ask for a discount
(C) To modify an order
(D) To confirm order status

2. Where does the man probably work?
(A) At a health clinic
(B) At a clothing retailer
(C) At a police station
(D) At a nursing home

3. Look at the graphic. What discount will the woman most likely receive?
(A) 5% off
(B) 15% off
(C) 20% off
(D) 30% off

PART 4

Piko Kitchen

Piko Kitchen is now available for booking.
Host your next party or function here.

15% discount if you book at least one month in advance.

Available times:
12 P.M. – 4 P.M.
6 P.M. – 10 P.M.

4. Why is the event being held?
(A) To open a new office
(B) To announce a new product
(C) To reward employees
(D) To celebrate an anniversary

5. Look at the graphic. Why is the speaker unable to use the coupon for the event?
(A) The event will take place next month.
(B) The event will run longer than the available times.
(C) The venue is located too far away for many guests.
(D) The venue will not be ready in time.

6. What does the speaker want the listener to do?
(A) Review a schedule
(B) Send out some invitations
(C) Research a venue
(D) Pay a deposit

Questions 1-3 refer to the following conversation and coupon.

W: Hello, this is Janie from Sacred Hearts Nursing Home. ❶ I placed an order for 25 uniforms last week, but ❶❸ I'll need 15 more. I was also hoping to get all of them by next Monday.

M: I'm sorry, Janie. We've been swamped lately, and ❷ we won't be able to add custom embroidery to our clothes until next Thursday.

W: Don't worry about it. ❸ I'll place a separate order then. Will you still be sending me the first 25 uniforms by next Monday?

M: Of course. They are ready for shipping.

W: That's great. Oh, right. ❸ I forgot I had this voucher. Could I use this for the new order?

M: Sure thing. I'll charge the amount on the credit card we have on file.

1-3번은 다음 대화와 쿠폰에 관한 문제입니다.

여: 안녕하세요, 저는 성심 양로원의 재니입니다. **지난주에 25개의 유니폼을 주문했는데요, 15개가 더 필요합니다.** 다음주 월요일까지 다 받았으면 좋겠는데요.

남: 재니, 죄송합니다. 최근에 주문이 쇄도해서요. **다음 주 목요일이 되어서야 옷에 맞춤화된 자수를 추가할 수 있을 것 같습니다.**

여: 걱정하지 마세요. **그렇다면 별도로 주문을 하겠습니다.** 다음 주 월요일까지 25개 유니폼은 보내주실 수 있는 거죠?

남: 물론이죠. 배송 준비가 다 되었습니다.

여: 좋습니다. 아, 맞아요. **이 바우처를 잊고 있었는데요. 새로 주문한 것에 이것을 사용할 수 있을까요?**

남: 물론이지요. 등록해 놓은 신용카드에 금액을 청구하겠습니다.

어휘 nursing home 양로원 | swamped 매우 바쁜 | embroidery 자수 | modify 수정하다 | status 상태 | retailer 소매점

1. Why is the woman calling?

(A) To change a delivery address
(B) To ask for a discount
(C) To modify an order
(D) To confirm order status

여자가 전화를 건 목적은 무엇인가?

배송 주소를 변경하기 위해서
할인을 요청하기 위해서
주문을 수정하기 위해서
주문 상태를 확인하기 위해서

해설 종전에 25개를 주문했는데 15개를 추가 주문하고 싶다고 하여(I placed an order for 25 uniforms last week, but I'll need 15 more.) 주문 수정을 한다는 정답은 (C)가 된다.

2. Where does the man probably work?

(A) At a health clinic
(B) At a clothing retailer
(C) At a police station
(D) At a nursing home

남자는 어디서 일할 것 같은가?

병원에서
옷 소매점에서
경찰서에서
요양원에서

해설 유니폼과 옷에 자수를 넣는다라는 내용을 통해서(we won't be able to add custom embroidery to our clothes until next Thursday.) 정답은 (B)이다. 남자와 여자를 헷갈리지 않도록 주의하자.

3. Look at the graphic. What discount will the woman most likely receive?

(A) 5% off
(B) 15% off
(C) 20% off
(D) 30% off

시각 정보를 보시오. 여자가 받게 되는 할인은 얼마인가?

5% 할인
15% 할인
20% 할인
30% 할인

해설 새 주문에 대해서 바우처를 사용할 수 있냐고 했으므로(I forgot I had this voucher. Could I use this for the new order?) 15개에 대한 할인율인 (B)가 정답이다.

Questions 4-6 refer to the following announcement and advertisement.

W: Hello, this is Mollie. ❹ I'm giving you an update on the appreciation party for our employees. I received the confirmed list of participants, and it says 55 people will be attending. ❺ I also looked at the tentative agenda, and it looks like the event will run for around four hours. If we start at 7 P.M. as planned, we won't be able to use the coupon for Piko Kitchen. Perhaps we should remove some of the items from the agenda. ❻ Can you check one more time? Otherwise, I'll look up other venues and see which ones are available.

4-6번은 다음 공지와 광고에 관한 문제입니다.

여: 안녕하세요. 저는 몰리입니다. **직원들에 대한 감사 파티에 대해 업데이트를 드리려고 합니다.** 참석자 명단을 확인했고, 55명이 참석할 것입니다. 또한 가안을 봤는데요, **잠정적인 안건을 살펴 보았을 때 이벤트가 약 4시간 정도 진행될 예정입니다. 만약 계획한 대로 저녁 7시에 시작한다면 피코 키친 쿠폰은 사용을 못할 것입니다.** 아마도 계획에서 몇 가지를 빼야 할지도 모릅니다. 다시 한번 확인해 주실 수 있을까요? **그렇지 않으면 다른 장소를 물색해서 이용가능한 곳이 어디인지를 찾아봐야 합니다.**

어휘 appreciation 감사 | tentative 일시적인 | reward 보상하다 | available 이용 가능한 | invitation 초대장 | venue 장소

4. Why is the event being held?
(A) To open a new office
(B) To announce a new product
(C) To reward employees
(D) To celebrate an anniversary

이벤트는 왜 개최되는가?
신규 사무실을 오픈하기 위해서
신제품을 발표하기 위해서
직원들에게 보상하기 위해서
기념일을 축하하기 위해서

해설 직원들을 위한 감사 파티라고 나와 있으므로(I'm giving you an update on the appreciation party for our employees.) 정답은 (C)가 된다.

5. Look at the graphic. Why is the speaker unable to use the coupon for the event?
(A) The event will take place next month.
(B) The event will run longer than the available times.
(C) The venue is located too far away for many guests.
(D) The venue will not be ready in time.

시각 정보를 보시오. 화자는 왜 이벤트를 위해 쿠폰을 사용할 수 없는가?
이벤트가 다음 달에 개최된다.
이벤트가 이용 가능한 시간보다 길게 진행된다.
장소가 많은 손님들에게 너무 멀다.
장소가 제 시간에 준비되지 못한다.

해설 행사가 7시에 시작되어 4시간 정도 진행된다면 할 수가 없다고 나와있고(I also looked at the tentative agenda, and it looks like the event will run for around four hours. If we start at 7 P.M. as planned, we won't be able to use the coupon for Piko Kitchen.) 광고에서 운영 시간이 오후 10시까지라고 나와 있으므로 시간 때문에 사용할 수 없는 정답은 (B)가 된다.

6. What does the speaker want the listener to do?
(A) Review a schedule
(B) Send out some invitations
(C) Research a venue
(D) Pay a deposit

화자는 청자가 무엇을 하기를 원하는가?
스케줄을 검토한다
초대장을 보낸다
장소를 찾는다
보증금을 낸다

해설 시간이 문제가 될 수 있으므로 다시 한번 확인해 달라고 했으므로(Can you check one more time? Otherwise, I'll look up other venues and see which ones are available.) 정답은 (A)가 된다.

고난도 실전 문제

DAY 05_06.mp3

PART 3

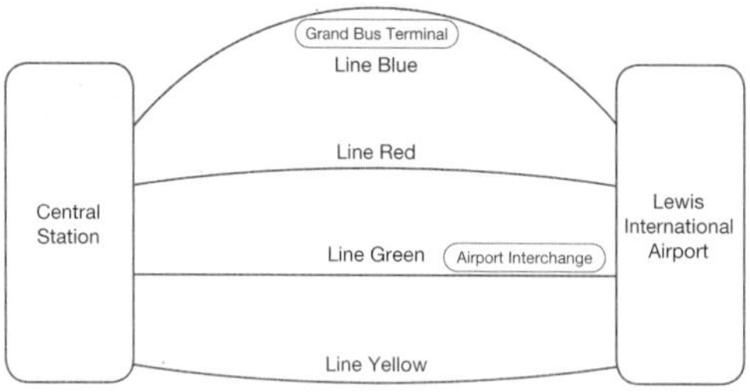

1. Where does the conversation take place?

(A) At an airport
(B) At a conference center
(C) At a subway station
(D) At a bus terminal

2. Look at the graphic. Which line does the woman suggest the man take?

(A) Line Blue
(B) Line Red
(C) Line Green
(D) Line Yellow

3. Why is the man going to Philadelphia?

(A) To attend a conference
(B) To meet a client
(C) To examine a facility
(D) To interview a candidate

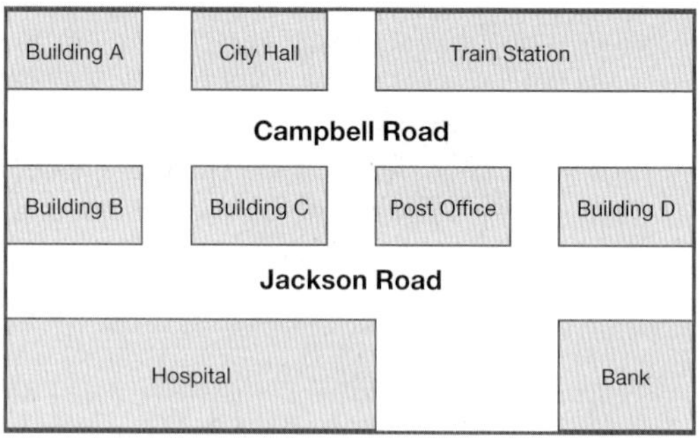

4. Who most likely is the man?

(A) A building manager
(B) A postal worker
(C) A delivery person
(D) A city official

5. What problem does the man mention?

(A) Some information is incorrect.
(B) Some equipment is malfunctioning.
(C) A road is under construction.
(D) A product has been damaged.

6. Look at the graphic. Where will the man go next?

(A) To Building A
(B) To Building B
(C) To Building C
(D) To Building D

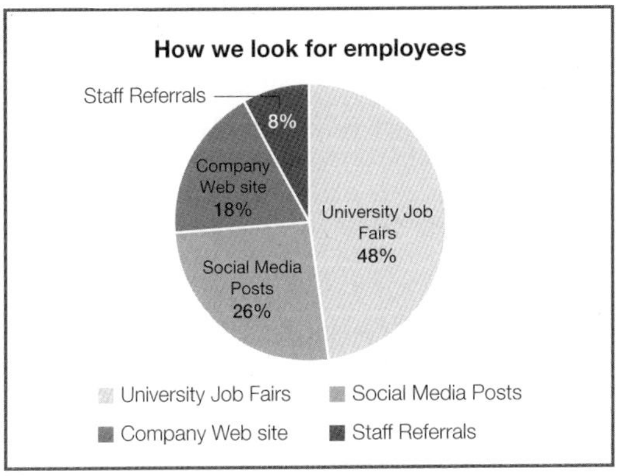

7. What would the woman like to do?

(A) Edit an online job posting
(B) Modify a recruitment tactic
(C) Confirm a travel itinerary
(D) Finalize a department budget

8. Look at the graphic. Which method does the man suggest using?

(A) University Job Fairs
(B) Social Media Posts
(C) Company Web site
(D) Staff Referrals

9. What does the woman ask the man to do?

(A) Design a personnel evaluation form
(B) Collaborate with a colleague
(C) Interview some potential candidates
(D) Revise an employment contract

PART 4

Request for Reimbursement	
Expenditure	**Amount**
Rental Car	$235.00
Accommodation	$675.00
Meals	$410.00
Flight	$750.00

10. What did the listener do last week?

(A) He attended a function.
(B) He toured an office building.
(C) He trained a new staff member.
(D) He purchased some equipment.

11. Look at the graphic. Which amount needs to be checked?

(A) $235
(B) $675
(C) $410
(D) $750

12. What does the speaker say was sent to the staff?

(A) An updated form
(B) A discount code
(C) A software manual
(D) Some contacts

고난도 실전 문제

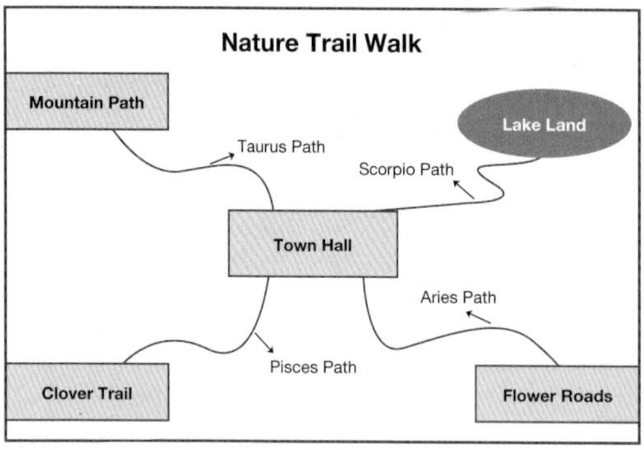

13. Look at the graphic. Which path does the speaker recommend?
(A) Taurus
(B) Scorpio
(C) Pisces
(D) Aries

14. According to the speaker, what will happen at 3 P.M.?
(A) A bus will arrive.
(B) A competition will begin.
(C) A group photo will be taken.
(D) A picnic will take place.

15. What does the speaker say she will do next?
(A) Distribute some maps
(B) Take a water bottle
(C) Call for help
(D) Assign a group leader

Company Name	Notes
TPP	Lowest prices
Grissom	Fastest delivery
Kovar	Widest selection
L-Train	Highest quality

16. What type of business is being launched?
(A) A fitness center
(B) A real estate agency
(C) A remodeling firm
(D) A dining establishment

17. What does the speaker say he is pleased about?
(A) Some employee applications
(B) Some shared facilities
(C) The neighboring buildings
(D) The price of some services

18. Look at the graphic. Which company does the speaker want to use?
(A) TPP
(B) Grissom
(C) Kovar
(D) L-Train

MEMO

PART 3&4

DAY 06

화자 의도 뭘 들어? 앞뒤 잘 들어!

음원 바로 듣기

동영상 강의 바로 보기

화자 의도 파악 문제는 화자의 숨은 의도를 파악해서 정답을 골라야 하기 때문에, PART 3&4 문제 유형 중 체감 난이도가 가장 높은 문제에 속한다. 따라서, 문장의 사전적인 의미로 문제를 풀기보다는 반드시 앞뒤 문맥을 잘 간파하면서 정답을 찾아야 한다. 보기에 나온 단어가 그대로 들린다면 일차적으로 오답일 가능성이 높다. 대부분의 화자 의도 파악 문제가 패러프레이징 되어 출제되기 때문이다. 또한, 세 문제 중 마지막 문제가 화자 의도 파악 문제라면 보기를 하나씩 읽고 답을 고를 시간적 여유가 있지만, 두 번째 문제로 출제된다면 해당 문제에 집중한 나머지 두 번째 문제뿐만 아니라 세 번째 문제까지도 놓칠 수가 있다. 따라서, 두 번째 문제로 출제될 경우에는 미리 보기의 키워드를 잡아서 빠르게 비교하면서 문제를 풀 수 있도록 해야 한다. 또한, 화자의 의도를 나타내는 문장이 나오고 나서 다시 한번 언급하므로 전반적인 흐름을 놓쳤더라도 화자 의도 문장 다음 문장부터 집중해서 잘 듣는 것도 좋은 방법이다.

만점 포인트

이것만 알면 만점!

1 화자 의도 파악 문제는 앞뒤에 정답이 있다.

만점 포인트 1 화자 의도 파악 문제는 앞뒤에 정답이 있다.

화자 의도 파악 문제는 주어진 문장이나 표현이 어떤 의도로 쓰였는지를 파악하는 문제로, 있는 그대로의 사전적인 의미로만 판단해서 정답을 찾지 말고 전반적인 문맥의 흐름을 이해하며 풀어야 하기 때문에 난이도가 높은 문제 유형에 속한다.

❶ 화자 의도 파악 문제를 먼저 읽고, 4개의 보기 키워드를 찾는다(주로 명사와 동사를 중심으로).
❷ 사전적인 의미만 생각해서 성급하게 답을 고르지 않는다.
❸ 앞뒤 문맥과 흐름을 잘 이해하여 정답을 찾는다.
❹ 화자 의도 다음에 나오는 문장을 집중해서 잘 듣는다.
❺ 보기에 나온 어휘가 반복해서 들린다면 오답일 가능성이 높다.

DAY 06_01.mp3

PART 3

1. Where do the speakers most likely work?
   (A) At a clothing store
   (B) At a construction company
   (C) At a sports center
   (D) At a manufacturing facility

2. What does Marjorie imply when she says, "I'll be meeting them at our office in 15 minutes"?
   (A) She is unhappy about a project.
   (B) She has yet to book a meeting room.
   (C) She will have the information soon.
   (D) She is unable to attend an event.

3. What may happen due to a delay?
   (A) Some overtime work may be required.
   (B) A business deal may be terminated.
   (C) A supplier will receive more orders.
   (D) Some staff members may be trained.

PART 4

4. Where does the speaker work?
   (A) In a manufacturing plant
   (B) In a laboratory
   (C) At a construction site
   (D) At a hospital

5. What does the speaker want to purchase?
   (A) Some appliances
   (B) Some protective gear
   (C) Some computers
   (D) Some light fixtures

6. What does the speaker imply when he says, "I heard you're finalizing the budget tomorrow"?
   (A) He wants to have a meeting with the budgeting committee.
   (B) He is apologizing for missing a deadline.
   (C) He is surprised at how quickly the listener finished a task.
   (D) He hopes the request will be approved soon.

Questions 1-3 refer to the following conversation.

M: Hello, Marjorie. ❶ I was just going through our plant's production schedule. It looks like we were supposed to begin production on the running shoes for Knight Sporting Goods this Monday.
W: I know. That's what I wanted to discuss with you.
M: The first batch of the product is supposed to be delivered at the end of April, right?
W: Exactly. The thing is, we still don't have the mesh fabric yet. ❷ I spoke with our vendor about the delay.
M: And what did they say?
W: Well, I'll be meeting them at our office in 15 minutes.
M: Alright. ❷ Keep me updated. ❸ If they can't make the shipment soon, we may have to end the contract and look for a new vendor.

1-3번은 다음 대화에 관한 문제입니다.

남: 마조리 안녕하세요. **공장 생산 일정에 대해서 방금 검토해 보았어요.** 이번 주 월요일에 기사 스포츠용품을 위한 운동화 생산을 시작하기로 되어있네요.
여: 압니다. 그 부분을 당신과 이야기하고 싶었습니다.
남: 첫 번째 제품분은 4월 말에 배송되기로 되어 있죠, 맞죠?
여: 정확합니다. 근데 문제는 메시 직물이 아직 없다는 것입니다. **그 지연 건에 관해 판매자와 이야기를 했습니다.**
남: 뭐라고 하던가요?
여: 그게, **15분 후에 사무실에서 그들과 미팅이 있습니다.**
남: 좋아요. **나중에 알려주세요. 만약 배송을 곧 하지 못한다면, 그 업체와의 계약은 끝내고 다른 새 업체를 찾아야 합니다.**

어휘 go through 검토하다 | production 생산성 | be supposed to ~하기로 계획되어있다 | vendor 판매자 | delay 지연 | terminate 종료하다

1. Where do the speakers most likely work?
(A) At a clothing store
(B) At a construction company
(C) At a sports center
(D) At a manufacturing facility

화자들은 어디에서 일할 것 같은가?
옷 가게에서
건설 회사에서
스포츠 센터에서
공장에서

해설 공장 생산 일정에 대해서 이야기하고 있으므로(I was just going through our plant's production schedule.) 정답은 (D)가 된다.

2. What does Marjorie imply when she says, "I'll be meeting them at our office in 15 minutes"?
(A) She is unhappy about a project.
(B) She has yet to book a meeting room.
(C) She will have the information soon.
(D) She is unable to attend an event.

마조리가 "15분 후에 사무실에서 그들과 미팅이 있습니다"라고 말할 때 무엇을 의미하는가?
그녀는 프로젝트에 대해서 마음에 안 든다.
그녀는 회의실 예약을 아직 안 했다.
그녀는 곧 정보를 알게 될 것이다.
그녀는 행사에 참여할 수 없다.

해설 앞에서 지연 건에 대해 판매자와 이야기를 했고, 그 뒤에 업데이트하겠다고 했으므로 정답은 곧 어떻게 되는지 정보를 알게 된다라는(I spoke with our vendor about the delay., Keep me updated.) 정답은 (C)가 된다.

3. What may happen due to a delay?
(A) Some overtime work may be required.
(B) A business deal may be terminated.
(C) A supplier will receive more orders.
(D) Some staff members may be trained.

지연 때문에 무슨 일이 일어날 것인가?
초과 근무가 필요할 수도 있다.
사업 거래가 종료될 수도 있다.
공급업체가 더 많은 주문을 받게 될 것이다.
몇몇 직원들은 교육받을 수도 있다.

해설 거래를 끝내고 새로운 업체를 찾아본다고 했으므로(If they can't make the shipment soon, we may have to end the contract and look for a new vendor.) 정답은 (B)가 된다.

해설 호주

Questions 4-6 refer to the following telephone message.

M: Good morning, Jeannette. ❹ This is Allen from the factory floor. I'm calling since you're in charge of purchasing, and ❺ I was wondering if I could get your authorization to buy some more air conditioners for the production line. This summer has been the hottest one we've experienced so far, and the machinery has been overheating frequently. This has caused the plant to shut down unexpectedly, affecting our productivity. It has negatively impacted employee morale, as they're feeling exhausted from working in the heat. ❻ I'm hoping you'll help us get the air conditioners as soon as possible. I heard you're finalizing the budget tomorrow. Let me know what you think. Thanks.

4-6번은 다음 전화 메시지에 관한 문제입니다.

남: 좋은 아침이에요, 자네트. **공장 작업 현장의 앨런입니다.** 제가 연락드린 이유는 당신이 구매를 담당하고 있기 때문이고, **생산 라인에 에어컨을 더 구매해야 하는 데 당신의 승인이 필요합니다.** 이번 여름이 여태까지 경험했던 것 중에 가장 더웠고, 기계가 자주 과열되었습니다. 이로 인해 공장이 예상치 못하게 문을 닫아야 했고, 생산성에도 영향을 미쳤습니다. 열기로 인해 직원들도 많이 지쳐서 직원들의 사기에도 부정적으로 영향을 미쳤습니다. **가능한 한 빨리 에어컨을 구매하는 데 도와주시면 감사하겠습니다. 제가 듣기로 예산 마감 날짜가 내일이라고 하던데요.** 어떻게 생각하시는지 알려주시기 바랍니다. 감사합니다.

어휘 in charge of ~를 담당하는 | wonder 궁금하다 | authorization 승인 | frequently 자주 | unexpectedly 예상치 못하게 | productivity 생산성 | exhausted 피곤한 | appliance 기기 | protective gear 안전장비

4. Where does the speaker work?

(A) In a manufacturing plant
(B) In a laboratory
(C) At a construction site
(D) At a hospital

화자는 어디에서 일하는가?

제조 공장에서
실험실에서
공사 현장에서
병원에서

해설 공장 작업 현장의 누구라고 이야기했으므로(This is Allen from the factory floor.) 정답은 (A)가 된다.

5. What does the speaker want to purchase?

(A) Some appliances
(B) Some protective gear
(C) Some computers
(D) Some light fixtures

화자가 구매하고 싶은 것은 무엇인가?

기기
안전장비
컴퓨터
조명

해설 여름에 너무 더웠기 때문에 에어컨을 구매하는 데 승인이 필요하다고 했으므로(I was wondering if I could get your authorization to buy some more air conditioners for the production line.) 정답은 (A)가 된다.

6. What does the speaker imply when he says, "I heard you're finalizing the budget tomorrow"?

(A) He wants to have a meeting with the budgeting committee.
(B) He is apologizing for missing a deadline.
(C) He is surprised at how quickly the listener finished a task.
(D) He hopes the request will be approved soon.

남자가 "제가 듣기로 예산 마감 날짜가 내일이라고 하던데요"라고 말할 때 무엇을 의미하는가?

그는 예산위원회와 회의를 하고 싶다.
그는 마감 날짜를 놓친 것에 대해 사과한다.
그는 청자가 얼마나 빨리 일을 끝냈는지에 대해 놀란다.
그는 요청이 빨리 승인되기를 원한다.

해설 앞에서 에어컨을 구매하는 데 승인이 필요하며, 또한 가능한 한 빨리 에어컨을 구매하는 데 도와달라고 했으므로(I'm hoping you'll help us get the air conditioners as soon as possible.) 정답은 빨리 승인되기를 원한다는 (D)가 된다.

PART 3&4 DAY 06

고난도 실전 문제

DAY 06_02.mp3

PART 3

1. What are the speakers planning?

(A) A team building day
(B) A company picnic
(C) An anniversary celebration
(D) A charity fundraiser

2. What does the man mean when he says, "we've been doing that for the last five years"?

(A) He does not enjoy watching sporting events.
(B) He does not want to repeat an activity.
(C) He believes an event was successful.
(D) He is unsure how to complete a procedure.

3. What is the woman worried about?

(A) Low registration numbers
(B) Employee well-being
(C) The department budget
(D) The tight deadline

---

4. What are the speakers mainly discussing?

(A) A building blueprint
(B) A construction material
(C) A cost estimate
(D) A renovation project

5. What does the woman say about the carpeting?

(A) It is made from recycled materials.
(B) It looks outdated.
(C) It is heavily stained.
(D) It will be delivered today.

6. What does the woman imply when she says, "This room is quite big"?

(A) The property has a good value.
(B) A job will take a long time to finish.
(C) More furniture should be purchased.
(D) She would like to hire more workers.

---

7. Where does the conversation take place?

(A) At a factory
(B) At a sporting goods store
(C) At an auto repair shop
(D) At a hardware store

8. Why does the woman say, "It's almost winter"?

(A) To purchase some new supplies
(B) To show excitement about traveling
(C) To stress an upcoming work deadline
(D) To express interest in a service

9. What does the man give to the woman?

(A) A brochure
(B) A receipt
(C) A work schedule
(D) A business card

PART 4

10. What department does the speaker most likely work in?
(A) Public Relations
(B) Information Technology
(C) Product Development
(D) Human Resources

11. What does the speaker want to purchase?
(A) Stationery
(B) Vehicles
(C) Furniture
(D) Electronics

12. What does the speaker imply when she says, "The budget is due on Wednesday, isn't it"?
(A) She will have to adjust the deadline.
(B) She would like to confirm the listener's availability.
(C) She is going on a business trip on Wednesday.
(D) She wants the approval to be processed quickly.

---

13. Who are the listeners?
(A) Professional recruiters
(B) Board members
(C) Department heads
(D) Administrative assistants

14. Why does the speaker say, "your staff is very professional"?
(A) To congratulate an employee
(B) To reassure the listeners
(C) To acknowledge a problem
(D) To ask for a recommendation

15. What does the speaker remind the listener to do?
(A) Submit some evaluation forms
(B) Update an employee directory
(C) Ask a lot of questions
(D) Show some appreciation

---

16. Who most likely is the speaker?
(A) A retail sales associate
(B) An executive
(C) A human resources manager
(D) A customer service representative

17. What does the speaker mean when she says, "it's the last week of June"?
(A) She must take an alternative approach.
(B) She is disappointed with her colleagues.
(C) She needs to submit an application soon.
(D) She has already completed a task.

18. According to the speaker, what will happen next month?
(A) A proposal will be revised.
(B) Internal communication will improve.
(C) Interviews will be conducted.
(D) A Web site will be shut down for maintenance.

PART 3&4

DAY 07

토익이 좋아하는 스토리는 따로 있다!

음원 바로 듣기

동영상 강의 바로 보기

PART 3&4 문제를 풀다 보면 스토리와 논리 전개가 반복적으로 출제된다는 것을 알 수가 있다. 즉, 토익에 출제되는 내용 자체가 매우 한정적이다. 그러므로 토익을 처음 공부할 경우에는 방대한 어휘와 표현을 암기해야 하기 때문에 어려움을 토로할 수 있겠지만, 공부를 하다 보면 매번 반복되는 주제와 테마에 익숙해지게 된다. 즉, 빈출되는 내용과 연관된 어휘와 스토리만 숙지해두면 충분히 고득점을 받을 수 있는 것이다.

만점 포인트

이것만 알면 만점!

1 회의 장소, 일정 취소 또는 변경은 매달 출제된다.

2 구인 광고, 신입 사원 교육, 면접 일정 및 결과는 토익이 좋아하는 주제다.

3 사무용품이나 기계에 관한 주문, 고장 및 수리 내용도 매달 출제된다.

4 전화 / 녹음 메시지에서 출제되는 스토리는 정해져 있다.

5 교통수단의 지연은 '악천후' 아니면 '기계적 결함'이다.

6 시상식, 퇴임식, 송별회에서는 그 인물의 소개와 업적을 반드시 물어본다.

7 교통 정체의 원인은 '사고' 또는 '도로 공사'라 '우회'를 하거나 '대중교통 이용'을 권한다.

8 인수합병이나 정책의 변화에는 반드시 끝에 '긍정적 효과'를 언급한다.

9 판매의 저조나 하락으로 인한 '문제점'과 '해결책'을 물어본다.

10 박물관, 미술관 투어, 공연장에서는 사진 촬영 금지나 기념품 가게 방문을 제안한다.

만점 포인트 1 회의 장소, 일정 취소 또는 변경은 매달 출제된다.

PART 3&4에 자주 출제되는 스토리와 논리 전개를 익히고, 단어의 패러프레이징 표현을 암기함으로써 보다 빠르고 효율성 있게 문제를 풀 수 있도록 하자.

review, look over, go over, check	검토하다
postpone, delay, push back, put off	미루다
reschedule	일정을 변경하다
conduct the survey / research	설문조사 / 연구를 하다
distribute, hand out, pass around	나누어 주다
document, report, paper, estimate, draft, contract, file	서류
outing, picnic, excursion	소풍, 야유회
process, procedure, protocol, steps	절차
employee benefits package	복지후생 제도
give / make / deliver a speech / presentation	연설 / 프레젠테이션을 하다
sales figures / numbers	판매 수치
change, update, revise	변화하다, 수정하다
come up with some idea, brainstorm ideas	아이디어를 생각해내다
release, launch, introduce, unveil	출시하다
register, enroll, sign up	등록하다
online, Web site, Internet, www.~, electronically, digitally	온라인으로
work, assignment, task, project	업무
change, switch, swap	바꾸다

Day 07_01.mp3

PART 3

1. What is the purpose of the phone call?
(A) To change an event venue
(B) To provide some directions
(C) To reschedule an appointment
(D) To confirm equipment rental

2. What does the man ask about?
(A) Seeing a different professional
(B) Adjusting an existing order
(C) Reviewing a business model
(D) Filling out some paperwork

3. Why does the man say a location is convenient?
(A) It has longer business hours.
(B) It offers free parking for visitors.
(C) It is near his house.
(D) It is located in the city center.

Questions 1-3 refer to the following conversation.

1-3번은 다음 대화에 관한 문제입니다.

W: Hello, ❶ I'm calling from Dr. Bradshaw's office about your appointment on Wednesday. I'm sorry to inform you that the doctor has an urgent matter to tend to, and she will be out of the office for the remainder of the week. We would like to set you up for next Wednesday at the same time. Will this day work for you?

M: Umm… I'll be away on a business trip next week. ❷ Can't I just meet another dentist this Wednesday?

W: Please hold on. Ah, Dr. Tanen has a spot open at 4 P.M., but she will be in our Somerville branch.

M: That'll work. ❸ I live in Somerville, so it should be easier for me to get there. Let's do that.

여: 안녕하세요. **브래드쇼 박사 사무실에서 수요일 예약에 관해서 연락드립니다. 죄송하지만 박사님이 긴급하게 처리해야 할 문제가 있어서, 그 주 나머지 동안 사무실에 안 계실 예정입니다. 저희는 다음 주 수요일 동일한 시간으로 예약을 해 드리고 싶은데요. 이 날짜가 괜찮으실까요?**

남: 음… 다음 주에 출장이라서요. **이번 주 수요일에 다른 치과 의사에게 진찰받을 수 없나요?**

여: 잠시만 기다려주세요. 아, 태넌 박사가 오후 4시에 비어있지만, 그녀는 서머빌 지점에 계실 겁니다.

남: 괜찮습니다. **저는 서머빌에 거주하고 있어서, 거기까지 가는 데 더 쉽습니다.** 그렇게 하지요.

어휘 appointment 약속 | inform 알리다 | urgent 긴급한 | remainder 나머지 | venue 장소 | reschedule 재조정하다

1. What is the purpose of the phone call?

(A) To change an event venue
(B) To provide some directions
(C) To reschedule an appointment
(D) To confirm equipment rental

전화를 건 목적은 무엇인가?

이벤트 장소를 변경하기 위해서
약도를 제공하기 위해서
예약을 재조정하기 위해서
장비 대여를 확인하기 위해서

해설 기존 예약이 수요일이었는데 다음 주 수요일로 예약 변경을 물어보는 것이므로(I'm calling from Dr. Bradshaw's office about your appointment on Wednesday. I'm sorry to inform you that the doctor has an urgent matter to tend to, and she will be out of the office for the remainder of the week. We would like to set you up for next Wednesday at the same time. Will this day work for you?) 정답은 (C)가 된다.

2. What does the man ask about?

(A) Seeing a different professional
(B) Adjusting an existing order
(C) Reviewing a business model
(D) Filling out some paperwork

남자가 요청하는 것은 무엇인가?

다른 전문가를 보는 것
기존 주문을 변경하는 것
비즈니스 모델을 검토하는 것
서류를 작성하는 것

해설 다른 치과 의사에게 진찰을 받아도 되냐고 물었으므로(Can't I just meet another dentist this Wednesday?) 정답은 (A)가 된다.

3. Why does the man say a location is convenient?

(A) It has longer business hours.
(B) It offers free parking for visitors.
(C) It is near his house.
(D) It is located in the city center.

남자는 왜 위치가 편리하다고 말하는가?

영업시간이 더 길다.
방문객들에게 무료 주차를 제공한다.
집 근처이다.
도심부에 위치하고 있다.

해설 다른 약속 장소가 서머빌인데 괜찮냐는 물음에 거기에 거주하고 있다고 이야기했으므로(I live in Somerville, so it should be easier for me to get there.) 정답은 (C)가 된다.

만점 포인트 2 구인 광고, 신입 사원 교육, 면접 일정 및 결과는 토익이 좋아하는 주제다.

job advertisement, job ad	취업 광고
Personnel Department, Human Resources Department	인사부
transfer, relocate, move	전근가다
fill out the form, complete the form	양식을 작성하다
short on staff, shorthanded, understaffed, not enough staff	직원이 부족하다
coworker, colleague, associate	직장 동료
job opening / vacancy	공석
hire / increase / recruit / expand / add employees	직원을 고용하다
performance evaluation	업무 평가
attend, make it, join	참석하다
mandatory	의무적인
input / enter the data	데이터를 입력하다

DAY 07_02.mp3

PART 3

4. Why is the woman meeting with the man?
(A) To tour the facilities
(B) To interview for a job
(C) To meet with a client
(D) To negotiate some terms

5. Why does the woman mention her former colleague?
(A) To make a complaint about him
(B) To explain how she learned about a company
(C) To describe how she developed her skills
(D) To request special treatment

6. What area does the woman want to focus on?
(A) Market research
(B) Brand positioning
(C) Digital marketing
(D) Public relations

Questions 4-6 refer to the following conversation.	4-6번은 다음 대화에 관한 문제입니다.
M: Thank you for coming into our office today, Ms. Moreno. The first question for you is, ❹ why are you interested in working here at Renteria?	**남:** 오늘 사무실에 방문해 주셔서 감사합니다. 모레노 씨. 일단 첫 번째 질문은 **렌테리아에서 일하는 데 관심을 가지시는 이유가 무엇입니까?**
W: Well, ❺ one of my former colleagues, Carter Keene, works here. He told me about the work he does in the Marketing Department, and he encouraged me to apply when there was an opening.	**여:** 음. **제 예전 동료 중에 한 명이었던 카터 킨이 여기에서 일하고 있습니다. 그는 마케팅 부서에서 하고 있는 일에 관해서 저에게 말했고, 공석이 생겼을 때 지원하라고 알려줬습니다.**
M: I see that you've been in your current company for more than five years. Why do you want to leave now?	**남:** 현재 회사에서 5년 이상 근무하고 계신데요. 왜 이직하시려고 합니까?
W: Working at Carrier Agency has been a great learning experience, but I currently work mainly on market research. ❻ My true passion is social media marketing, and I would like to focus more on that area.	**여:** 캐리어 에이전시에서 일한 것은 굉장히 좋은 배움의 경험이었지만, 저는 현재 시장조사에만 주로 중점을 두고 일하고 있습니다. **제가 하고 싶은 것은 소셜 미디어 마케팅이고, 그 분야에 대해서 좀 더 집중해서 하고 싶습니다.**

어휘 come into 방문하다 | apply 지원하다 | facility 시설 | complaint 불평

4. Why is the woman meeting with the man? — 여자는 왜 남자를 만나는가?

(A) To tour the facilities — 시설을 견학하기 위해서
(B) To interview for a job — 면접을 보기 위해서
(C) To meet with a client — 고객을 만나기 위해서
(D) To negotiate some terms — 몇 가지 조건을 협상하기 위해서

해설 남자의 질문에서 왜 여기서 일하고 싶냐고 물어봤으므로(why are you interested in working here at Renteria?) 면접을 보는 것임을 알 수 있으므로 정답은 (B)가 된다.

5. Why does the woman mention her former colleague? — 여자는 왜 예전 직장 동료를 언급하는가?

(A) To make a complaint about him — 그에 대해 불평을 하기 위해서
(B) To explain how she learned about the company — 그녀가 어떻게 회사에 대해서 알게 되었는지를 설명하기 위해서
(C) To describe how she developed her skills — 그녀가 어떻게 기술을 발전시켰는지를 설명하기 위해서
(D) To request special treatment — 특별한 처리를 요청하기 위해서

해설 예전에 일했던 동료가 마케팅 부서에 공석이 생겼으니 지원해보라고 해서, 즉 회사를 알게 된 이유를 설명하고 있으므로(one of my former colleagues, Carter Keene, works here. He told me about the work he does in the Marketing Department, and he encouraged me to apply when there was an opening.) 정답은 (B)가 된다.

6. What area does the woman want to focus on? — 여자가 집중하고 싶은 것은 어떤 분야인가?

(A) Market research — 시장조사
(B) Brand positioning — 브랜드 포지셔닝
(C) Digital marketing — 디지털 마케팅
(D) Public relations — 홍보

해설 원래 하고 싶은 분야는 소셜 미디어 마케팅이라고 했으므로(My true passion is social media marketing, and I would like to focus more on that area.) 정답은 (C)가 된다.

만점 포인트 3 사무용품이나 기계에 관한 주문, 고장 및 수리 내용도 매달 출제된다.

technical support	기술적 지원
cost estimate, price quote	가격 견적
assemble, put together	조립하다
disassemble, take apart	해체하다
damaged, cracked, scratched, torn, defective	하자가 있는
custom-made, customized, tailored, individualized	고객 맞춤의
fix, repair	수리하다
replace	교체하다
broken, malfunctioning, not working, out of order	고장 난
storage room, warehouse	창고
repairperson, technician, mechanic, expert	수리공, 기술자
express / rush / expedited / overnight delivery	빠른 배송

DAY 07_03.mp3

PART 3

7. What is the main topic of the conversation?
(A) A delayed delivery
(B) A doctor's appointment
(C) A business consultation
(D) A defective machine

8. Why does the man say, "Many of our patients use this room"?
(A) To express interest in purchasing some equipment
(B) To suggest renovating a room
(C) To describe the urgency of a request
(D) To imply that the room is too small

9. What will the woman do next?
(A) Visit another customer
(B) Make a phone call
(C) Process a refund
(D) File a complaint

Questions 7-9 refer to the following conversation.	7-9번은 다음 대화에 관한 문제입니다.
M: Thank you for coming on such short notice, Katherine. ❼ Your team just installed a radiator in one of our consultation rooms a few hours ago, but we're having trouble with it. Could you take a look?	**남:** 캐서린, 갑작스러운 공지에 와 주셔서 감사합니다. **당신의 팀이 몇 시간 전에 우리 컨설팅 룸 중에 하나에 라디에이터를 설치하셨는데, 문제가 생겼습니다.** 한번 봐주시겠어요?
W: I'm sorry for the inconvenience. You're a loyal customer, and we want you to be fully satisfied with our products. Let me check the unit now.	**여:** 불편을 끼쳐 죄송합니다. 단골 고객이시므로 우리 제품에 만족할 수 있도록 해드리고 싶습니다. 지금 확인하러 가겠습니다.
M: Well, I turned up the temperature to the highest setting. ❽ It's been on for the last hour, but the room's still cold. Many of our patients use this room.	**남:** 그게, 온도를 가장 높게 올렸습니다. **한 시간 동안 켜져 있었는데, 방이 여전히 춥습니다.** 우리의 많은 환자들이 이 방을 사용합니다.
W: Again, I sincerely apologize. We'll take care of this right away. ❾ Let me call the store and have one of my employees deliver a new unit as soon as possible.	**여:** 다시 한번 진심으로 사과드립니다. 당장 이 문제를 해결해 드리겠습니다. **가게에 전화해서 우리 직원 중 한 명에게 가능한 한 빨리 새것으로 배송하게 하겠습니다.**

어휘 install 설치하다 | inconvenience 불편 | sincerely 진심으로 | defective 하자 있는 | urgency 긴급

7. What is the main topic of the conversation? / 대화의 주된 주제는 무엇인가?

(A) A delayed delivery / 지연된 배송
(B) A doctor's appointment / 의사와의 예약
(C) A business consultation / 비즈니스 컨설팅
(D) A defective machine / 하자가 있는 기계

해설 설치한 라디에이터가 문제가 있다고 이야기하는 내용이므로(Your team just installed a radiator in one of our consultation rooms a few hours ago, but we're having trouble with it.) 정답은 (D)가 된다.

8. Why does the man say, "Many of our patients use this room"? / 남자는 왜 "우리의 많은 환자들이 이 방을 사용합니다"라고 말하는가?

(A) To express interest in purchasing some equipment / 장비를 구매하는 것에 관심을 보이기 위해서
(B) To suggest renovating a room / 방을 보수하는 것을 제안하기 위해서
(C) To describe the urgency of a request / 요청사항이 급하다는 것을 설명하기 위해서
(D) To imply that the room is too small / 방이 매우 협소하다는 것을 내포하기 위해서

해설 한 시간이나 틀어놨는데 여전히 춥고, 많은 환자들이 사용하므로(It's been on for the last hour, but the room's still cold.) 좀 더 빨리 해결해 주기를 바라는 것을 내포하는 정답은 (C)가 된다.

9. What will the woman do next? / 여자가 다음으로 할 것은 무엇인가?

(A) Visit another customer / 다른 고객을 방문한다
(B) Make a phone call / 전화를 건다
(C) Process a refund / 환불을 처리한다
(D) File a complaint / 불만을 제기한다

해설 가게에 전화해서 직원에게 새것을 배송하도록 시킨다고 했으므로(Let me call the store and have one of my employees deliver a new unit as soon as possible.) 정답은 (B)가 된다.

만점 포인트 4 전화 / 녹음 메시지에서 출제되는 스토리는 정해져 있다.

전화 / 녹음 메시지의 대부분은 병원 / 면접 일정, 고장 난 제품 변경 및 수리, 호텔이나 식당의 예약 변경, 배송 지연 및 변경에 관한 것이다.

place / make an order	주문하다
receptionist	접수담당자
remodel, renovate, improve	개조하다
sold out, unavailable, out of stock	매신된, 품절된
real estate, property	부동산
software, computer program	소프트웨어
receipt, proof of purchase, payment record	영수증
expired, out of date	만료된
clinic, hospital, medical facility, doctor's office	병원
restaurant, cafeteria, bistro, eatery, dining establishment	식당
be out of town, go on a business trip	출장 가다
visit, drop / stop / come by	들르다, 방문하다
ahead of schedule, in advance	예정보다 빨리
on schedule, on time	제시간에
behind schedule, late	예정보다 늦은
refund, money back, cash back	환불하다
reimburse, compensate	배상하다
discount, price reduction, special deal, special offer, mark down, saving, ~% off, reduced price / rate	할인

DAY 07_04.mp3

PART 3

10. Who most likely is the woman?
(A) A receptionist
(B) A pharmacist
(C) A sales associate
(D) A factory supervisor

11. What does the woman suggest doing?
(A) Registering for a promotion
(B) Postponing a business trip
(C) Filling out a reimbursement form
(D) Rescheduling an appointment

12. What will the man do next?
(A) Talk to a manager
(B) Ask for a discount
(C) Print out an invoice
(D) Provide some personal information

Questions 10-12 refer to the following conversation.

W: Good morning, ⑩ you've reached Wilkerson Dentistry. How may I help you today?

M: Hello. This is Lucas Barnes. ⑪ I'm calling about my appointment next Monday afternoon at 4 P.M. I'm afraid I won't be able to make it then. I'll be going on a business trip all week next week.

W: Thank you for letting us know in advance, Mr. Barnes. ⑪ Would you like to meet with the doctor this week, then? The doctor will be available to see you this Thursday morning at 10.

M: I might be busy preparing for the trip then. ⑫ But I'll speak with my supervisor first and call you back.

10-12번은 다음 대화에 관한 문제입니다.

여: 좋은 아침입니다. **윌커슨 치과입니다. 오늘 무엇을 도와드릴까요?**

남: 안녕하세요. 저는 루카스 반즈입니다. **다음 주 월요일 오후 4시의 예약 때문에 전화드렸는데요. 죄송하지만 못 갈 것 같습니다. 다음 주 내내 출장을 가게 돼서요.**

여: 반즈 씨 미리 말씀해 주셔서 감사합니다. **그러면 이번 주에 예약해 드릴까요? 이번 주 목요일 아침 10시에 가능합니다.**

남: 그때는 출장 준비 때문에 바쁠 것 같아요. **하지만 우선 상사에게 이야기해보고 다시 연락 드리겠습니다.**

어휘 available 가능한 | receptionist 접수 담당자 | pharmacist 약사 | associate 직원 | postpone 연기하다

10. Who most likely is the woman?

(A) A receptionist
(B) A pharmacist
(C) A sales associate
(D) A factory supervisor

여자가 누구일 것 같은가?

접수 담당자
약사
영업 직원
공장 관리자

해설 치과에서 전화를 받고 예약에 관련된 업무를 하는 사람은 접수 담당자이므로(you've reached Wilkerson Dentistry. How may I help you today?) 정답은 (A)가 된다.

11. What does the woman suggest doing?

(A) Registering for a promotion
(B) Postponing a business trip
(C) Filling out a reimbursement form
(D) Rescheduling an appointment

여자가 제안하는 것은 무엇인가?

프로모션을 등록하는 것
출장을 연기하는 것
상환서를 작성하는 것
예약을 변경하는 것

해설 다음 주 월요일 예약에서 이번 주 목요일로 변경을 물어보는 내용이 나오므로(I'm calling about my appointment next Monday afternoon at 4 P.M. I'm afraid I won't be able to make it then. I'll be going on a business trip all week next week., Would you like to meet with the doctor this week, then? The doctor will be available to see you this Thursday morning at 10.) 정답은 (D)가 된다.

12. What will the man do next?

(A) Talk to a manager
(B) Ask for a discount
(C) Print out an invoice
(D) Provide some personal information

남자가 다음으로 할 것은 무엇인가?

상사에게 이야기한다.
할인을 요청한다.
송장을 프린트한다.
개인 정보를 제공한다.

해설 예약을 변경하기 전에 상사에게 물어본다고 이야기했으므로(But I'll speak with my supervisor first and call you back.) 정답은 (A)가 된다.

만점 포인트 5 교통수단의 지연은 '악천후' 아니면 '기계적 결함'이다.

bad / poor / severe / unfavorable / inclement weather	악천후
until further notice	추후 공지가 있을 때까지
snowstorm, blizzard	눈보라
inconvenience	불편
bound for	~행
flight attendant, cabin crew	승무원
missing luggage	분실된 수하물
lost and found center	분실물 센터
mechanical problem / issue	기계적 결함
heavy rain	폭우
heavy snow	폭설
delay, push back, postpone, put off	미루다, 연기하다
overhead compartment	머리 위 짐칸
carry-on luggage	기내 휴대 수하물
airplane, plane, aircraft	비행기
baggage claim area	짐 찾는 곳

DAY 07_05.mp3

PART 3

13. What does the woman say has caused a problem?

(A) Heavy traffic
(B) Some damaged ticket machines
(C) Inclement weather conditions
(D) An old booking system

14. What is the man scheduled to do tomorrow?

(A) Attend a convention
(B) Inspect a factory
(C) Deliver a presentation
(D) Repair some machinery

15. Why does the woman say, "There's a flight leaving at 10 P.M."?

(A) To apologize for a delay
(B) To recommend an alternative
(C) To correct an error
(D) To offer a seat upgrade

해설 호주 - 미국

Questions 13-15 refer to the following conversation.

M: Hi. I'd like to purchase a ticket on flight 628 to New York departing at 3 P.M. today.

W: Please wait as I check our system. ⑬ Many people have been forced to make sudden changes to their travel arrangements due to the blizzard.

M: I thought so. ⑭ My bosses just told me that I need to give a presentation to a client in New York tomorrow. That's why I'm flying out last minute.

W: ⑮ I'm checking to see if there are any seats available for the 3 o'clock flight. Umm... There's a flight leaving at 10 P.M.

M: That will do. Could you get me a ticket for that flight? I just need to fly out today.

13-15번은 다음 대화에 관한 문제입니다.

남: 안녕하세요. 오늘 오후 3시에 출발해서 뉴욕으로 가는 비행기 628편의 티켓을 구매하고 싶습니다.

여: 시스템을 확인하는 동안 기다려주세요. **많은 사람들이 눈보라 때문에 어쩔 수 없이 갑작스럽게 여행 계획을 변경할 수밖에 없었습니다.**

남: 그럴 것 같아요. **제 상사가 방금 저에게 내일 뉴욕에 있는 고객을 위해 프레젠테이션해야 한다고 말해주어서요.** 막판에 급하게 비행기를 타려고 합니다.

여: **3시 비행기의 좌석이 있는지 확인하고 있습니다. 음… 밤 10시에 출발하는 게 있는데요.**

남: 괜찮습니다. 그 비행 편 티켓으로 해주시겠어요? 오늘 비행기를 타면 돼요.

어휘 purchase 구입하다 | depart 출발하다 | sudden 갑작스러운 | inclement 좋지 못한 | alternative 대안

13. What does the woman say has caused a problem?

(A) Heavy traffic
(B) Some damaged ticket machines
(C) Inclement weather conditions
(D) An old booking system

여자는 문제를 야기시킨 것이 무엇이라고 말하는가?

교통 정체
손상된 티켓 판매기
악천후
노후된 예약 시스템

해설 눈보라 때문에 갑작스럽게 변경사항이 많아졌다는 내용이 나오므로(Many people have been forced to make sudden changes to their travel arrangements due to the blizzard.) 정답은 (C)가 된다. blizzard(눈보라)가 결정적인 단어인데 이것을 놓치면 답을 할 수가 없으므로 잘 기억해 두자.

14. What is the man scheduled to do tomorrow?

(A) Attend a convention
(B) Inspect a factory
(C) Deliver a presentation
(D) Repair some machinery

남자가 내일 하기로 예정된 것은 무엇인가?

컨벤션에 참석한다
공장을 검사한다
프레젠테이션을 한다
기계를 수리한다

해설 뉴욕에 있는 고객에게 프레젠테이션을 하라고 상사로부터 연락을 받았으므로(My bosses just told me that I need to give a presentation to a client in New York tomorrow.) 정답은 (C)가 된다.

15. Why does the woman say, "There's a flight leaving at 10 P.M."?

(A) To apologize for a delay
(B) To recommend an alternative
(C) To correct an error
(D) To offer a seat upgrade

여자는 왜 "밤 10시에 출발하는 게 있는데요" 라고 말하는가?

지연에 사과하기 위해서
다른 대안책을 제안하기 위해서
에러를 수정하기 위해서
좌석 업그레이드를 제공하기 위해서

해설 앞에서 남자가 원한 비행편은 오후 3시이지만, 대신에 밤 10시를 이야기하고 있어(I'm checking to see if there are any seats available for the 3 o'clock flight.) 다른 대안책을 이야기하는 정답은 (B)가 된다.

만점 포인트 6 시상식, 퇴임식, 송별회에서는 그 인물의 소개와 업적을 반드시 물어본다.

win an award / prize	상을 받다
accomplishment, achievement	성취 / 성과
keynote speaker	기조연설자
recognize	인정하다
in recognition of	인정하여
reception, welcoming party	환영회
proceeds	수익금
fundraiser, fundraising event	모금행사
outstanding, excellent, exceptional, prestigious	훌륭한
farewell party	송별회
retirement party	은퇴식
well-known, famous, renowned, notable	유명한
nominees	후보자
nomination	후보
charity event	자선행사
Employee of the Year, best employee	올해의 직원
non-profit organization	비영리 단체

DAY 07_06.mp3

PART 4

16. What event is being held?

(A) A retirement party
(B) A charity fundraiser
(C) A career expo
(D) A trade convention

17. According to the speaker, what is Lauren Soto's greatest accomplishment?

(A) She expanded a client base.
(B) She founded a charitable organization.
(C) She relocated to a company's overseas office.
(D) She designed the most successful product.

18. What does the speaker ask Lauren Soto to do?

(A) Watch a presentation
(B) Introduce a special guest
(C) Present an award
(D) Accept a gift

Questions 16-18 refer to the following excerpt from a meeting.

M: [16] Thank you, everyone, for taking the time out of your busy schedules to come and celebrate Lauren Soto's last day at our company. She is loved and respected by all her colleagues, especially because we all know how dedicated and professional Lauren is about her job. Our client numbers grew significantly thanks to Lauren's hard work. [17] Her most outstanding achievement at McKinney Incorporated is securing more business contracts than any other employee in history. We are grateful for you, Lauren. [18] Now, we would like to invite you up to the stage so that we can present you with a special engraved watch. Everyone, please give Lauren a big round of applause.

16-18번은 다음 회의 발췌록에 관한 문제입니다.

남: **여러분들, 바쁘신 와중에 로렌 소토의 우리 회사에서 마지막 날을 축하하기 위해서 시간을 내어 와주셔서 감사합니다.** 그녀는 직원들이 좋아하고 존경하는 사람입니다, 특히 그녀가 얼마나 헌신적이고 전문적으로 일해 왔는지를 모두 알기 때문입니다. 로렌이 열심히 일한 덕분에 고객의 숫자가 현저하게 증가했습니다. **맥키니 사에서 그녀의 가장 훌륭한 업적은 역사상 어느 직원들보다 많은 사업 계약을 체결한 것입니다.** 로렌, 감사합니다. **지금, 특별히 새긴 시계를 당신에게 드릴 수 있도록 당신을 무대에 모시고 싶습니다.** 여러분들, 로렌에게 큰 박수 부탁드립니다.

어휘 dedicate 헌신하다 | significantly 현저하게 | outstanding 훌륭한 | engraved 새겨진 | charity 자선 | found 설립하다 | charitable 자선의

16. What event is being held?

(A) A retirement party
(B) A charity fundraiser
(C) A career expo
(D) A trade convention

어떤 이벤트가 개최되고 있는가?

은퇴식
자선기금
취업 엑스포
무역 컨벤션

해설 로렌 소토의 마지막 날을 축하하러 모인 것이므로(Thank you, everyone, for taking the time out of your busy schedules to come and celebrate Lauren Soto's last day at our company.) 정답은 (A)가 된다.

17. According to the speaker, what is Lauren Soto's greatest accomplishment?

(A) She expanded a client base.
(B) She founded a charitable organization.
(C) She relocated to a company's overseas office.
(D) She designed the most successful product.

화자에 따르면, 로렌 소토의 가장 큰 업적은 무엇인가?

그녀는 고객층을 넓혔다.
그녀는 자선 기관을 창립했다.
그녀는 회사 해외 지사로 옮겼다.
그녀는 가장 성공적인 제품을 디자인했다.

해설 고객들과 계약을 체결했다는 내용이 나오므로(Her most outstanding achievement at McKinney Incorporated is securing more business contracts than any other employee in history.) 정답은 (A)가 된다.

18. What does the speaker ask Lauren Soto to do?

(A) Watch a presentation
(B) Introduce a special guest
(C) Present an award
(D) Accept a gift

화자가 로렌 소토에게 무엇을 하라고 요청하는가?

프레젠테이션을 본다.
특별한 손님을 소개한다.
상을 준다.
선물을 받는다.

해설 무대에 모셔서 특별히 새겨진 시계를 준다고 했으므로(Now, we would like to invite you up to the stage so that we can present you with a special engraved watch.), 로렌이 그 시계를 받는다는 (D)가 정답이다. watch가 나온다고 해서 (A)를 하지 않도록 주의하자.

만점 포인트 7 교통 정체의 원인은 '사고' 또는 '도로 공사'라 '우회'를 하거나 '대중교통 이용'을 권한다.

under construction	공사 중
transit service, public transportation	대중교통
traffic jam, traffic congestion, heavy traffic	교통 체증
driver, motorist	운전자
take a detour / side street, take an alternate / different route	우회 도로를 이용하다
road repavement	도로 재포장
road work, road repair	도로 공사
crash, collision	충돌
overpass	고가도로, 육교

DAY 07_07.mp3

PART 4

19. What is the broadcast mainly about?

(A) A broken traffic signal
(B) A power outage
(C) A car accident
(D) A derailed train

20. What will be completed in five days?

(A) Construction of a new highway
(B) Renovation of a bridge
(C) Redevelopment of a commercial area
(D) Extension of a subway line

21. According to the speaker, what should the listeners do?

(A) Check for weather updates
(B) Avoid driving during rush hours
(C) Use public transportation
(D) Take an alternate route

해설 미국

Questions 19-21 refer to the following radio broadcast.

W: Thank you for tuning in to WKFM's *The Morning Central* with Sandy Morrison. It's time for local news. ⑲ A multiple collision occurred on the overpass leading to Calmar Bridge this morning at 8:27 A.M. A total of 12 vehicles were involved in this crash, and at least 20 people were taken to the nearest hospital. No fatalities have been reported. ⑳ There is evidence of major structural damage to the bridge as a result, and the bridge will be closed for urgent repairs. The repairs will take five days to complete. Meanwhile, ㉑ please make sure to take a detour when planning your commute. We will keep you posted if we have any updates.

19-21번은 다음 라디오 방송에 관한 문제입니다.

여: WKFM의 샌디 모리슨과 함께하는 〈모닝 센트럴〉에 채널 고정해 주셔서 감사합니다. 지역 뉴스 시간입니다. **오늘 오전 8시 27분에 카머 다리로 가는 고가도로에서 여러 건의 충돌 사고가 있었습니다. 총 12개의 차량이 충돌되었고,** 적어도 20명의 사람들이 근처 병원으로 옮겨졌습니다. 사망자는 없는 것으로 보고 되었습니다. **그 결과 다리가 크게 손상되어 긴급한 복구를 위해 폐쇄될 것입니다. 수리는 완료되는 데 5일 정도 소요가 될 것입니다.** 그러는 동안에, **통근을 계획하실 때 우회 도로를 이용하시기 바랍니다.** 만약 변경사항이 있으면 계속해서 알려드리겠습니다.

어휘 collision 충돌 | urgent repair 긴급 수리 | detour 우회 도로 | commute 통근하다 | power outage 정전 | extension 연장

19. What is the broadcast mainly about?

(A) A broken traffic signal
(B) A power outage
(C) A car accident
(D) A derailed train

방송은 주로 무엇에 관한 이야기인가?

고장 난 신호등
정전
차 사고
탈선 열차

해설 충돌 사고로 총 12개의 차량이 충돌되었다는 이야기가 나오므로(A multiple collision occurred on the overpass leading to Calmar Bridge this morning at 8:27 A.M. A total of 12 vehicles were involved in this crash.) 정답은 (C)가 된다.

20. What will be completed in five days?

(A) Construction of a new highway
(B) Renovation of a bridge
(C) Redevelopment of a commercial area
(D) Extension of a subway line

5일 이후면 어떤 것이 완성될 것인가?

새 고속도로 공사
다리 보수 공사
상업지구 재개발
지하철 노선 연장

해설 다리를 긴급하게 복구하기 위해 폐쇄하고 5일이면 끝난다고 했으므로(There is evidence of major structural damage to the bridge as a result, and the bridge will be closed for urgent repairs. The repairs will take five days to complete.) 정답은 (B)가 된다.

21. According to the speaker, what should the listeners do?

(A) Check for weather updates
(B) Avoid driving during rush hours
(C) Use public transportation
(D) Take an alternate route

화자에 따르면, 청자들이 해야 하는 것은 무엇인가?

일기예보 정보 확인하기
러시아워 동안에 운전 피하기
대중교통 이용하기
우회 도로 이용하기

해설 우회해서 가라고 했으므로(please make sure to take a detour when planning your commute.) 정답은 (D)가 된다.

만점 포인트 8 인수합병이나 정책의 변화에는 반드시 끝에 '긍정적 효과'를 언급한다.

acquire, merge, buy, purchase	인수 / 합병하다
plant, factory, manufacturing facility, production facility	공장
mayor, city official, local politician	시장
staff cutbacks	직원 감축
competitor, rival	경쟁업체
president, executive officer, CEO	회장
release, launch, introduce, unveil, put on the market	출시하다
dismiss	해고하다

DAY 07_08.mp3

PART 4

22. What is the broadcast mainly about?

(A) An advertising campaign
(B) A technology convention
(C) A corporate merger
(D) A global business trend

23. According to the speaker, who is June Palmer?

(A) An executive officer
(B) An engineer
(C) A reporter
(D) A writer

24. What will BG Electronics most likely do next year?

(A) Expand to an overseas market
(B) Launch an e-commerce Web site
(C) Launch a new battery
(D) Build a manufacturing facility

Questions 22-24 refer to the following broadcast.

W: You're listening to KACL's *Business Update*. ㉒ Yesterday, BG Electronics, the nation's top manufacturer of smartphones, announced a much-anticipated acquisition of Conquest Global. After the takeover, BG Electronics will be able to utilize Conquest Global's high-capacity batteries designed for smartphones. This is a result of a five-year-long discussion. ㉓ The CEO of BG Electronics, June Palmer, hopes that this change will help the company develop into a multi-billion-dollar corporation. With Conquest Global's unrivaled battery technology, ㉔ BG Electronics plans to construct a new plant next year to make a new line of smartphones. These phones would only need to be charged once every 48 hours.

22-24번은 다음 방송에 관한 문제입니다.

여: 여러분들은 KACL의 〈비지니스 업데이트〉를 듣고 계십니다. **어제 우리나라에서 가장 최고의 스마트폰 제조업체인 BG 일렉트로닉이 콘퀘스트 글로벌과 고대하던 인수를 발표했습니다.** 인수 이후에, BG 일렉트로닉은 스마트폰을 위해 디자인된 콘퀘스트 글로벌의 대용량 배터리를 활용할 수 있게 될 것입니다. 이것은 5년간의 긴 협상의 결과입니다. **BG 일렉트로닉의 CEO인 준 파머**는 이 변화가 수십억 달러의 회사로 발전하는 데 도움을 주기를 바랍니다. 콘퀘스트 글로벌의 비할 데 없는 배터리 기술을 가지고, **BG 일렉트로닉은 내년에 새로운 라인의 스마트폰을 만들기 위해 새 공장을 지을 계획입니다.** 이 핸드폰은 48시간마다 한 번만 충전하면 되는 것입니다.

어휘 manufacturer 제조업체 | acquisition 인수 | unrivaled 비할 데 없는 | executive officer 임원

22. What is the broadcast mainly about?

(A) An advertising campaign
(B) A technology convention
(C) A corporate merger
(D) A global business trend

방송은 무엇에 관한 것인가?

광고 캠페인
기술 컨벤션
회사 합병
세계 비즈니스 트렌드

해설 BG 일렉트로닉이 콘퀘스트 글로벌을 인수한다는 내용이므로(Yesterday, BG Electronics, the nation's top manufacturer of smartphones, announced a much-anticipated acquisition of Conquest Global.) 정답은 (C)가 된다.

23. According to the speaker, who is June Palmer?

(A) An executive officer
(B) An engineer
(C) A reporter
(D) A writer

화자에 따르면, 준 파머는 누구인가?

임원
엔지니어
기자
작가

해설 BG 일렉트로닉의 CEO라고 했으므로(The CEO of BG Electronics, June Palmer,) 정답은 (A)가 된다.

24. What will BG Electronics most likely do next year?

(A) Expand to an overseas market
(B) Launch an e-commerce Web site
(C) Launch a new battery
(D) Build a manufacturing facility

BG 일렉트로닉이 내년에 무엇을 할 것 같은가?

해외시장으로 확장한다
이커머스 웹사이트를 출시한다
새 밧데리를 출시한다
공장을 건설하다

해설 새로운 공장을 지어서 새로운 라인의 스마트폰을 만들겠다고 이야기했으므로(BG Electronics plans to construct a new plant next year to make a new line of smartphones.) 정답은 (D)가 된다.

만점 포인트 9 판매의 저조나 하락으로 인한 '문제점'과 '해결책'을 물어본다.

cut costs, reduce expenses	비용을 줄이다
increase, rise, soar, go up	증가하다
feedback, opinion, survey, questionnaire	의견, 설문조사
revise, edit, amend, update, change	수정하다, 고치다, 바꾸다
income, revenue, earnings, proceeds	수익
quarterly sales records	분기별 매출액
decrease, decline, drop, slow	감소 / 하락하다
environmentally friendly, eco-friendly	친환경적인
cheap, inexpensive, affordable, reasonable, less expensive	가격이 싼
long-lasting, durable	내구성이 있는

DAY 07_09.mp3

PART 4

25. What problem is being discussed?
(A) Customers are unhappy with a product.
(B) Productions have been delayed.
(C) Incorrect findings were presented.
(D) Sales targets were not met.

26. What solution does the speaker suggest?
(A) Conducting market analysis
(B) Hiring a business consultant
(C) Lowering the price of a product
(D) Expediting a shipment

27. What can customers do to receive a discount?
(A) Register for a store membership
(B) Participate in a survey
(C) Purchase an item online
(D) Refer a friend or a family member

Questions 25-27 refer to the following excerpt from a meeting.

W: The last item I'd like to discuss with you today is our quarterly figures. ㉕ I'm afraid the sales in all of our supermarket branches have declined quite significantly in the second quarter. Needless to say, this is well below our projected target. Now, to regain a competitive edge over our rivals, ㉖ I propose carrying out extensive market research. This will be done in a total of three phases, first starting with an analysis of our current customers. We will design a customer satisfaction questionnaire. We plan to distribute these forms in our branches. We will also post the same form online. ㉗ To encourage our customers to complete the survey, we will give out prizes and discount coupons to all participants as an incentive.

25-27번은 다음 회의 발췌록에 관한 문제입니다.

여: 오늘 여러분들과 함께 논의하고 싶은 마지막은 분기 수치입니다. **유감스럽게도, 우리 슈퍼마켓의 모든 지점의 판매가 2분기에 현격하게 급감했습니다. 말할 필요도 없이, 우리가 예상했던 목표 보다 훨씬 이하입니다.** 이제, 우리의 라이벌보다 경쟁적 우위를 되찾기 위해서, **대대적인 시장조사를 실행할 것을 제안합니다.** 이것은 총 3단계로 이루어질 것입니다. 첫 번째로는 현재 고객들을 분석하는 것입니다. 우리는 고객만족도 조사를 디자인할 것입니다. 우리는 지점에 이 양식을 모두 배포할 예정입니다. 우리는 또한 온라인상에도 똑같은 양식을 게재할 것입니다. **고객들이 설문조사를 완성할 수 있도록 하기 위해서, 모든 참석자들에게 상품과 할인 쿠폰의 혜택을 드릴 것입니다.**

어휘 quarterly figures 분기 수치 | decline 감소하다 | significantly 현격하게 | Needless to say 말할 필요 없이 | competitive 경쟁적인 | questionnaire. 조사 | expedite 신속히 처리하다

25. What problem is being discussed?
(A) Customers are unhappy with a product.
(B) Productions have been delayed.
(C) Incorrect findings were presented.
(D) Sales targets were not met.

어떤 문제가 논의되고 있는가?
고객들은 제품에 불만족하고 있다.
생산이 지연되었다.
잘못된 조사 결과를 제시했다.
판매 목표가 충족되지 못했다.

해설 2분기에 판매가 급감했고, 예상했던 목표 보다 훨씬 못 미쳤다고 했으므로(I'm afraid the sales in all of our supermarket branches have declined quite significantly in the second quarter. Needless to say, this is well below our projected target.) 정답은 (D)가 된다.

26. What solution does the speaker suggest?
(A) Conducting market analysis
(B) Hiring a business consultant
(C) Lowering the price of a product
(D) Expediting a shipment

화자가 제안한 해결책은 무엇인가?
시장분석을 하는 것
비즈니스 컨설턴트를 고용하는 것
제품 가격을 낮추는 것
배송을 신속하게 처리하는 것

해설 대대적인 시장 조사를 제안했으므로(I propose carrying out extensive market research.) 정답은 (A)가 된다.

27. What can customers do to receive a discount?
(A) Register for a store membership
(B) Participate in a survey
(C) Purchase an item online
(D) Refer a friend or a family member

고객들은 할인을 받기 위해서 무엇을 할 수 있는가?
가게 멤버십에 가입한다
설문조사에 참여한다
물건을 온라인으로 구매한다
친구 혹은 가족에게 추천한다

해설 설문조사를 완료하는 사람에게 할인 쿠폰을 준다고 했으므로(To encourage our customers to complete the survey, we will give out prizes and discount coupons to all participants as an incentive.) 정답은 (B)가 된다.

만점 포인트 10 박물관, 미술관 투어, 공연장에서는 사진 촬영 금지나 기념품 가게 방문을 제안한다.

refrain from, prohibit A from	금하다, 삼가다
auditorium	강당
intermission	중간 휴식
recording, album	앨범
souvenir	기념품
preview	시사회
performance, show	공연
event, function	행사

DAY 07_10.mp3

PART 4

28. What most likely is the speaker's profession?

(A) Museum guide
(B) Store manager
(C) Craft artist
(D) Graphic designer

29. What does the speaker say about the ceramics exhibit?

(A) It can be viewed online.
(B) It contains over 200 pieces of art.
(C) It is closed to the public.
(D) It is the longest-running exhibit.

30. What does the speaker recommend that listeners do?

(A) Visit a souvenir shop
(B) Purchase some ceramics
(C) Read an exhibition catalog
(D) Take photos of the artwork

Questions 28-30 refer to the following speech.

M: Hello, everyone. ㉘ Welcome to Carroll Museum of Art. I'll be leading you on tour today. Before we begin, ㉙ I know that some of you may be here to see our famous ceramics exhibit, which is the largest collection in the state. I'm sorry to inform you that the East Wing, where the exhibit is located, is closed for maintenance today. We do have many other pieces of art for you to enjoy, though. During the tour, I'll give you plenty of time to enjoy the artwork on your own. You can also choose to explore the museum on your own at any time. ㉚ On your way out, you should definitely visit the museum gift shop where you can buy exhibition catalogues as well as souvenirs from the museum.

28-30번은 다음 연설에 관한 문제입니다.

남: 여러분, 안녕하세요. **캐럴 미술 박물관에 오신 것을 환영합니다. 제가 오늘 여러분들 투어를 이끌게 됩니다.** 우리가 시작하기에 앞서서, **여러분들 중 몇 분들은 주에서 가장 많은 컬렉션이 있는 유명한 세라믹 전시회를 보기 위해 오셨을 겁니다. 유감스럽게도 전시가 되고 있는 이스트 윙이 오늘 유지 보수로 인해 문을 닫았습니다.** 하지만 여러분들이 즐기실 수 있는 많은 다른 예술작품들이 있습니다. 투어가 진행되는 동안, 여러분들 스스로 예술작품을 감상하실 수 있는 시간을 충분히 드릴 것입니다. 또한 언제든지 혼자서 박물관을 둘러보실 수도 있습니다. **나가시기 전에,** 박물관에서 나오는 전시 카탈로그뿐만 아니라 **기념품들도 구매하실 수 있는 박물관 기념품점에 들리세요.**

어휘 exhibit 전시 | maintenance 유지 보수 | souvenir 기념품

28. What most likely is the speaker's profession?

(A) Museum guide
(B) Store manager
(C) Craft artist
(D) Graphic designer

화자의 직업이 무엇이겠는가?

박물관 가이드
가게 매니저
공예가
그래픽 디자이너

해설 박물관에 오신 것을 환영하고 오늘 투어를 이끈다고 했으므로(Welcome to Carroll Museum of Art. I'll be leading you on tour today.) 정답은 (A)가 된다.

29. What does the speaker say about the ceramics exhibit?

(A) It can be viewed online.
(B) It contains over 200 pieces of art.
(C) It is closed to the public.
(D) It is the longest-running exhibit.

화자는 세라믹 전시회에 대해서 뭐라고 말하는가?

온라인상에서 볼 수 있다.
200점이 넘는 예술작품을 소장하고 있다.
대중들에게 오픈되지 않는다.
가장 오래 전시되고 있다.

해설 세라믹 전시회가 열리는 이스트 윙이 문을 닫았다고 나와 있으므로(I know that some of you may be here to see our famous ceramics exhibit, which is the largest collection in the state. I'm sorry to inform you that the East Wing, where the exhibit is located, is closed for maintenance today.) 정답은 (C)가 된다.

30. What does the speaker recommend that listeners do?

(A) Visit a souvenir shop
(B) Purchase some ceramics
(C) Read an exhibition catalog
(D) Take photos of the artwork

화자가 청자들에게 추천하는 것은 무엇인가?

기념품점을 방문한다
세라믹을 구매한다
전시회 카탈로그를 읽는다
예술 작품 사진을 찍는다

해설 기념품점에 들리라고 했으므로(On your way out, you should definitely visit the museum gift shop) 정답은 (A)가 된다.

MEMO

고난도 실전 문제

DAY 07_11.mp3

PART 3

1. What are the speakers discussing?
   (A) Purchasing a new vehicle
   (B) Fulfilling an order
   (C) Visiting a client
   (D) Revising an agreement

2. What does the woman say about Rivermont Street?
   (A) Traffic signs are broken there.
   (B) It connects to the city center.
   (C) It is closed to traffic.
   (D) A parking facility is being built nearby.

3. What does the man suggest doing?
   (A) Checking the traffic report
   (B) Using public transportation
   (C) Leaving the office right away
   (D) Postponing an appointment

---

4. What problem does the woman mention?
   (A) There was a delivery oversight.
   (B) A vehicle was in an accident.
   (C) Some machinery is sold out.
   (D) Some products are malfunctioning.

5. What does the man say will take place on Thursday?
   (A) A grand opening
   (B) A cooking class
   (C) A store inspection
   (D) A product launch

6. What does the woman say she will do?
   (A) Contact a driver
   (B) Transfer a call
   (C) Check the inventory
   (D) Extend a warranty

Seminar Schedule

Title	Date
Clear Communication	Monday, September 16
Advanced Business Writing	Tuesday, September 17
Effective Speaking	Wednesday, September 18
Strategies for Customer Satisfaction	Thursday, September 19

7. According to the man, what has recently changed?
   (A) An office layout
   (B) An employee handbook
   (C) A scheduling conflict
   (D) A corporate policy

8. What does the woman say about the seminars?
   (A) Topics will change monthly.
   (B) Attendance is mandatory.
   (C) Seating is on a first-come, first-served basis.
   (D) Sessions will be led by the personnel manager.

9. Look at the graphic. What session will the man attend?
   (A) Clear Communication
   (B) Advanced Business Writing
   (C) Effective Speaking
   (D) Strategies for Customer Satisfaction

PART 4

10. What is the message mainly about?
(A) A temporary move
(B) A technology conference
(C) A business news center
(D) A laboratory renovation

11. According to the speaker, what can be accessed on a Web site?
(A) A map
(B) A directory
(C) An events calendar
(D) A reservation form

12. How can the listeners borrow a laptop?
(A) By paying a fee in advance
(B) By submitting a credit card
(C) By showing an ID badge
(D) By subscribing to a service

---

13. What is the broadcast mainly about?
(A) Highway construction
(B) Road closure
(C) Inclement weather
(D) A vehicle accident

14. What are the motorists advised to do?
(A) Use public transportation
(B) Reduce their speed
(C) Follow detour signs
(D) Carpool with others to work

15. What will happen on October 15?
(A) Some roadwork will be finished.
(B) A new bus terminal will open.
(C) Some drivers will be stopped for a license check.
(D) A toll fee will be increased.

---

16. What is the broadcast mainly about?
(A) The relocation of a local company
(B) The expansion of the apartment complex
(C) The construction of an office complex
(D) The remodeling of a shopping center

17. What is mentioned about the project?
(A) It has yet to receive proper permits.
(B) It will commence this week.
(C) It will be finished in a year.
(D) It is located in the outskirts of the city.

18. What advantage of the project does the speaker mention?
(A) Business activity will increase.
(B) A city's population will grow.
(C) A city will receive more funding.
(D) More jobs will be created.

MEMO

PART 5

토익 950점 이상이 되기 위해서는 PART 5&6의 고득점이 전제되어야 한다. 즉, PART 5&6가 거의 만점에 가깝게 나와야 하는 것이다. 토익은 시험 출제자의 의도를 파악해서 답을 찾는 시험 영어이므로 출제 유형을 제대로 알고 대비하는 것이 매우 중요하다.

DAY 01-05

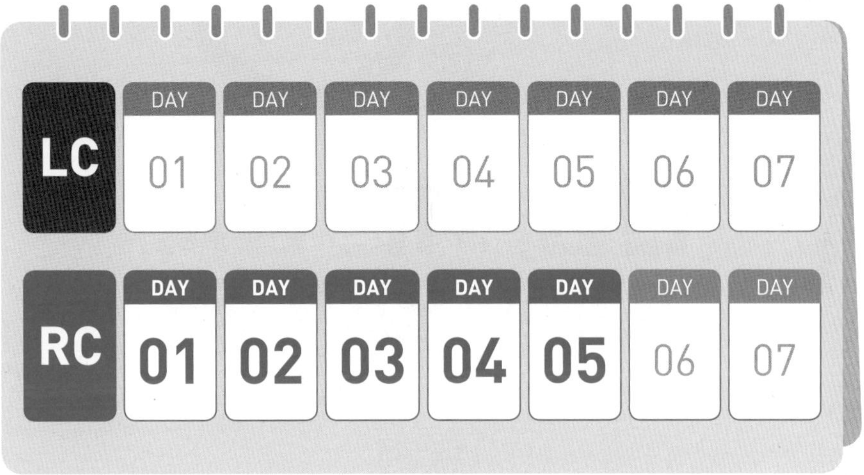

PART 5 만점 핵심 공략

1. 기본 품사 무시하지 마라
2. 빈출 문제에 주목하라! 토익이 사랑하는 문제는 따로 있다.
3. 1초 짜리 문제, PART 5의 대부분은 해석이 필요 없는 문제이다.
4. 토익은 점차 진화하고 있다, 느낌과 감은 버리고 답이 되는 이유를 확실히 알자!

PART 5

DAY 01

만점, 기본 품사 4개만 알면 끝!

동영상 강의 바로 보기

토익 시험에서 가장 빈출도가 높은 대표적인 품사는 '명사, 동사, 형용사, 부사'이다. 이 품사들의 자리를 물어보는 문제가 매달 출제되며, 이러한 문제의 특징은 별도의 해석 없이도 빠르게 풀 수 있다는 것이다. 그러므로 이 4가지 주요 품사만 섭렵하더라도 PART 5의 60~70%는 수월하게 해결할 수 있다. 고득점자라고 하더라도 이러한 기본 품사 부분을 쉽다고 간과하여 종종 오답을 고르는 실수를 범할 수가 있으므로 이번 기회를 통해 시험에 잘 나오는 기본 품사 자리를 완벽히 마스터하도록 하자.

만점 포인트

이것만 알면 만점!

1 명사: 가산이냐? 불가산이냐? 그것이 문제로다.
2 동사: 토익이 사랑하는 동사는 따로 있다.
3 형용사: 헷갈리지만 의외로 쉬운 것이 형용사다.
4 부사: 딱 2가지만 알면 끝난다.

만점 포인트 1 명사: 가산이냐? 불가산이냐? 그것이 문제로다.

적중! 유형 정리

Franzia Inc. now has ------- with 28 major automobile companies all over the world.

(A) contracts
(B) contract
(C) contractor
(D) contracting

프란지아 사는 전 세계적으로 28개 주요 자동차 회사와 계약을 맺고 있다.

해설 has라는 타동사의 목적어 자리로 명사인 (A), (B), (C)가 들어갈 수 있는데, 명사에서 가장 중요한 핵심은 가산 명사와 불가산 명사를 구분하는 것이다. (B), (C)의 경우는 가산 명사이므로 괄호 앞에 관사 a(n) 혹은 괄호 뒤에 (e)s가 없어서 오답이다. 따라서, 정답은 (A) contracts가 된다.

만점 전략 1 가산 명사 vs. 불가산 명사

1. 가산 명사 vs. 불가산 명사

명사의 핵심은 '종류'와 '수'이다. 그러므로 명사의 종류, 즉, '가산'인지 '불가산'인지 먼저 확인하고, 가산 명사일 경우에는 반드시 단수인지 복수인지를 구분해야 한다. 단수일 때는 앞에 부정관사 a(n)을, 복수일 때는 뒤에 (e)s를 붙인다. 하지만 불가산 명사는 앞뒤에 아무것도 붙이지 않는다.

가산 명사		불가산 명사	
a permit	허가(증)	permission	허가(증), 승인
a certificate	증명(서)	certification	증명(서)
an approach	접근 (방법)	access	접근
a survey	설문조사	research	연구
a detail	세부사항	information	정보
a suggestion	제안	advice	조언

2. -ing로 끝나는 불가산 명사

-ing로 끝나는 것을 흔히 동명사로 착각하기 쉬우나, -ing로 끝나는 명사도 있다. 다음은 시험에 자주 출제되는 -ing로 끝나는 명사이므로 익혀두자. 참고로, -ing로 끝나는 명사는 불가산 명사로 쓰인다.

-ing로 끝나는 불가산 명사			
understanding	이해	accounting	회계(학)
planning	계획	training	교육, 훈련
widening	확장	photocopying	복사
advertising	광고, 광고업	housing	주택
cleaning	청소	handling	처리
seating	좌석	banking	은행 업무
shipping	배송	dining	식사
writing	글쓰기	ticketing	티켓 발급

만점 전략 2 명사 자리

1. 명사 자리

명사는 문장에서 주어, 목적어, 보어 역할을 하며, 명사를 수식하는 '형용사, 분사' 또는 한정사인 '관사'와 '소유격' 뒤에 온다.

❶ 명사 + 동사
The elevator was temporarily out of order. 엘리베이터가 일시적으로 고장 났다.

❷ 타동사 + 명사
Mr. Kim made **an effort** to reach an agreement. 김 씨는 합의에 도달하기 위해 노력했다.

❸ 전치사 + 명사
The building is under **construction**. 그 건물은 공사 중이다.

❹ 5형식 동사 + 목적어 + 명사
The manager considers Ally a dedicated **worker**. 매니저는 앨리를 헌신적인 노동자로 여긴다.

❺ 관사 a(n) / the + 명사
The **registration** for the program is easy. 프로그램 등록은 쉽다.

❻ 소유격 + 명사
My **assistant** will answer the telephone. 내 비서가 전화를 받을 것이다.

❼ 형용사 / 분사 + 명사
Ms. Lee submitted relevant / revised **documents**. 이 씨는 관련 / 개정 서류를 제출했다.

❽ 한정사 + 부사 + 형용사 + 명사
The newly renovated **factory** will resume operations. 새로 개조된 공장이 재개될 것이다.

❾ 명사 + 명사(복합 명사)
For **safety reasons**, you should wear masks. 안전을 위해, 마스크를 착용해야 한다.

❿ 명사, 추가 설명
Clayton Sinclair, **a famous writer**, will visit Korea soon.
유명한 작가인 클레이턴 싱클레어가 한국을 방문할 예정이다.

2. 복합 명사 (명사 + 명사)

복합 명사란 명사 다음에 명사가 따라 나와 하나의 뜻을 만드는 경우를 말한다. 최근 들어 복합 명사 문제는 출제 빈도수가 점차 낮아지는 추세로, 시험에 자주 출제되었던 표현을 암기해두면 쉽게 해결할 수 있다. 명사 앞에 빈칸이 있는 경우 무조건 형용사를 고르기보다는 복합 명사 문제인지를 확인할 필요가 있다.

training session	교육 기간	bank transaction	은행 거래
contingency plan	비상사태 대책	delivery company	배송 업체
travel arrangement	여행 준비	office supplies	사무용품
job opportunity	고용 기회	employee productivity	직원 생산성
safety standards	안전 기준	customer satisfaction	고객 만족
job opening	공석	awards ceremony	시상식

만점 전략 3 혼동하기 쉬운 명사

보기에 형태가 비슷한 명사가 나온다면 '사람 명사(가산 명사)'와 '추상 명사(불가산 명사)'를 구분하는 문제이거나 '의미(뜻) 차이'를 구분하는 문제이므로 평소에 차이를 미리 공부해 둘 필요가 있다.

attendant	안내원	attendance	참석, 참석자 수
attendee	참석자	attention	주의(집중), 주목
production	생산	product	제품, 결과 / 부산물
produce	농산물	productivity	생산성
installation	설치	installment	할부, 권, 판
correspondent	특파원	correspondence	서신 왕래
architect	건축가	architecture	건축
accountant	회계사	accounting	회계
authority	권한, 권위자	authorization	허가, 승인
professional	전문가	profession	직업

만점 전략 4 명사 vs. 동명사

전치사 뒤에 빈칸이 나오는 경우는 보통 전치사의 목적어로 명사와 동명사를 구분하는 문제이다. 빈칸에 들어갈 단어가 명사인지 동명사인지를 빠르게 구분하는 방법은 빈칸 뒤에 '목적어의 유무'와 빈칸 앞에 '수식하는 어구(형용사 / 부사)'로 알아낼 수 있다.

– 명사가 답인 경우: 빈칸 앞에 형용사가 오며, 뒤에 목적어가 없다. (단, 복합 명사는 제외)

~ for careful **planning**
전치사 형용사 명사

– 동명사가 답인 경우: 앞에 부사가 오며, 뒤에 타동사의 동명사의 경우 목적어가 있다.

~ for carefully **planning** the upcoming events
전치사 부사 동명사 명사

명사 앞에는 한정사의 종류인 관사(a(n), the)와 소유격이 올 수 있지만, 동명사 앞에는 올 수 없다.

만점 포인트 2 동사: 토익이 사랑하는 동사는 따로 있다.

적중! 유형 정리

Severe weather conditions and technical issues ------- airplanes to be delayed for over three hours.

(A) made
(B) followed
(C) postponed
(D) caused

악천후와 기계적 문제는 비행기로 하여금 세시간 이상 지체를 야기했다.

해설 동사 어휘 문제로 목적어인 airplanes 다음에 목적격 보어로 to부정사가 와야 하는 5형식 동사를 찾는 문제이다. 그런 동사로는 ask, urge, encourage, allow, enable, cause 등이 있으며, 따라서 정답은 (D) caused가 된다. 해석에 의존해서 다른 보기를 정답으로 고르지 않도록 주의하자. 토익이 사랑하는 동사를 암기해두는 것이 중요하다.

만점 전략 1 토익이 사랑하는 동사 (2형식 vs. 5형식)

토익 시험에서 자주 출제되는 동사는 2형식과 5형식 동사로, 2형식의 경우는 '주격 보어', 5형식의 경우 '목적격 보어' 자리를 묻는 문제가 주로 출제된다. 요즘에는 반대로 그러한 종류의 보어를 가지는 2형식 또는 5형식 동사를 묻는 문제가 출제되는 경우가 더러 있으므로 그 종류를 모두 숙지하고 있어야 한다.

1. 2형식 「주어 + 동사 + 주격 보어」

주격 보어 자리에는 주로 '형용사'가 답으로 출제된다.

2형식 동사	
become, grow, turn, get	~이 되다
be, remain, prove, seem, appear, stay	~이다

2. 5형식 「주어 + 동사 + 목적어 + 목적격 보어」

❶ 주어 + 동사 + 목적어 + 형용사

목적격 보어로 형용사를 취하는 5형식 동사			
make	~을 ~하게 만들다	find	~가 ~한 것을 알게 되다
leave	~을 ~한 채로 두다	consider	~을 ~ 하다고 여기다
keep	~을 ~하도록 유지하다	deem	~을 ~로 여기다

위의 동사는 수동태 문장으로 바꿀 경우 be p.p. 다음에 '형용사'가 와야 하므로 주의한다.

be made / found / left / considered / kept / deemed + 형용사

Mr. Park **considers** your complaints **unacceptable.** 박 씨는 당신의 불만을 받아들일 수 없다고 생각한다.

→ Your complaints **are considered unacceptable** by Mr. Park.

주로 '요구 / 설득 / 허락' 등의 동사

❷ 주어 + 동사 + 목적어 + to부정사

목적격 보어로 to부정사를 취하는 5형식 동사			
ask, urge, request, require	요구하다	want	원하다
allow, permit	허락하다	enable	가능하게 하다
cause	야기시키다	advise	조언하다
expect	기대하다	encourage	장려하다

위의 동사는 수동태 문장으로 바꿀 경우 be p.p. 다음에 전치사 to가 아닌 'to부정사'가 와야 하므로 주의한다.

be encouraged / reminded / allowed / required + to부정사

The CEO **encouraged** employees **to enhance** productivity. 대표는 직원들의 생산성 향상을 독려했다.

→ Employees **were encouraged to enhance** productivity by the CEO.

만점 전략 2 provide vs. offer

provide와 offer 모두 '제공하다'의 의미이지만 provide는 3형식 동사로, offer는 4형식으로 사용된다.

1. 3형식 동사

3형식 동사인 provide는 동사 다음에 사람이 올 경우와 사물이 올 경우 각각 쓰이는 전치사가 다르니 구분을 해서 알아두자.

provide somebody **with** something something을 somebody에게 주다

provide something **to / for** somebody somebody에게 something을 주다

2. 4형식「주어 + 동사 + 간접 목적어(에게) + 직접 목적어(을 / 를)」 ~에게 ~을 / 를 주다

대표적인 4형식 동사			
give	주다	send	보내다
offer	제공하다	grant	승인하다
award	수여하다		

만점 전략 3 announce vs. notify

announce와 notify 둘 다 '공지하다'의 의미이지만, 3형식 동사인 announce는 목적어로 명사 또는 that절을 바로 취하며, notify의 경우는 사람 목적어가 나오고 of / that을 취한다.

3형식 동사 + 목적어(that절)
say / **mention** / **announce** / **suggest** / **recommend** / **explain** + (to me) + **that**

4형식 동사 + 목적어(사람) + that절
inform / **notify** / **advise** / **remind** / **assure** + me + **of** / **that**

4형식 동사의 경우, 수동태 문장으로 바꿀 경우 be p.p. 다음에 of / that절이 와야 하므로 주의한다.

be informed / notified / advised / reminded / assured + of / that

만점 전략 4 준사역동사 help

help라는 준사역동사는 3형식 문장과 5형식 문장에 모두 쓰이지만, 토익 시험에서는 주로 5형식 문장으로 출제된다.

3형식 help + to부정사 / 동사원형

5형식 help + 목적어 + to부정사 / 동사원형

This information will **help** you **(to) choose** the best product.
이 정보는 귀하가 최고의 제품을 선택하는 데 도와줄 것이다.

만점 전략 5 should가 생략된 동사원형 구문 「(should) + 동사원형」

should가 생략되어 동사원형을 쓰는 경우가 두 가지가 있다.

1. '주장, 요구, 명령, 추천, 제안'을 나타내는 동사 + that + 주어 + (should) + 동사원형

주장, 요구, 명령, 추천, 제안을 나타내는 동사			
insist	주장하다	ask	요청하다
demand	요구하다	request	요청하다
require	요구하다	recommend	추천하다
suggest	제안하다		

Travis Restaurant **requests** that customers (should) make reservations for a table at least one day in advance.
트레비스 레스토랑은 고객들에게 하루 전에 테이블 예약을 해야 한다고 요청합니다.

2. It is '필요성 / 당위성'을 나타내는 형용사 + that + 주어 + (should) + 동사원형

필요성, 당위성을 나타내는 형용사			
advisable	추천할만한	essential	필수적인
imperative	반드시 해야 하는	critical	중요한
important	중요한	necessary	필수적인

It is **imperative** that the deadline (should) be extended until next month.
마감 날짜가 다음 달로 연장되어야만 합니다.

만점 포인트 3 형용사: 헷갈리지만 의외로 쉬운 것이 형용사다.

적중! 유형 정리

The system implemented by Tanika Inc. should be ------- all domestic and international standards.

(A) complied
(B) complying
(C) in compliance
(D) compliant with

타니카 사에서 실행한 시스템은 국내와 해외 기준을 준수해야 한다.

해설 빈칸은 be동사의 보어 자리이므로 형용사가 와야 해서 정답은 (D) be complaint with '~ 를 지키는 / 준수하는'이 된다. (A)의 경우는 뒤에 목적어가 나와서 수동태로 쓸 수 없으며, 또한 자동사는 수동태가 안되므로 오답이 된다. 또한, (B), (C)의 경우는 with를 동반해야 하므로 오답이다.

만점 전략 1 형용사 자리: '명사 수식'과 '보어(주격 보어 / 목적격 보어)' 자리

1. 명사 수식

------- + 명사 (명사를 앞에서 수식)

This is an increasingly **important** factor. 점점 더 중요한 요소가 있습니다.

명사 + -------: (명사를 뒤에서 수식)

There are more seats **available**. 이용 가능한 좌석이 더 있습니다.

> **고득점 포인트**
> 명사를 뒤에서 수식하는 후치 수식의 형용사 **available, possible, imaginable**이 출제된 적이 있다.

2. 보어(주격 보어 / 목적격 보어)

주격 보어로 형용사를 취하는 2형식 동사		
become, grow, turn, get	+ 형용사	~이 되다
be, remain, prove, seem, appear, stay		~이다

목적격 보어로 형용사를 취하는 5형식 동사		
make	+ 목적어 + 형용사	~을 하게 만들다
find		~가 ~한 것을 알게 되다
leave		~을 ~한 채로 두다
consider		~을 ~하다고 여기다
keep		~을 ~하도록 유지하다
deem		~을 ~로 여기다

만점 전략 2 시험에 자주 출제되는 형용사 문제

1. 혼동하기 쉬운 형용사 어휘

비슷하게 생긴 형용사의 의미 차이를 물어보는 경우

considerate considerable	사려 깊은 상당한	confident confidential	자신감 있는, 확신한 기밀의, 비밀의
favorite favorable	좋아하는 호의적인, 유리한	beneficial beneficent	유익한 자비로운
respectful respectable respective	공손한, 예의 바른 존경할 만한 각각의, 각자의	weekly weeklong	매주의 일주일간의

2. 형용사 숙어 표현 「be + 형용사 + 전치사 / to부정사」

토익에 출제되는 대부분의 형용사 문제는 다음과 같은 숙어 표현이다.

be capable of	~할 능력을 갖다	be valid for	~이 유효하다
be complaint with	~를 준수하다	be optimistic about	~에 낙관적이다
be eligible for / to부정사	~할 자격이 있다	be appreciative of	~에 감사하다
be aware of / that	~을 인식하다 / 알다	be subject to	~하기 쉽다, 영향을 받다
be equivalent to	~에 상응하다	be accustomed to	~에 익숙하다
be eager to부정사	~하기를 열망하다	be bound to부정사	반드시 ~하다
be willing to부정사	기꺼이 ~하다	be reluctant to부정사	~을 주저하다

3. 한정사 + 형용사 + 형용사 + 명사

일반적으로 「한정사 + 부사 + 형용사 + 명사」의 어순이지만, 부사 대신에 형용사가 쓰이는 다음의 경우를 주의하자.

a (professionally / **professional**) financial advisor

빈칸에 professionally가 아니라 professional이 온 이러한 경우에는 두 형용사가 뒤의 명사를 수식하므로 나란히 올 수 있다.

4. 명사 + ly → 형용사

일반적으로 -ly는 부사이다. 「형용사 + ly」는 부사이지만, 「명사 + ly」는 형용사이다.

costly	값비싼	friendly	친절한
timely	시기적절한	orderly	질서 있는, 정돈된
daily	매일의	monthly	매달의

만점 포인트 4 부사: 딱 2가지만 알면 끝난다.

적중! 유형 정리

Lomita Cosmetics ------- offers regular customers a 20% discount on its new products.

(A) occasionally
(B) recently
(C) previously
(D) lately

로미타 코스메틱 사는 종종 신제품에 대해 단골 고객들에게 20퍼센트 할인을 제공한다.

해설 빈칸은 동사 offer를 수식하는 부사 문제로, (B), (D)의 경우는 '최근에'라는 의미로 '과거 / 현재완료'와 잘 쓰이며, (C)는 '이전에 / 예전에'라는 의미로 '과거 시제'와 쓰여야 한다. 문제에서는 현재 동사가 사용되어 현재 시제와 잘 어울리는 occasionally '이따금씩 / 종종'이라는 부사가 적합하므로 정답은 (A) occasionally가 된다.

만점 전략 1 부사 자리

부사는 동사, 형용사, 부사, 문장 전체를 수식한다. 대부분의 부사 문제는 '위치'를 물어보는 문제로 보통 수식하는 단어의 앞에 위치한다.

e.g. They **finally** decided to reform the law. 그들은 마침내 그 법을 개혁하기로 결정했다. 동사 앞 수식
I'll send the statistics **immediately**. 제가 바로 통계를 보내드리겠습니다. 완전한 문장 뒤, 동사 수식
It was an **absolutely** successful project. 그것은 완전히 성공적인 프로젝트였다. 형용사 수식
The lawyer knows civil rights **very** well. 그 변호사는 시민의 권리에 대해 매우 잘 알고 있다. 부사 수식
Actually, he quit the job. 사실, 그는 그 일을 그만뒀어요. 문장 전체 수식

만점 전략 2 시험에 출제되는 부사 문제 딱 2가지

1. 완전한 문장 뒤가 밑줄이라면, 부사 자리

– 자동사 + **부사**: The profits have risen **significantly**. 수익이 크게 증가했다.
– be p.p. + **부사**: The machine was repaired **immediately**. 그 기계는 즉시 수리되었다.

2. 동사구 사이에 들어가는 부사 자리

– 주어 + **(부사)** + 동사
The CEO **finally** decided to expand into European market.
사장은 마침내 유럽 시장으로 확장할 것을 결정했다.

– be + **(부사)** + -ing / p.p.
be + -ing / p.p. + **(부사)**
The new supermarket is (~~convenient~~, **conveniently**) located on La Trobe Street.
새로 생긴 슈퍼마켓은 편리하게 라 트로브 가에 위치해 있습니다.

– have + (**부사**) + p.p.
have + p.p. + (**부사**)
The company has (~~substance~~, ~~substantial~~, **substantially**) expanded its profit margins.
그 회사는 이익률이 상당히 확대되었다.

만점 전략 3 부사 vs. 접속부사

「-------, 주어 + 동사」에서 빈칸에 들어갈 수 있는 단어는 '부사' 역할을 하는 단어이다.

1. -------, 주어 + 동사.

❶ 부사: **Unfortunately**, Mr. Max couldn't make it on time.
유감스럽게도, 맥스 씨는 제시간에 도착할 수 없었습니다.

❷ 전치사 + 명사: **By the way**, I want to discuss this report in detail.
그나저나, 이 보고서에 대해 자세히 논의하고 싶습니다.

❸ to부정사: **To serve** you better, we need to hire more staff.
당신을 더 잘 모시려면, 직원을 더 뽑아야 합니다.

❹ 분사 구문: **Traveling abroad**, Ms. Lee reserved a seat in business class.
해외 여행을 하면서, 이 씨는 비즈니스석 좌석을 예약했다.

❺ 접속부사: **Nevertheless**, more employees will be assigned to the new project.
그럼에도 불구하고, 더 많은 직원들이 새로운 프로젝트에 배치될 것이다.

❻ 부사절: **Unless you meet the deadline**, you will be in trouble.
당신이 납기를 지키지 않으면 당신은 곤란해질 것입니다.

2. 접속부사: 접속사는 두 문장을 연결해 주지만, 접속부사의 품사는 부사이다.

❶ 주어 + 동사 + ~. -------, 주어 + 동사.
Your store is among our loyal clients. **Therefore**, we will refund the total cost of the defective items.
귀하의 가게는 저희 충성 고객들 중에 한 분 이십니다. 그래서, 하자가 있는 물건에 대한 전체 비용을 환불해 드릴 것입니다.

❷ 주어 + 동사 + ~; -------, 주어 + 동사.
Mr. Gonzales applied for the sales position; **however**, his previous jobs were all in marketing.
곤잘레스 씨는 영업직에 지원했습니다. 하지만, 그 이전일들은 모두 마케팅에 관련된 것이었습니다.

❸ 주어 + 동사 + ~ and therefore / thereafter / then 주어 + 동사.
KG Logistics ships sensitive documents locally **and therefore**, requires a strictly secure tracking system.
케이지 로직스는 민감한 자료를 지역에 배송합니다. 그래서, 엄격한 안전한 추적 시스템이 요구됩니다.

❹ 주어 + ------- + 동사.
The bank **therefore** will hire four new tellers.
은행은 그래서 네 명의 은행원을 고용할 것입니다.

인과 / 결과	therefore, thus, hence 그러므로, as a result 그 결과, in conclusion 결론적으로, consequently 결과적으로, for this reason 이러한 이유로, accordingly 따라서, namely 즉 다시 말해
부가 / 추가	also 또한, in addition, additionally, moreover, furthermore, besides 게다가 / 더욱이
역접 / 대조 / 양보	however 그러나, on the contrary 그와는 반대로, on the other hand 반면에, if not, otherwise 그렇지 않으면, even so 그렇다 하더라도, unfortunately 안타깝게도, nevertheless, nonetheless 그럼에도 불구하고, in the mean time 그동안에, 한편
대신 / 대안	instead 대신에, alternatively 대안으로
강조	in particular, particularly 특히, in fact, in deed 사실상
순서	previously, formerly 이전에, afterwards 그 이후에, since then 그때 이후로
예시	for example, for instance 예를 들어
기타	if so 그렇다면, if possible 가능하면, likewise 마찬가지로

만점 전략 4 고득점자의 발목을 잡는 부사 어휘

1. 수사를 수식하는 부사

nearly, approximately	거의, 대략	around, about	약
more than, over	~이상	at least, up to	적어도, 최대 ~까지

2. still vs. yet

have (be) yet to ~하지 못하고 있다

Mr. Lim **has yet to** place an advertisement in the newspaper for the senior analyst position.
임 씨는 시니어 분석가 자리를 신문의 광고에 아직 게재하지 않았습니다.

still ~ not

You **still** do **not** understand. 당신은 아직도 이해하지 못하는 군요.

The television was taken to the repair center a week ago, but it (**still**, ~~yet~~) has not been repaired. 텔레비전이 일주일 전 수리센터로 옮겨졌는데, 아직도 수리가 안 됐어요.

→ not을 중심으로 not 앞에는 still, 뒤에는 yet을 사용하므로 여기서 정답은 still이 된다.

3. otherwise: 다르게, 그 외에는, 그렇지 않으면

❶ unless **otherwise** indicated / mentioned / stated / specified 별다른 언급 / 명시되지 않으면
= unless indicated / mentioned / stated / specified **otherwise**

❷ You should record working hours after shifts; **otherwise**, you will not be paid appropriately.
교대 후 작업 시간을 기록해야 해요. 그렇지 않으면 알맞게 보수가 지급되지 않을 거예요.

4. 그 외 부사 어휘 문제

주로 수식하는 것들과의 궁합(collocation) 문제가 출제된다.

arrive punctually	정각에 도착하다	explicitly state	명료하게 명시하다
readily accessible	쉽게 접근할 수 있는	meticulously plan	꼼꼼하게 계획하다
adversely affect	악영향을 주다	conveniently located	편리하게 위치한
heavily discounted	대폭 할인된	highly recommended	강력하게 권하다
mutually beneficial	상호 간의 이해된	inspect thoroughly	철저하게 검사하다
be awarded accordingly	알맞게 받다	deeply sorry / regret	몹시 미안한 / 유감인
well attended	출석률이 좋은	travel extensively	두루 여행하다
proceed cautiously	조심스럽게 진행되다	work collaboratively	협조적으로 일하다
speak eloquently	유창하게 말하다	work closely	면밀하게 일하다

5. 증가 / 감소를 수식하는 부사

considerably, substantially, significantly, greatly	상당히
unexpectedly, surprisingly	뜻밖에, 의외로
sharply, dramatically	급격하게
remarkably, markedly	두드러지게
quickly, rapidly	빠르게
slowly	느리게
steadily	꾸준히
gradually	점차적으로

The profit margin at Concord Broadcasting has increased **significantly** over the 3 years.
콩코드 방송사의 수익이 지난 3년동안 급격하게 증가했다.

MEMO

고난도 실전 문제

1. The time needed to obtain all relevant skills ------- on numerous elements.
(A) depend
(B) depends
(C) depending
(D) to depend

2. ------- to William Street is expected to be limited to one lane when the road construction project starts next June.
(A) Access
(B) Accessing
(C) Accesses
(D) Accessible

3. The international sales department has ------- valuable to our operations overseas since its foundation five years ago.
(A) proved
(B) searched
(C) told
(D) achieved

4. For safety reasons, a city official must inspect your newly built restaurant ------- before allowing you to open for business.
(A) powerfully
(B) extremely
(C) solidly
(D) thoroughly

5. Due to urgent road repairs, drivers must use ------- when driving on Highway 25.
(A) cautious
(B) cautiously
(C) cautioned
(D) caution

6. The conversation with Mr. Davidson was ------- *Biznet Magazine*'s best interview of the year.
(A) easy
(B) easiest
(C) easily
(D) easing

7. Even though his presentation is long and detailed, Travis Kim thinks viewers will ------- find it interesting.
(A) still
(B) quite
(C) too
(D) ever

8. The conference organizers will ------- all attendees with complimentary lunch and refreshments.
(A) offer
(B) donate
(C) provide
(D) suggest

9. According to the annual employee questionnaire, morale at the JTB Toy factory has become ------- better over the last three years.
(A) progresses
(B) progressive
(C) progressing
(D) progressively

10. Ms. Adeel, HR director at Roxen Inc., considers punctuality an important ------- for all newly hired employees to have.
(A) device
(B) type
(C) action
(D) trait

11. Although only department managers were required to attend, Ms. Salito ------- all staff members to come to last week's meeting.
(A) to have urged
(B) had urged
(C) will have urged
(D) was urged

12. Before deciding to invest in the property market, Ms. Min ------- that Mr. Xian consider the potential risks more carefully.
(A) requested
(B) announced
(C) reported
(D) notified

13. Our experienced accountants offer solutions to help companies like yours ------- issues that may affect a company's success.
(A) address
(B) addressed
(C) can address
(D) are addressing

14. The marketing manager was ------- of the team members' efforts to make the new advertising campaign a success.
(A) willing
(B) appreciative
(C) fulfilled
(D) decisive

15. The advertisement team's ideas were presented so ------- that the clients have already agreed to work with us.
(A) skill
(B) skilled
(C) skillful
(D) skillfully

16. The recent survey indicates that most people ------- Sweet Candy's cookies very appetizing.
(A) find
(B) feel
(C) take
(D) like

17. In order to advertise your brands, please contact Macmore Inc., which specializes in ------- promotional merchandise.
(A) personally
(B) personalized
(C) personality
(D) personalizes

18. It is my great pleasure to ------- you that the new vice president will be appointed by the board of directors.
(A) announce
(B) mention
(C) inform
(D) say

19. Applications from potential candidates remain active for ten years and ------- are kept in our filing system.
(A) thereafter
(B) instead
(C) unless
(D) rather

20. GDX Inc. will try to attract a lot of potential buyers by ------- advertising its Web site.
(A) effective
(B) effectively
(C) more effective
(D) most effective

PART 5

DAY 02

1초 문제: 매달 빠짐없이 나오는 문제를 찍어주마!

동영상 강의 바로 보기

토익에서 자주 출제되는 4가지 품사(명사, 동사, 형용사, 부사)의 자리 문제 이외에, 매달마다 빠짐없이 출제되는 문제 유형이 있다. 이러한 유형의 문제는 해석도 필요 없이 1초 안에 풀 수 있는 문제들이다. 그러므로 어떤 유형이 출제되는지를 미리 파악한다면 PART 7까지 무난하게 시간 관리를 잘하면서 문제를 풀 수 있게 되어 자연스럽게 RC 고득점으로 이어질 수 있다.

만점 포인트

이것만 알면 만점!

1 대명사: '소유격'이 주로 단골 정답이다.
2 동사 어휘: '자동사'와 '타동사'를 제일 먼저 떠올려라!
3 동사: 동사는 3가지만 집중하자! 수, 시제, 태 일치!
4 전치사 vs. 접속사 vs. 접속부사: 구분만 할 줄 알면 거저 주는 문제

만점 포인트 1 대명사: '소유격'이 주로 단골 정답이다.

적중! 유형 정리

As a demand for ------- chocolate-flavored ice cream declines, local merchants earn less income than ever.

(A) they
(B) their
(C) themselves
(D) theirs

초콜릿 맛 아이스크림 제품에 대한 수요가 감소함에 따라, 지역 상인들은 전보다 수입이 적어진다.

해설 빈칸은 대명사 문제로 중간에 명사를 수식하는 chocolate-flavored가 들어간다고 하더라도 결국에는 ice cream이라는 명사 앞에 들어가야 하므로 소유격이 적합하다. 따라서, 정답은 (B) their가 된다.

만점 전략 1 인칭대명사

1. 주격 대명사: 주어 자리

------- + 동사

After you review all the documents, **you** can contact us for more information.
귀하께서 모든 서류를 검토한 이후에, 더 많은 정보를 위해서 우리에게 연락하실 수 있습니다.

2. 소유격 대명사: 명사 앞자리

------- + (부사) + (형용사) + 명사

Mr. Lee's fans are looking forward to reading **his** newly released novel.
이 씨의 팬들은 그의 새로 나온 소설을 읽는 것에 기대하고 있습니다.

전치사 + ------- + 명사

I will send you an itinerary to **your** e-mail. 귀하의 이메일로 여행 일정표를 보내드리겠습니다.

3. 목적격 대명사: 타동사 / 전치사의 목적어 자리

타동사 + -------

전치사 + -------

If your order is defective, please send **us** the product immediately. 타동사의 목적어 자리
만약 주문에 하자가 있다면, 제품을 빨리 보내주세요.

I will report back to **him**. 전치사의 목적어 자리
그에게 보고를 할 것이다.

4. 소유대명사(소유격 + 명사): 주어, 목적어, 보어 자리

Bobby wanted to meet with a friend of **mine**. (mine = my friend) 바비는 내 친구 중에 한 명을 만나고 싶어 했다.

주어 Her house and **mine** are located on Oak Street.
(mine: my house)
그녀의 집과 저의 집은 오크 가에 위치합니다.

목적어 Duran completed the report, but Jane has not finished **hers**.
her report

듀란은 보고서를 완성했지만, 제인은 아직 그녀의 것을 완성하지 못했습니다.

보어 This apartment is **his**.
his apartment

이 아파트는 그의 것입니다.

만점 전략 2 재귀대명사

1. 재귀 용법

타동사 / 전치사의 목적어로 주어와 목적어의 내용이 같을 때 사용하며, 생략할 수 없다.

Ms. Linda has shown **herself** to be friendly. (Ms. Linda = herself)

린다 씨는 자기 자신을 친절한 사람으로 보여줬다.

2. 강조 용법

주어나 목적어를 강조할 때 쓰이며, 주로 주어 뒤 혹은 완전한 문장 끝에 위치하며, 생략할 수 있다.

I **(myself)** am a stranger here **(myself)**. 저는 여기에 초행입니다.

3. 관용 표현

주로 by / for라는 전치사와 사용되어 다음과 같은 뜻을 나타낸다.

by oneself (= on one's own) 혼자서, 혼자의 힘으로

for oneself 스스로, 혼자 힘으로

Ms. Peterson has to train the new staff **by herself**. 피터슨 씨는 신입 직원을 혼자서 교육해야만 한다.

만점 포인트 2 동사 어휘: '자동사'와 '타동사'를 제일 먼저 떠올려라!

적중! 유형 정리

Mr. Tao, the head of the HR Department, ------- responsibility for providing training to all new employees.

(A) adheres
(B) undertakes
(C) consults
(D) assumes

인사부장인 타오 씨는 모든 신입 직원들에게 교육을 할 책임을 갖고 있다.

해설 빈칸은 동사 어휘 자리로, 목적어로 responsibility를 갖는 타동사는 보기에서 (D)가 있다. (B)도 '떠맡다 / 책임지다'의 의미가 있지만 목적어로 '일 / 업무'의 의미를 갖는 단어가 와야 한다. title / responsibility와 잘 어울리는 타동사는 assume이다.

만점 전략 자동사 vs. 타동사

동사에는 두 가지 종류가 있으며 목적어의 유무에 따라 자동사와 타동사로 구분할 수 있다. 자동사는 목적어를 취할 수 없지만, 전치사를 동반해서 목적어를 취할 수도 있다. 타동사는 주로 '~을 / 를 하다'로 해석되어 '목적어'를 가진다. 자동사는 자주 쓰이는 전치사 혹은 부사와 함께, 타동사는 목적어와 함께 암기해 두면 좋다.

1. 「자동사 + 부사」

arrive late / punctually	늦게 / 정각에 도착하다
function / work properly	제대로 작동하다
grow rapidly / steadily	빠르게 / 꾸준하게 성장하다
speak eloquently	유창하게 말하다
travel extensively	널리 여행하다
work closely	긴밀하게 일하다
increase / decrease dramatically	급격하게 증가 / 감소하다
rise / decline considerably / significantly	상당히 증가 / 감소하다
behave responsibly	책임감 있게 처신하다
proceed steadily	꾸준히 나아가다
start / begin promptly	즉시 시작하다

2. 「자동사 + 전치사」

object to(=oppose)	반대하다	adhere to, comply with, conform to	지키다, 준수하다
refer to(=consult)	참조하다	belong to	~에 속하다
lead to(=cause)	결과를 초래하다	reply / respond to	~에 응답하다
proceed to	나아가다	succeed to	~을 이어받다
proceed with	계속하다	succeed in	성공하다
agree to / with / on / upon	동의하다	enroll in, register for	~에 등록하다
appeal to	호소하다	specialize in	전문으로 하다
inquire about	문의하다	remark / comment on	언급하다, 말하다
account for	설명하다, 처리하다	deal with(=address, handle)	처리하다, 다루다
refrain from	삼가다, 자제하다	contribute to	~에 기여하다
collaborate on / with	~에 / ~와 협력하다	benefit from	~로부터 이익을 얻다
expand into	~로 확장하다	rely / depend / count on	~에 의지 / 의존하다

3. 「타동사 + 목적어」

meet, satisfy, fulfill 충족시키다	**meet** the needs / requirements / deadline / expectations / goals 필요 / 자격 요건 / 마감 날짜 / 기대 / 목표를 충족시키다
implement 실행 / 시행하다	**implement** the plan / policy / program / system / procedure 계획 / 정책 / 프로그램 / 시스템 / 절차를 실행 / 시행하다
reach 도달하다	**reach** an agreement / a conclusion / a compromise 합의 / 결론 / 협상에 도달하다
address 다루다	**address** the issues / problems / concerns / requests / complaints 문제 / 우려 / 요구 / 불평 불만을 다루다
consult 참조하다	**consult** the e-mail / manual 이메일 / 매뉴얼을 참조하다
assume 떠맡다, 책임지다	**assume** the title / responsibility 직책 / 책임을 떠맡다
suspend 중단 / 중지하다	**suspend** the production / service 생산 / 서비스를 중단하다
enhance, improve 향상시키다, 개선하다	**enhance** / **improve** the productivity / efficiency 생산성 / 효율성을 향상시키다 / 개선하다

만점 포인트 3 동사: 동사는 3가지만 집중하자! 수, 시제, 태 일치!

적중! 유형 정리

Once next year's financial plans -------, department supervisors will make their final decision about adding more employees.

(A) have been approved
(B) approves
(C) will approve
(D) approved

일단 내년 예산이 승인되면, 부서장들은 직원들을 더 충원할지에 대한 마지막 결정을 할 것이다.

해설 빈칸은 동사 자리로 동사 문제가 나오면 '수, 시제, 태'를 고려해야 한다. 주어는 financial plans로 복수이고, 시제는 once 조건의 부사절에서 주절의 시제가 미래(will make)일 때 종속절은 현재를 쓴다. 또한, 뒤에 목적어가 없기 때문에 수동태가 와야 하므로 종합적으로 모두 부합하는 (A)가 정답이 된다. 가장 오답률이 높은 (B)의 경우는 수일치도 안 되고, 목적어도 없으므로 정답이 될 수 없다.

만점 전략 1 동사의 수일치: 주어와 동사 사이에 교란시키는 수식어를 조심하라!

주어가 단수 / 복수인지에 따라 동사도 수를 일치시켜준다. 하지만 고난도 문제의 경우 주어 뒤에 동사가 바로 나오기 보다는 주어와 동사 사이에 다양한 수식어를 등장시켜 교란시키므로 함정에 빠지지 않기 위해서는 평소에 다양한 수식어의 종류를 알아야 한다.

주어(S)	형용사	동사(V)
	전치사 + 명사	
	분사: 현재분사, 과거분사	
	형용사절: 관계대명사, 관계부사	
	to부정사 형용사적 용법	
	목적격 관계대명사(that) + 주어 + 동사	
	동격	

1. 주어 + (형용사) + 동사

Customers **(unfamiliar with the new system)** should contact the customer service center.
새로운 시스템에 익숙하지 않은 고객들은 고객 서비스 센터에 연락을 해야 한다.

2. 주어 + (전치사 + 명사) + 동사

The new CEO **(from the headquarters)** is planning to visit the factory in Seoul.
본사에서 온 새로 부임한 사장은 서울에 있는 공장을 방문할 예정이다.

3. 주어 + (현재분사 / 과거분사) + 동사

Any employee **(taking extra vacations)** has to receive approval from the supervisor.
추가 휴가를 내는 직원은 상사로부터 승인을 얻어야만 한다.

Those **(interested in participating in the upcoming fundraising event)** should tell Mr. Kim.
다가오는 기금 행사에 참석을 원하는 사람들은 김 씨에게 말해야 한다.

4. 주어 + (관계대명사 / 관계부사) + 동사

The man **(who is standing next to the podium)** is my boss.
연단 옆에 서 있는 남자가 내 상사이다.

The city **(where the Gallop Convention Center will be relocated)** is expected to be more convenient. 갤럽 컨벤션 센터가 이전할 도시는 더욱 편리해질 전망이다.

5. 주어 + (to부정사) + 동사

The machines **(to be sent to Las Vegas)** will be ready by next Monday.
라스베이거스에 보내질 기계가 다음 주 월요일까지 준비될 것이다.

6. 주어 + (that + S + V) + 동사

생략 가능

The budget report **(that you requested)** has been approved by Mr. Russell.
귀하가 요청하신 예산 보고서는 러셀 씨에게 승인되었습니다.

7. 주어 + , (동격), + 동사

Richard Clements, **(the well-known singer)**, will visit Paris next month.
유명한 가수인 리처드 클레멘츠는 다음 달 파리를 방문할 것이다.

만점 전략 2 동사의 시제 일치: 시간 어구(시간 부사, 시간 전치사, 시간 접속사)를 주목해라!

동사의 시제 일치 문제는 해석으로 문제를 풀기보다는 특정 시제와 잘 쓰이는 시간 어구 즉 시간 부사, 시간 전치사, 시간 접속사를 빠르게 파악해서 문제를 풀도록 하자.

1. 시간 / 조건의 부사절

시제에서 출제 빈도수가 높은 문제로, 시간 / 조건의 부사절에서 주절의 시제가 '미래'라고 할지라도, 종속절은 '현재 시제'가 나온다.

시간 접속사: when, by the time, as soon as, until
조건 접속사 : if, unless, once, as long as

When she **comes**, I **will tell** her about it. 그녀가 올 때, 나는 그녀에게 그것에 대해 말할 것이다.
···› when이라는 시간의 접속사가 와서, 주절의 시제가 will tell(미래)이라고 할지라도, 종속절은 comes(현재 시제)를 사용한다.

I **will conclude** the meeting **unless** you **have** further questions. 만약 더 질문이 없다면 미팅을 종료할 것입니다.
···› unless라는 조건의 접속사가 와서, 주절의 시제가 will conclude(미래)라고 할지라도, 종속절은 have(현재 시제)를 사용한다.

고득점 포인트
by the time은 토익에 두 가지 유형으로 출제가 된다.
By the time + S + 현재, S + will have p.p.
By the time + S + 과거, S + had p.p.

2. 현재완료

since라고 해서 다 같은 since가 아니다. since는 '때문에', '이래로'의 의미로 사용이 된다. '때문에'의 의미일 때는 접속사로 쓰이며, '이래로'일 때는 전치사와 접속사 둘 다 사용이 된다. 특히, '이래로'일 때는 현재완료 시제와 함께 사용한다.

❶ since ~이래로(전치사 / 접속사)

S + have p.p. + since + S + 과거 동사 / 과거 시점 명사

Ten years **have passed since I saw** you. 내가 너를 본 이후로 10년이 지났다.

The employees at Carlson have gone through many formidable challenges **since last May.** 칼슨 사의 직원들은 지난 5월부터 많은 힘든 도전을 해왔다.

Since + S + 과거 동사 / 과거 시점 명사, S + have p.p.

Since I saw you, ten years **have passed.** 내가 너를 본 이후로 10년이 지났다.

Since last summer, the CZ Advertising Agency has produced more than 20 TV commercials. CZ 광고 대행사는 지난 여름부터 20개 이상의 TV 광고를 제작했다.

❷ over / in / for / during the past / last 기간 명사

Over the past five years, many things **have changed.** 지난 5년간에 걸쳐, 많은 것들이 변했다.

❸ recently (최근에) 부사는 '과거' 혹은 '현재완료'와 잘 쓰인다.

K Electronics **has** recently **lowered** the prices of its newly released products.
케이 일렉트로닉은 최근에 새롭게 출시된 제품의 가격을 낮췄다.

3. 현재 진행

현재 진행은 현재 진행의 의미도 있지만 '가까운 미래'를 나타낼 수도 있다.

Mr. Anderson **is coming** for the groundbreaking ceremony **next week.**
앤더슨 씨는 다음 주에 기공식을 위해 올 것이다.

4. 미래 완료(will have p.p.)

미래 완료 시제는 미래 완료 시점을 나타내는 시간 어구와 잘 쓰인다.

by next + 시간 표현: 다음 ~까지

by the end of + 시간 표현: ~말까지

by the time: ~할 때 / 즈음

Mr. Kwon **will have worked** for ten years at this company **by next March.**
내년 3월이면 권 씨는 이 회사에서 일한 지 10년이 된다.

만점 전략 3 동사 태: 뭘 봐! 뒤를 봐! (뒤에 목적어의 유무를 빨리 확인하라!)

1. 수동태는 목적어의 유무를 빨리 파악하는 것이 중요하다. 수동태 뒤에는 명사가 오지 않는다.

be p.p. + 명사 ⓧ

be p.p. + 전치사, X, 부사 ⓞ

A revised expense report should **be submitted** to Mr. Potter.
수정된 경비 보고서는 포터 씨에게 제출되어야 한다.
→ be p.p. 수동태 뒤에 전치사 to

2. be p.p. + 명사가 가능한 경우 (4형식, 5형식 동사)

일반적으로 수동태 be p.p. 뒤에는 명사가 오지 않지만, 4형식과 5형식 동사는 가능하다.

4형식 동사					
give	주다	send	보내다	offer	제공하다
grant	수여하다	award	수여하다	assign	맡기다

5형식 동사			
consider	~을 ~라고 여기다	name	~을 ~로 명명하다
elect	~를 ~로 뽑다	appoint	~을 ~로 임명하다

DMK Inc. **was awarded the contract** due to competitive prices. (4형식 동사 award의 수동태)
DMK 사는 경쟁적 가격 때문에 계약을 따냈다.

3. 감정 동사 → "나 피곤해!(I am tired!)"만 기억하자!

사람의 감정 동사는 주어가 '사람'일 때 '수동태', '사물'일 때는 '능동태'를 쓴다.

satisfy	만족시키다	interest	흥미를 일으키다	excite	신나게 만들다
disappoint	실망시키다	fascinate	매혹시키다	concern	걱정스럽게 만들다
confuse	혼동시키다	please, delight, gratify		기쁘게 하다	

Ms. Klein **is pleased** to announce that her company is opening another branch in Seoul.
클레인 씨는 그녀의 회사가 서울에 또 다른 지점을 열게 될 것을 알리게 되어 기쁩니다.

만점 포인트 4 전치사 vs. 접속사 vs. 접속부사: 구분만 할 줄 알면 거저 주는 문제

적중! 유형 정리

------- the extra days Ms. Moore dedicated to her project, she was not able to meet the deadline.

(A) During
(B) In spite of
(C) Even though
(D) However

무어 씨가 프로젝트에 헌신했던 추가적인 날에도 불구하고, 마감 날짜를 맞출 수가 없었다.

해설 Ms. Moore에서 project까지가 앞에 나오는 the extra days를 수식하고, 결국은 the extra days라는 명사 앞에 들어가는 전치사 문제로, 보기에서 (C) Even though는 접속사라서 탈락, (D) However는 접속부사이므로 답이 될 수 없다. 전치사 (A), (B) 중에서 해석상 '~에도 불구하고'의 의미가 적합하므로 정답은 (B)가 된다.

만점 전략 1 전치사 vs. 접속사

매달 전치사와 접속사 구분 문제가 출제된다. 일반적으로 전치사, 접속사, 접속부사가 보기에 섞여서 출제되므로, 해석에 의존해서 풀기보다는 평소에 전치사, 접속사, 접속부사의 문법적 쓰임과 종류를 알면 해석하지 않고도 쉽게 문제를 해결할 수 있다.

1. 전치사 vs. 접속사

전치사와 접속사는 뒤에 무엇이 나오는지에 따라 쉽게 구분할 수 있다.

전치사 + 명사 or 동명사
접속사 + 주어 + 동사

2. 전치사 vs. 부사절 접속사

의미는 비슷하지만, 문법적 쓰임이 다르므로 종류를 확실히 구분할 수 있도록 하자.

종류	전치사	부사절 접속사	의미
양보	despite, in spite of, notwithstanding	although, even though	비록 ~이지만
이유	because of, due to	because, as, since	~때문에
시간	during + 특정 기간, for + 기간 명사	while	~하는 동안
	following, after	after → 전치사, 접속사 둘다 가능	~후에
	prior to, before	before	전에
	on / upon -ing	as soon as	~하자마자
	by (완료), until (계속 / 지속)	by the time	~할 때까지
조건	without	unless	만약 ~가 아니라면
	in case of, in the event of	in case (that)	~한 경우에, 대비하여
목적	so as to, in order to + 동사원형	so that, in order that	~하기 위해서
기타	given	given that	~을 고려하면
	like	as if, as though	마치 ~처럼

만점 전략 2 접속부사

접속부사는 두 문장을 연결해 주는 의미에서 접속사와 비슷하지만, 실제 품사는 접속사가 아니라 '부사'이다. 특히 접속부사가 쓰이는 시험에 잘 나오는 문장의 패턴이 있으므로 잘 익혀두도록 하자.

접속부사

❶ 주어 + 동사 ~. 접속부사, 주어 + 동사.
❷ 주어 + 동사 ~; 접속부사, 주어 + 동사.
❸ 주어 + 동사 ~ and therefore / thereafter / then 주어 + 동사.
❹ 주어 + 접속부사 + 동사.

인과 / 결과	therefore, thus, hence 그러므로, as a result 그 결과, in conclusion 결론적으로, consequently 결과적으로, for this reason 이러한 이유로, accordingly 따라서, namely 즉 다시 말해
부가 / 추가	also 또한, in addition, additionally, moreover, furthermore, besides 게다가 / 더욱이
역접 / 대조 / 양보	however 그러나, on the contrary 그와는 반대로, on the other hand 반면에, if not, otherwise 그렇지 않으면, even so 그렇다 하더라도, unfortunately 안타깝게도, nevertheless, nonetheless 그럼에도 불구하고, in the mean time 그동안에, 한편
대신 / 대안	instead 대신에, alternatively 대안으로
강조	in particular, particularly 특히, in fact, in deed 사실상
순서	previously, formerly 이전에, afterwards 그 이후에, since then 그때 이후로
예시	for example, for instance 예를 들어
기타	if so 그렇다면, if possible 가능하면, likewise 마찬가지로

만점 전략 3 헷갈리기 쉬운 전치사

by vs. until (~까지): 같이 쓰이는 동사로 구분		
by	동작의 완료 (마감 / 기한)	finish, submit, return, deliver, receive, postmark
until	동작 상태 (지속 / 계속)	postpone, last, open, stay

for vs. during (~하는 동안): 뒤에 기간 / 특정 기간으로 구분		
for	for + 기간 명사	for two days
during	during + 특정 기간	during winter vacation

MEMO

고난도 실전 문제

1. The excellent service and food are the ------- gourmets flock to this restaurant.
(A) reasonable
(B) reasoning
(C) reasoned
(D) reason

2. For the past 10 years, Olive Tech. ------- approximately 3,000 books to the public libraries.
(A) will be donated
(B) is donated
(C) was donated
(D) has donated

3. ------- recent system errors, the Finance Department completed the next year's budget ahead of schedule.
(A) Although
(B) Whereas
(C) Notwithstanding
(D) Moreover

4. After taking a vacation for two weeks, Ms. Apana ------- to her office on September 9.
(A) returning
(B) returned
(C) was returned
(D) to return

5. ------- Ms. Choi returns from her business trip in Tokyo, the weekly department meeting will resume.
(A) That
(B) Once
(C) As well
(D) Then

6. Mr. Carlton from Piwan Inc. will be using conference room C while he ------- the company's market research data.
(A) specializes
(B) proceeds
(C) responds
(D) compiles

7. The position of office manager at PCS Inc. is highly recommended by a former colleague of -------, Ms. Jenkins.
(A) my
(B) me
(C) mine
(D) myself

8. ------- KCX Supermarket was founded in 1993, its sales have increased dramatically.
(A) Instead
(B) While
(C) However
(D) Since

9. Ms. Suharman from the accounting department ------- the updated policy for travel expenses at tomorrow's meeting.
(A) will be addressed
(B) had addressed
(C) is addressing
(D) address

10. All application forms and references for the marketing manager position must be postmarked ------- May 5 to be eligible.
(A) until
(B) within
(C) before
(D) recently

11. Bellevue Cookware's promotional offer ------- from March 31 until June 30.

(A) extends
(B) extending
(C) extensive
(D) extensively

12. Given the comfortable seats, overnight travel on the West Connect bus is never -------.

(A) tired
(B) tires
(C) tiring
(D) tiredly

13. ------- a newly designed system, Brooks Inc.'s profits will increase by 15 percent next year.

(A) Even though
(B) Since
(C) Due to
(D) Besides

14. Please ------- from playing loud music after midnight so as not to disturb neighbors in residential areas.

(A) refrain
(B) emerge
(C) prohibit
(D) differ

15. ------- Mr. Fahad is ready to make another order, Brig Office Supplies will have provided a new pricing chart.

(A) By the time
(B) In order for
(C) So that
(D) Moreover

16. The enclosed brochure contains detailed information Mr. Corson -------.

(A) correct
(B) has been corrected
(C) to correct
(D) will correct

17. When registering for the upcoming Modiva Expo in Hong Kong, be sure to help ------- to a name tag and brochure.

(A) you
(B) your
(C) yours
(D) yourself

18. Employees interested in attending the company excursion are asked to register by next Monday ------- we can prepare sufficient refreshments for all attendees.

(A) unless
(B) in order to
(C) in case
(D) so that

19. A recent survey indicates that some employees check their work-related e-mails regularly ------- on vacation.

(A) so that
(B) during
(C) whether
(D) while

20. Mr. Alfredo recently ------- Employee of the Year due to his outstanding achievements.

(A) named
(B) was named
(C) is named
(D) has named

PART 5

DAY 03

이걸 알아야 진정한 토익 고수

동영상 강의 바로 보기

토익 시험에 출제되는 문법 중에서 학생들이 가장 어려워하는 것 중에 하나가 '분사'와 '형용사절(관계대명사 / 관계부사)'이다. 그 이유는 한글에서 명사를 수식하는 형용사 종류는 주로 명사 앞에 위치하는 반면, 영어에서는 명사를 뒤에서 수식하는 경우가 대부분이기 때문이다. 특히, 그중에서 '분사'와 '형용사절(관계대명사 / 관계부사)'이 대표적이다. 영어 어순에 익숙해짐에 따라 고득점이 결정되고, 특히 '분사'와 '형용사절'을 잘 이해한다면 PART 7에서 직독직해도 자연스럽게 이루어져 PART 5&6 뿐만 아니라 독해 실력도 향상할 수 있다.

만점 포인트

이것만 알면 만점!

1 분사: 어렵게 생각했지만 의외로 쉬운 것이 분사다.
2 분사 구문: 시험에 빈출되는 분사 구문은 따로 있다.
3 관계대명사: 앞과 뒤만 잘 챙기자.
4 관계부사: 뒤가 완전한지 불완전한지만 따져보자.

만점 포인트 1 분사: 어렵게 생각했지만 의외로 쉬운 것이 분사다.

적중! 유형 정리

All employees ------- in the office after 7 P.M. are advised to inform the security officer at the front desk.

(A) remain
(B) remains
(C) remaining
(D) remained

저녁 7시 이후에 사무실에 남아 있는 모든 직원들은 프런트 데스크에 있는 경비원에게 알려야 한다.

해설 문장의 주어는 All employees, 동사는 are advised to로 이미 동사가 나와 있으므로 (A), (B)는 오답이 되며, 빈칸은 앞의 주어인 All employees를 수식하는 분사 자리이고, '남아있는'의 의미이면서 자동사의 현재분사인 (C)가 정답이 된다.

만점 전략 1 분사 역할

분사는 동사의 역할을 하는 형용사이므로 형용사 역할과 같은 '명사 수식'과 '보어 자리'에 쓰인다. 분사에는 '현재분사'와 '과거분사' 두 가지가 있는데 이들은 각각 '능동 혹은 수동'의 개념에 따라 구분한다.

1. 분사의 종류

현재분사(동사 + -ing): ~하고 있는(능동, 진행)
과거분사(동사 + -ed / p.p.): ~된(수동, 완료)

2. 분사의 역할: 명사 수식, 보어(주격 / 목적격 보어)

❶ 명사 수식

수식 받는 명사와 분사가 능동 관계이면 현재분사, 수동 관계이면 과거분사를 사용한다.

------- + 명사
A (~~breaking~~, **broken**) window 깨진 창문

명사 + -------
The shoes (~~ordering~~, **ordered**) by Mr. Kim are expensive. 김 씨에 의해 주문된 신발은 비싸다.

❷ 보어

2형식(주격 보어): 주어 + 동사(be / become / remain) + **분사**
Dr. Lee's keynote speech was **inspiring**. 이 박사의 기조연설은 감동적이었다.

5형식(목적격 보어): 주어 + 동사(make / find / leave / consider / keep / deem) + 목적어 + **분사**
To keep our customers **satisfied**, Mr. Stein always tries to do his best.
고객들을 만족시키기 위해서, 스테인 씨는 항상 최선을 다하려고 노력한다.

만점 전략 2 현재분사 vs. 과거분사

분사에는 '현재분사'와 '과거분사'가 있다. 현재분사와 과거분사의 차이는 수식하는 명사와의 관계가 '능동' 혹은 '수동'의 의미 차이로 구분한다. 시험에서는 명사를 수식하는 현재분사와 과거분사를 구분하는 문제가 출제되므로, 출제율이 높은 '현재분사 + 명사', '과거분사 + 명사' 궁합을 암기해두면 답을 빨리 고를 수 있다.

자동사는 수동태가 안되므로 p.p. 형태의 과거분사가 아니라 -ing의 현재분사 형태로만 쓰이는 것들이 있다.

1.

현재분사 + 명사			
existing building	기존 건물	rising cost	증가하는 비용
remaining period	남은 기간	leading company	일류 회사
lasting impression	지속적인 인상	promising employee	전도유망한 직원
opening ceremony	개회식	demanding job	힘든 일
missing luggage	분실한 짐	challenging work	어려운 업무
emerging market	떠오르는 시장(신흥 시장)	mounting pressure	증가하는 압력

2.

과거분사 + 명사			
enclosed document	동봉된 서류	designated parking lot	지정된 주차장
written consent	서면 동의	qualified applicant	자격요건을 갖춘 지원자
attached file	첨부된 파일	accomplished artist	기량이 뛰어난 화가
damaged item	손상된 물건	detailed information	상세한 정보
revised report	수정된 보고서	dedicated crew	헌신적인 직원
proposed project	제안된 프로젝트	reduced price	할인된 가격

3. 현재분사 vs. 동명사

「동사 + -ing」는 '현재분사' 또는 '동명사'로 볼 수 있는데, 형태가 같기 때문에 간혹 현재분사와 동명사의 사용을 헷갈리는 경우가 종종 있으므로 이번 기회를 통해서 확실히 구분할 수 있도록 하자.

(**Updating** / Updated) documents is ~

문장의 동사가 is 단수이므로 주어는 documents가 아닌 괄호 안에 있는 것이 된다. 주어가 될 수 있는 것은 동명사인 Updating이며, 해석은 '서류를 업데이트하는 것은 ~이다'가 된다.

(Updating / **Updated**) documents are ~

문장의 동사가 are 복수이므로 주어는 documents가 된다. 즉, 괄호 안에 있는 것이 명사인 documents를 수식해야 하며 의미상 '업데이트된 서류들'이 되어야 하므로 정답은 과거분사 Updated가 된다.

To (**revising** / **revised**) plans ~

revising은 동명사와 현재분사로 볼 수 있는데, 이 경우 뒤에 plans를 목적어로 받을 수 있는 동명사 revising은 올 수 있다. 하지만 분사의 경우에는 현재분사 revising, 과거분사 revised 중에서 의미상 '수정된'이란 의미가 적합하므로 revised인 과거분사만 가능하다. 즉, 동명사 revising, 과거분사 revised 둘 다 올 수 있게 된다. 만약, 이처럼 문법적으로 둘 다 가능한 경우에는 해석으로 구분하면 된다. To revising plans는 '계획을 수정하는 것에 대한', To revised plans는 '수정된 계획들에 대한'으로 해석된다.

To a (~~revising~~ / **revised**) plan
a라는 한정사와 plan이라는 명사 사이에는 형용사 또는 분사가 올 수 있으며, 해석상 '수정된'이라는 수동의 의미가 적합하므로 정답은 과거분사 revised가 된다.

To (**revising** / ~~revised~~) the plans
the plans를 받는 동명사 revising이 올 수 있고, the라는 '한정사' 앞에는 어순상 형용사나 분사가 들어갈 수 없으므로 현재분사 revising, 과거분사 revised는 답이 될 수가 없다. 참고로 「한정사(관사) + 형용사 + 명사」 어순이 되어야 하므로, 형용사 / 분사는 한정사(관사) 뒤에 와야 한다.

PART 5 DAY 03

만점 포인트 2 분사 구문: 시험에 빈출되는 분사 구문은 따로 있다.

적중! 유형 정리

As ------- in the contract, customers will be charged a late fee if the bill is overdue.

(A) indicative
(B) indication
(C) indicated
(D) indicating

계약서에 명시된 대로, 청구서가 기한이 지난다면 고객들은 연체료가 부과될 것이다.

해설 as는 전치사 또는 접속사로 쓰이는데, 이 문장에서는 접속사로 사용되었다. 접속사 뒤에는 '주어+동사'가 나와야 하지만, 주어와 동사가 생략된 분사 구문으로 사용되었다. 빈칸 뒤에 목적어가 없고 바로 전치사가 나왔으므로 수동의 개념이 들어가야 하기 때문에 정답은 (C) indicated가 된다. as indicated(명시된 대로)를 관용적인 분사 구문 표현으로 암기하면 빠르게 답을 찾을 수가 있다.

만점 전략 1 분사 구문

분사 구문은 「접속사 + 주어 + 동사」의 부사절을 분사가 이끄는 분사구로 간결하게 나타낸 것이다. 토익에서 출제되는 분사 구문은 '현재분사' 혹은 '과거분사'를 선택하는 문제가 나오는데, 주절의 주어와의 관계가 '능동'이면 '현재분사', '수동'이면 '과거분사'로 선택하면 된다. 분사 구문의 관용적인 표현을 암기해두면 시험장에서 보다 빨리 답을 찾을 수가 있다.

1. 접속사 + 주어 + 동사, 주어 + 동사 → 접속사 + -ing / p.p., 주어 + 동사

After Mr. Kim reviewed the agreement, he finally signed the contract.
→ **(After) reviewing** the agreement, he finally signed the contract.
김 씨는 계약서를 검토한 후, 마침내 계약서에 서명했다.

TIP! 명사를 뒤에서 수식하는 분사 빨리 알아내는 방법

분사 구문에서 현재분사와 과거분사를 빠르게 선택할 수 있는 방법은 뒤에 목적어가 나온다면 현재분사가 답이 되고, 전치사 / X / 부사가 나오면 과거분사가 답이 된다. 물론 예외도 존재한다. 뒤에 전치사가 나오더라도 '자동사'의 경우는 과거분사가 아니라 '현재분사' 형태로 사용해야 한다.

(Briefing / Briefed) the group, the manager began the meeting.
매니저가 그룹에게 브리핑한 다음에, 미팅을 시작했다.
⋯› 주절의 주어인 the manager와의 능동 / 수동 관계를 통해서 구별해도 되고, 뒤에 the group이라는 목적어가 나오므로 바로 Briefing을 답으로 고를 수 있다.

(Disappointing / Disappointed) with the merger, Mr. Singh quit.
싱 씨는 합병에 실망했기 때문에 그만뒀다.
⋯› 주어 Mr. Singh과의 관계를 봐도 '실망되다'라는 수동이며, 뒤에 at이라는 전치사를 동반하므로 과거분사인 Disappointed가 정답이다.

All personnel **working** from home need to report their working hours.
재택근무하는 모든 직원들은 근무 시간을 보고해야 한다.
⋯› All personnel을 수식하는 분사로 뒤에 전치사인 from이 나오지만, work는 자동사이므로 과거분사가 아닌 현재분사가 와야 한다.

2. 주어 + 동사 + 접속사 + 주어 + 동사 → 주어 + 동사, 접속사 + -ing / p.p.

Muller Inc. announced it would visit Willis Co. next month, and Muller Inc. confirmed rumors that it plans to expand into Europe.

→ Muller Inc. announced it would visit Willis Co. next month, (**confirming** / confirmed) rumors that it plans to expand into Europe.

뮬러 사는 다음 달에 윌리스 사를 방문할 것이라고 발표하면서, 유럽 지역으로 확장할 것이라는 소문을 확인시켜주었다.

…› 완전한 문장 뒤에 콤마로 연결된 분사 구문으로 뒤에 rumors라는 명사가 나오므로 현재분사 confirming이 정답이다.

PART 5

DAY 03

만점 전략 2 시험에 잘 나오는 분사 구문

토익 시험에서는 분사 구문의 과정을 물어보기보다는 분사 구문의 결과로 굳혀진 관용적인 표현이 자주 출제되므로 평소에 분사 구문의 관용적인 표현을 익혀두면 정답을 쉽게 찾을 수가 있다.

시간 접속사 when / while / after / before + 현재분사
when / while / after / before interviewing 인터뷰할 때 / 할 동안에 / 하고 나서 / 하기 전에

조건 접속사 if / unless / once + 과거분사
unless otherwise mentioned / indicated / stated / specified / instructed 달리 언급 / 명시 / 지시받지 않으면 = unless mentioned / indicated / stated / specified / instructed otherwise * otherwise는 뒤에 적을 수 있다.

as + 과거분사
as discussed / mentioned / stated / indicated / noted 논의된 / 언급된 / 명시된 대로

만점 포인트 3 관계대명사: 앞과 뒤만 잘 챙기자.

적중! 유형 정리

Bernard Miller, ------- work had a significant influence on literature, is one of the most notable novelists in the world.

(A) that
(B) whose
(C) who
(D) what

문학에 지대한 영향을 미친 업적을 가진 버나드 밀러는 세계에서 가장 유명한 소설가 중에 하나이다.

해설 빈칸은 앞에 나오는 명사 Bernard Miller를 수식하는 관계대명사 자리로, 콤마 다음에 쓸 수 없는 (A)는 탈락이 되고, 앞에 선행사가 나오므로 (D) what도 탈락이 된다. 빈칸 뒤에 work라는 명사가 나와서 사람 선행사를 받는 소유격 관계대명사가 적합하므로 정답은 (B) whose가 된다.

만점 전략 1 관계대명사

관계대명사 문제는 거의 매달 출제되는 출제 빈도가 높은 문제로 주로 who, which, whose가 정답으로 많이 출제된다. 하지만 요즘에는 다른 관계대명사도 출제되고 있으니 두루두루 학습하는 것이 중요하다.

1. 관계대명사 종류

종류	선행사	주격	소유격	목적격
who	사람	who	whose	whom
which	사물, 동물	which	of which / whose	which
that	사람, 사물, 동물	that	x	that

❶ 주격 관계대명사: 선행사 + 주격 관계대명사 + 동사

The hotel staff **who** is standing near the front desk will help you.
프린트 데스크 옆에 서있는 호텔 직원이 당신을 도와 드릴 것입니다.

❷ 소유격 관계대명사: 선행사 + 소유격 관계대명사 + 명사 (명사를 포함해서 완전한 문장이 나온다)

Jason Lee is the author **whose** novels are very famous.
제이슨 리는 작가인데 그분의 소설은 유명하다.

❸ 목적격 관계대명사: 선행사 + 목적격 관계대명사 + 주어 + 동사
목적격 관계대명사: 선행사 + 목적격 관계대명사 + 주어 + 동사 + 전치사
목적격 관계대명사: 선행사 + 전치사 + 목적격 관계대명사 + 주어 + 동사

This is a revised schedule, **which** you can find on the Web site.
이것은 귀하가 웹사이트에서 찾을 수 있는 수정된 스케줄입니다.

The Extell Center, **which** KCG Inc. has resided **in**, needs to repair the elevators soon.
The Extell Center, **in which** KCG Inc. has resided, needs to repair the elevators soon.
KCG 사가 들어가 있는 엑스텔 센터는 곧 엘리베이터를 수리할 필요가 있다.
⋯› 첫 번째 문장에서 in이라는 전치사는 앞으로 나올 수가 있다.

만점 전략 2 관계대명사 that vs. what

1. 관계대명사 that 이것만 조심하라!

관계대명사 that은 소유격이 없고, 전치사 뒤에 나올 수 없으며, 계속적 용법으로 사용할 수 없다(콤마 다음에 사용할 수 없다).

The client, **that** I met yesterday, liked the revised project. ⊗ ···› 콤마 다음에 that이 올 수 없다.
→ The client, **whom** I met yesterday, liked the revised project. ⓞ
내가 어제 만났던 고객이 수정된 프로젝트를 마음에 들어 했다.

2. 관계대명사 what 이것만 조심하라!

what 안에 선행사를 포함하고 있으므로 앞에 선행사가 나오면 what을 쓸 수 없다.
what = the thing which

I purchased the apartment (**that** / what) my family wanted. 내 가족이 원했던 아파트를 구입했다.
···› 선행사가 나와있고 wanted의 목적어가 없으므로 목적격 관계대명사 that이 온 것이다.

I purchased (that / **what**) my family wanted. 내 가족이 원했던 것을 구입했다.
···› 선행사가 없고, purchased 타동사의 목적어 역할을 하면서 뒤에 불완전한 문장이 나오므로 what이 필요하다.

만점 포인트 4 관계부사: 뒤가 완전한지 불완전한지만 따져보자.

적중! 유형 정리

In recognition of your continued support, we have sent you a $50 gift certificate for Bonjour Bistro, ------- you can enjoy various French dishes.

(A) who
(B) where
(C) what
(D) which

귀하의 지속적인 지원에 보답하고자, 봉주르 비스트로에서 여러 가지 프랑스 음식을 즐기실 수 있는 50달러 상품권을 보내드렸습니다.

해설 빈칸 앞에 나오는 장소 Bonjour Bistro를 수식하며 뒤에 완전한 문장을 동반하는 관계부사가 적합하므로 정답은 (B)가 된다. (A)는 선행사가 사람이 아니고, (C)는 앞에 선행사가 나왔으므로, (D)는 뒤가 불완전한 문장이 아니라서 오답이다.

만점 전략 1 관계부사

관계부사 문제는 관계대명사에 비해 출제율이 낮은 편이다. 관계대명사가 출제율이 높지만 문제를 풀 때는 관계부사의 특징도 같이 알고 있어야 확실하게 관계대명사의 정답을 고를 수 있으므로, 관계부사의 특징과 관계대명사와의 차이점을 아는 것은 굉장히 중요하다.

종류	선행사	전치사 + 관계대명사
when	시간	at / on / in which
where	장소	at / on / in which
why	이유	for which
how	방법	in which

This is the bookstore **which / that** I purchased the newly published novel in. 목적격 관계대명사
This is the bookstore **in which** I purchased the newly published novel. 전치사 + 목적격 관계대명사
This is the bookstore **where** I purchased the newly published novel. 관계부사
이 곳은 내가 새롭게 출간된 소설을 산 서점이다.
where = in which 즉, 「전치사 + 관계대명사 = 관계부사」가 성립한다.

만점 전략 2 관계대명사 vs. 관계부사

관계대명사와 관계부사의 차이는 앞에 나오는 선행사에 따라 구별하고, 뒤에 나오는 문장이 완전한지 불완전한지에 따라 구별할 수 있다.

- 관계대명사 + **불완전한** 문장
- 관계부사 + **완전한** 문장

The Lizzy Shoe company, (**which** / ~~where~~) is located on Queens Blvd, is the second oldest shoe company in the country.
퀸스 도로에 위치한 리지 신발 회사는 나라에서 두 번째로 오래된 신발 회사이다.
⋯› 앞의 회사를 수식하며 뒤에 불완전한 문장이 나오므로 관계대명사인 which가 정답이다.

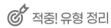

MEMO

고난도 실전 문제

1. Monetary contributions ------- by Hartford Co. will be given to charities throughout the city.
(A) generating
(B) generated
(C) have generated
(D) are generating

2. The customer service center called Mr. Schwartz yesterday to tell him that the camera ------- ordered is not available until next week.
(A) he
(B) that
(C) were
(D) until

3. A recent survey has shown that those ------- regularly check food ingredients on labels are likely to be healthy.
(A) what
(B) where
(C) who
(D) when

4. Due to its proximity to the highway, Dayton could be a very ------- location to build a plant.
(A) offering
(B) proposing
(C) promising
(D) identifying

5. Mr. Rudriguez will send a copy of the presentation ------- the marketing manager gave at the meeting last week.
(A) then
(B) what
(C) that
(D) when

6. When ------- prospective candidates, the interviewers need to ask as many questions as possible.
(A) interviewing
(B) interviews
(C) interviewed
(D) interview

7. Mr. Parkston, ------- donations have helped build the new community center, will deliver a speech at the opening ceremony.
(A) who
(B) whom
(C) whoever
(D) whose

8. The Hartford Photography Contest will provide an ------- deadline for candidates who were not able to submit their entries.
(A) extensive
(B) extends
(C) extension
(D) extended

9. We had a series of workshops with five speakers yesterday, most of ------- are renowned in the field.
(A) who
(B) them
(C) that
(D) whom

10. Any staff members ------- in joining the fitness program should complete an enrollment form by next Friday.
(A) interest
(B) interests
(C) interesting
(D) interested

11. Technicians at BYF Inc. take ongoing safety training sessions, ------- fulfilling the company's requirements.
(A) throughout
(B) between
(C) thereby
(D) such as

12. Unless instructed -------, all employees should turn off electronic devices like computers and fax machines at the end of each workday.
(A) indeed
(B) meanwhile
(C) accordingly
(D) otherwise

13. When applying for a managerial position, make sure that you understand ------- the job involves.
(A) which
(B) what
(C) how
(D) when

14. ------- met this week's sales goals, all sales associates in PCA Publishing received a $100 gift certificate.
(A) Being
(B) To have
(C) Having
(D) To be

15. Mrs. Robinson chose the place ------- the company will hold its 20th anniversary.
(A) where
(B) which
(C) until
(D) during

16. The founder of Rocco Services, Mr. Lester, always stresses that the primary goal of the company is to keep customers -------.
(A) satisfied
(B) satisfyingly
(C) satisfaction
(D) satisfying

17. According to the recently released survey, most customers respond to the questions regarding their shopping habits, ------- to spend more money online.
(A) prefer
(B) preferring
(C) preferred
(D) preference

18. Fifteen buildings on Flamingo Road, five of ------- were over 100 years old, were recently remodeled.
(A) what
(B) which
(C) them
(D) these

19. KG Consulting helps ------- retail owners to have a competitive advantage over other companies by offering business strategies.
(A) emerged
(B) emerging
(C) emerge
(D) emerges

20. The building manager will explain the ------- paper recycling policy at the monthly meeting.
(A) revising
(B) revision
(C) revised
(D) revise

PART 5

DAY 04

출제 빈도 낮다고 무시하지 마라!

동영상 강의 바로 보기

토익 문제 중에서 매달 출제되지 않고, 몇 개월에 한 번, 혹은 몇 년에 한 번 출제될 정도로 빈도가 낮은 문제들이 있다. 출제 빈도가 낮다고 해서 간과하여 틀리는 경우가 종종 있는데, 토익 고득점을 위해서는 이러한 문제도 놓치지 않아야 하므로 이번 기회를 통해서 확실히 정리할 수 있도록 하자. 명사절과 비교급은 1년에 2-3번 정도 출제되며, 가정법의 경우는 1년 혹은 2년에 한 번 꼴로 출제된다. 도치의 경우는 거의 출제되지 않지만 출제된 경우 오답을 고를 확률이 높으므로 유의하자.

만점 포인트

이것만 알면 만점!

1 명사절: 약간 어렵지만 나오는 종류는 정해져 있다.
2 to부정사와 동명사: 시간 낭비하지 말고 이것만 알자.
3 비교급: 의외로 간단하다.
4 가정법: 고민 없이 두 가지만 기억하자.

만점 포인트 1 명사절: 약간 어렵지만 나오는 종류는 정해져 있다.

적중! 유형 정리

------- Bennet Tech. expands into Asia depends on the costs estimated by its financial department.

(A) While
(B) Whether
(C) Although
(D) Moreover

베넷 테크의 아시아로 확장 여부는 회계부서에서 예상하는 비용에 따라 달라진다.

해설 문장의 동사가 expands와 depends on 두 개가 나오므로 접속사가 필요하다. 접속사 역할을 하지 못하는 접속부사 (D)는 오답이 되며, 문장의 동사는 depends on이 되고 그 앞 전체가 주어가 되는데, 주어인 Bennet Tech와 동사인 expands를 이끄는 명사절 접속사를 찾는 문제이다. (A)와 (C)는 부사절 접속사이므로 오답이다. 따라서, 정답은 (B)가 된다.

PART 5
DAY 04

만점 전략 1 명사절

명사절은 출제 빈도가 낮은 편이며, 토익 시험에 출제되는 명사절도 거의 정해져 있으므로 출제율이 높은 명사절 중심으로 확실히 익혀 두자.

1. 명사절 자리

주어 자리 **Whether Ms. Choi has arrived from Beijing or Shanghai** is not known.
최 씨가 베이징에서 도착할지 상하이에서 도착할지는 아직 알려지지 않았다.
…› is not known이라는 동사 앞의 주어 자리에 들어가는 명사절

목적어 자리 Lucy announced yesterday **that her company would not merge with Vista Co.**
루시가 어제 그녀의 회사는 비스타 사와 합병하지 않는다고 발표했다.
…› 타동사 announced의 목적어 자리에 들어가는 명사절

보어 자리 The problem is **that we will not be able to conduct the inspection tomorrow.**
문제는 우리는 내일 검사를 할 수 없을 것이라는 것이다.
…› be동사의 보어 자리에 들어가는 명사절

2. 명사절을 이끄는 접속사 that vs. what

- that + 완전한 문장 (*cf.* 관계대명사 that + 불완전한 문장)
- what + 불완전한 문장

The board of directors announced **that** performance evaluations will be conducted every month.
이사진은 업무 평가를 매달 진행할 것이라고 공지했다
…› 타동사 announced의 목적어 자리로 뒤에 완전한 문장이 오므로 명사절의 that이 온다.

What Mr. Clements needs is helpful comments on his report.
클레멘츠 씨가 필요한 것은 그의 보고서에 대한 도움이 되는 코멘트이다.
…› 문장의 동사 is의 앞 전체가 명사절로, 명사절 내의 needs의 목적어가 없는 불완전한 문장이므로 what이 온다.

3. 명사절을 이끄는 접속사 whether

The customer needs to choose **whether he will get a full refund or exchange the defective item**.

고객은 전액 환불을 받을 것인지 아니면 결함이 있는 제품을 교환할 것인지를 선택해야 한다.

··· 타동사 choose의 목적어 자리에 들어가는 명사절을 이끄는 접속사로 whether이 온다.

Department managers will decide **whether to nominate Mr. Kent for the Employee of the Year**.

부서장들은 켄트 씨를 올해의 직원 후보로 임명할지를 결정할 것이다.

··· 타동사 decide의 목적어 자리에 들어가는 명사절을 이끄는 접속사로 whether이 온다. 「whether + to부정사」

부사절의 whether

Whether the orders are large or small, the customers receive the same discount on them.

주문한 것이 크든 작든, 고객들은 동일한 할인을 받는다.

··· whether는 명사절을 이끄는 접속사이나, or 혹은 or not과 쓰여서 부사절로 사용되기도 한다.

4. 동격의 that

the fact / opinion / news / rumor **that** ~라는 사실 / 견해 / 뉴스 / 소문

Everybody on the marketing team is aware of **the fact that** Mr. Liam will quit.

마케팅 팀 모두가 리암 씨가 그만둘 것이라는 사실을 알고 있다.

만점 포인트 2 to부정사와 동명사: 시간 낭비하지 말고 이것만 알자.

적중! 유형 정리

Please make sure that the latest model of KZ 2080 laptop computers ------- sent to the trade show in Tokyo are ready by Monday.

(A) to be
(B) was
(C) are
(D) have been

도쿄 무역 쇼에 보낼 KZ 2080 최신 모델의 노트북이 월요일까지 준비가 될 수 있도록 해주세요.

해설 that 이하에서 이미 are라는 동사가 나와 있으므로 (B), (C), (D)는 오답이며, 빈칸 앞의 명사 laptop computers를 수식하는 to 부정사의 형용사적인 용법이 적합하므로 정답은 (A)가 된다.

만점 전략 1 to부정사와 동명사

to부정사와 동명사는 토익에서 자주 출제되지는 않지만, 출제된다 하더라도 주로 관용적인 표현으로 출제되기 때문에 to부정사와 동명사를 취하는 품사들과 함께 숙어적인 표현으로 익혀두자.

1. to부정사가 답이 되는 경우

• **to부정사를 목적어로 취하는 동사**

intend to부정사	~하는 것을 의도하다	plan to부정사	~하는 것을 계획하다
decide to부정사	~을 결정하다	aim to부정사	~을 목표로 하다
strive to부정사	고군분투하다	hesitate to부정사	~하는 것을 망설이다
promise to부정사	~하는 것을 약속하다	manage to부정사	가까스로 해내다

• **to부정사를 목적격 보어로 취하는 동사**

allow + 목적어 + to부정사	~하는 것을 허락하다	require + 목적어 + to부정사	~하라고 요구하다
intend + 목적어 + to부정사	~하도록 의도하다	encourage + 목적어 + to부정사	~하라고 격려하다
cause + 목적어 + to부정사	~하는 것을 야기하다	enable + 목적어 + to부정사	~할 수 있게 하다
remind + 목적어 + to부정사	~하라고 상기시키다	urge + 목적어 + to부정사	~하도록 권고하다

• **to부정사를 취하는 형용사**

be able to부정사	~할 수 있다	be reluctant to부정사	~하기를 꺼리다
be about to부정사	막 ~하려고 하다	be likely to부정사	~할 가능성이 있다
be eager to부정사	~하는 것을 열망하다	be willing to부정사	기꺼이 ~하다
be proud to부정사	~을 자랑스럽게 여기다	be hesitant to부정사	~하는 것을 망설이다
be ready to부정사	~할 준비가 되어 있다	be eligible to부정사	~할 자격이 있다

• **be to가 답이 되는 경우**

goal, purpose, job, aim, objective, mission이 주어로 나오면 동사는 be to가 나온다.

The **purpose** of the workshop **is to** provide participants with new sales strategies.
이 워크숍의 목적은 참가자들에게 새로운 판매 전략을 제공하는 것이다.

2. to부정사의 to vs. 전치사 to

to라고 해서 다 같은 to가 아니다. to부정사의 to로 볼 수도 있고, 전치사의 to로도 볼 수 있으므로 평소에 구분해서 암기를 해 두면 쉽게 문제를 풀 수 있다.

to부정사: to + 동사원형
전치사 to: to + 명사 or 동명사

전치사 to ← 뒤에 명사 or 동명사가 온다.

be subject to	~에 영향을 받기 쉽다	be committed to	~에 헌신하다
be accustomed to	~에 익숙하다	be dedicated to	~에 헌신하다
be opposed to	~에 반대하다	be devoted to	~에 전념하다
in addition to	~하는 것 이외에도	look forward to	학수고대하다

3. 동명사를 목적어로 취하는 동사

consider -ing	~하는 것을 고려하다	recommend -ing	~하는 것을 추천하다
suggest -ing	~하는 것을 제안하다	avoid -ing	~하는 것을 피하다
mind -ing	~하는 것을 꺼리다	include -ing	~하는 것을 포함하다
enjoy -ing	~하는 것을 즐기다	discontinue -ing	~하는 것을 중단하다
finish -ing	~하는 것을 끝내다	postpone -ing	~하는 것을 연기하다

만점 포인트 3 비교급: 의외로 간단하다.

적중! 유형 정리

Of the stationery stores located in the city, KC Stationery is the ------- to get to from our office.

(A) easily
(B) easiest
(C) more easily
(D) most easily

시에 있는 문구점 중에서, KC 문구점이 사무실에서 가장 쉽게 접근할 수 있는 곳이다.

해설 비교급 / 최상급을 물어보는 문제로 빈칸 앞에 the가 있으므로 최상급인 (B)와 (D)가 답이 될 수 있다. 빈칸은 is라는 be 동사의 보어 자리로 형용사가 들어가야 하므로, 형용사의 최상급인 (B) easiest가 정답이 된다. (D)는 부사의 최상급이다.

만점 전략 1 비교급

비교 구문은 '원급, 비교급, 최상급'으로 구성이 되며, 비교적 출제 빈도가 낮고 난이도도 쉬운 편이지만, 종종 성급하게 틀리는 경우가 있으므로 쉽더라도 바로 넘어가지 말고 각 비교급에 잘 쓰이는 어구를 확인하고 넘어가자.

1. 원급 비교: ~만큼 ~한 / 하게

as 형용사 / 부사 as
the same ~ as: ~와 같은

The newly purchased fax machine is **as efficient as** the previous one.
새롭게 구입한 팩스는 그 이전 것만큼이나 효율적이다.

The new DX300 model has almost **the same** features **as** the previous one.
새로 나온 DX 300 모델은 이전 모델과 거의 똑같은 특징을 가지고 있다.

2. 비교급 비교: ~보다 더 / 덜 ~한 / 하게

형용사 / 부사 -er + than
more 형용사 / 부사 + than

Please submit the application form **no later than** midnight. 자정까지 신청서를 내주세요.
Ms. Lee's new album is **more** popular **than** the last one. 이 씨의 새 앨범은 마지막 것 보다 더 유명하다.

비교급 강조 부사: even, much, still, far

Replacing the broken equipment would be **much cheaper than** buying a new one.
고장 난 기계를 교체하는 것이 구매하는 것보다 훨씬 저렴하다.

3. 최상급 비교: ~ 중에서 / ~에서 가장 ~한 / 하게

the / 소유격 / 's -est / most ~ 비교 범위 (in / of / among)

Brown Enterprise, one of **the largest** companies **in** the US, will introduce a variety of new programs next month.
미국에서 가장 큰 회사 중에 하나인 브라운 기업은 다음 달 여러 가지 새 프로그램을 소개할 것이다.

만점 포인트 4 가정법: 고민 없이 두 가지만 기억하자.

적중! 유형 정리

Georgia Interior may charge additional fees ------- extra hours be required to repair the elevator.

(A) in fact
(B) when
(C) should
(D) through

엘리베이터를 수리하는 것에 대한 추가적인 시간이 필요하다면 조지아 인테리어에서 추가적인 요금을 부과할 수 있다.

해설 빈칸 뒤에 주어와 동사가 나와서 단순하게 접속사인 (B)를 고르지 않도록 조심한다. 이 문장은 가정법 미래 도치 구문으로 원래 If extra hours should be required to ~이지만 if가 생략되면서 도치가 되어 should가 들어가야 하므로 정답은 (C)가 된다.

만점 전략 가정법

가정법은 1년 혹은 2년에 거의 한 문제 정도 출제된다고 보면 된다. 토익에 출제되는 가정법은 두 가지 종류로 '가정법 과거완료'와 '가정법 미래'이다. 난이도가 높은 가정법 도치 구문도 종종 출제되므로 제대로 익혀두자.

1. 가정법 과거완료: 과거에 ~했었더라면, ~었을 텐데(과거 상황에 대한 아쉬움이나 후회 표현)

가정법 과거완료 If + had p.p., 주어 + would / could / should / might + have p.p.

If 생략 도치 Had + 주어 + p.p., 주어 + would / could / should / might + have p.p.

If Ms. Lee **had arrived** earlier, she **could have helped** the keynote speaker.
이 씨가 일찍 도착했었더라면, 기조 연설자를 도울 수 있었을 텐데.

> **고득점 포인트**
> must have p.p.는 '~임에 틀림없다'로 해석된다. '~했어야만 했는데'로 해석하지 않도록 조심하자.

2. 가정법 미래: (혹시) 미래에 ~라면, 미래에 ~일 것이다.

가정법 미래 If + 주어 + should + 동사원형, 주어 + will / can / may + 동사원형
If + 주어 + should + 동사원형, 명령문 (please)

If 생략 도치 Should + 주어 + 동사원형, 주어 + will / can / may + 동사원형 or 명령문

If you **should decide** to join our club, **please** take advantage of a special offer.
저희 클럽에 가입을 결정하신다면, 특별 할인을 이용하세요.

MEMO

고난도 실전 문제

1. Taking pictures during musical performances is strictly prohibited, so audiences ------- to turn off their cameras or mobile phones.
(A) had urged
(B) will be urging
(C) were urging
(D) are urged

2. A recent poll indicates ------- the popularity of Mr. Han's latest film has been decreasing since the harsh reviews were revealed in the local newspaper.
(A) that
(B) which
(C) what
(D) those

3. Despite the inclement weather conditions, the shipment we ordered last week will arrive ------- earlier than expected.
(A) much
(B) more
(C) as
(D) like

4. The department supervisor should explicitly state ------- is in charge of assigning a new task.
(A) when
(B) everything
(C) who
(D) some

5. ------- Carlton's newly released song will be as enthusiastically received as his previous one remains to be seen.
(A) As though
(B) Whether
(C) Regarding
(D) Moreover

6. Sales representatives should remind customers ------- the device cautiously before purchasing it.
(A) handling
(B) handled
(C) to handle
(D) handles

7. KJ International Arts Festival will award the prize to ------- submission gets the most votes from the judges.
(A) some
(B) whichever
(C) these
(D) whoever

8. Sakamoto Footwear produces its ------- handmade leather boots of any manufacturer in Italy.
(A) finely
(B) finest
(C) finer
(D) fine

9. ------- is interested in joining this year's Christmas party should speak to Mr. Chen in the marketing department.
(A) Whoever
(B) Anyone
(C) Them
(D) Some

10. The safety manual explains ------- new technicians need to know about handling hazardous materials.
(A) which
(B) where
(C) how
(D) what

11. Please note that a special request for an ocean view room is ------- to availability at the time of check-in.

(A) current
(B) likely
(C) subject
(D) standard

12. Additional information ------- to the upcoming workshop next week was emailed to those who had expressed interest in participating.

(A) granted
(B) pertaining
(C) receiving
(D) similar

13. Of all the bids submitted by various contractors, it can be difficult to choose ------- would best meet the company's budget.

(A) when
(B) why
(C) which
(D) where

14. In addition to ------- residential complexes, Harim Construction also builds commercial buildings.

(A) construct
(B) constructing
(C) construction
(D) constructed

15. The fact ------- the local farmers expanded their land area by 10 percent last year was surprising.

(A) because
(B) that
(C) which
(D) unless

16. The primary goal of the customer service center ------- all customer inquiries and complaints in a timely manner.

(A) had addressed
(B) is to address
(C) is addressed
(D) address

17. Profits increased after the acquisition, so the board of directors will consider ------- another factory.

(A) build
(B) to build
(C) building
(D) built

18. If the hotel reservation ------- sooner, it must have been possible to accommodate all participants at one hotel.

(A) had made
(B) was made
(C) had been made
(D) made

19. Once the renovation projects have been reviewed by the management, the accounting team will determine ------- proposal will be chosen.

(A) whatever
(B) which
(C) why
(D) who

20. We at O'Neil Law Firm ------- to make our legal services available to as many clients as possible.

(A) encourage
(B) strive
(C) disregard
(D) recognize

PART 5

DAY 05

너만 틀리는 고난도 어휘 문제

동영상 강의
바로 보기

토익 고득점의 발목을 잡는 것 중에 하나가 바로 어휘 문제이다. 보통 한글로 해석해서 답을 찾는 경우가 대부분인데, 단순하게 한글로 해석해서 의미가 맞는다고 해서 답을 고르다가 낭패를 보는 경우가 종종 있다. 그러므로 평소에 한글로 해석해서 이해하기 보다는 영어 표현을 그대로 익히는 것이 중요하다. 또한, 대부분의 토익 문제에 등장하는 어휘 문제는 굳이 해석하지 않더라도 풀 수 있는 어휘 문제들이다. 예를 들어, 연어(collocation)라고 해서 흔히 함께 쓰이는 단어들의 결합이 그것이다. 따라서 평소에 연어(collocation) 중심으로 어휘를 암기하고, 자주 빈출되었던 어휘 문제, 그리고 고득점자들도 오답률이 높은 고난도 어휘가 어떤 것이 있는지 이번 기회를 통해서 확실히 익혀두어 어휘 문제 만점을 받도록 하자.

만점 포인트

이것만
알면 만점!

1 해석이 필요 없는 1초짜리 어휘 문제
2 나만 해석하다가 틀릴 수 있는 어휘 문제
3 고수도 틀리는 고난도 어휘 문제
4 시력이 안 좋거나 나 혼자 착각하다 틀리는 어휘 문제

만점 포인트 1 해석이 필요 없는 1초짜리 어휘 문제

적중! 유형 정리

Due to ------- conditions in the market, the launch of the newest sports vehicle should be postponed.

(A) unfavorable
(B) unwilling
(C) opposing
(D) reluctant

시장의 악조건 때문에, 최신 스포츠카 출시가 연기 되어야만 한다.

해설 unfavorable condition은 '악조건'이라는 뜻으로, 문장 전체를 해석하지 않고 평소에 collocation으로 암기를 하면 충분히 빠르게 정답 (A) unfavorable를 찾을 수가 있다.

만점 전략 궁합으로 암기(collocation)

1. 명사 궁합 「전치사 + 명사」, 「명사 + 전치사」

전치사 + 명사		명사 + 전치사	
under construction	공사 중	rise / increase in	~에 대한 증가
under consideration	고려 중	decline / decrease in	~에 대한 감소
under the supervision of	~의 관리 감독 하에	effect / impact on	~에 대한 영향
(up)on request	요청하자마자	workshop / class on	~에 대한 워크숍 / 수업
(up)on receipt	수령하자마자	access to	~에 대한 접근
(up)on arrival	도착하자마자	contribution to	~에 대한 공헌
out of order	고장 난	commitment to	~에 대한 헌신 / 전념
out of stock	재고가 떨어진	investment in	~에 대한 투자
until further notice	추후 공지가 있을 때까지	advance in	~에 대한 진보
on schedule	예정대로	demand for	~에 대한 수요
behind schedule	예정보다 늦게	qualification for	~에 대한 자격요건
ahead of schedule	예정보다 빨리	preference for	~에 대한 선호
in advance	미리, 앞서서	request for	~에 대한 요청

2. 형용사 궁합 「형용사 + 명사」

tentative agreement	잠정적인 합의	tight schedule	빡빡한 일정
unfavorable condition	악조건	notable economist	저명한 경제학자
substantial bonus	상당한 보너스	competitive salary	높은 연봉
generous donation	후한 기부	exhaustive research	철저한 조사
formidable challenge	힘든 도전	unprecedented rise	전례가 없는 증가
established customer	기존 고객	extensive knowledge	광범위한 지식

3. 부사 궁합 「동사 + 부사」, 「부사 + 동사」, 「부사 + 형용사」

arrive punctually	정각에 도착하다	travel extensively	두루두루 여행하다
fall behind considerably	상당히 뒤처지다	adversely affect	악영향을 미치다
meticulously plan	꼼꼼하게 계획하다	conveniently located	편리하게 위치한
well attended	출석률이 좋은	highly recommended	강력하게 권하는
explicitly state	명료하게 명시하다	heavily discounted	대폭 할인된
mutually beneficial	상호 이익이 되는	readily accessible	쉽게 접근할 수 있는

만점 포인트 2 나만 해석하다 틀릴 수 있는 어휘 문제

적중! 유형 정리

Chloe Ltd. has a good reputation for providing employees with a ------- salary and the best benefits packages in the industry.

(A) satisfied
(B) preventable
(C) competitive
(D) experienced

클로에 사는 직원들에게 높은 연봉과 최고의 복지후생 혜택을 제공하는 것으로 업계에서 좋은 평판을 가지고 있다.

해설 한국말로 해석할 경우 '만족된 연봉'이라고 해서 (A)를 답으로 고르기 쉽지만, (A)는 사람의 감정 동사로 뒤에 사람이 나와야 하므로 오답이 된다. 정답은 competitive salary '높은 연봉'이라고 해서 (C) competitive가 답이 된다.

만점 전략 해석하다가 낭패 볼 수 있는 어휘 문제

한글로 해석하기보다는 영어적인 표현을 평소에 익혀두자.

❶ Yesterday's (**unusually** / ~~dangerously~~) heavy rain makes commuters in the city concerned about traffic congestion during rush hours.

어제 유난히 많은 비가 내리면서 시내 통근자들은 출근 시간대의 교통 혼잡을 우려하고 있다.

→ '폭우'라는 단어를 보고 '위험하게'가 연상이 되어 dangerously를 고르지 않도록 조심하자. '평소와는 다르게 폭우가 와서 ~하다'라는 의미가 적합하므로 정답은 unusually가 된다.

❷ Dubio Cafe's new cakes are (~~cautious~~ / **perishable**) and should be stored in the fridge.

두비오 카페의 새로운 케이크는 상하기 쉬우므로 냉장고에 보관되어야 한다.

→ 냉장고에 보관해야 한다고 해서 '조심성 있는'의 cautious를 고르지 않도록 조심하자. '상하기 쉽기 때문에 냉장 보관해야 한다'는 의미가 적합하므로 정답은 '상하기 쉬운'의 perishable이 된다.

❸ Please call Mr. Fabio in the customer service center if you think you have received the e-mail in (**error** / ~~mistake~~).

이메일을 잘못 받았다고 생각되면, 고객센터에 있는 파비오 씨에게 연락 주세요.

→ 해석만을 봤을 때는 '실수로'라는 의미로 둘 다 답이 될 수 있을 것 같지만, in error 그리고 by mistake로 쓰이기 때문에 정답은 error가 된다.

만점 포인트 3 고수도 틀리는 고난도 어휘 문제

적중! 유형 정리

With her broad knowledge in the industry, Ms. Zen will be a valuable ------- to the marketing team at Oakmont Co.

(A) inquiry
(B) addition
(C) position
(D) pattern

젠 씨가 가진 그 분야의 폭넓은 지식으로 오크먼트 회사의 마케팅팀에 좋은 추가 인재가 될 것이다.

해설 a valuable / fine / welcome addition / asset to '~에 좋은 추가 인원 / 자산'이란 의미로 해석상 '지식이 광범위하므로 좋은 추가 인원 / 인재 / 자산이다'라는 말이 적합하므로 정답은 (B) addition이 된다.

만점 전략 고난도 어휘 문제

토익 시험에 출제되는 어휘는 한번 출제되었던 것들이 반복해서 출제되는 경우가 많으므로, 이번 기회를 통해서 출제되었던 고난도 어휘를 익혀두자.

❶ GX Solutions and TA Chemicals reached an agreement to work (~~together~~ / **alongside**) one another on a new project.

GX 솔루션과 TA 케미칼은 새 프로젝트에 서로 함께 작업하는 것에 대해 합의를 했다.

⋯› 해석상 '함께 일하다'의 의미로 together를 고르기 쉽고, one another가 없다면 답이 될 수 있다. 하나의 숙어적인 표현으로 work alongside one another '서로 함께 일하다'의 의미가 있으므로 정답은 alongside가 된다.

❷ Delta Electricity appreciates your (**prompt** / ~~missed~~) payment of this month's bill, which is due by July 1.

델타 전력은 7월 1일까지인 이번 달 요금의 즉각적인 지불에 감사드립니다.

⋯› 뒤에 due라는 '마감'이라는 단어가 나온다고 해서 '놓친'의 뜻을 가진 missed를 연상하여 고르지 않도록 조심하자. '즉각적인 지불'이라고 해서 prompt payment가 되므로 정답은 prompt이다.

❸ Amber Airline passengers bound for Sydney are (**welcome** / ~~expectant~~) to use the outlets in the lounge in order to recharge their mobile phones.

시드니 발 앰버 항공 승객들은 휴대폰을 충전하기 위해서 라운지에서 콘센트를 사용해도 좋습니다.

⋯› 해석상 '~를 해도 좋다'가 적합하므로 정답은 be welcome to인 welcome이 된다.

만점 포인트 4 시력이 안 좋거나 나 혼자 착각하다 틀리는 어휘 문제

적중! 유형 정리

The 5th annual award ceremony has been ------- scheduled for May 13.

(A) abundantly
(B) temperately
(C) steadily
(D) tentatively

매년마다 개최되는 다섯 번째 시상식이 잠정적으로 5월 13일로 예정되었다.

해설 빈칸은 scheduled를 수식하는 부사 자리로 '일시적으로'라는 의미의 부사인 temporarily를 (B) temperately '적당하게'로 착각해서 답을 고르지 않도록 조심하자. 정답은 '잠정적으로 예정되다'라고 해서 (D)가 된다.

PART 5
DAY 05

만점 전략 혼자 헷갈려서 틀리는 어휘

❶ Sienna Bistro does not take responsibility for personal belongings left (~~nonreturnable~~ / **unattended**) in the dining room.

시에나 비스트로는 식당에 방치된 채로 남겨진 개인 소지품에 대해서 책임을 못 집니다.

⋯› '개인 소지품'이라는 단어가 나와서 nonreturnable '반납할 수 없는'을 연상해서 정답으로 고르지 않도록 조심하자. '방치된 채로'의 의미가 적합한 정답은 left unattended가 된다.

❷ The recent survey indicates that our company has competitive advantage (**over** / ~~than~~) others regarding software programs.

최근 설문조사에서 말해주는 바는 우리 회사가 소프트웨어 프로그램에 관한한 다른 경쟁업체보다 경쟁적 우위에 있다는 것이다.

⋯› 해석상 '~보다'라고 해석된다고 해서 무조건 than을 고르지 않도록 조심하자. '~보다 경쟁적 우위'는 competitive advantage over가 되어 정답은 over이다.

❸ This year's CEMA Electronics Convention in Seattle was (~~many~~ / **well**) attended by industry experts and buyers.

올해 시애틀의 CEMA 전자 컨벤션은 업계 전문가들과 구매자들이 많이 참석했다.

⋯› 해석상 '많이 참석했다'라고 해서 many를 답으로 고르지 않도록 조심하자. many는 형용사이므로 attended를 수식할 수 없을 뿐만 아니라, '출석률이 좋다'라고 할 때 well attended가 되므로 정답은 well이 된다.

고난도 실전 문제

1. According to the new data, MG Automobile's latest vehicle in the European market will be only ------- successful.
(A) suspiciously
(B) regrettably
(C) marginally
(D) permanently

2. Savers Supplies provides a ------- selection of personalized partitions to organize office areas for its customers.
(A) diverse
(B) prolonged
(C) several
(D) various

3. Due to additional tourist attractions, the city of Milford drew much larger groups of visitors in ------- years.
(A) subsequent
(B) next
(C) followed
(D) late

4. The lawyers working at the Fitz and Gerald Law Firm are reminded that they cannot comment on any ------- cases.
(A) dependent
(B) attentive
(C) practical
(D) pending

5. Regardless of the size of purchases, Peer Store customers ------- the same high quality of service.
(A) satisfy
(B) deserve
(C) complete
(D) produce

6. Please keep in mind that all employees in the sales department should avoid ------- of customers' personal information.
(A) permission
(B) confession
(C) allowance
(D) disclosure

7. All new technicians should complete a ------- safety training course before dispatching.
(A) various
(B) rigorous
(C) prosperous
(D) spacious

8. Renowned novelist Anton Hales ------- the plot for his recent detective story, *Into The Mirror*, during his travel to London last winter.
(A) lectured
(B) conceived
(C) resemble
(D) motivated

9. Starting next Monday, there will be a brief ------- in the electronic service in A Building for regular maintenance.
(A) statement
(B) outline
(C) interruption
(D) production

10. Mr. Lanner was finally chosen for a senior analyst position because his research was very -------.
(A) qualified
(B) knowledgeable
(C) pleased
(D) impressive

11. In order to promote the company's products and services, ------- from satisfied regular customers are very helpful.

(A) intervals
(B) testimonials
(C) technology
(D) solidity

12. Ms. Maseratti, the chief marketing officer, is recruiting a focus group to ------- consumers' needs.

(A) gauge
(B) administer
(C) settle
(D) comply

13. Even though the parts may be purchased online, the production of the printer has been -------.

(A) notified
(B) suspended
(C) deducted
(D) expired

14. Based on a recent survey, consumers reacted ------- to the newly released software program, Whiz 3.2.

(A) unfavorably
(B) probably
(C) potentially
(D) unlikely

15. A retired executive who has a ------- of expertise across a wide range of industries decided to deliver a speech for our employees next week.

(A) wealth
(B) height
(C) labor
(D) fame

16. The City Transportation Official announced yesterday that a ten-kilometer ------- between Park Avenue and Queens Road will be widened in September.

(A) journey
(B) stretch
(C) duration
(D) instance

17. The red dots ------- Watanabe's book are helpful for readers to understand the important information described in it.

(A) among
(B) throughout
(C) during
(D) toward

18. Valentino Restaurant will remodel the interior and an ------- courtyard for an outdoor terrace.

(A) entertained
(B) assessed
(C) enclosed
(D) accidental

19. Despite harsh reviews from customers, SC Electronics' remote control is ------- with most television brands.

(A) reportable
(B) reflective
(C) compatible
(D) conclusive

20. Barnum Co.'s increased profits resulted from the recent ------- to use environmentally friendly materials.

(A) restrictions
(B) inquiries
(C) explanation
(D) initiatives

PART 6

PART 6에서 여러 가지 문법, 구조, 어휘를 물어보는 문제가 골고루 출제되지만, 한 지문당 1문제는 반드시 빈칸에 알맞은 문장을 고르는 유형인 '문장 삽입' 문제가 출제된다. PART 6는 PART 5와 PART 7의 중간 단계로, PART 5에서의 문법과 어휘 토대 위에 PART 7으로 가기 전 전체적인 문맥을 파악해야 하는 능력을 요구한다.

DAY 06

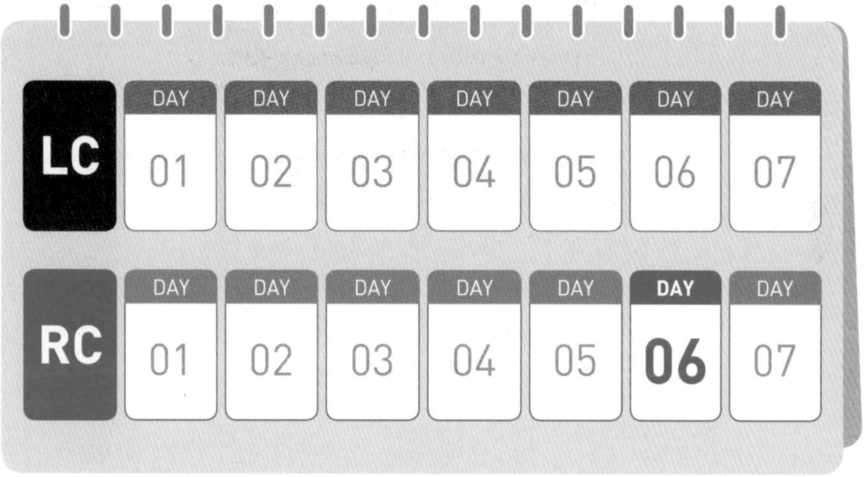

PART 6 만점 핵심 공략

- 문장 삽입 문제는 빈칸 앞뒤 문장의 대명사나 연결어 등을 최대한 이용하자.
- PART 6에 나오는 시제 문제는 감이나 느낌으로 풀지 말자.
- 접속부사만 알아도 PART 6 어렵지 않다.

PART 6

DAY 06

단골 문제를 찍어주마!

동영상 강의
바로 보기

문장 삽입 문제의 경우 토익 학습자들이 어렵게 느끼는 문제 중에 하나이기도 하지만, 문장 삽입의 위치에 따라 자주 출제되는 정답 패턴과 정답을 찾는 전략을 잘 이해한다면 어렵지 않게 답을 찾을 수 있다. 또한, 지시어, 시제, 연결 어구 문제의 경우도 느낌이나 감에 의존하다가 오답을 고를 수가 있으므로, 전체적인 지문의 흐름과 단서를 파악한 후 정답을 찾도록 해야 한다. 지시어의 경우는 앞에 나오는 명사를 빠르게 찾아서 대명사 형태를 찾는 문제로, 일단 앞의 어떤 명사를 받는지를 빨리 찾아내는 것이 관건이다. 시제 문제의 경우에는 시간 어구가 나오지 않은 채 문제를 풀어야 한다면 그 문장을 중심으로 앞뒤 문장의 시제를 알려주는 단서를 통해서 답을 선택해야 한다. 연결 어구의 문제로는 접속부사가 매달 출제된다. 앞 문장과 뒤 문장의 맥락을 보고 결정을 해야 하고, 해석에만 너무 의존한 나머지 접속부사 자리에 접속사를 답으로 고르지 않도록 유의해야 한다.

만점 포인트
이것만 알면 만점!

1. 문장 삽입: 이것만 알면 더 이상 어렵지 않다!
2. 지시어(대명사): 앞에 나오는 명사를 빨리 확인해라!
3. 시제: 빈칸 앞, 뒤 문장의 시제를 알려주는 단서를 찾아라!
4. 연결 어구: 접속부사만 마스터해라!

만점 포인트 1 문장 삽입: 이것만 알면 더 이상 어렵지 않다!

적중! 유형 정리

Thank you again for your registration and participation in the 15th Annual Clark Art Spring Exhibition, which will be held from December 3 through December 17. As a returning exhibitor, your painting, *Ocean Road*, will be displayed in Room A. Please note that new requirements will be implemented. This year, all artwork must be delivered to the exhibition center for installation by 9 P.M. on December 2. -------. We ask that you confirm the dimensions of your work via e-mail as soon as possible.

Adele Hansen, Event Coordinator

(A) These include that paintings should be ready to be framed and wired to hang.
(B) The number of artists has increased in recent years.
(C) The exact schedule will be announced later.
(D) Clark Art Center will be located next to the Flaming Rd.

12월 3일부터 17일까지 매년마다 개최되는 15번째 클라크 아트 스프링 전시회에 등록하고 참석하시는 것에 대해 다시 한번 감사드립니다. 재참가 전시자로서, 귀하의 〈오션 로드〉 그림은 룸 A에 전시될 예정입니다. 새로운 요구사항들이 있음을 알아주시기 바랍니다. 올해, 모든 전시 작품은 12월 2일 저녁 9시까지 설치를 위해서 전시 센터로 배송되어야 합니다. **이것은 그림들이 액자에 넣어져 바로 걸 수 있는 상태가 되어야 하는 것을 포함합니다.** 가능한 한 빨리 귀하의 작품의 사이즈를 확인해서 이메일로 부탁드립니다.

아델 한센, 이벤트 코디네이터

(A) 이것은 그림들이 액자에 넣어져 바로 걸 수 있는 상태가 되어야 하는 것을 포함합니다.
(B) 최근 몇 년 동안 예술가의 수가 증가했습니다.
(C) 정확한 일정은 추후 공지할 것입니다.
(D) 클라크 아트 센터는 플라밍 로 옆에 위치할 것입니다.

해설 빈칸 앞에 12월 2일이라는 날짜가 나왔기 때문에 뒤에도 날짜에 관련된 것이 언급될 것이라고 생각하고 (C)를 고르는 경우가 있다. 하지만 이미 날짜를 정확하게 언급했으므로 더 이상 정확한 날짜 이야기는 나올 필요가 없다. 앞 부분에서 new requirements가 실행된다고 했고, 이 부분에 대한 자세한 설명이 필요하므로 그것을 받는 these로 시작하는 (A)가 정답이 된다.

만점 전략 문장 삽입 이렇게 풀어라!

❶ 주어진 지문의 전체적인 구성을 확인하고, 처음부터 끝까지 읽으며 전체적인 맥락을 파악하여 답을 찾는다.
❷ 빈칸 앞뒤 문장의 키워드를 확인한다. 주로 **this, these, also, however, in addition, in fact, therefore**가 정답이거나 정답을 알려주는 단서로 많이 출제된다.
❸ 보기를 하나씩 대입해서 오답을 소거한 다음 정답을 찾는다.

1. 처음부터 끝까지 맥락을 파악해서 푼다.

The Cowen Theater announced yesterday that its run of *Winter Magic*, a recently released film by Adam Munrrow, would be extended. Due to a sudden demand for the movie, the last performance will be on August 15. Given the poor reviews written by critics after the opening, this move surprised everybody. -------. The movie, however, gained sudden popularity with children under 12 years old, many of whom like animations. They are apparently interested in the movie's story and characters.

(A) Moreover, the Cowen Theater was founded 13 years ago.
(B) Also, the initial ticket sales had been weak.
(C) The opening show was well-attended by local business owners.
(D) The main actors were local residents.

코웬 극장은 최근에 출시된 아담 문로우의 영화 〈윈터 매직〉의 상영이 연장될 것이라고 어제 발표했다. 영화에 대한 갑작스러운 수요 때문에, 마지막 상영이 8월 15일이 될 것이다. 개봉 이후 비평가들의 혹평을 고려해 보면, 이것은 모든 사람을 놀라게 만들었다. **또한, 초기 티켓 판매도 저조했다.** 하지만 그 영화는 애니메이션을 좋아하는 12세 미만의 아이들 사이에서 갑자기 인기를 얻었다. 그들은 분명히 영화의 줄거리와 캐릭터에 관심을 보였다.

(A) 게다가, 코웬 극장은 13년 전에 설립되었다.
(B) 또한, 초기 티켓 판매도 저조했다.
(C) 개막 전에는 지역 업주들의 참석이 뜨거웠다.
(D) 주연 배우들은 지역 주민들 출신이었다.

해설 지문 전체를 읽어봐야 하는 문장 삽입 문제로, 정답의 단서가 되는 부분은 빈칸 뒤에 나오는 however이다. however를 중심으로 뒤에는 인기를 얻었다는 긍정적 내용이 나오므로 앞에는 부정적인 내용이 나와야 하는데, 이미 poor reviews라는 부정적인 내용이 나왔기 때문에 더 추가하는 내용을 연결하는 Also가 들어가는 (B)가 정답이 된다.

2. 앞뒤 키워드를 찾는다.

Starting next Thursday, the company will be holding a training workshop for all new customer service staff on how to better serve customers. By doing so, we can meet our recently revised policies. -------. All relevant employees should register for the session by this Friday. Those who participate in the workshop can pick up a copy of the detailed workshop schedule in the employee cafeteria on the fifth floor at any time. Please check the company Web site for further updates.

(A) The same speakers as last time will be invited.
(B) All employees required to attend the event.
(C) The purpose of these policies is to better build relationships with customers.
(D) Unfortunately, the deadline for registration has passed.

다음 주 목요일부터, 회사에서 어떻게 하면 고객들을 더 잘 응대할 수 있을지에 대한 신입 고객서비스 담당 직원 교육 워크숍을 개최합니다. 워크숍을 함으로써, 최근에 수정된 방침들을 충족시킬 수 있게 됩니다. **이 정책의 목적은 고객과의 더 나은 관계 구축을 위한 것입니다.** 모든 관련된 직원들은 이번 주 금요일까지 등록하셔야 합니다. 참석하는 분들은 워크숍에 관한 상세한 스케줄을 5층에 있는 직원 휴게실에서 언제든 가져가실 수 있습니다. 또한, 더 자세한 업데이트는 회사 웹사이트를 확인해 주세요.

(A) 지난번과 같은 연사가 초대될 것입니다.
(B) 모든 직원은 그 행사에 의무적으로 참석해야 합니다.
(C) 이 정책의 목적은 고객과의 더 나은 관계 구축을 위한 것입니다.
(D) 유감스럽게도 등록 마감일이 지났습니다.

해설 빈칸 앞에서 recently revised policies '최근에 수정된 방침들'이 나와 있으므로, 방침들에 대한 구체적인 내용이 나와야 하므로 (C)가 적합하다. 키워드인 this, these와 같은 단어를 주의해서 보는 것도 답을 빠르게 찾을 수 있는 하나의 방법이다.

3. 보기를 하나씩 대입해서 오답을 소거한다.

Any employees who have been working full time for three years in Lawson Ltd. are eligible to apply for promotion and internal transfers. -------. Then candidates applying from outside the company will be considered. In-house applicants who have the necessary qualifications and skills will be given preference.

(A) We, Lawson Ltd., are happy to welcome new recruits.
(B) For instance, a competitive bonus will be given to full-time employees.
(C) In addition, all employees are encouraged to promote new products.
(D) Employees who are interested in applying should notify their immediate supervisor.

로슨 사에서 3년 동안 풀타임으로 일해온 직원들은 승진과 내부 인사이동에 지원할 자격이 됩니다. **지원하는 데 관심 있는 직원은 직속상관에게 보고해야 합니다.** 그러고 나서, 그들은 외부에서 지원한 이들과 함께 고려 대상이 될 것입니다. 필요한 자격요건과 기술을 가진 내부 지원자들에게는 우선권이 주어집니다.

(A) 저희 로슨 사는 신입사원을 환영합니다.
(B) 예를 들어, 경쟁적인 상여금은 풀타임 직원에게 주어질 것입니다.
(C) 또한, 전 직원이 신제품을 홍보할 것을 권장합니다.
(D) 지원하는 데 관심 있는 직원은 직속상관에게 보고해야 합니다.

해설 이 문제의 경우는 보기를 하나씩 대입해 본다. 빈칸의 앞 문장과 뒤 문장은 지원에 관한 이야기가 나오므로, 빈칸도 지원에 관련된 문장이 나와야 하는데, (A), (B), (C)는 지원과는 관련이 없어 소거시켜 정답은 '지원에 관심 있는 직원들은 직속상관에 보고해야 한다'는 의미의 (D)가 적합하다.

만점 포인트 2 지시어(대명사): 앞에 나오는 명사를 빨리 확인해라!

적중! 유형 정리

Next Wednesday, there will be technical crews from the maintenance team in the office setting up our new door entry system. It is mandatory that all employees set aside time that afternoon to register their personal identification code and scan their fingerprints into the new system. ------- will be required when arriving at work and leaving the office.

(A) Much
(B) Both
(C) Another
(D) Those

다음 주 수요일, 관리팀에서 새로운 출입 시스템을 설치할 기술자들이 사무실에 올 것입니다. 그날 오후에, 모든 직원들은 개인 신상 코드를 등록하고, 지문을 스캔하기 위한 시간을 꼭 비워두셔야 합니다. **이 두 가지는** 모두 출근과 퇴근 시에 필요합니다.

해설 빈칸 앞에서 언급한 personal identification code와 fingerprints를 받는 (B) Both가 정답이다.

만점 전략 앞 문맥에서 언급된 명사를 받는 대명사

❶ 빈칸 앞에 언급된 명사가 '단수'인지 '복수'인지를 확인한다.
❷ 가산 명사를 받는 부정대명사에는 another, every, each, many, both, all, several, a few가 있다.
❸ 불가산 명사를 받는 부정대명사에는 much, little, a little이 있다.
❹ 가산 / 불가산 명사를 모두 받는 부정대명사에는 some, any, most, all이 있다.

1 If you fail to deliver your e-mail, please check that the address you sent is correct and resend it. However, if constant pop-up errors continue to appear during transmission, it is possible that the problem can be an error in our system rather than the address you entered. If you are not able to send e-mail to ------- address, please contact our Customer Support Center immediately.

(A) their
(B) his
(C) other
(D) any

만약 이메일을 전송하는 데 실패했다면, 보낸 주소가 올바른지 확인하고 이메일을 다시 전송하세요. 하지만, 전송하는 동안에 계속해서 에러 메시지가 뜬다면, 아마도 주소를 잘못 입력했기보다는 우리 시스템의 문제일 가능성도 있습니다. 만약 귀하께서 이메일을 **어떤** 주소로도 보내실 수 없다면, 고객 지원 센터로 즉시 연락 주세요.

해설 빈칸 앞의 내용을 보면 '계속해서 에러가 뜨면 그건 시스템의 문제일 가능성이 있다'라고 하며, 어떠한 주소로 보내도 안된다면 연락을 달라는 의미로 '어떠한 ~라도'의 의미를 나타내는 (D)가 정답이 된다.

2

We are writing to let you know that our company is updating the new client directory to have the most recent contact information. This information includes your business address and office phone number. I'd appreciate if you review the attached e-mail, and let us know if ------- has changed.

(A) whatever
(B) anyone
(C) either
(D) another

저희 회사는 가장 최근 연락처를 포함하는 새 고객 주소록을 만들고 있다는 것을 알려드리려고 메일을 드립니다. 이 정보는 귀하의 사업체 주소와 사무실 전화번호를 포함합니다. 첨부된 이메일을 확인하시고, **둘 중 하나에** 변경사항이 있으시면 알려주시면 감사하겠습니다.

해설 빈칸은 주어 자리로 이미 접속사 if가 있으므로 접속사인 (A)는 들어갈 수 없으며, 앞에서 사업체 주소와 사무실 전화번호 두 가지 중에 변경사항이 있으면 알려달라고 했으므로, 두 가지의 의미를 나타내는 (C)가 적합하다.

3

Since the new system for reporting daily working hours was introduced last month, we have received many inquiries from staff members. To address the many questions we got, we have arranged two training sessions on Monday, April 5, at 10 A.M. and on Friday, April 9, at 2 P.M. Employees are not required to attend. For ------- who are interested in learning more about the newly introduced system, please contact Jullie Choi to request an appointment.

(A) that
(B) anyone
(C) those
(D) them

근무시간을 매일 보고하는 새 시스템이 지난달에 도입된 이후로, 직원들로부터 많은 질문을 받았습니다. 저희가 받은 많은 질문을 해결하기 위해서, 두 개의 교육 세션을 4월 5일 월요일 오전 10시와 4월 9일 금요일 오후 2시에 잡았습니다. 모든 직원들이 참석할 필요는 없습니다. 새로 도입된 시스템에 대해서 알고 싶으신 **분들은**, 예약하기 위해서 줄리 최에게 연락 주세요.

해설 who와 잘 쓰이는 anyone 또는 those who가 답이 될 수 있지만, anyone은 단수 취급, those는 복수 취급한다. '관심 있는 사람들'이란 의미가 되어야 하므로 people을 받는 대명사인 (C) those가 정답이 된다.

만점 포인트 3 시제: 빈칸 앞, 뒤 문장의 시제를 알려주는 단서를 찾아라!

적중! 유형 정리

From: Gonzales Rodrigues
To: Hasting Paper employees
Date: March 2

As you may know, Travis Lee is retiring after 25 years of service at Hasting Paper. In honor of his long career and his dedication to our company, the retirement party will be held on Friday, March 23 at 5 P.M.

I recommend that all suggestions about the parting gift ------- by Monday, March 19.

Please leave your ideas with my administrative assistant, Michelle Kim.

(A) makes
(B) will have made
(C) be made
(D) make

발신: 곤살레스 로드리게스
수신: 해스팅 페이퍼 직원들
날짜: 3월 2일

여러분들도 아시다시피, 트래비스 리는 해스팅 페이퍼에서 25년간 근무하시고 은퇴하십니다. 그의 오랜 근무와 회사에 대한 공헌에 감사하고자, 은퇴식이 3월 23일 금요일 오후 5시에 개최될 것입니다.

3월 19일 월요일까지 작별 선물로 어떤 것이 좋을지 의견 부탁드립니다.

제 비서인 미셸 김에게 의견을 남겨주세요.

해설 빈칸은 동사 자리로 주어가 all suggestions이고, 시제는 글 쓴 날짜가 3월 2일이고 3월 19일을 언급하기 때문에 미래 시제인 (B)를 고르지 않도록 조심해야 한다. 빈칸 앞에 recommend라는 동사가 나오고 that절이 나오면 뒤에 should가 생략된 동사원형이 나와야 하며, 뒤에 목적어가 아닌 전치사 by가 나왔으므로 빈칸은 수동태의 원형이 와야 한다. 따라서, 정답은 (C)가 된다. 「주장, 요구, 명령, 추천, 제안 동사(insist, ask, recommend, suggest) + that + 주어 + (should) + 동사원형」의 구문을 기억하자.

만점 전략 1 토익이 좋아하는 PART 6 빈출 시제, '현재 시제'

❶ 공연, 대중교통 등의 고정된 시간표나 일정은 현재 시제를 사용한다.
❷ 업무 등의 주기적, 일상적, 반복적인 일의 경우는 현재 시제를 사용한다.
❸ 확정된 미래, 정해진 사실, 진리, 상식, 규칙, 계약 등 문서화되는 내용은 현재 시제를 사용한다.
❹ 계약서, 품질보증서, 규칙 등 강제성을 가지고 있는 경우는 현재 시제를 사용한다.

One of the most well-known tour companies in the country, Best Travel Tours ------- in helping travelers to have an enjoyable travel experience. Every tour package includes transportation, guides, and complimentary lunch. If you have further questions, please contact operation manager Russell Kelly.

(A) specializes
(B) will specialize
(C) specialized
(D) specializing

우리나라에 가장 잘 알려진 여행사 중에 하나인 베스트 여행사는 여행객들이 즐거운 여행 경험을 할 수 있도록 도와주는 것을 **전문적으로 하고 있습니다**. 모든 여행 패키지는 교통, 가이드 및 무료 점심을 포함하고 있습니다. 만약 더 질문이 있으시면, 운영 매니저인 러셀 켈리에게 연락 주세요.

해설 베스트 여행사라는 회사가 제공하는 서비스는 사실을 설명하는 문장이기 때문에 현재 시제가 적합하므로 (A)가 정답이 된다.

만점 전략 2 토익이 좋아하는 PART 6 빈출 시제, '현재완료 시제'

현재완료는 과거에서 현재까지의 경험, 결과, 완료, 계속을 나타낸다.

I am writing to remind you that we ------- some feedback from our consumers regarding the recently released JCB cabinet. Most of these comments show that customers are frustrated because the cabinet door does not close properly.

(A) have received
(B) will receive
(C) receiving
(D) receive

최근에 출시된 JCB 캐비닛에 관해 고객들로부터 피드백을 **받았음을** 상기시키고자 글을 씁니다. 이 피드백 언급의 대부분은 고객들이 캐비닛 문이 완전히 닫히지 않아 당황해한 것을 보여주고 있습니다.

해설 빈칸은 동사 시제 문제로, 지문의 내용은 고객들로부터 피드백을 받았고 빈칸 다음 문장에서 피드백 내용에 대해 언급한다. 현재까지 영향을 미치는 현재완료가 적합하므로 정답은 (A)가 된다.

만점 전략 3 PART 6의 시제 문제는 빈칸 앞, 뒤의 시제 단서를 파악하자.

The Exotic Food Exhibition ------- to southern Williamstown on October 15. During the past five years, this popular event has gone on tour around the state from July to September. This year, the event coordinator decided to make more room for exhibitors. As planned, 25 more participants showed up to demonstrate a variety of tasty dishes.

(A) will come
(B) came
(C) comes
(D) was coming

이국적인 음식 전시회가 10월 15일 윌리엄스타운 남부에서 **개최되었다**. 지난 5년 동안, 이 유명한 이벤트는 7월부터 9월까지 주 전역을 순회했다. 올해, 이벤트 주최자는 전시자들을 위해 더 넓은 공간을 제공하기로 결정했다. 계획한 대로, 25명의 더 많은 전시 참가자가 여러 가지 맛있는 음식을 선보이기 위해 참가했다.

해설 '행사가 ~할 것 같다'라는 미래 시제를 쓰지 않도록 조심해야 한다. 중후반부의 decided to와 showed up을 통해서 알 수 있듯이, 이미 일어난 행사를 언급하므로 과거 시제인 (B)가 정답이 된다.

만점 포인트 4 연결 어구: 접속부사만 마스터해라!

적중! 유형 정리

You can rent our office for a four-hour time period during chosen hours of operation. The rent includes the exclusive use of the entire facility, including printer and copy machines. The rent for up to 15 people is $800 a month. You will be offered a 10 percent discount at our snack bar. -------, if you want, you can bring your own food as long as you get approval from the supervisor. Please let me know the specific date and time you would like so that we can make the reservation for you.

(A) Therefore
(B) For instance
(C) However
(D) Subsequently

선택한 운영 시간 동안에 4시간 정도 사무실을 렌트하실 수 있습니다. 렌트는 전체 시설을 독점으로 이용하실 수 있으며, 프린터와 복사기도 포함이 됩니다. 15명까지 렌트하는 비용은 한 달에 800달러입니다. 저희 스낵바를 이용하실 경우 10퍼센트 할인을 해드립니다. **하지만,** 만약 원하시면, 담당자의 허가가 있는 한 음식을 가지고 오셔도 됩니다. 예약을 해드리기 위해서 명확한 날짜와 시간을 알려주세요.

해설 빈칸을 중심으로 해서 앞 문장은 snack bar를 이용하는 것이고, 뒤에 나오는 문장은 본인의 음식을 가지고 오는 것이므로 상반된 연결 어구를 나타내는 (C) However가 정답이 된다.

만점 전략 1 PART 6에 매달 출제되는 연결 어구, '접속부사'

대표적인 연결 어구에는 '전치사, 접속사, 접속부사'가 있으며, PART 6에서 '접속부사' 문제는 매달 출제된다. 전체의 문맥을 보기보다는 앞뒤 문장 사이의 관계를 먼저 파악하는 것이 중요하다. 설사 해석으로 잘 파악했다 하더라도 접속부사 자리에 전치사나 접속사를 고르는 실수를 범하지 않도록 조심해야 한다.

1. 전치사 vs. 접속사 vs. 접속부사

보통 세 가지를 쉽게 구분하는 방법은 뒤에 무엇이 나오느냐의 문법적 쓰임에 따라 쉽게 결정된다.

전치사 + 명사 or 동명사
접속사 + 주어 + 동사
접속부사, + 주어 + 동사

2. 전치사 vs. 부사절 접속사

의미는 비슷하나, 문법적 쓰임이 다르므로 확실히 구분할 수 있도록 하자.

종류	전치사	부사절 접속사	의미
양보	despite, in spite of, notwithstanding	although, (even) though	비록 ~이지만
이유	because of, due to	because, as, since	~때문에
시간	during + 특정 기간, for + 기간 명사	while	~하는 동안
	prior to	before	~전에
	following	after	~후에

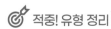

3. 접속부사

인과, 결과	therefore, thus, hence 그러므로, as a result 그 결과, in conclusion 결론적으로, consequently 결과적으로, for this reason 이러한 이유로, accordingly 따라서, namely 즉, 다시 말해
부가, 추가	also 또한, in addition, additionally, moreover, furthermore, besides 게다가, 더욱이
역접, 대조, 양보	however 그러나, on the contrary 그와는 반대로, on the other hand 반면에, if not, otherwise 그렇지 않으면, even so 그렇다 하더라도, unfortunately 안타깝게도, nevertheless, nonetheless 그럼에도 불구하고, in the mean time 그동안에, 한편
대신, 대안	instead 대신에, alternatively 대안으로
강조	in particular, particularly 특히, in fact, in deed 사실상
순서	previously, formerly 이전에, afterwards 그 이후에, since then 그때 이후로
예시	for example, for instance 예를 들어
기타	if so 그렇다면, if possible 가능하면, likewise 마찬가지로

1 I would like to remind you that we will retake an advertisement featuring horses at Thomas Ranch on Friday. ------- the policies outlined in our contract, we will not charge any fees for retaking. When filming animals, we have to be ready for any unexpected situations. Unfortunately, even though we are well aware of that, we were previously not able to film the scene we needed. If possible, I would like to start at 7:00 A.M. so that we can film the scene from various angles before lunch.

(A) Otherwise
(B) Under the circumstances
(C) In accordance with
(D) However

우리가 금요일에 토마스 랜치에서 말이 등장하는 광고를 재촬영해야 할 것을 상기시켜드리려고 합니다. 우리 계약서에 나온 조항에 **따라**, 우리는 재촬영에 대해서 어떠한 금액도 청구하지 않을 것입니다. 동물을 촬영할 때, 예상치 못한 상황에 준비해야 합니다. 유감스럽게도, 그것을 모두 인지했음에도 불구하고 우리가 필요했던 장면을 못 찍었습니다. 가능하면 오전 7시부터 시작해서 점심시간 전에 여러 가지 각도에서 촬영할 수 있게 하고 싶습니다.

해설 policies라는 명사 앞에 들어가는 전치사 문제로 (A), (B), (D)는 접속부사 자리에 들어가는 부사 역할을 하므로 오답으로 제거하면 전치사 (C)가 남는다. 해석상으로도 '~에 따라'가 적합하므로 (C) In accordance with가 정답이 된다.

2 Richard Clements, CEO of GX Automobile in Detroit, announced yesterday that its innovative technology will make electric vehicles more attractive will produce longer lasting batteries. Mr. Clements predicts the number of electric cars in GX Automobile will more than double in the coming years. -------, he believes that in 10 years only electric cars will be sold here in Detroit.

(A) Nonetheless
(B) In fact
(C) As a result of
(D) Even if

디트로이트에 있는 GX 자동차의 최고 경영자인 리처드 클레멘츠는 회사의 혁신적인 기술이 전기차를 더 매력적이고, 오래가는 배터리를 만들게 해줄 것이라고 어제 발표했다. 클레멘츠 씨는 다가오는 해에는 GX 자동차의 전기차 숫자가 두 배가 넘을 것으로 예상한다. 실제로, 그는 10년 후에는 디트로이트에서 전기차만 팔릴 것이라고 믿는다.

해설 빈칸은 접속부사 자리로, 보기에서 전치사인 (C) As a result of와 접속사인 (D) Even if를 제외하면 (A)와 (B)가 남는다. 해석상 앞에 나와있는 것을 구체적으로 강조 설명하는 In fact가 적합하므로 (B)가 정답이 된다.

3

Effective June 1, Katsuro Shoes will implement a new policy regarding refunds. We guarantee that our customers can get a full refund for unused items purchased at our store. Items may be returned within a month of purchase and refunded ------- they are unopened or show no signs of wear.

(A) moreover
(B) provided
(C) in particular
(D) whereas

6월 1일부로, 카츠로 슈즈는 환불에 관한 새로운 방침을 시행할 것입니다. 저희는 고객님들이 저희 가게에서 구매한 사용하지 않은 물건에 대해 전액 환불받을 수 있게 보장합니다. 물건은 구매한지 한 달 안에 교환할 수 있으며, 사용하지 않았거나 개봉되지 않은 물건**이라면** 환불할 수 있습니다.

해설 빈칸은 주어와 동사(it shows) 앞에 들어가는 접속사 자리이다. 따라서, 접속부사 자리에 들어갈 수 있는 (A)와 (C)가 오답이다. 해석상 '~한다면'의 조건의 의미가 들어가야 하므로 (B) provided (that)가 정답이 된다.

MEMO

고난도 실전 문제

Questions 1-4 refer to the following e-mail.

To: Triton Jackson <tjackson@strategiescomn.org>
From: Amy Torres <atorres@torresmanufacturing.com>
Date: May 7
Subject: April 30 Workshop

Dear Mr. Jackson,

I would like to share our -------(1.) for the workshop Anita Huxley led at our headquarters on April 30. Several employees -------(2.) their concerns about the usefulness of the workshop. However, they participated actively throughout the day and even asked about whether there will be follow-up sessions. We requested that participants fill out our firm's evaluation form -------(3.) in order to better evaluate the effectiveness of the workshop. Mostly, the results are very positive, with 89 percent of participants reporting that their communication skills have become stronger. -------(4.). Please contact me if you would like to talk about the workshop in more detail.

Best regards,

Amy Torres

1. (A) appreciate
   (B) appreciative
   (C) appreciated
   (D) appreciation

2. (A) express
   (B) is expressing
   (C) were to be expressed
   (D) had expressed

3. (A) afterwards
   (B) often
   (C) since
   (D) instead

4. (A) The workshop will be held again later in the week.
   (B) A few participants mentioned the workshop would have been more useful with practices included.
   (C) Another workshop in team building is occasionally provided.
   (D) We will offer you an invoice requesting a payment.

Questions 5-8 refer to the following letter.

Morrison Bakery
12 Main Street
Broadway, New York 31034

Dear Customers,

Over the last two years, we have offered our baked goods, including cakes, pies, cookies, and brownies, at low prices. We regret to inform you that soaring costs for ingredients, such as yeast and sugar, have compelled us to increase our prices by 7 percent, -------(5.) July 1. We have made all possible efforts not to increase our prices so far. -------(6.), we never want to compromise on the quality of our baked goods. Using the best ingredients available on the market will enable us to offer delicious desserts that meet your expectations. -------(7.). We appreciate your -------(8.) and look forward to serving you the best quality products.

Sincerely,

Tony Corelli, Owner

5. (A) actual
(B) promising
(C) practical
(D) effective

6. (A) Similarly
(B) Therefore
(C) However
(D) Accordingly

7. (A) We think you will find that our products are still of great value.
(B) Our efforts to stay profitable have failed.
(C) We hope our competitors will raise their prices as well.
(D) Our products are much healthier than traditional baked goods.

8. (A) supportive
(B) support
(C) supporter
(D) supports

고난도 실전 문제

Questions 9-12 refer to the following excerpt from a manual.

This manual contains procedures for quality control at Tuckman Inc. Our up-to-date manufacturing system relies on ------- (9.) quality control. Only by keeping an accurate monitoring system ------- (10.) minimize unnecessary costs and meet customer satisfaction. To achieve this goal, we must avoid defects. When items are delivered in good condition, we can reduce costs for returns and exchanges. ------- (11.). Therefore, all the processes need to be correctly ------- (12.).

9. (A) precise
(B) seasonal
(C) extensive
(D) mechanized

10. (A) is able to
(B) to be able
(C) our ability to
(D) are we able to

11. (A) It will take at least seven days for shipment.
(B) Unfortunately, some products are damaged.
(C) However, this might not be possible if unexpected defects occur.
(D) We could estimate the costs for you.

12. (A) implemented
(B) revised
(C) extended
(D) copied

Questions 13-16 refer to the following letter.

1 April
Ricky Howe
3519 Patrick Rd.
Toronto, ON 4877

The Jessop Community Association (JCA) is pleased to ------- (13.) that its annual Spring Festival, will be held at Central Park on April 30 from 3 P.M. to 9 P.M. This event will feature a variety of exciting activities and a tasty barbecue dinner that will be offered at 6 P.M. Visitors must pay a $10 entrance fee. The proceeds from the event will ------- (14.) go towards a park renovation project. This project will include hiring a construction company to remodel the park, and the remaining funds will be used for a city cleaning campaign.

This special event ------- (15.) to be a lot of fun. ------- (16.).

Regards,

Justin Charles
Director, The Jessop Community Association (JCA)

13. (A) announce
(B) comment
(C) remember
(D) state

14. (A) entirely
(B) often
(C) primarily
(D) together

15. (A) promise
(B) promises
(C) promising
(D) promised

16. (A) You are welcome to help by disposing of all garbage.
(B) The park is nearly 75 years old.
(C) We hope you will be able to join us.
(D) Central Park attracts over 15,000 visitors annually.

PART 7

PART 7은 모든 수험자들이 어려워하는 파트이다. 800점대 이하의 대부분의 학생들의 경우에는 시간 부족으로 마지막 3~4지문, 즉 15~20 문제 정도를 전혀 풀지 못한 채 시험이 끝나는 경우가 허다하다. 800점이 넘는 학생들의 경우라 하더라도 1~2지문을 풀지 못하거나, 문제를 모두 풀었다 하더라도 정확도가 떨어져서 점수로 잘 이어지지 않는 경우가 종종 있다. RC 고득점을 위해서는 PART 5&6를 빠르고 정확하게 풀어야 하는 것이 가장 중요하며, 그렇게 절약한 시간을 PART 7에 안배해야 한다. 독해의 경우는 충분한 시간이 주어진다면 문제를 다 풀 수 있으며, 이는 고득점으로 이어질 수 있기 때문에 시간 관리 전략을 잘 세워야 한다.

RC 100 문제에서 보통 PART 5&6(46 문제)를 15분 내에 해결하고, PART 7의 경우에는 단일 지문(29 문제)은 30분 내에, 이삼중 지문(25 문제)은 25분 내에 풀어야 한다. 그렇게 되면 70분 내에 모든 문제를 풀고 여유롭게 마킹까지 할 수가 있다. 즉, 토익 고득점으로의 관건은 PART 5&6의 빠른 속도와 정확한 문제 풀이로 생긴 시간을 PART 7에 최대한 활용하여 정확도를 높이는 것이다.

DAY 07

LC	DAY 01	DAY 02	DAY 03	DAY 04	DAY 05	DAY 06	DAY 07
RC	DAY 01	DAY 02	DAY 03	DAY 04	DAY 05	DAY 06	**DAY 07**

PART 7 만점 핵심 공략

- PART 7의 정답은 지문 안에 있다. 독해 4독을 통한 정확도를 높이자!
- 무조건 많이 읽는다고 좋은 게 아니다. 시험에 나오는 빈출 유형을 알고 익히자.
- PART 7의 고득점은 패러프레이징이 정답이다.
- PART 7은 어휘력, 빠르고 정확한 독해력, 집중력 이 세 박자가 다 갖춰져야 한다.

PART 7

DAY 07

PART 7으로 고득점 거듭나기!

동영상 강의 바로 보기

PART 7 고득점을 얻기 위해서는 다독이 중요하다. 하지만, 출제 유형과 출제자의 의도를 모른 채 양으로만 승부하려 하지 말고 시험에 출제되는 독해 부분을 여러 번 읽음으로써(독해 4독) 응용력을 키우는 게 단기간에 PART 7 고득점을 받는 가장 바람직한 공부 방법이다.

만점 포인트

이것만 알면 만점!

1 독해 이렇게 공부해라.
2 시험 전 알아야 할 독해 십계명
3 동의어 & 패러프레이징
4 단일 지문 & 이삼중 지문

만점 포인트 1 독해 이렇게 공부해라.

만점 전략 1 공부 전, 이것만 명심하자!

1. 독해의 기본은 '패러프레이징(paraphrasing)'이다.

영어에서는 어휘 반복을 좋아하지 않는다. 지문에 나온 어휘나 표현을 동의어 또는 비슷한 표현으로 바꿔서(패러프레이징) 질문에서 출제된다. 그러므로 평소에 시험에 자주 출제되는 동의어와 비슷한 표현을 공부해 두자.

예) a receipt from the hospital = a proof of treatment

2. 정답은 반드시 '지문 안'에 있다. (지문 속 키워드 파악)

다른 공인 영어 시험에 비해서 토익 독해가 비교적 쉬운 이유는 지문 속에 정답의 근거가 모두 있다는 것이다. 그렇다면 왜 점수로 이어지지 않을까? 첫 번째는 시간이 부족해서이며, 두 번째는 시간 부족으로 인해 성급하게 답을 찾거나 확대 해석해서 답을 찾는 경우이며, 세 번째는 전체 지문을 이해할 수 있는 능력이 부족해서이다. 또한, 설사 정답의 근거 문장을 찾았다고 하더라도 패러프레이징 표현을 알지 못하면 오답을 고를 수 있다.

3. 문제를 푸는 효과적인 순서가 있다.

처음부터 무턱대고 지문을 읽어 내려가는 것이 아니라, 먼저 '지문의 유형'을 확인한다. 예를 들어, 이메일과 기사는 지문 논리 전개 방식이 다르므로 평소에 지문 유형별 전략을 파악해두면 도움이 된다. 두 번째로는 문제를 먼저 읽고 그 문제에서 '고유명사'나 '키워드'를 먼저 파악한다. 세 번째로는 파악한 고유명사나 키워드를 의식하면서 지문을 읽어 내려간다. 마지막으로는 지문을 다 읽고 문제를 풀이하는 것이 아니라, 지문을 읽어 내려가면서 동시에 문제를 같이 풀어야 한다.

지문 유형 확인 → 문제 유형 확인 → 지문 읽기 → 문제 풀이 (지문 읽으면서 번갈아 문제 풀기)

만점 전략 2 독해 이렇게 공부하라! (독해 4독)

독해를 잘하는 방법으로 많은 지문을 읽고 문제를 풀어보는 다독이 중요하지만, 단기간 안에 독해 고득점을 받기 위한 가장 좋은 방법 중에 하나는 시험에 자주 출제되는 지문의 유형을 반복해서 읽음으로써 토익 출제자의 의도를 파악하는 것이 중요하다.

1. 시간 안에 풀기(실제 시험처럼 문제를 푼다.)

시간 안배는 단일 지문은 30분, 이삼중 지문은 25분이며, 단일 지문의 경우에는 한 지문당 3분, 이삼중 지문의 경우에는 한 세트를 5분 안에 풀어야 한다. 초과되는 시간은 늘 기록해 두자.

2. 근거 찾기(한번 보고 두 번 보고 자꾸 봐서 근거를 찾아라!)

답지를 보고 바로 채점하지 말고, 다시 한번 읽으면서 질문의 근거가 되는 부분을 밑줄이나 형광펜으로 색깔을 달리해서 표시해 보자. 1번에서 2번으로 가는 단계가 굉장히 중요하다. 예컨대, 문제를 처음 풀었을 때는 정답을 (A)로 선택했는데, 다시 읽고 근거를 찾아보니 답이 (B)라면 왜 처음에 (A)로 답을 잘못했는지를 체크해 봐야 한다. 이를 파악해야 다음에는 보완해서 정답을 빠르게 찾을 수 있기 때문이다.

3. 문장 분석(독해 지문에 쓰인 문법과 어휘를 토대로 문장 분석을 익혀라!)

세 번째 읽을 때는 전체적인 지문의 내용보다는 지문 내에 쓰인 문법과 어휘를 신경 쓰면서 읽어 내려간다. 예를 들어, help라는 준사역동사가 쓰이면 뒤에는 동사원형이 나오고, conduct라는 동사는 survey와 잘 쓰임을 확인하면서 읽어 내려가다 보면 PART 5&6도 자연스럽게 학습할 수 있는 일석이조의 효과를 볼 수 있다. PART 5&6 문제는 PART 7에서 발췌해서 빈칸을 내는 경우가 대부분이므로 PART 7을 공부함과 동시에 PART 5&6도 유기적으로 공부할 수 있다.

4. 배경 상식(지문 유형에 따라 잘 나오는 내용이 따로 있다.)

토익 공부를 오래 한 학생이라면 알고 있겠지만, 토익에 출제되는 독해 내용은 반복되어서 출제되는 경우가 많다. 예컨대, '이메일'에서 자주 출제되는 내용은 '불평, 불만, 회의 변경' 등이며, 지문 유형에 따라 논리 전개도 비슷하므로 지문의 내용과 논리 전개를 다시 한번 생각하며 정리를 해나가다 보면, 실제 시험에서 유사한 문제가 나왔을 때 공부했던 배경지식을 바탕으로 답을 쉽게 찾을 수 있게 된다.

시간 맞춰 풀기 → 근거 찾기 → 문장 분석 → 배경 상식

Questions 1-2 refer to the following memo.

To: All employees at KC Sports Complex
From: Michael Taylor, General Manager
Subject: Renovation

I would like to remind you that the planned renovations to the sports complex will commence next month.

The first phase of the renovation will be completed by mid-May. There will be a second and final phase of renovations from early July to late September. Please note that we will be closing for two weeks, beginning on September 2.

We are confident that you will enjoy the new facilities. Also, we apologize in advance for any inconveniences caused during the renovation period.

1-2번은 다음 회람에 관한 문제입니다.

수신: KC 종합 운동장의 전 직원
발신: 총무부장 마이클 테일러
제목: 수리

여러분에게 예정되었던 **종합운동장의 보수공사가 다음 달에 시작될 것임을** 알려드리고자 합니다.

보수의 첫 단계는 5월 중순까지 완료될 것입니다. 두 번째 및 마지막 단계의 수리는 7월 초부터 9월 말까지 있을 것입니다. 9월 2일부터 시작해서 2주 동안은 문을 닫게 됨을 유의하세요.

새 시설을 좋아하시리라 확신합니다. 그리고 수리 기간 동안에 야기되는 불편함에 대해 미리 사과드립니다.

1. What is the purpose of the memo?

(A) To inform staff of the upcoming building remodeling
(B) To announce the completion of building work
(C) To explain the new facilities
(D) To apologize for the cause of the renovation

2. When are all the renovations due to be finished?

(A) By mid-May
(B) By early July
(C) By late September
(D) By early September

1. 회람의 목적은 무엇인가?
(A) 곧 있을 건물 보수공사에 대해 직원들에게 공지하기 위해서
(B) 건물 작업이 끝났음을 공지하기 위해서
(C) 새로운 시설을 설명하기 위해서
(D) 보수공사의 원인을 사과하기 위해서

2. 모든 보수공사가 언제 끝나는가?
(A) 5월 중순
(B) 7월 초
(C) 9월 말
(D) 9월 초

해설 **1.** 글의 목적은 첫 번째 단락에서 거의 좌우된다. 보수공사가 다음 달에 시작된다는 것을 공지하는 글이므로 renovation의 패러프레이징 remodeling이 들어가는 정답은 (A)가 된다.

2. 두 번째 단락에 9월 말에 끝난다는 말이 있으므로 정답은 (C)가 된다.

독해 지문 문제풀이 순서

1단계 지문 유형 파악

글의 지문 유형은 '회람'이다. 제목(subject)과 더불어 보내는 사람과 받는 사람을 확인한다.

2단계 문제 유형 파악

두 가지 문제가 출제되어, 1번은 글의 목적(주로 첫 번째 문단에 답이 있을 것이며), 2번은 보수공사가 언제 끝나는지 물어보는 세부정보 문제이다.

3단계 지문 읽으면서 문제 풀기

첫 문장을 읽으면서 the planned renovation ~ 1번 문제인 renovation을 remodeling으로 패러프레이징한 (A)를 답으로 고른다. 계속 읽으면서 두 번째 문단의 There will be ~ late September를 통해서 늦은 9월인 (C)를 답으로 고른다.

독해 4독 적용

1단계 시간 안에 풀기

시간 안에 답을 고른다.

2단계 근거 찾기

답의 근거가 되는 문장을 밑줄 혹은 형광펜으로 표시한다.

3단계 문장 분석

읽으면서 문법과 어휘를 확인한다. 예를 들어, remind라는 동사는 목적어 다음에 that을 취하는 동사로 쓰이며, commence는 자동사이기 때문에 뒤에 목적어가 올 수 없다.

4단계 배경 상식

'회람 글'로써, 보내는 사람과 받는 사람을 확인하면서 회사 내에서 보내는 회람이라는 것을 확인한다. 이러한 회람 글의 논리 전개는 첫 번째 문단에서 회사 보수공사가 진행할 것이라는 것을 알린다. 두 번째 문단에서는 주로 보수공사에 대한 구체적인 내용이 언급된다(보수공사 이유, 공사 기간, 시작 날짜, 끝나는 날짜). 마지막 문단은 주로 보수공사에 대한 질문이나 요청 혹은 불편함에 대한 사과로 마무리한다. 지문 유형별로 논리 전개 방식과 내용의 배경 상식을 이해하면 추후에 비슷한 지문이 나왔을 때 쉽게 응용할 수가 있다.

만점 포인트 2 시험 전 알아야 할 독해 십계명

1. 글을 쓴 목적(주제)만 알아도 독해의 반은 해결! (매회 7~8 문제)

❶ 이메일: 제목(Subject, Re:)을 주목하라!

❷ 회람(Memo), 편지(Letter), 공지문(Notice)이면 다음을 주목하라!

– I am writing to ~, This letter is to ~, I am pleased to ~, Thank you ~

– inform, notify, should, must, announce, confirm

❸ 반전(but, however, unfortunately, by the way)을 주목하라!

2. '요청 문제'는 주로 후반부에 정답이 있다. (매회 2~4 문제)

❶ 명령문(Please ~)을 주목하라!

❷ You must / should, I would like you to, Would you ~?, Why don't you ~? 등의 표현을 주목하라!

❸ recommend, hope, want, expect, require, encourage 단어를 주목하라!

3. 'NOT 문제'는 여기를 조심해서 보자! (매회 2~4 문제)

❶ 숫자, 날짜, 기호가 열거된 곳에 답이 있다.

❷ 등위 접속사(and, as well as, but)를 조심하자!

❸ '추가'를 나타내는 접속부사(moreover, in addition, also)를 주목하라!

4. '추론 문제'는 나중에 풀어라! (매회 3~5 문제)

❶ 시간이 많이 걸리는 추론 문제(indicate, imply, suggest, mention, true가 나오는 문제)는 나중에 풀어라!

❷ 질문의 키워드를 파악한 후 지문을 의식하며 읽어라!

❸ 확대 해석해서 느낌이나 감으로 정답을 찾지 마라!

❹ 지문에서 본 단어가 그대로 보기에 나왔다고 해서 바로 정답을 체크하지 말자!

5. '고유명사' 문제는 거저 주는 문제다! (매회 4~6 문제)

❶ 문제에서 고유명사(사람 / 지명 / 회사 이름)를 먼저 파악하고, 지문에 미리 표시하라!

❷ 표시된 고유명사를 의식하면서 읽어 내려가라!

❸ 고유명사를 서로 헷갈리지 말자! (남자를 여자로, 여자를 남자로 착각하지 말자!)

6. '방법, 연락처, 수단'에 관련된 정답은 지문 후반부에 있다. (매회 1~3 문제)

❶ how 유형은 연락처, 할인, 예약, 참가, 구매 방법 등을 묻는 문제이다.

❷ 답이 뻔하게 나오는 문제로 가장 빨리 풀 수 있는 문제이다.

❸ if 조건절과 by -ing, to부정사(~하기 위해서)가 있는 부분을 유심히 봐라!

7. '동의어 어휘 문제'는 무조건 동의어를 찍지 말자. (매회 1~2 문제)

❶ 사전적 동의어로 풀 수 있는 문제가 있다. **ex** survey 설문조사 – questionnaire

❷ 문맥을 통해서 풀 수 있는 문제가 있다. **ex** assess 평가하다 – analyze 분석하다

❸ 다의어 즉, 여러 가지 의미를 가지고 있지만 지문에서 쓰인 의미를 묻는 경우도 있다.

ex case 상황, 사건, 용기, 사례

8. '동봉, 첨부 문제'는 지문 전체를 읽지 않아도 쉽게 풀 수 있는 문제다. (매회 0~2 문제)

❶ Enclosed, Attached, Included '동봉된 / 첨부된 / 포함된'로 시작하는 단어를 주목하라!

❷ 지문 중후반부에 답이 있다.

❸ be provided, be sent with, come with, along with 단어를 주목하라!

9. 이삼중 지문: 날짜, 숫자, 종류 열거, 사람이 나오면 연계 지문 문제이다. (매회 8~10 문제)

❶ 보기에서 날짜, 숫자, 종류나 사람 이름이 열거되어 있으면 90% 이상은 연계 지문 문제이다.

❷ 다섯 문제 중 거의 네 번째, 다섯 번째 문제가 연계 지문 문제일 가능성이 높다.

❸ 지문 하나에서 답을 성급하게 고르지 말고, 연계해서 문제를 풀어라!

10. 제일 마지막 하단에 나와있는 부분도 간과하지 말자! (매회 0~2 문제)

❶ 제일 하단에 폰트가 작은 글씨로 되어 있는 부분도 간과하지 말자!

❷ 설문조사 제일 하단에 comment 부분은 반드시 정답으로 출제된다.

❸ NOTE, *로 표시한 부분은 주목해서 보자!

❹ 제약이나 제한적인 어휘(only, limited, not all, all)를 조심하자!

❺ 상기 또는 강조하는 부분(please remember, don't forget, don't miss)에 정답이 있다.

만점 포인트 3 동의어 & 패러프레이징

만점 전략 1 동의어

1. 동의어의 3가지 유형

❶ '사전적 의미의 동의어'를 찾는 유형이 있다. **ex** free 무료 – complimentary

❷ 해당 지문에서 사용된 '문맥과의 조화'를 보고 찾는 유형이 있다. **ex** locate 위치를 찾아내다 – find

❸ 한 단어에 여러 가지 의미가 있는 '다의어' 유형이 있다. **ex** term – 조건, 기간, 용어

2. 동의어 문제 풀이법

❶ 성급하게 사전적인 의미 그대로의 동의어를 고르지 않도록 주의한다.

❷ 주어진 어휘를 포함하는 문장을 정확하게 해석해서, 문맥에 어울리는 것을 정답으로 찾는다.

❸ 혹시 모르는 어휘이거나 뜻이 애매한 경우는, 보기를 하나씩 대입해서 답을 찾아본다.

3. 동의어 문제 유형

In order to gain a competitive **advantage** over rival companies in Beijing, Colton Inc. decided to construct a new manufacturing facility there.

(A) market
(B) edge
(C) boundary
(D) urgency

베이징에 있는 다른 경쟁업체들보다 경쟁적 우위를 얻기 위해서, 코튼 사는 새로운 공장을 건설하기로 결정했다.

해설 '~보다 경쟁적으로 우위'라는 표현으로 competitive advantage over에서 advantage 대신 edge로도 바꿔서 쓸 수 있으므로 정답은 (B)가 된다.

4. 동의어 출제 패턴

consent 동의, 허가	permission, approval
outstanding 뛰어난	excellent, exceptional
decline 감소 / 거절하다	decrease, reject, turn down
keep 유지하다, 보유하다	retain, maintain
entry 출품작	submission to contest
locate 위치하다, 위치를 찾아내다	find
serve 제공하다, 근무하다	provide, act to work

만점 전략 2 패러프레이징

1. 패러프레이징 문제 유형

Forte Co. acquired Lorenza Inc. to strengthen its position in the computer software market.

(A) Lorenza Inc. was purchased by Forte Co. to reinforce its status in the industry.

(B) Forte Co. bought Lorenza Inc. in order to make it the largest manufacturer in the industry.

포르테 사는 컴퓨터 소프트웨어 시장에서 입지를 공고히 하기 위해서 로렌자 사를 인수했다.

해설 acquire '인수하다'의 패러프레이징으로 purchase가 나왔으며, strengthen '강화하다' its position의 패러프레이징으로 reinforce its status가 나온 정답은 (A)가 된다.

2. 패러프레이징 출제 패턴

be held every Monday 매주 월요일에 열리다	take place once a week 일주일에 한 번 열리다
refer to the attached schedule 첨부된 스케줄을 참조하다	consult the enclosed document 동봉된 서류를 참고하다
register for the workshop early 워크숍에 미리 등록하다	advance registration 사전 등록
move headquarters to New York 본사를 뉴욕으로 옮기다	relocate the main office to New York 본사를 뉴욕으로 이전하다
previously owned car 이전에 소유되었던 차	used car, second-hand car 중고차
a receipt from the hospital 병원 영수증	a proof of treatment 치료 증명서
last a long time 오래가다	durability 내구성
acquire NBS Manufacturing NBS 제조업을 인수하다	purchase a company 회사를 매입하다
confidential document 기밀 문서	sensitive material 민감한 자료

3. 시험에 자주 출제되는 패러프레이징 100선

1. 광고	flyer, post, advertisement, ads, commercial, publicity
2. 구입 / 구매하다, 인수합병하다	buy, purchase, acquire, merge, buyout
3. 거절하다	decline, reject, turn down
4. 할인	discount, reduced rates, sale, savings, ~% off, markdown, discounted price
5. 해외	overseas, international, abroad, worldwide, all over the world
6. 보수 공사	remodeling, renovation, redesign, upgrade, change, improvement
7. 시작하다, 효력을 발생하다	begin, start, initiate, kick off, launch, commence, initiate, effective + 날짜
8. 평가하다	assess, evaluate, review, critique
9. 돈, 자금	fund, funding, money, budget, finance
10. 추가의	additional, extra, more, further
11. 소득, 수입	income, revenue, earnings
12. 무료 견적	free quote, free estimate
13. 증가하다	increase, rise, surge, double, soar

14. 회사	firm, company, corporate, enterprise, business
15. 돈을 대다	finance, sponsor, fund, pay
16. 무료의	free, complimentary, at no charge / cost
17. 송장, 명세서	invoice, receipt, bill, statement
18. 설문조사	survey, market research, questionnaire, feedback, opinion, input, view
19. 생산 시설, 공장	production facility, factory, plant, manufacturing facility
20. 본사	headquarters, main offices, head office, ~ based
21. 가격이 합리적인, 저렴한	cheap, less expensive, affordable, low-cost, reasonable, moderate, competitive
22. 질긴, 오래가는	durable, outlast, long-lasting
23. 계약	contract, agreement
24. 식당	restaurant, bistro, cafeteria, dining establishment, eatery, eating establishment
25. 책자, 안내서	brochure, pamphlet, booklet, handbook, manual, instructions
26. 폐업하다	go out of business, shut down, close down, go bankrupt, discontinue, halt its operation, stop
27. 차량	vehicle, car, transportation
28. 대회	tournament, competition, contest
29. 환불하다	refund, money back, issue a refund
30. 사교 모임	party, function, social gathering, reception
31. 들르다	drop by, come by, stop by, visit
32. 자격 요건	qualification, prerequisite, must, necessary
33. 의사 전달 기술	communication skills, interact with others, interpersonal skills
34. 생산(량)	output, production, yield
35. 기부(금)	donation, (financial) contribution
36. 옷	apparel, clothing, garment, attire
37. 1년에 2번	twice a year, once every six months, biannual
38. 미리	ahead of time, beforehand, in advance, early
39. 정교한, 복잡한	elaborate, sophisticated, detailed, complicated, complex
40. 용기주다, 격려하다	encourage, motivate, promote
41. 노력하다, 애쓰다	endeavor, strive, try, struggle
42. (가치) 높이다, 강화하다	enhance, improve, strengthen, elevate
43. 거대한	enormous, huge, vast, tremendous, immense
44. 보증 / 확실히 하다	ensure, guarantee, promise
45. 특히	especially, notably, specifically
46. 중요한	essential, crucial, vital, important, fundamental
47. 설립 / 확립하다	establish, institute, organize, found, set up
48. 분명한, 명백한	evident, apparent, clear, obvious
49. 조사, 검사	examine, inspect, investigate
50. 능가 / 월등하다	exceed, go beyond, surpass, excel
51. 뛰어난	excellent, outstanding, exceptional

52. 실현가능한, 있을법한	feasible, possible
53. 작은, 미세한, 섬세한	fine, tiny, delicate
54. 충족시키다	meet, satisfy, fulfill, accommodate, suit, fit
55. 측정 / 평가하다	measure, gauge, judge, assess, analyze
56. 위험한, 모험적인	hazardous, dangerous, risky
57. 유지하다, 지속하다	maintain, keep, retain, sustain
58. 첨부하다	attach, send, enclose, include
59. 온라인, 인터넷	Web site, internet, online, www.~, digital, electronic
60. 인수하다, 떠맡다	take over, assume, undertake
61. 이사가다, 이전하다	move, transfer, relocate
62. 조사하다, 검토하다	examine, study, look into, review, look over, go over
63. 연기하다	delay, set back, postpone, put off, defer
64. 임원, 경영진	executives, management, administration, CEO, Vice President
65. 중고의	used, secondhand, pre-owned
66. 수용하다	accommodate, hold, lodge, board
67. 오직	only, just, solely, exclusively
68. 회사 동료	coworker, colleague, companion, associate
69. 상품	product, merchandise, goods, commodity
70. 담당하다, 책임지다	be responsible for, be in charge of, take care of
71. 다루다	cover, handle, deal with, address
72. 최신의	newest, brand-new, all new, latest
73. 상당한 할인, 상당히 할인된	huge discount, substantial discount, heavily discounted
74. 공개하다, 폭로하다, 출시하다	unveil, release, show, disclose, launch
75. 맞춤 제작의	custom-made, made-to-order, customized, tailored, individualized, one-of-a-kind
76. 제출하다	submit, turn in, hand in, present, forward, send
77. 특별 할인	special discount, special deal, special offer, promotional offer
78. 연설하다	make a delivery / presentation, deliver a speech / talk
79. 다양한	a variety of, a wide range / selection of, diverse, various
80. 현장에서	on site, on-the-spot, on the premises
81. 유명한	known, popular, well-known, renowned, famous
82. 준비하다	arrange, prepare, make arrangements
83. 매력적인	attractive, eye-catching, inviting
84. 책임	responsibility, obligation, role, duty
85. 수정하다	change, revise, modify, update
86. 서류	paper, document, file, certificate, certification
87. 요구사항	requirement, necessity, prerequisite
88. 즉시	immediately, promptly, instantly
89. 할당하다	allot, allocate, assign
90. 참조하다	refer to, consult, lookup
91. 사진	photograph, picture, image
92. 지키다, 준수하다	comply with, adhere to, conform to, observe

93. 실행하다, 실시하다	conduct, implement, execute, carry out, put into action
94. 보여주다	show, reveal, present
95. 포함하는	including, involving, containing
96. 이전의	previous, former, prior
97. 위임하다, 대표자	delegate, delegation, give an authority, representative
98. 단점	disadvantage, drawbacks, flaw, fault, shortcomings, demerits
99. 기록, 정보, 수치	data, figure, record, information
100. 배부하다	hand out, distribute, give out, pass out

1

Vernon Entertainment is pleased to have such a dedicated group of employees join our growing firm. Over the next few weeks, we hope that you will become familiar with the requirements and policies. Please note that any computer-related issues are handled by our Technical Department, so if you have any problems, please contact them directly. They can be reached at extension 810.

버논 엔터테인먼트는 헌신적인 직원들이 **성장하는** 회사에 합류하게 된 것을 기쁘게 생각합니다. 향후 몇 주간에 걸쳐서, 귀하가 요구사항과 정책에 익숙해지기를 바랍니다. 컴퓨터와 관련된 어떠한 문제라도 기술부서에서 다룬다는 것을 알아두시고, 문제가 있다면 그쪽으로 바로 연락을 하시기 바랍니다. 내선번호는 810입니다.

The word "growing" in paragraph 1, line 2, is closest in meaning to

(A) producing (B) spreading (C) expanding (D) gaining

해설 '성장하는 회사'라는 것은 회사의 규모가 커지고 증가한다는 의미이므로 보기에서 가장 적합한 답은 (C)가 된다.

2

Many companies have been forced to reduce their workforces over the past several years. This has resulted in having staff members sacrifice their personal time to deal with more assignments. Unfortunately, this practice has also led to reduced motivation and lower productivity in the long term.

많은 회사에서 지난 몇 년간 인력을 감축시켜와야 했다. 이 결과로 직원들이 개인적인 시간을 더 많은 일을 처리하는 데 희생하도록 했다. 불행하게도, 이렇게 **실행**하는 것은 결국에는 또한 동기 저하와 낮아진 생산성으로 이어졌다.

The word "practice" in paragraph 1, line 4, is closest in meaning to

(A) rule (B) profession (C) activity (D) rehearsal

해설 practice만 봤을때는 (D)도 답이 될 수 있겠지만, 이 문맥에서는 앞에서 '그렇게 행한 행동, 실행, 실천'을 의미하므로 정답은 (C)가 된다.

3

I ordered a variety of office supplies from your company, which arrived yesterday. It arrived three days earlier than your online catalog said. However, I was surprised by the low quality of the items. I ordered matte printer paper, but the coating was not as good as I expected. The staplers are also difficult to turn on. Although I have bought office supplies from Hayden Office Supplies several times before, I am so disappointed this time. So, I think I have to go for another brand.

저는 귀하의 회사에서 여러 가지 사무 용품을 주문했고, 그 물건들은 어제 도착했습니다. 귀하의 온라인 카탈로그에 쓰인 것보다 3일이나 일찍 도착했습니다. 하지만, 물건의 품질이 낮은 것을 보고 놀랐습니다. 무광의 프린터 용지를 주문했는데, 코팅이 제가 예상했던 것만큼 좋지 않았습니다. 스테이플러 또한 켜기 힘들었습니다. 비록 제가 하이든 사무 용품에서 전에도 몇 번 주문한 적이 있었지만, 이번에는 매우 실망입니다. 그래서 다른 브랜드를 **선택할** 생각입니다.

The phrase "go for" in paragraph 1, line 8, is closest in meaning to

(A) move (B) rush (C) reach (D) choose

해설 go for만 봤을 때는 사전적 의미로 '~를 향해 가다'가 되겠지만, 여기서는 '제품에 불만족하기 때문에 다른 브랜드로 간다'라는 뜻이다. 다른 브랜드를 선택한다는 의미이므로 정답은 (D)가 된다.

4

The McAllister Flavor is a popular online magazine with over 25,000 subscribers who want up-to-date information on cooking and food shopping. This year, we have launched our first contest for readers. Send in photos of food or recipes you made, and our panel of experts will select the three best ones. Winning contestants will receive a $500 gift certificate and a one-year subscription to our magazine. Entries must be received by March 3. We may use submissions for promotional or advertising purposes. We will never disclose a participant's personal information to other parties.

〈맥앨리스터 플레이버〉는 요리와 음식 구매에 관한 최신 정보를 알고 싶어 하는 25,000명 이상의 구독자를 가진 유명한 온라인 잡지책입니다. 올해, 우리는 독자들을 위해 처음으로 행사를 시작했습니다. 음식 혹은 음식을 만든 요리법을 사진으로 보내주시면, 전문가 위원들이 최고의 3장을 뽑을 것입니다. 우승자는 500달러의 상품권과 일 년 정기구독권을 받게 되실 겁니다. 제출은 3월 3일까지입니다. 제출하신 것은 홍보 또는 광고 목적으로 사용될 수 있습니다. 참가자들의 개인 정보는 공개되지 않을 것입니다.

What does the McAllister Flavor promise its readers?

(A) It offers a weekly online article.
(B) It checks work references.
(C) It keeps private information secure.
(D) It will respond to a post within one day.

맥앨리스터 플레이버는 독자들에게 무엇을 약속하는가?

(A) 매주 온라인 기사를 제공한다.
(B) 작업 참조를 확인합니다.
(C) 개인 정보를 안전하게 지켜줍니다.
(D) 하루 안에 게시물에 응답할 것입니다.

해설 제일 마지막 문장에서 개인 정보는 공개되지 않을 것이라는 것을 패러프레이징하면 personal information을 private information으로 never disclose를 secure로 표현한 정답은 (C)가 된다.

5 Have you been considering ways to make your business internationally successful? Are you thinking of advertising your business on foreign Web sites? If so, join the Edinburgh Institute to register for a series of lectures on overseas digital marketing. The lectures will start on Monday, October 3. A lot of professional marketing veterans from all over the world will deliver various lectures.

귀하의 사업을 세계적으로 성공하게 만드는 방법을 고려하고 계신가요? 해외 웹사이트에 귀하의 사업을 광고할 생각이 있으신가요? 만약 그렇다면, 해외 디지털 마케팅에 관한 여러 가지 수업에 등록하기 위해서 에딘버그 시설에 합류하세요. 수업은 10월 3일 월요일에 시작할 예정입니다. 전 세계에서 온 많은 전문 마케팅 베테랑들이 다양한 수업을 할 예정입니다.

What is implied about the lecturers?

(A) They are marketing professors.
(B) They are organizing the international conference every month.
(C) They have all been previously employed by Edinburgh Institute.
(D) They have extensive experience in advertising abroad.

강사에 대해 시사하는 바는?

(A) 그들은 마케팅 교수들입니다.
(B) 그들은 매달 국제회의를 조직하고 있습니다.
(C) 그들은 모두 이전에 에딘버그 연구소에 고용되었었다.
(D) 그들은 해외 광고 경험이 풍부하다.

해설 강사에 대한 질문인데 지문에서 veteran을 extensive experience로, from all over the world를 abroad로 패러프레이징 한 정답은 (D)가 된다.

만점 포인트 4 단일 지문 & 이삼중 지문

❶ 단일 지문은 총 29문제, 총 10지문으로 시간은 30분, 즉 한 지문마다 3분을 넘어서는 안된다.

❷ 이삼중 지문 총 25문제, 총 5세트(이중 지문 2세트 + 삼중 지문 3세트), 한 세트당 5분을 넘어서는 안된다.

❸ 이삼중 지문의 경우 연계하여 푸는 문제는 보통 1~2 문제로 마지막 두 문제에서 출제되는 경향이 있다.

만점 전략 1 지문 유형

1. 문자 대화문 & 온라인 채팅(매회 2개 지문)

❶ 비즈니스 또는 일상생활에 관련된 정보를 여러 사람이 나누는 대화

❷ 회사 동료들 사이 업무에 관한 내용

❸ 회의나 일정 변경에 관한 내용

❹ 고객과 고객을 응대하는 사람과의 문제 해결에 관한 내용

2. 이메일 & 편지(매회 3~5개 지문)

❶ 회의 / 행사 참석 요청, 연설을 요청하는 내용

❷ 서비스의 이용이 뜸한 고객 혹은 구독권 만료가 된 고객에게 보내는 할인 혜택 제공

❸ 상품이나 서비스에 대한 항의 / 불평 / 불만 내용

❹ 배송 지연에 따른 사과 내용

❺ 예약이나 일정을 취소 또는 확정하는 내용

❻ 구직자의 합격 또는 불합격을 통보하는 내용

3. 광고(매회 2~3개 지문)

❶ 근무 경력이 있는 경력직 구인 광고

❷ 신규 회원 모집 광고

❸ 호텔이나 리조트 등의 숙박 시설 이용 광고

❹ 제품 / 서비스 광고

❺ 점포 이전, 재고 정리 할인, 기념일 할인 광고

4. 공지 / 회람(매회 0~2개 지문)

❶ 인사발령, 사내 세미나 교육 공지

❷ 안전 수칙이나 공공시설 이용 안내 공지

❸ 제품이나 서비스 구매 후 설문조사 부탁 공지

❹ 회사 내 정책 혹은 시설(주차장 공사) 공지

❺ 버스 / 열차 / 항공기 승객에 관한 공지

5. 기사(매회 1~3개 지문)

❶ 인수합병에 관한 기사

❷ 외부 인물 영입 혹은 인사이동에 관한 기사

❸ 산업 전망 혹은 특정 사업 성장에 관한 기사
❹ 성공한 특정 인물이나 업체의 기사
❺ 새로운 다리 / 도로 / 지하철 노선 건설에 관한 건설 혹은 공사에 관한 기사

6. 양식(매회 2~3개 지문, 이삼중 지문 포함)

❶ 물품 거래 내역서인 청구서 혹은 송장(invoice)
❷ 행사에 초대하는 초대장(invitation)
❸ 행사 일정 혹은 항공편 일정(schedule)
❹ 제품 또는 서비스 구매 후 고객 만족도 조사(survey form)
❺ 전화 메시지 메모(telephone message)
❻ 제품이나 서비스에 대한 보증서(warranty)
❼ 계약 조항(contract)

만점 전략 2 문제 유형

1. 주제 / 글을 쓴 목적 찾기

보통 글의 도입부에 정답이 위치하는 경우가 대부분이지만, 난이도가 있는 문제의 경우 전체 지문을 포괄하거나 마지막 부분에 글의 목적을 나타내는 경우가 있으므로 주의해야 한다.

2. 세부사항 / 추론 문제

세부사항 문제의 경우는 본문에 그대로 나와 있는 경우가 많아 쉽게 풀 수 있는 경우도 있지만, 난이도가 있는 문제에서는 동의어로 패러프레이징 되어 나와 있는 경우가 대부분이다. 추론 문제의 경우는 전체 지문을 다 읽고 이해해야 하므로 다소 시간이 오래 걸리는 문제이므로 다른 문제를 먼저 풀고 나중에 푸는 것이 좋다.

3. 화자 의도 파악 문제

문자 메시지와 온라인 채팅에서 나오는 문제로, 보통 화자 의도 파악 문제는 앞뒤 문장에 단서가 나와있는 게 일반적이지만, 처음부터 끝까지 전체적인 맥락을 이해하면서 푸는 경우가 있으므로 지문의 흐름을 따라가는 것이 중요하다. 간혹 화자 간의 관계를 혼동하여 오답을 선택할 수 있으므로 주의하자.

4. 문장 삽입 문제

문장 삽입 문제는 주어진 문장 안에서 핵심이 되는 키워드를 빨리 파악한다. 예컨대, 지시어(this, these, it, they 등)나 연결어(however, therefore, also) 등을 최대한 활용한다. 지문 전체의 흐름을 파악하면서 앞뒤 문장에 자연스럽게 이어질 수 있도록 앞에 나와 있는 문제들을 먼저 풀어 이해한 정보를 바탕으로 문장을 대입해서 마지막으로 풀이하는 것이 좋다.

5. 동의어 문제

제시하는 어휘와 동의어를 찾는 문제로, 일반적으로 우리가 알고 있는 동의어를 매치시켜서 답을 고르는 문제가 출제가 되지만, 여러 가지 의미로 사용되는 어휘가 그 문맥 안에서 자연스럽게 어울리는 답을 골라야 하는 문제가 대부분이다. 그러므로 반드시 동의어를 많이 안다고 해서 해석 없이 바로 답을 구하지 않도록 주의하자.

MEMO

고난도 실전 문제

Questions 1-3 refer to the following advertisement.

LUNCHEON AT RYERSON MUSEUM

We, Ryerson Museum, invite residents of Harrington to attend a luncheon on May 8. The museum houses a large collection of artwork from the 18th and 19th centuries as well as a wide range of paintings produced by innovative artists here in Harrington. One of the special features is the private sculpture collection donated by the late Arthur Fleury, who used to live in this elegant building with his family before it was renovated in 1938.

Advance registration is needed. Tickets for the luncheon are priced at $50, and the reservation can be made by calling 555-2598. All proceeds from this event will go toward the upcoming renovation of the west wing of the museum. After the luncheon, attendees can enjoy live music by the famous local band The Gravey. Moreover, most exhibitions will be open to every attendee for viewing, including Mr. Fleury's special private collection. The event is scheduled to begin at 12 P.M. and last approximately one hour. There will be plenty of time for attendees to enjoy the luncheon and view the artwork.

1. What is the advertisement about?

(A) A museum opening
(B) A local fundraiser
(C) A speech by a sculptor
(D) An artwork workshop

2. What is indicated about Ryerson Museum?

(A) It provides an array of art classes to local people.
(B) It is currently under construction.
(C) It was once used as a residence.
(D) It mainly displays contemporary art.

3. What is NOT scheduled to happen at the May 8 event?

(A) A speech will be held one hour before the luncheon.
(B) A meal will finish around 1 P.M.
(C) A sculpture collection will be on display.
(D) Guests can enjoy the entertainment.

Questions 4-6 refer to the following online chat discussion.

Ana Cruz [2:13 P.M.]
Today, we need to talk about the annual skills workshop, which will be held on April 10.

Dylan Reynolds [2:14 P.M.]
Janet, you were working at the Carlton branch last April during this event, weren't you?

Janet Lee [2:17 P.M.]
Right, I was. I'm so excited to see how to handle the professional development event here at the Dayton branch.

Dylan Reynolds [2:18 P.M.]
Please remember that you'd better register in advance. The main conference can only accommodate 80 people.

Ana Cruz [2:19 P.M.]
Oh, okay. That's a good reminder. Now, let's move on to the next item on the agenda. Kate Erickson has finally selected the topic for the small group session, right?

Janet Lee [2:19 P.M.]
Yes. I got her e-mail. The title of the topic is "How to Save Your Time by Using E-mail Tools". It will be added to the schedule now.

Ana Cruz [2:21 P.M.]
Elizabeth Wilson, who is scheduled to speak in the morning session, called me this morning. She can't make it in the morning, but she can come to the afternoon session. I think I need to change her time rather than cancel her presentation. What do you think?

Dylan Reynolds [2:22 P.M.]
Hmm. Why don't we just have Grace McLean switch times with her? If so, the problem will be solved.

Janet Lee [2:23 P.M.]
That's a good idea. That will work. I know Grace will be present in both the morning and afternoon sessions.

Ana Cruz [2:24 P.M.]
Then we're all in agreement. I'll ask Grace about changing times.

SEND

4. What can be inferred about Ms. Lee?
(A) She has not received the updated schedule.
(B) She has invited Ms. McLean to an event.
(C) She asked for advice on the workshop.
(D) She has worked at this branch for less than a year.

5. What is suggested about the workshop?
(A) It will be open to people around the world.
(B) There is a deadline to be filled.
(C) It has a limited seating capacity.
(D) It will be hosted at a convention center.

6. At 2:24 P. M., what does Ms. Cruz mean when she writes, "Then we're all in agreement"?
(A) She thinks all problems have been solved.
(B) She will hire another speaker.
(C) She supports trading two speaking times.
(D) She confirms the cancellation of Wilson's workshop.

Questions 7-10 refer to the following article.

Boden Clothing to open Asian stores

October 8 - At a today's press conference, Gale Banks, CEO of Boden Clothing, announced his plan to expand the thriving local clothing business into international markets by opening flagship retail stores in Hong Kong, Korea, and Japan. Construction for a new manufacturing plant has already begun. The distribution warehouses in China and Indonesia are scheduled to begin operations in early March, just one month before the opening of the flagship stores. –[1]–.

For Boden Clothing, this year was a successful year, and Mr. Banks attended the grand opening of the company's largest retail location in Melbourne. "Thanks to the employees' hard work and dedication, we've seen unprecedented growth over the last five years", he told journalists at the press conference today. –[2]–. "Our company aims to establish itself as one of the world's leading clothing companies by expanding operations into foreign markets for the first time." –[3]–.

Financial analysts predict that today's announcement will make Boden Clothing's share price increase. This will undoubtedly bring more attention to the company, and its sales will continue to soar over the coming year. –[4]– .

7. What is indicated about Boden Clothing?
(A) Its international sales have increased considerably.
(B) It was founded in Hong Kong.
(C) It has previously focused on domestic sales.
(D) It considers opening a factory in Melbourne.

8. What is suggested about Boden Clothing's Asian stores?
(A) They are scheduled to open for business next April.
(B) They have recently been visited by Gale Banks.
(C) They will be the largest location of the company.
(D) They will only sell world-famous clothing brands.

9. According to the article, what has Boden Clothing accomplished this year?
(A) It launched a new line of clothing.
(B) It opened its new fashion retail store.
(C) It made a business contract with a foreign company.
(D) It achieved more sales than its rival companies.

10. In which of the positions marked [1], [2], [3], and [4] does the following sentence best belong?
"If Boden Clothing continues to expand so quickly, Mr. Banks' goal may become a reality."
(A) [1]
(B) [2]
(C) [3]
(D) [4]

고난도 실전 문제

Questions 11-15 refer to the following e-mails.

To:	Julia Soto <jsoto@jcreviews.net>
From:	Oliver Ventura <oventura@kokomagazine.com>
Subject:	More work
Date:	April 30

Dear Ms. Soto

After receiving your review of *The Guideline for Successful Home-Cooking*, I was so impressed with your evaluation of the book. So, I have requested a personal interview with the author for future books.

We always try to find which books will attract more interest among our readers even though we publish all kinds of reviews. I think most *Koko Magazine*'s readers are likely to read about nutrition and health.

In the June issue, we will feature a story about healthy lifestyles. Norman Bright, the well-known nutritionist, has coincidentally written a book called *The Importance of Nutrition*. So, I would like to highlight this book alongside.

We would also like to cover a review of Jackson Barham's *Successful Gardening*, which is a practical handbook for gardening enthusiasts.

As a keen reader of books, we were hoping that you would have time to review both books by May 15 for our June edition. Please respond to confirm as soon as possible whether you would be available. If you would consider writing one rather than both, please let me know your preference for which one you would be able to review by the above deadline.

Regards,

Oliver Ventura, Editor-In-Chief
Koko Magazine

To:	Oliver Ventura <oventura@kokomagazine.com>
From:	Julia Soto <jsoto@jcreviews.net>
Subject:	RE: More work
Date:	May 1

Dear Mr. Oliver Ventura

Based on my previous reviews on a variety of books, I would enjoy reviewing the books you mentioned. However, regarding the second book you listed, I have doubts. Actually, I have already reviewed the author's previous books. Honestly, I am simply not a fan of his writing style. Therefore, I might not be able to evaluate his book.

I am still interested in reviewing two books. If possible, I would like to propose a different book for my second submission: *From Garden to Table* by Rowan Charles.

And lastly, regarding the May 15 deadline, due to the tight schedule, would it be possible to extend this by a week? As far as I know, the magazine will hit shelves on the last day of the month. So I would really appreciate it if you could extend my deadline to May 22.

Regards,

Julia Soto, JC Reviews

11. Why did Mr. Ventura write the first e-mail?

(A) To propose that Ms. Soto write new book reviews
(B) To promote Ms. Soto's new novel
(C) To give Ms. Soto a magazine
(D) To ask Ms. Soto for a job interview

12. What is true about *Koko Magazine*?

(A) It mainly focuses on home improvement.
(B) Much of its audience seems to be influenced by nutrition and health.
(C) It has won several awards for its book review.
(D) One of its well-read articles was about history.

13. What can be inferred about Jackson Barham?

(A) He has worked on a writing project with Ms. Soto.
(B) His reviews were covered in *Koko Magazine*.
(C) His previous work was critiqued by Ms. Soto.
(D) His new book has been critically acclaimed.

14. What does Ms. Soto suggest Mr. Ventura do?

(A) Ask for a personal interview with Rowan Charles
(B) Allow her to review a different book
(C) Revise her latest reviews
(D) Arrange a meeting with Norman Bright

15. When is the June issue of the magazine likely to be published?

(A) May 19
(B) May 22
(C) May 30
(D) June 1

Questions 16-20 refer to the following notice, letter, and Web site.

Renew your TBA membership!

As a reminder, it is time for you to renew your membership with TBA Broadcasting. As a membership holder, you are aware that we have provided incredible benefits that come with membership fees.

- A three-month free trial subscription to our magazine about the broadcast
- Weekly e-mail updates about upcoming events and exclusive offers for our members
- Provide an opportunity to join "First Listens" to new programs

Recently, we have added new membership categories listed below. You can renew at the same level or choose to change to another.

Annual Membership Category

Blue Level – $55	**Crown Level – $150**
All the membership benefits listed above	All the benefits listed above for up to five guests
Red Level – $85	**Diamond Level – $250**
Blue Level benefits plus two guest passes to any TBA event	Crown Level benefits plus four guest passes and a 15% discount on our online products

Ms. Caroline Clark
365 Ridgeway Road
Cincinnati, OH 45201

Dear Ms. Clark,

We really appreciate that you decided to renew your TBA membership. As a network, one of the biggest networks in the country, we are not able to continue providing high-quality programming to our listeners without supporters like yourself. Also, you will find your new membership card and guest passes enclosed with this letter.

Moreover, in order for members to provide feedback easily, you can find the our comment section for each of our programs on our Web site at www.feedbacktbabroadcasting.org. We have also created a survey form to evaluate our membership program. We would greatly appreciate if you would take five minutes to fill it out.

Best Wishes,

James Clear, TBA Broadcasting

TBA Membership Survey Form

Name: Caroline Clark

Do you think the membership fee is reasonable?

I think $85 is a little high. But, the main reason why I decided to choose that membership is to support the broadcasting you provide rather receive the benefits.

What is the most important benefit of membership?

Broadcasting magazine is quite interesting, and it contains useful information. So I really enjoy reading it.

Do you have any other comments?

I recently renewed my membership, but I only got free passes. I would really appreciate it if you check one more time and send me the item that I am still missing.

16. What is indicated about TBA Broadcasting?

(A) It has a Web-based store.
(B) It sends out monthly e-mails.
(C) It hosts four events annually.
(D) Its membership can be canceled at any time.

17. What is Ms. Clark's membership level?

(A) Blue Level
(B) Red Level
(C) Crown Level
(D) Diamond Level

18. In the letter, the word "network" in paragraph 1, line 1, is closest in meaning to

(A) structure
(B) community
(C) station
(D) connection

19. What does Ms. Clark suggest about the TBA Broadcasting membership?

(A) It could upgrade another membership level.
(B) Its fee is reasonably priced.
(C) Its complimentary publication is educational.
(D) It may remove the comment section from its Web site.

20. What item did Ms. Clark ask to be sent?

(A) A free guest pass
(B) A membership card
(C) A discount voucher
(D) A program calendar

실전 모의고사 1

MP3 바로 듣기

해설서 바로 가기

- **준비물:** OMR 카드, 연필, 지우개, 시계
- **시험시간:** LC 약 45분 RC 75분

나의 점수		
	LC	RC
맞은 개수		
환산 점수		
총점: _______________ 점		

점수 환산표			
LC		RC	
맞은 개수	환산 점수	맞은 개수	환산 점수
96-100	475-495	96-100	460-495
91-95	435-495	91-95	425-490
86-90	405-475	86-90	395-465
81-85	370-450	81-85	370-440
76-80	345-420	76-80	335-415
71-75	320-390	71-75	310-390
66-70	290-360	66-70	280-365
61-65	265-335	61-65	250-335
56-60	235-310	56-60	220-305
51-55	210-280	51-55	195-270
46-50	180-255	46-50	165-240
41-45	155-230	41-45	140-215
36-40	125-205	36-40	115-180
31-35	105-175	31-35	95-145
26-30	85-145	26-30	75-120
21-25	60-115	21-25	60-95
16-20	30-90	16-20	45-75
11-15	5-70	11-15	30-55
6-10	5-60	6-10	10-40
1-5	5-60	1-5	5-30
0	5-35	0	5-15

TEST 1

Actual Test_1.mp3

LISTENING TEST

In the Listening test, you will be asked to demonstrate how well you understand spoken English. The entire listening test will last approximately 45 minutes. There are four parts, and directions are given for each part. You must mark your answers on the separate answer sheet. Do not write your answers in your test book.

PART 1

Directions: For each question in this part, you will hear four statements about a picture in your test book. When you hear the statements, you must select the one statement that best describes what you see in the picture. Then find the number of the question on your answer sheet and mark your answer. The statements will not be printed in your test book and will be spoken only one time.

Statement (B), "A man is pointing at a document," is the best description of the picture, so you should select answer (B) and mark it on your answer sheet.

1.

2.

GO ON TO THE NEXT PAGE

3.

4.

5.

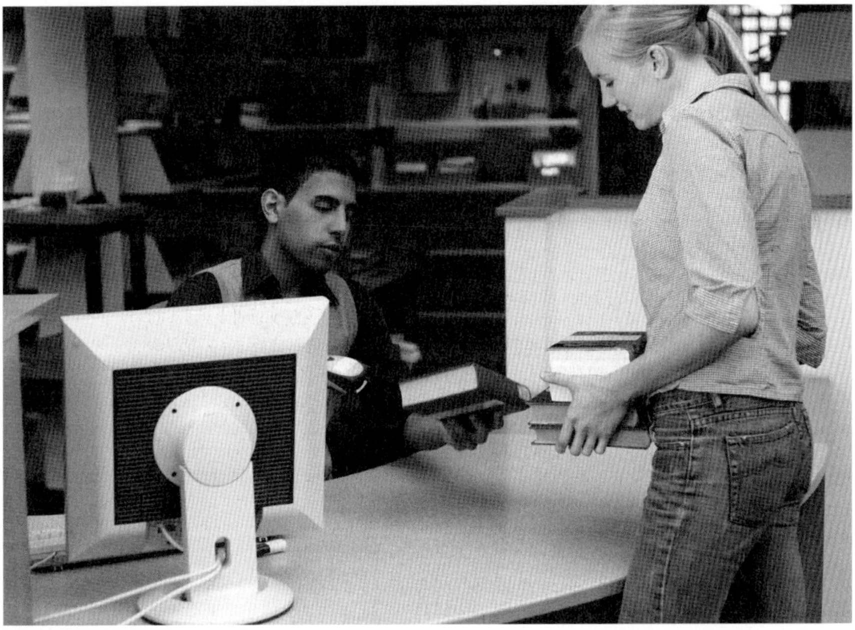

6.

GO ON TO THE NEXT PAGE

PART 2

Directions: You will hear a question or statement and three responses spoken in English. They will not be printed in your test book and will be spoken only one time. Select the best response to the question or statement and mark the letter (A), (B), or (C) on your answer sheet.

7. Mark your answer on your answer sheet.
8. Mark your answer on your answer sheet.
9. Mark your answer on your answer sheet.
10. Mark your answer on your answer sheet.
11. Mark your answer on your answer sheet.
12. Mark your answer on your answer sheet.
13. Mark your answer on your answer sheet.
14. Mark your answer on your answer sheet.
15. Mark your answer on your answer sheet.
16. Mark your answer on your answer sheet.
17. Mark your answer on your answer sheet.
18. Mark your answer on your answer sheet.
19. Mark your answer on your answer sheet.
20. Mark your answer on your answer sheet.
21. Mark your answer on your answer sheet.
22. Mark your answer on your answer sheet.
23. Mark your answer on your answer sheet.
24. Mark your answer on your answer sheet.
25. Mark your answer on your answer sheet.
26. Mark your answer on your answer sheet.
27. Mark your answer on your answer sheet.
28. Mark your answer on your answer sheet.
29. Mark your answer on your answer sheet.
30. Mark your answer on your answer sheet.
31. Mark your answer on your answer sheet.

PART 3

Directions: You will hear some conversations between two or more people. You will be asked to answer three questions about what the speakers say in each conversation. Select the best response to each question and mark the letter (A), (B), (C), or (D) on your answer sheet. The conversations will not be printed in your test book and will be spoken only one time.

32. Why does the man thank the woman?
(A) She is leading a training session.
(B) She recommended a potential job applicant.
(C) She finished a project ahead of schedule.
(D) She is covering a coworker's shift.

33. According to the man, what has changed?
(A) A project deadline
(B) A menu item
(C) A service fee
(D) An event location

34. What will the man most likely do next?
(A) Organize a stock room
(B) Contact a client
(C) Visit a local store
(D) Make a purchase

---

35. What does the man want to hold for his staff?
(A) A music performance
(B) A training session
(C) A company anniversary
(D) A sports festival

36. What is the man concerned about?
(A) Bad weather
(B) A cost
(C) Heavy traffic
(D) A regulation

37. What does Justine give to the man?
(A) A sample item
(B) A brochure
(C) An invoice
(D) A building map

38. Where do the speakers work?
(A) At a theater
(B) At a community center
(C) At an art museum
(D) At a university

39. What will happen on June 8?
(A) A cooking demonstration will be given.
(B) A dance performance will be presented.
(C) A painting class will be offered.
(D) A music concert will be held.

40. What will the man do tomorrow?
(A) Buy some supplies
(B) Meet with a client
(C) Go to the airport
(D) Participate in a tour

---

41. What are the speakers mainly discussing?
(A) A hiring process
(B) A budget report
(C) A charity event
(D) A holiday sale

42. What does the woman inform the man about?
(A) A potential investor
(B) A local law
(C) An upcoming inspection
(D) A renovation project

43. What does the woman say she will do?
(A) Review some applications
(B) Inquire about a date
(C) Compare some costs
(D) Attend a conference

GO ON TO THE NEXT PAGE

44. What kind of business do the speakers own?
(A) A gym
(B) A supermarket
(C) A farm
(D) A café

45. Why does the woman say, "I'm not sure we have enough management experience to do that"?
(A) To decline an invitation to an event
(B) To express frustration about a process
(C) To suggest taking some classes
(D) To show doubt about an idea

46. What does the man recommend doing?
(A) Revising contract terms
(B) Acquiring more funds
(C) Using a consulting firm
(D) Attending a convention

---

47. What is the reason for the woman's visit?
(A) To interview for a job
(B) To inspect a building
(C) To drop off a package
(D) To fix a machine

48. What did the man's employees do?
(A) They watched some videos.
(B) They examined a refrigerator.
(C) They moved some equipment.
(D) They cleaned an area.

49. What will the woman do after 20 minutes?
(A) Fill out a survey
(B) Unload a vehicle
(C) Contact a manager
(D) Give a price estimate

50. Where do the speakers work?
(A) At a law office
(B) At a convention center
(C) At a recruiting company
(D) At an engineering firm

51. What does the man say he needs to do?
(A) Return an ID
(B) Purchase a parking pass
(C) Review a job contract
(D) Join a celebration

52. What does the woman imply when she says, "I have another meeting to attend right now"?
(A) She forgot about an appointment.
(B) She will book a meeting room.
(C) She cannot provide assistance.
(D) She would like the man to wait.

---

53. Where do the speakers most likely work?
(A) At a photo studio
(B) At an electronics manufacturer
(C) At a newspaper company
(D) At a law firm

54. What are the speakers worried about?
(A) Exceeding a budget
(B) Providing confidential details
(C) Increasing some sales figures
(D) Acquiring a contract

55. What will the man probably do next?
(A) Send out some e-mails
(B) Contact a client
(C) Talk to an executive
(D) Review a manual

56. What is the man doing today?

(A) Moving some furniture
(B) Meeting some customers
(C) Training some interns
(D) Revising some documents

57. What problem does the man mention?

(A) An event has been delayed.
(B) An employee is not available.
(C) A device is not working.
(D) An item has been misplaced.

58. What does the woman recommend doing?

(A) Changing menu items
(B) Revising a schedule
(C) Calling a manufacturer
(D) Switching locations

---

59. What are the speakers mainly talking about?

(A) Some potential job applicants
(B) An event to promote some new merchandise
(C) A new way to communicate with clients
(D) Some defective products

60. Why was a decision made?

(A) To attract investors
(B) To expand overseas
(C) To extend a deadline
(D) To save money

61. What does Betty say will be available next week?

(A) A meeting space
(B) Some research findings
(C) Some extra phones
(D) An expanded parking lot

Line 1	HALIFAX THEATER'S *Star-crossed Lovers*

Line 2	Admission: $18
Line 3	Date: March 3
Line 4	Location: Lee Auditorium
Line 5	Time: 7 P.M.

62. What most likely is the man's profession?

(A) Scriptwriter
(B) Maintenance worker
(C) Theater director
(D) Graphic designer

63. Look at the graphic. What line should be changed?

(A) Line 2
(B) Line 3
(C) Line 4
(D) Line 5

64. What does the woman say she has to do?

(A) Review an agreement form
(B) Get a supervisor's approval
(C) Update a budget report
(D) Contact a performer

GO ON TO THE NEXT PAGE

Trail Name	Length
Calim Trail	6km
Hudson Trail	8km
Rafter Trail	10km
Senco Trail	12km

65. Why does the woman want her colleagues to go on a hike?

(A) To conduct some research
(B) To improve their teamwork
(C) To learn about nature
(D) To increase their stamina

66. Look at the graphic. How long is the trail that the speakers agree on?

(A) 6 kilometers
(B) 8 kilometers
(C) 10 kilometers
(D) 12 kilometers

67. What does the man recommend the woman do later?

(A) Review an invoice
(B) Create a poll
(C) Make a purchase
(D) Email a park agency

Renay Resort: Event Halls		
Bronze Hall	$2,000	Fits up to 100 guests
Silver Hall	$4,000	Fits up to 300 guests
Gold Hall	$5,000	Fits up to 500 guests
Diamond Hall	$6,000	Fits up to 600 guests

68. What kind of event is the woman organizing?

(A) A marketing conference
(B) A retirement party
(C) An anniversary celebration
(D) A product demonstration

69. Look at the graphic. Which event hall will the speakers most likely use?

(A) The Bronze Hall
(B) The Silver Hall
(C) The Gold Hall
(D) The Diamond Hall

70. What does the woman say she will do next?

(A) Download a program
(B) Revise an itinerary
(C) Make a booking
(D) Print a map

PART 4

Directions: You will hear some talks given by a single speaker. You will be asked to answer three questions about what the speaker says in each talk. Select the best response to each question and mark the letter (A), (B), (C), or (D) on your answer sheet. The talks will not be printed in your test book and will be spoken only one time.

71. Who most likely is the speaker?
(A) A supermarket manager
(B) A local farmer
(C) A TV show producer
(D) A head chef

72. What is the talk mainly about?
(A) Grocery shopping
(B) Internet research
(C) A supply order
(D) A recipe book

73. What does the speaker want the listeners to do on Monday morning?
(A) Submit a review
(B) Build a garden
(C) Compare some data
(D) Cook some food

---

74. What kind of team does the speaker coach?
(A) Soccer
(B) Baseball
(C) Hockey
(D) Golf

75. What does the speaker mention about her players?
(A) Many of them live far away.
(B) Most of them work late.
(C) They are going to participate in a tournament.
(D) They need to practice more often.

76. Why does the speaker say, "Your team has the field from 6 to 7"?
(A) To request a switch
(B) To extend a game time
(C) To praise a team member
(D) To verify an appointment

77. What field does the speaker most likely work in?
(A) Hospitality
(B) Finance
(C) Transportation
(D) Manufacturing

78. What does the speaker imply when he says, "I have to inform the client about this by 5 P.M. today"?
(A) He needs employees to make a quick decision.
(B) He wants to reschedule a client meeting.
(C) He was unable to complete a project on time.
(D) He will be out of the office tomorrow.

79. What will the company do for some employees?
(A) Provide a company vehicle
(B) Give additional vacation days
(C) Present some awards
(D) Supply some food

---

80. What does Garlow produce?
(A) Office supplies
(B) Sporting goods
(C) Organic beverages
(D) Home electronics

81. What will Garlow do?
(A) Host a fundraiser for charity
(B) Design a new line of products
(C) Open branches overseas
(D) Reduce water usage

82. What will the listeners hear after the commercial break?
(A) A discussion
(B) A weather update
(C) Customer testimonials
(D) Business advice

GO ON TO THE NEXT PAGE

83. What is the speaker mainly talking about?
(A) The importance of communication
(B) Performance evaluation meetings
(C) A project deadline
(D) A corporate policy

84. According to the speaker, why do the listeners need to use a company's Web portal?
(A) To adjust their work hours
(B) To request a new badge
(C) To reserve a conference room
(D) To download a security update

85. What should the listeners do if a Web portal is not working?
(A) Restart a machine
(B) Buy some new equipment
(C) Contact an IT staff member
(D) Visit the security office

---

86. What is the main topic of the broadcast?
(A) Online shopping trends
(B) Home improvement
(C) Saving money
(D) Healthy eating

87. Why does the speaker say, "It doesn't even take much time"?
(A) To express a benefit of a program
(B) To schedule a consultation
(C) To announce a commercial break
(D) To recommend an express service

88. According to the speaker, what should the listeners do first?
(A) Contact a friend
(B) Speak with an expert
(C) Sign up for a membership
(D) Record their goal

89. What will happen at the Morey Art Gallery next Friday?
(A) Some remodeling work will be completed.
(B) A workshop will be held.
(C) A new exhibit will be opened.
(D) Some artwork will be unavailable.

90. What does the speaker say about some Morey University students?
(A) They will give a demonstration at the gallery.
(B) They will start their internship at the gallery this month.
(C) They created some of the artwork.
(D) They organized a gallery display.

91. According to the speaker, what should the listeners do in advance?
(A) Sign up on a Web site
(B) Purchase an annual pass
(C) Take some photographs
(D) Visit a nearby university

---

92. Why is the speaker calling?
(A) To schedule a meeting
(B) To make a job offer
(C) To confirm a travel itinerary
(D) To review a contract

93. What does the speaker say the listener will be required to do?
(A) Approve an application
(B) Finish a certification course
(C) Relocate to a new country
(D) Renew a passport

94. What does the speaker say will happen next week?
(A) Reservations will be made.
(B) Event invitations will be sent.
(C) A board member will retire.
(D) A business will not open.

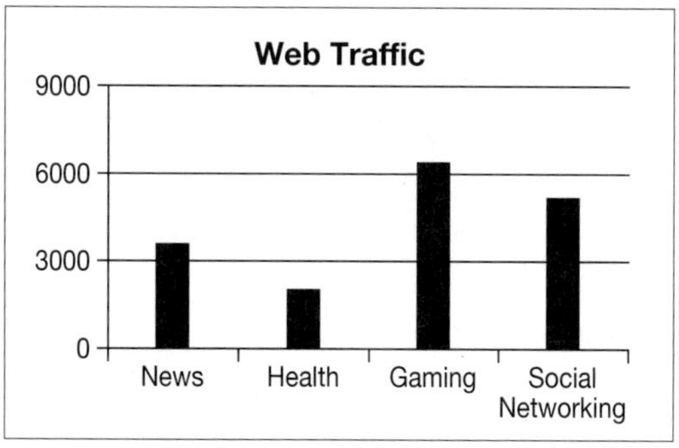

95. In what department does the speaker most likely work?
(A) Information Technology
(B) Human Resources
(C) Finance
(D) Marketing

96. Look at the graphic. Which type of Web site does the speaker recommend?
(A) News
(B) Health
(C) Gaming
(D) Social Networking

97. What will the listeners most likely do next?
(A) Read some testimonials
(B) Break into small groups
(C) Have some refreshments
(D) Complete a survey

Volcano Pizza
Summer Hours

Monday-Thursday	12 P.M. - 10 P.M.
Friday	12 P.M. - 11 P.M.
Saturday	12 P.M. - 12 A.M.
Sunday	12 P.M. - 8 P.M.

98. Look at the graphic. When is the speaker leaving the message?
(A) On Thursday
(B) On Friday
(C) On Saturday
(D) On Sunday

99. Why does the speaker leave the message?
(A) To confirm a reservation
(B) To inquire about a location
(C) To apologize for a misunderstanding
(D) To make a complaint

100. What does the speaker request?
(A) An extension to get a special price
(B) An addition to the menu
(C) A late-night delivery of some food
(D) An address of another branch

This is the end of the Listening test. Turn to Part 5 in your test book.

GO ON TO THE NEXT PAGE

READING TEST

In the Reading test, you will read a variety of texts and answer several different types of reading comprehension questions. The entire Reading test will last 75 minutes. There are three parts, and directions are given for each part. You are encouraged to answer as many questions as possible within the time allowed.

You must mark your answers on the separate answer sheet. Do not write your answers in your test book.

PART 5

Directions: A word or phrase is missing in each of the sentences below. Four answer choices are given below each sentence. Select the best answer to complete the sentence. Then mark the letter (A), (B), (C), or (D) on your answer sheet.

101. Most doctors at Grant Hospital ------- only patients with appointments.

(A) grant
(B) accept
(C) start
(D) resolve

102. The IT crew is in charge of setting up the latest programs as soon as developers request -------.

(A) theirs
(B) them
(C) you
(D) yours

103. Next spring, Genesee's Flower Festival will take place in May, although it ------- is held in April.

(A) traditionally
(B) tradition
(C) traditions
(D) traditional

104. Installing the new climate control system could take ------- much as a month.

(A) in
(B) also
(C) as
(D) not

105. Mr. Zhukov replaced his car remote since it had not been working -------.

(A) lastly
(B) earnestly
(C) properly
(D) moderately

106. All commuter bus drivers are required to have their type 1 ------- renewed every three years.

(A) application
(B) license
(C) permission
(D) enrollment

107. Pyreen kitchen appliances will help your restaurant run ------- no matter what cuisine you serve.

(A) smoothly
(B) smoothed
(C) smoothing
(D) smooth

108. Hella Fashion's line of business apparel tripled following its ------- in the first quarter.

(A) expanded
(B) expand
(C) expandable
(D) expansion

109. New lawyers at Tran and Nguyen Associates should ------- attend the evening seminar on October 14.

(A) frequently
(B) definitely
(C) exactly
(D) explicitly

110. Ms. Palmieri asked us to tell her ------- of the three investment accounts was most profitable.

(A) that
(B) what
(C) which
(D) such

111. Citronar Beverages Ltd. introduced a novel ------- for gathering customer feedback by providing free samples at sports events.

(A) audience
(B) selection
(C) advantage
(D) strategy

112. The goal of the conference is to define ------- what targets we need to achieve before the end of the season.

(A) specification
(B) specifically
(C) specific
(D) specifying

113. All second-hand non-fiction books will be ------- an additional 25 percent on Thursday and Friday.

(A) assigned
(B) purchased
(C) suggested
(D) discounted

114. Mr. Vanger wished to be present at the grand opening, but he had other ------- that morning.

(A) obligates
(B) obligation
(C) obligated
(D) obligations

115. Abkhazia Airlines altered its a... to ------- meals to long-distance i... flights.

(A) impose
(B) limit
(C) claim
(D) export

116. Paran Resorts managed to bring its talks about the merger to a satisfactory ------- last weekend.

(A) resolved
(B) resolving
(C) resolution
(D) resolute

117. Grander is seeking a certified accountant, whose ------- responsibility will be to document the company's financial transactions.

(A) acceptable
(B) compatible
(C) primary
(D) eligible

118. The seminar organizers ------- out dozens of invitations, but only a few guest speakers have answered back.

(A) send
(B) are sending
(C) sent
(D) will send

119. Visitor numbers at the Natural History Museum increased ------- following the opening of the new dinosaur exhibit.

(A) restrictively
(B) originally
(C) rapidly
(D) correctly

120. Although she ------- the complete sales report, Ms. Orrin was still satisfied with the results of the recent online promotion.

(A) had not seen
(B) was not seen
(C) is not seen
(D) is not seeing

GO ON TO THE NEXT PAGE

121. The Rapport Magazine phone application will be updated ------- the hours of 2 A.M. and 8 A.M.
(A) between
(B) among
(C) before
(D) upon

122. ------- working for a decade on the R&D team, Ms. Trockner was promoted to team leader.
(A) Often
(B) Both
(C) Later
(D) After

123. Given the ------- cost of petroleum products, companies are being advised to decrease the availability of free shipping.
(A) appealing
(B) informative
(C) rising
(D) constructive

124. The research findings are posted on the company's Web site for participants to read ------- their convenience.
(A) with
(B) in
(C) at
(D) until

125. Chez Marseille's patrons must give at least 24 hours' ------- when canceling a table reservation.
(A) absence
(B) termination
(C) release
(D) notice

126. Ms. Benitez never fails to find ------- ways to deal with unexpected delays.
(A) pragmatically
(B) pragmatism
(C) pragmatist
(D) pragmatic

127. Mauna Kona Coffee reported a significant rise in coffee bean production ------- an exceptionally hot and wet monsoon season.
(A) whereas
(B) caused by
(C) apart from
(D) since

128. Some company directors choose to implement ------- management approach.
(A) visibility
(B) visibly
(C) visible
(D) vision

129. The package courier may arrive as early as 3 o'clock ------- how heavy traffic is.
(A) dependent
(B) to depend
(C) depended
(D) depending on

130. Kunst Web Service's designers have been ------- to the changing expectations of customers.
(A) attentive
(B) available
(C) relevant
(D) prepared

PART 6

Directions: Read the texts that follow. A word, phrase, or sentence is missing in parts of each text. Four answer choices for each question are given below the text. Select the best answer to complete the text. Then mark the letter (A), (B), (C), or (D) on your answer sheet.

Questions 131-134 refer to the following Web page.

Renovating a commercial location can seem -------, but Spruce Designworks will help to make the experience swift and painless. Whether you are upgrading a restaurant, a hotel, or a boutique shop, our expert team has the experience, skill, and dedication to ------- your remodeling effectively.
131. **132.**

Our staff will consult with you closely to make sure that your dream for your business can become a reality. -------, we go out of our way to work only with suppliers and subcontractors with track records of high quality and good results. -------.
133. **134.**

131. (A) complicates
(B) complication
(C) complicate
(D) complicated

132. (A) manage
(B) manages
(C) managed
(D) managing

133. (A) Whenever possible
(B) As long as
(C) Likewise
(D) But

134. (A) The remodeling process should take six to eight weeks.
(B) Our Web site provides more details about the companies we partner with.
(C) We specialize in building modern kitchen spaces.
(D) We pride ourselves on handling all phases of your project in-house.

GO ON TO THE NEXT PAGE

Questions 135-138 refer to the following e-mail.

From: customerservice@locality.com

Date: October 9

Subject: What can we do better?

To: Christian Sale <csale81@lwmail.com>

Dear Mr. Sale,

According to our computer system, you have used locality.com to find accommodations ------- (135.) over the past two years. We're interested in hearing what you have to say about our Web site and hope you can take the time to fill out a brief feedback form made up of five questions. Please answer ------- (136.) as completely as you can. We would appreciate it if you would send your ------- (137.) by 8 P.M. this Friday. ------- (138.). To get started, click on the link below and follow the instructions that pop up.

Best Regards,

The Locality Team

135. (A) regular
(B) regulation
(C) regularly
(D) regulate

136. (A) whichever
(B) everyone
(C) them
(D) her

137. (A) authorization
(B) evaluation
(C) priority
(D) booking

138. (A) If you do so, we will offer a discount on your next stay.
(B) As a priority club member, you are entitled to special amenities, including free parking.
(C) You may cancel your reservation at no additional charge.
(D) This special offer won't last for long, so make your arrangements today!

Questions 139-142 refer to the following memo.

Date: 7 July
Subject: Pettis to make needed electrical repairs
From: Kilmarnock Management
To: All Employees

------- (139.) the last few months, you have likely noticed buzzing and sparking electrical outlets on the 6th through 10th floors. As this is a potential safety issue, we have called Pettis Inc., a local electrical contractor, who ------- (140.) renovation and rewiring for us.

This e-mail is to bring your attention to the fact that Pettis crew members will be in the building from tomorrow through the weekend. They aim to make the repairs on a floor by floor basis so that the work causes fewer disruptions. However, for the next few ------- (141.), some areas may be obstructed, and there will be some additional noise. ------- (142.).

Don't hesitate to reach out to the management team if you have any concerns or suggestions. We will do our best to make needed accommodations.

139. (A) While
(B) Over
(C) Among
(D) Before

140. (A) will be performing
(B) is now performing
(C) may perform
(D) was performing

141. (A) weeks
(B) hours
(C) months
(D) days

142. (A) Pettis is one of the best-known local electricians.
(B) Floors 11-20 will require their own repairs in the near future.
(C) If necessary, temporary office space can be made available.
(D) This unfortunate flaw is common in older buildings.

GO ON TO THE NEXT PAGE

Questions 143-146 refer to the following article.

DUBLIN (January 14) Mischance Media is excited to introduce the next President of its publishing wing: Vineeta LaVine, who will officially take over the position on February 21. Her strong background in the ------- **143.** made her an appealing candidate for the job. Ms. LaVine is a graduate of Midlands University, where she received both a Bachelor's and a Master's degree in English Literature. She then ------- **144.** her career in publishing as an assistant editor at Stockhausen-Cobain Books. After 15 years, she left to join Mischance Media. ------- **145.**. In Dublin, Lavine will exercise creative control over the company's European publishing as well as Earshot Audiobooks, in ------- **146.** Mischance recently purchased a controlling stake.

143. (A) novel
(B) grade
(C) subject
(D) field

144. (A) will launch
(B) launches
(C) had launched
(D) launched

145. (A) A market downturn has forced many publishers to lay off staff.
(B) She worked most recently as a managing editor at Mischance's New York office.
(C) She says she became passionate about reading as a middle school student.
(D) The firm is currently expanding into Asian markets.

146. (A) that
(B) which
(C) what
(D) when

PART 7

Directions: In this part, you will read a selection of texts, such as magazine and newspaper articles, e-mails, and instant messages. Each text or set of texts is followed by several questions. Select the best answer for each question and mark the letter (A), (B), (C), or (D) on your answer sheet.

Questions 147-148 refer to the following advertisement.

Geum Wol Presents: Winter Wonders

It has been more than five decades since our founder DB Kim first began designing necklaces and rings. Over the years, we have developed a reputation throughout the world for excellence. This winter, we are proud to present a chic, modern line of accessories targeting younger customers. As always, we use the finest available diamonds, emeralds, opals, and amethysts sourced from our trusted partners. Starting August 16, we will accept orders for the new line, with shipment guaranteed by November anywhere in Asia. To get in touch with your local Geum Wol wholesaler, visit www.geumwol.co.kr.

147. For whom is the advertisement intended?

(A) Accessory makers
(B) Jewelers
(C) Fashion designers
(D) Advertisers

148. What is suggested about Geum Wol?

(A) It recently began selling necklaces and rings.
(B) It markets its merchandise in several countries.
(C) It is looking for a new partner to collaborate with.
(D) It will open a new location in the coming months.

GO ON TO THE NEXT PAGE

Questions 149-150 refer to the following Web page.

www.toledocommerce.org/opportunities

With investments in our community at an all-time high, now is the ideal time to submit your business proposals. Whether your company is well-established or just getting started, there are clients who need your services. The Toledo Chamber of Commerce has found over 100 firms that need suppliers to provide everything from raw materials to specialized software and to help find temporary staff. This is the revised directory, including contact information of all interested companies, and is current as of May 4. Look through the directory to find clients whose needs match up with your expertise.

Submit soon—before these opportunities are gone!

Revised: May 4

149. What is the purpose of the Web page?

(A) To help suppliers looking for clients
(B) To detail updated business regulations
(C) To advertise a local company
(D) To promote an investment opportunity

150. According to the Web page, what has recently been updated?

(A) A directory of firms
(B) A software program
(C) A proposal form
(D) A list of vendor guidelines

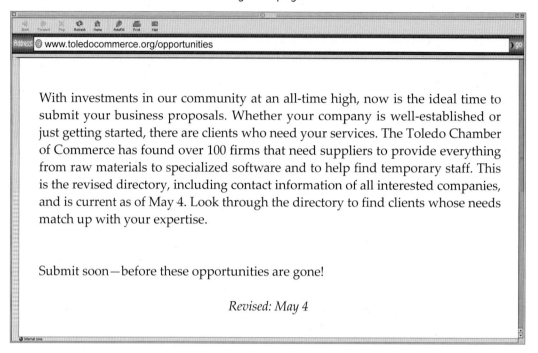

Questions 151-153 refer to the following e-mail.

From:	Geraldine Watson <gwatson@off.org>
Re:	Film Festival Arrangements
Date:	October 16
To:	Participating Panelists

Thank you for your participation in the upcoming 7th annual Oshawa Film Festival. Please remember to register in room 302 of Juniper Hall, located at 404 Grandview Avenue, when you arrive on-site. Our booth will open at 8 A.M. on the 18th. There you will pick up your event ID card, a guide to the festivals, as well as a meal voucher.

Panel discussions will be held following screenings in lecture auditoriums 2 and 3, while local film students and sponsors will make presentations in conference room C of Birch Hall. Each room will be furnished with podiums, wireless microphones, and a PC which can be connected to the auditorium's projector and sound system. If you require special assistance, including wheelchair access or sign language interpretation, get in touch with Kelvin Sunderland as soon as possible. You can call him at 555-919-3690.

With some panelists canceling at the last minute, alterations have been made to the festival guide. These cancellations will not alter your panel times, but since they may not be reflected in your printed versions, please refer to our Web site for the most current information.

Best regards,

Geraldine Watson

Festival Director

151. Where will festival materials for panelists be available?

(A) In Room 302
(B) In Lecture Auditorium 2
(C) In Lecture Auditorium 3
(D) In Conference Room C

152. When should participants call Mr. Sunderland?

(A) If they have to reschedule a panel discussion
(B) If they need specific accommodations
(C) If they want additional meal vouchers
(D) If they find misprinted information in the guide

153. What information will be listed online?

(A) What time sponsor presentations begin
(B) Where to find local screenings
(C) How to register for some multimedia equipment
(D) Which panels will not attend

GO ON TO THE NEXT PAGE

Questions 154-157 refer to the following article.

Oahu Observer

HONOLULU (July 22) — The Four Points Mall in Honolulu will be undergoing major renovations—and getting a new name, too. –[1]–. The Four Points Mall will soon be known as the Cosgood Galleria, Honolulu. Cosgood Enterprises, the retail property management chain headquartered in Geneva, Switzerland, has announced a multimillion-dollar plan to modernize the mall. The ambitious makeover will feature a new east wing, as well as a high-end dining experience at the Cosgood Grill. According to industry insiders, chef Rachel Gillis, who hosts the popular television series Hottest Eats, has agreed to head up its kitchen. –[2]–. Other new options will include a Greek restaurant, an artisanal salad bar, and a chic brunch spot.

Since it started operating 20 years ago, Cosgood Enterprises has been a leading light in luxury retail management around the globe. –[3]–. The Honolulu mall will be the company's first in Oahu.

Cosgood Gallerias can now be found in Canada, Brazil, Argentina, and Mexico. In addition to their signature Cosgood brand, they operate properties under the names Sunset Services and Sylvester's as well.

The remodeling in Honolulu will require a large team of construction workers from the local community. –[4]–. Cosgood representatives say the renovation should be complete within 18 months. The Vice President, Tabatha O'Brien, is confident that it will be well worth the wait.

Mark Kahale, Contributor

154. What is the purpose of the article?
(A) To report the construction of a building
(B) To discuss changing retail trends
(C) To announce changes at a property
(D) To profile a famous restaurant chain

155. What is indicated about Cosgood Grill?
(A) It will be located in the east wing.
(B) It will be Cosgood Galleria's only dining option.
(C) It will only offer breakfast and lunch service.
(D) It will be run by a celebrity.

156. Where is the main office of Cosgood Enterprises?
(A) In Canada
(B) In the United States
(C) In Switzerland
(D) In Argentina

157. In which of the positions marked [1], [2], [3], and [4] does the following sentence best belong?

"Many more employees are expected to be hired on as store staff when the galleria opens."

(A) [1]
(B) [2]
(C) [3]
(D) [4]

Questions 158-160 refer to the following information.

We are excited to present the December Issue of our complimentary monthly paper, Emerald Vistas. The periodical provides insights into some of the destinations we sail to, including detailed information about where to explore when you're in port or even on your next holiday. In this edition, we count down our top 20 favorite museums and galleries.

We also preview several great new trails and must-see mountain trekking paths, tips for vacationing solo, and the conclusion of the last month's article on finding healthy dining options while traveling. We hope you enjoy Emerald Vistas and invite you to take this issue with you at the conclusion of your voyage.

158. Who most likely produces *Emerald Vistas*?
(A) A regional tourism office
(B) A cruise line
(C) A travel Web site
(D) A hotel chain

159. When was the original article about dining published?
(A) October
(B) November
(C) December
(D) January

160. What topic is NOT discussed in the current issue of *Emerald Vistas*?
(A) Places to hike
(B) Traveling by yourself
(C) Cultural attractions
(D) Admission discounts

GO ON TO THE NEXT PAGE

Questions 161-164 refer to the following text message chain.

Sid Auckerman 12:21 P.M.
I'm at Water Street Bistro, and my table happened to be right next to Luca Moretti's from Avarici Automotive. We might win the renovation contract for their flagship store.

Emma Ali 12:22 P.M.
Fantastic! Are you with him currently?

Sid Auckerman 12:23 P.M.
He's out on the patio talking with Harold Koeman, Marketing Director at Avarici, but he'll be right back. Would we be able to finish all of the flooring work by August?

Emma Ali 12:24 P.M.
Our next project is the one with Williamstown Vocational College, then the new residence hall at the national training facility,(164) then nothing major. I can't see why we wouldn't.

Sid Auckerman 12:30 P.M.
To be safe, can we move back the residence hall work?

Emma Ali 12:31 P.M.
Let me message Alan Lazard from the training facility and tell him there might be a delay. But they won't be using the residence hall until September.

Sid Auckerman 12:32 P.M.
Understood. Looks like they're coming inside. Call me when you hear from Alan. This would be a huge deal for us, so let's make it our priority.

161. What is Mr. Auckerman hoping to do?
(A) Enter into an agreement
(B) Meet with an executive
(C) Attend a training seminar
(D) Reserve a restaurant table

162. Who will Mr. Auckerman talk to soon?
(A) Mr. Moretti
(B) Mr. Koeman
(C) Ms. Ali
(D) Ms. Lazard

163. At 12:24 P.M., what does Ms. Ali most likely mean when she writes, "I can't see why we wouldn't"?
(A) She is confident about meeting a deadline.
(B) She wants to speak with a colleague.
(C) She does not understand how a plan will work.
(D) She needs to see more details before making a decision.

164. What is suggested about the training facility?
(A) It currently houses famous student-athletes.
(B) It plans to construct an indoor track and field complex.
(C) It does not need a project to be completed immediately.
(D) It is being relocated to Williamstown.

GO ON TO THE NEXT PAGE

Questions 165-166 refer to the following memo.

Date: January 18
From: Dana Beckham
To: All Carmichael Insurance Team Members

We are revising our protocol in regards to personal expenses used by employees while traveling on behalf of the firm. As before, all expenses of over $100 will still need to be pre-approved. Please email me your requests 72 hours in advance.

Purchases of less than $100 while traveling should now be made using the discretionary spending card, one of which will be issued to each department. Remember, however, that any expenses charged to this card must be logged and reported using our accounting software, with brief explanations of the reason for each specific purchase. Also, note that all purchases must qualify under the company's expense guidelines, or the amount will be deducted from your salary. You can refer to these in detail on our Web site. If you have any questions, contact the Accounting team.

Department heads will submit the card statements and printed expense reports to Diontae Angelo on the 25th of every month, which will be evaluated by the 30th of the month at the latest.

165. What is the purpose of the memo?

(A) To explain why a budget was amended
(B) To introduce new department heads
(C) To request a report be submitted promptly
(D) To discuss changes to a company policy

166. According to the memo, what happens on the 25th of every month?

(A) Ms. Beckham approves purchase requests.
(B) Mr. Angelo receives expense reports.
(C) Credit card payments must be made.
(D) Travel expenses are logged.

Questions 167-168 refer to the following online chat discussion.

Paul Lin **[4:00 P.M.]**
Deirdre, management wants me to conduct your department performance reviews before the end of the month. Which date is best for you?

Deirdre Foyle **[4:01 P.M.]**
Would September 28 work? I'll need to be in the Incheon office for most of next week.

Paul Lin **[4:04 P.M.]**
I don't think so. I need time to conduct the reviews and then submit a 2-page report on each team member. Will you have a free afternoon on Thursday or Friday?

Deirde Foyle **[4:16 P.M.]**
I'll arrange for someone to cover for me on the 20th. I can be there by 11:30 A.M. Is that OK?

Paul Lin **[4:19 P.M.]**
Great. I am emailing you a list of documents you'll need to bring with you. Let me know if you have any questions.

SEND

167. Why did Mr. Lin contact Ms. Foyle?
(A) To discuss performance review results
(B) To arrange for a conference call
(C) To inform her about a business trip
(D) To set up a meeting with her

168. At 4:04 P.M., what does Mr. Lin most likely mean when he writes, "I don't think so"?
(A) He approves of a travel plan.
(B) He cannot travel to the Incheon office.
(C) Ms. Foyle needs to file a different form.
(D) Ms. Foyle should choose another time.

GO ON TO THE NEXT PAGE

Questions 169-171 refer to the following contract.

DMLT Terms of Service

A down payment of 30 percent of the total price will be required in advance. The remainder is due when the project is complete. The application will not become functional until the account is settled entirely. All back-end development, including the source code and server management protocols created for the project, are exclusively owned by DMLT LLC. DMLT may not be held responsible for any copyright claims pertaining to front-end use.

The client's input is welcomed in the design process, but excessive requests for modifications will result in a surcharge.

When the app goes live, it is advisable to hire an outside IT firm as a safety measure to protect your and your client's data.

DMLT provides complimentary Web-based technical training to assist with maintaining the app. Tutorials must be scheduled within a month of the app's launch.

If the client wishes to cancel the project, they must inform DMLT at least 45 days in advance of the scheduled release date. Failing to do so will result in forfeiting the down payment.

By signing this form, I am acknowledging that I understand and accept the terms of service above.

Name (please print): Akram Tagaev
Signature: Akram Tagaev

169. What type of service did Mr. Tagaev most likely request?

(A) Mobile banking
(B) IT training
(C) Online advertising
(D) App development

170. According to the contract, why would a client be charged an additional fee?

(A) Scheduling a tutorial
(B) Using DMLT's code
(C) Failing to make a payment on time
(D) Requesting too many changes

171. What topic is NOT mentioned in the contract?

(A) Cyber security
(B) A cancellation procedure
(C) Intellectual property
(D) Troubleshooting support

Questions 172-175 refer to the following article.

Financial Update

CHICAGO (November 5) — Claudia Jardine, who has overseen the longest period of growth in Daubert Industries' history, made her retirement plans public at a shareholder meeting yesterday.

Jardine, who was born in Paris, received degrees in English and economics from Suttree University in New York. She then worked for an investment firm back home in Paris. After a successful decade there, she was hired to manage Daubert's Montreal branch.

At Daubert, Jardine became a rising star, moving up the ranks quickly and soon arriving at the firm's headquarters in Chicago, where she eventually secured the position of company president. Her passion for eliminating inefficiencies boosted Daubert's bottom line and made her an icon in the field.

Daubert's CFO, Jeremy Levi, has been named the provisional president while the search for a replacement takes place. Insiders at the company, however, have often speculated that given his three-year term as the firm's second in command, he will likely succeed Ms. Jardine.

Ms. Jardine plans to stay in the city. By remaining close, she will be able to retain a presence in the firm as an advisor.

172. What is the purpose of the article?
(A) To introduce a newly-hired manager
(B) To report on a company's expansion
(C) To explain the success of a business strategy
(D) To discuss the retirement of an executive

173. The word "secured" in paragraph 3, line 4, is closest in meaning to
(A) reassured
(B) guaranteed
(C) acquired
(D) shielded

174. What is suggested about Mr. Levi?
(A) He will move to a different city for his new position.
(B) He will likely become the permanent CEO.
(C) He received a degree from the same university as Ms. Jardine.
(D) He has worked for Daubert Industries for his entire career.

175. Where does Ms. Jardine currently live?
(A) In Paris
(B) In New York
(C) In Chicago
(D) In Montreal

GO ON TO THE NEXT PAGE

Questions 176-180 refer to the following e-mail and Web page.

To	: Ji-Young Kim
From	: Patricia Boggs
Date	: September 20
Subject	: Info

Dear Mr. Kim,

Because you were on holiday during the past week, you may not have been informed about the status of our Web site. A member of our Web development team, Roger Chark, was implementing some new features when an earthquake hit, and we experienced a power outage. It took a full day for us to get electricity back, which meant users were unable to access our Web site.

You mentioned wanting to email our members today to inform them of our fundraiser, so we can reach our goal amount before the new financial year begins on October 1.The site is up and running with a new section where patrons can discuss all matters related to the event. If you need anything else, please do not hesitate to contact me.

Best,

Patricia Boggs
IT Supervisor
Greenstone Library

http://www.greenstonelibrary.com/discussion

September 20

I love the Greenstone Library! Because of the library's many events, I have a newfound joy for reading. During this month's book club, we read a book by Adam Dent. I had never read a single science fiction book in my life, but I was pleasantly surprised to see how enjoyable the genre could be. I'm excited about next month's Author's Talk series, where I'll have a chance to meet my new favorite writer.

As a member of the library, I've made donations in the past. But since receiving a fundraising e-mail from the library's president, I decided to make another contribution today. I had some issues connecting to the Web site a few days ago but had no problems this afternoon. I encourage people to support the library by making a donation before October 1st. Keep the Greenstone Library events coming!

-Walter Minshew

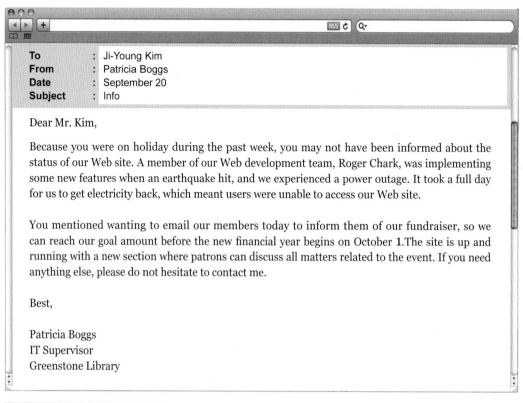

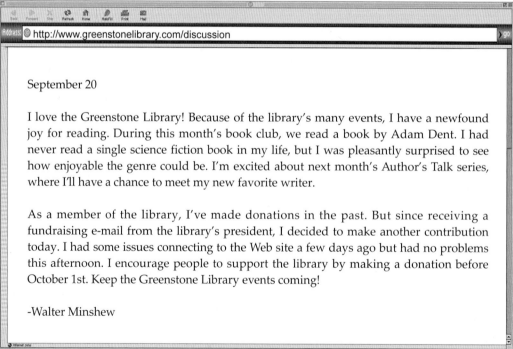

176. Why did Ms. Boggs contact Mr. Kim?

(A) To inquire about an event
(B) To announce a weather warning
(C) To recommend a job candidate
(D) To share a recent update

177. In the e-mail, the word "reach" in paragraph 2, line 2, is closest in meaning to

(A) contact
(B) stretch
(C) achieve
(D) extend

178. Who is Mr. Kim?

(A) A Web developer
(B) A local author
(C) The library president
(D) The IT supervisor

179. What is Mr. Minshew eager to do?

(A) Post on a Web page
(B) Attend a lecture series
(C) Organize a book club
(D) Sign up for a membership

180. What does Mr. Minshew suggest in his comment?

(A) He has met Adam Dent before.
(B) He recently downloaded a book from the library's online collection.
(C) He has read many science fiction novels in the past.
(D) He made a contribution before the end of a financial year.

GO ON TO THE NEXT PAGE

Questions 181-185 refer to the following e-mail and invoice.

DATE	: July 19
FROM	: freemandebbie@paulsoncc.org
TO	: rkipling@kiplingbros.net
SUBJECT	: Invoice no. 354789

Dear Mr. Kipling,

This e-mail is to notify you of some issues that I encountered with my most recent order. I've been using your business for years and have not experienced any errors before. Thus, I was shocked when I received my shipment yesterday. To start with, only one set of dumbbells arrived, which is not the quantity stated on the invoice. I read the note about the barbell set, but nothing was mentioned about the dumbbells.

Furthermore, product number 2985CM is $9 according to your Web page and brochure, but I was not charged that amount. Could you please take a look through your records and email me back as soon as possible?

I look forward to hearing from you soon.

Debbie Freeman

FOR	**FROM**
Debbie Freeman Paulson Community Center 4 Market Lane Hillsborough, NJ 08844	Kipling Brothers 8579 Pheasant Court Saint Albans, NY 11412

INVOICE MUST BE PAID WITHIN 24 HOURS OF RECEIPT

Invoice Number: 354789

Product Description	Product Number	Quantity	Price per Unit	Price
Dumbbell Weight Set with Emblem (2.5kg – 75kg)	136BE	2	$2,500	$5,000
Barbel Weight Set with Emblem (200kg)	832XZ	3	$850	$2,550
Microfiber towel, assorted color	4801YV	150	$2.50	$375
½ inch thick Yoga Mat with an emblem	2985CM	50	$12.00	$600

*Only two full barbell sets were in our inventory. Those two have been sent, and the final set will arrive within the next week. The additional delivery has been upgraded to express shipping.

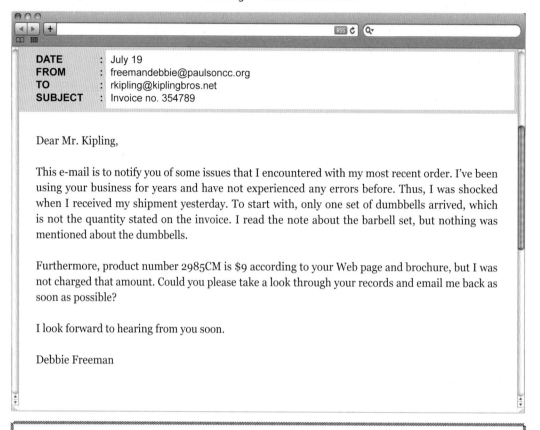

181. Kipling Brothers is most likely what type of business?

(A) A fitness center
(B) A physical therapy clinic
(C) A sporting goods supplier
(D) A fashion retailer

182. What is indicated about Ms. Freeman?

(A) She has purchased items from Kipling Brothers before.
(B) She requested express shipping.
(C) She is opening a new business location.
(D) She is a professional weightlifter.

183. What does Ms. Freeman request?

(A) Delivery to a different address
(B) A revised brochure
(C) An updated emblem design
(D) An e-mail response

184. According to the invoice, what is true about the barbell sets?

(A) Some of them will be delivered separately.
(B) Some of them were missing parts.
(C) They are made of different materials.
(D) They were in the sale.

185. What is one problem that Ms. Freeman identifies?

(A) The emblem on the dumbbells is too small.
(B) The barbells are not the correct weight.
(C) She was overcharged for the yoga mats.
(D) She did not receive enough towels.

GO ON TO THE NEXT PAGE

Questions 186-190 refer to the following chart, e-mail, and article.

Lissack Wallpaper – Farrow Collection
Products Available (updated 2 hours ago)

Name	Roll Size	Weight	Available for Purchase (today)	Available for Purchase (in 1 month)	Available for Purchase (in 2 months)
Samphire	50 sq. ft	1.8 kg	15	25	0
Golden Gate	50 sq. ft	1.8 kg	0	0	15
Fornasetti Bastoni	57 sq. ft	2 kg	12	12	12
Hallowtail	70 sq. ft	2.2 kg	25	30	0

To : Maxwell Vaughn
From : Ines Ronaldo
Date : 1 August
Subject : Operational measures
Attachment : Pictures.zip

Dear Mr. Vaughn,

I regretfully inform you that our wallpaper supplier, Lissack Wallpapers, will not have the pattern that we have selected for the Kraft Theater's concession stand and box office areas until after our anticipated grand opening date of September 3. I have attached pictures of possible substitutes that should match our interior designs, and they are competitively priced. With the opening about a month away, we need you to make a decision quickly. Although the change is unfortunate, I am positive that the Kraft Theater will still be able to provide the atmosphere we strive to achieve.

Sincerely,

Ines Ronaldo

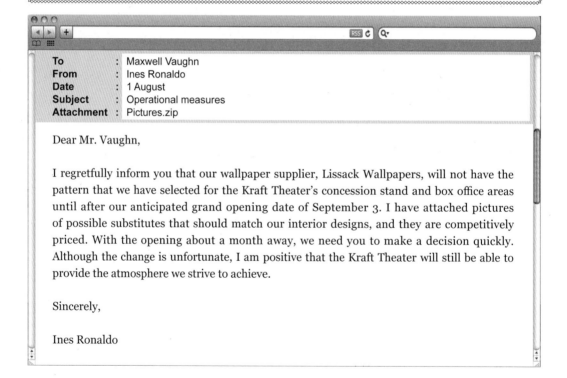

Kraft Theater Grand Opening

By Omar Blank

(Willowbrook—4 September) Local entrepreneur Crason Bayard joined former city mayor Sam Littleton yesterday to celebrate the first-ever showing at the new Kraft Theater located in the city center, across the street from Willowbrook Bank and the library. Previously the City Hall building and Mr. Littleton's place of employment, the original structure had been deserted for the last decade. Newly renovated, the building now houses 12 movie screens, a spacious concessions area with various snacks and beverages, and an open box office. An accompanying garden is scheduled to open in the spring. The layout, designed by Ines Ronaldo, keeps many original elements of the architecture, such as the marbled floors and domed ceiling, while adding a modern twist.

186. What does the chart indicate about all the wallpaper styles in the Farrow Collection?

(A) They are the same weight.
(B) They come in different sizes.
(C) They are currently available for purchase.
(D) They will be delivered in two months.

187. What wallpaper did Ms. Ronaldo originally order?

(A) Samphire
(B) Golden Gate
(C) Fornasetti Bastoni
(D) Hallowtail

188. What does Ms. Ronaldo ask Mr. Vaughn to do?

(A) Postpone the theater's opening
(B) Take pictures of a concession area
(C) Contact a supplier directly
(D) Make an alternate selection

189. According to the article, what occupied the building prior to the Kraft Theater?

(A) Some government offices
(B) Some dining facilities
(C) A bank
(D) A library

190. What is indicated about the Kraft Theater?

(A) It was constructed 10 years ago.
(B) It opened as planned.
(C) It is the site of a new film festival.
(D) It is owned by Mr. Littleton.

GO ON TO THE NEXT PAGE

Questions 191-195 refer to the following memo, schedule, and e-mail.

To	: All Markieff employees
From	: Markieff Facilities Department
Date	: 13 March
Subject	: Improvements to the company charter bus system

To directly implement your feedback from the recent questionnaire, we have decided to make improvements to the company's charter bus system that transports employees to Markieff laboratory and central office from the designated pickup point. The changes will take effect in the beginning of April:

(1) A fourth bus will be purchased to make sure that buses run as scheduled in case one breaks down. In addition, buses will now run every 30 minutes, not every hour.

(2) A second pickup location has also been added. As of now, we only stop at the Huntington Parking Garage at the south end of the city. However, the second stop will provide many employees with a more convenient commute.

(3) A late-night service has been implemented. The final bus will depart from the central office at 9 P.M.

We appreciate everyone's suggestions and concerns. We pride ourselves in being an employee-first company, and we are more than happy to accommodate as much of you as possible with our upgraded charter bus system.

Charter Bus Timetable—Weekday (mornings)

(Revised 1 April)

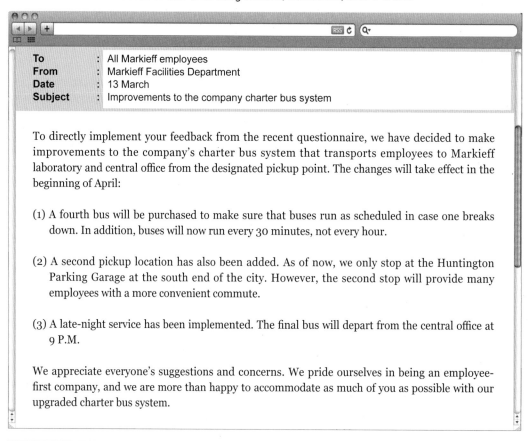

South Side Parking Garage	North Side Parking Garage	Markieff Laboratory	Markieff Central Office
5:30	5:41	5:54	5:58
6:00	6:11	6:24	6:28
6:30	6:41	6:54	6:58
7:00	7:11	7:24	7:28
7:30	7:41	8:54	7:58
8:00	8:11	8:24	8:28
8:30	8:41	8:54	8:58

To	:	Khayri Hariri <khariri@markieff.net>
From	:	David Berglund <dberglund@nowmail.com>
Date	:	17 April
Subject	:	Candidate interview at Markieff

Dear Mr. Hariri,

I appreciate the opportunity to interview Ms. Parnas this week on the Markieff grounds. I am delighted to have been chosen as a final candidate for the position in clinical research. I have received the timetable for the company charter bus. I plan to park at the north side garage at 8:30 A.M. and wait for the next bus to pick me up and drop me off at the central office, just in time for our meeting.

Best,

David Berglund

191. What reason is given for updating the charter bus system?

(A) Markieff is trying to reduce its environmental footprint.
(B) Markieff staff members provided feedback.
(C) The current buses are breaking down.
(D) A new building is being constructed on company grounds.

192. What will be one change to the bus system in April?

(A) Buses will run later at night.
(B) Buses will be accessible by wheelchair.
(C) A second bus route will be added.
(D) Buses will be powered by electricity.

193. What bus stop will be added to the route?

(A) South Side Parking Garage
(B) North Side Parking Garage
(C) Markieff Laboratory
(D) Markieff Central Office

194. Why will Mr. Berglund visit the Markieff grounds?

(A) To pursue an employment opportunity
(B) To present some research findings
(C) To finalize a merger of his company with Markieff
(D) To receive some on-site training

195. What time does Mr. Berglund expect to get off his bus at Markieff?

(A) At 7:28 A.M.
(B) At 7:58 A.M.
(C) At 8:28 A.M.
(D) At 8:58 A.M.

GO ON TO THE NEXT PAGE

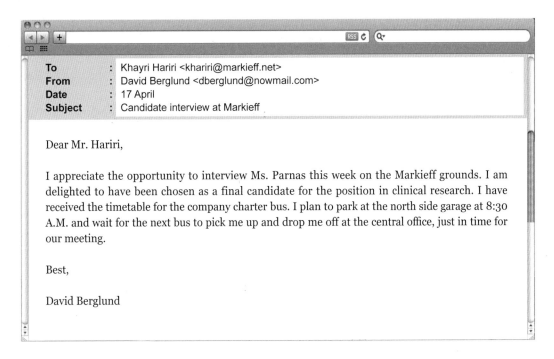

Questions 196-200 refer to the following invoice, review, and e-mail.

Nari Refresh

Invoice Number: 423689
Name: Denise Lett
Location Preference: Southwest branch

Product ID	**Product Detail**	**Total Amount**	**Price**
GS–103	Soho Gentle	150 sq. ft.	$450
GS-104	Brown Basketweave	45 sq. ft.	$225
GS-112	Sage Basketweave	20 sq. ft.	$100
GS-135	Zurro Floral	100 sq. ft.	$455
GS-136	Solstice Floral	75 sq. ft.	$320
			Grand Total $1,550
Pick up Location:	Nari Refresh—Southwest branch 915 Pine Avenue (404)555-7839 info@narirefresh.com		

Other stores:
Northwest main branch: 41 Grant Lane
Northeast branch: 834 Corona St.
Southeast branch: 173 King Dr.

Address: http://www.setimes.org/business/nari_refresh

25 June

After recently hearing about Nari Refresh's new in-store pickup service, I decided to give it a try last week. I was delighted with the efficiency of the whole process. Having paid through their Web site, I was able to pick up my items without having to wait in line.

Unfortunately, I was in a rush and did not have time to check my items at the store. As I was preparing to install the tiles at my client's house, I noticed that only half of product GS-135 was included. I contacted the store right away. Luckily, the supervisor located the missing items and arranged for me to pick them up at the branch closest to me. In addition, he gave me a coupon to be used for my next purchase. All in all, this service was a great help, and I'll be using it again in the future.

Denise Lett

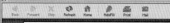

To:	Denise Lett <dlett@lettsmake.net>
From:	Keith Peters <keithpeters@narirefresh.com>
Date:	26 June
Subject:	Pick-up service

Dear Ms. Lett,

Thank you for the review on the SE Times Web site. We sincerely appreciate your business. We are relieved to hear that you could conveniently access our main branch from your work site so that you could retrieve the rest of your tiles without experiencing too much trouble.

Our goal is to provide excellent customer service to match our high-quality products, and I hope to serve you again soon. As you know, spring is right around the corner, which means it is the perfect time to pick up supplies for all your gardening needs!

Keith Peters
Customer Service Agent
Nari Refresh

196. For what industry does Ms. Lett most likely work?

(A) Home improvement
(B) Real estate
(C) Transport
(D) Food and beverage

197. What item did Ms. Lett need more of?

(A) Brown Basketweave
(B) Sage Basketweave
(C) Zurro Floral
(D) Solstice Floral

198. Where did Ms. Lett pick up the item missing from her order?

(A) At the southwest store
(B) At the northwest store
(C) At the northeast store
(D) At the southeast store

199. What is indicated about Nari Refresh?

(A) It sells landscaping equipment.
(B) It offers discounts for customers who write online reviews.
(C) It provides an overseas delivery service.
(D) It hires design professionals for in-house consultation.

200. What is one purpose of Mr. Peters's e-mail?

(A) To show appreciation to a customer
(B) To introduce a new product
(C) To detail reasons for a company policy change
(D) To inform clients about a seasonal promotion

Stop! This is the end of the test. If you finish before time is called, you may go back to Part 5, 6, and 7 and check your work.

실전 모의고사 2

MP3 바로 듣기

해설서 바로 가기

• **준비물:** OMR 카드, 연필, 지우개, 시계
• **시험시간:** LC 약 45분 RC 75분

나의 점수		
	LC	**RC**
맞은 개수		
환산 점수		
총점: ______________ 점		

점수 환산표			
LC		**RC**	
맞은 개수	환산 점수	맞은 개수	환산 점수
96-100	475-495	96-100	460-495
91-95	435-495	91-95	425-490
86-90	405-475	86-90	395-465
81-85	370-450	81-85	370-440
76-80	345-420	76-80	335-415
71-75	320-390	71-75	310-390
66-70	290-360	66-70	280-365
61-65	265-335	61-65	250-335
56-60	235-310	56-60	220-305
51-55	210-280	51-55	195-270
46-50	180-255	46-50	165-240
41-45	155-230	41-45	140-215
36-40	125-205	36-40	115-180
31-35	105-175	31-35	95-145
26-30	85-145	26-30	75-120
21-25	60-115	21-25	60-95
16-20	30-90	16-20	45-75
11-15	5-70	11-15	30-55
6-10	5-60	6-10	10-40
1-5	5-60	1-5	5-30
0	5-35	0	5-15

TEST 2

Actual Test_2.mp3

LISTENING TEST

In the Listening test, you will be asked to demonstrate how well you understand spoken English. The entire listening test will last approximately 45 minutes. There are four parts, and directions are given for each part. You must mark your answers on the separate answer sheet. Do not write your answers in your test book.

PART 1

Directions: For each question in this part, you will hear four statements about a picture in your test book. When you hear the statements, you must select the one statement that best describes what you see in the picture. Then find the number of the question on your answer sheet and mark your answer. The statements will not be printed in your test book and will be spoken only one time.

Statement (B), "A man is pointing at a document," is the best description of the picture, so you should select answer (B) and mark it on your answer sheet.

1.

2.

GO ON TO THE NEXT PAGE

3.

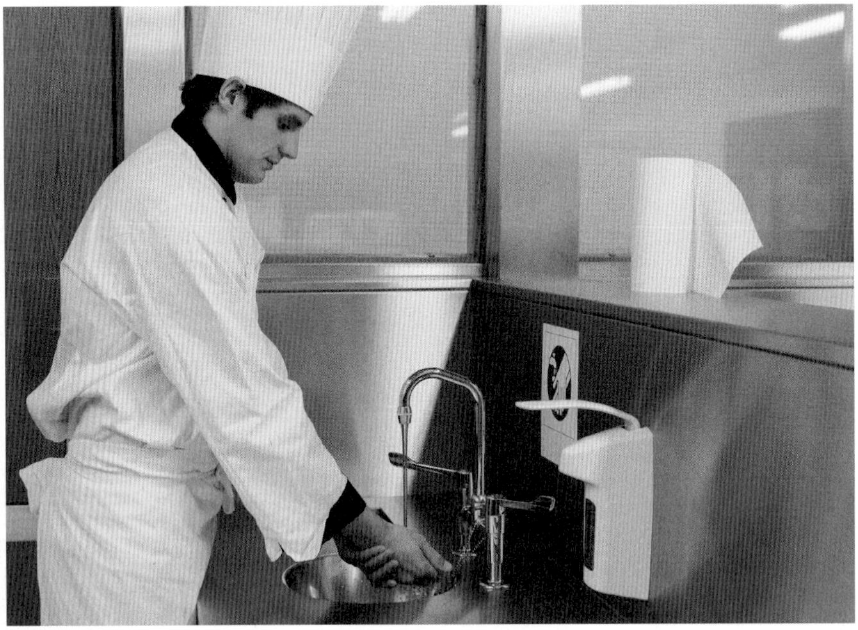

4.

5.

6.

GO ON TO THE NEXT PAGE

PART 2

Directions: You will hear a question or statement and three responses spoken in English. They will not be printed in your test book and will be spoken only one time. Select the best response to the question or statement and mark the letter (A), (B), or (C) on your answer sheet.

7. Mark your answer on your answer sheet.
8. Mark your answer on your answer sheet.
9. Mark your answer on your answer sheet.
10. Mark your answer on your answer sheet.
11. Mark your answer on your answer sheet.
12. Mark your answer on your answer sheet.
13. Mark your answer on your answer sheet.
14. Mark your answer on your answer sheet.
15. Mark your answer on your answer sheet.
16. Mark your answer on your answer sheet.
17. Mark your answer on your answer sheet.
18. Mark your answer on your answer sheet.
19. Mark your answer on your answer sheet.
20. Mark your answer on your answer sheet.
21. Mark your answer on your answer sheet.
22. Mark your answer on your answer sheet.
23. Mark your answer on your answer sheet.
24. Mark your answer on your answer sheet.
25. Mark your answer on your answer sheet.
26. Mark your answer on your answer sheet.
27. Mark your answer on your answer sheet.
28. Mark your answer on your answer sheet.
29. Mark your answer on your answer sheet.
30. Mark your answer on your answer sheet.
31. Mark your answer on your answer sheet.

PART 3

Directions: You will hear some conversations between two or more people. You will be asked to answer three questions about what the speakers say in each conversation. Select the best response to each question and mark the letter (A), (B), (C), or (D) on your answer sheet. The conversations will not be printed in your test book and will be spoken only one time.

32. What product is being discussed?
(A) A personal device
(B) A medical instrument
(C) A kitchen appliance
(D) A computer software

33. What caused a delay?
(A) A lack of materials
(B) A staffing shortage
(C) A reduced budget
(D) A design change

34. What will happen early next year?
(A) An inspection will be performed.
(B) An upgrade will be available.
(C) A product will be launched.
(D) A store will open.

---

35. Where do the speakers most likely work?
(A) At a printing shop
(B) At a photography studio
(C) At an art gallery
(D) At a department store

36. What has the woman decided to do?
(A) Find a new supplier
(B) Provide additional discount
(C) Ensure a service
(D) Open for longer hours

37. What does the man expect will happen?
(A) Profits will increase.
(B) More online purchases will be made.
(C) Another employee will be hired.
(D) Customer reviews will improve.

38. Where does the man work?
(A) At a department store
(B) At a furniture shop
(C) At an engineering firm
(D) At a car dealership

39. What is the woman concerned about?
(A) A specification
(B) A price
(C) A checkup
(D) A component

40. What will the woman do tomorrow morning?
(A) Make a payment
(B) Revise a document
(C) Try out a product
(D) Visit a client

---

41. What event are the speakers discussing?
(A) A retirement celebration
(B) An anniversary party
(C) An award ceremony
(D) A fundraising dinner

42. Why does the man say, "They're using this room for a board meeting first thing tomorrow"?
(A) To reject an idea
(B) To make an invitation
(C) To suggest another venue
(D) To emphasize an advantage

43. What does the man suggest doing?
(A) Using some cleaning supplies
(B) Calling another office branch
(C) Getting assistance from a coworker
(D) Ordering some extra food

GO ON TO THE NEXT PAGE

44. Where does the man work?

(A) At a shipping firm
(B) At a travel agency
(C) At a fitness center
(D) At a car rental company

45. According to the man, what event will take place later this month?

(A) A movie premiere
(B) A sports competition
(C) An industry convention
(D) A theater performance

46. What does the man suggest?

(A) Taking a shuttle
(B) Completing an application
(C) Booking a flight
(D) Using a credit card

---

47. What does the company need the woman for?

(A) Restoring a historical building
(B) Creating a training manual
(C) Organizing a grand opening
(D) Designing a smartphone app

48. Why is the woman the first applicant to be interviewed?

(A) She has worked for the company before.
(B) She submitted the best proposal.
(C) Her work has won an award.
(D) Her educational background was impressive.

49. What do the men mention about the museum?

(A) It offers amazing scenery.
(B) It is conveniently located.
(C) It has a unique architecture.
(D) It used to be a government office.

50. What does the woman say will happen this weekend?

(A) Some walls will be painted.
(B) Some products will be on sale.
(C) Some items will be given away.
(D) Some demonstrations will be held.

51. What does the man mean when he says, "I'll be in here often"?

(A) He is impressed by a new shop.
(B) He needs some products for his job.
(C) He passes by a location daily.
(D) He knows several store employees.

52. Why does the woman apologize?

(A) She is unable to provide some information.
(B) She failed to prepare some documents.
(C) She charged too much for an item.
(D) She cannot accept a payment method.

---

53. What type of product is being discussed?

(A) A bathroom fixture
(B) A musical instrument
(C) A household appliance
(D) An automobile part

54. What is the woman's complaint about the product?

(A) It is the wrong size.
(B) It is too loud.
(C) It is defective.
(D) It is missing some accessories.

55. What does Nelson suggest the woman do?

(A) Contact a supervisor
(B) Use a factory warranty
(C) Read a user's manual
(D) Purchase a different model

56. Where do the speakers most likely work?
(A) At a technical support center
(B) At a vocational school
(C) At a boat repair store
(D) At a home improvement shop

57. What are the speakers talking about?
(A) An air conditioning system
(B) A navigation device
(C) An emergency alarm
(D) An electric engine

58. What does the man ask the woman to do?
(A) Create a poster
(B) Consult a professional
(C) Check some inventory
(D) Confirm a work schedule

---

59. Where does the woman work?
(A) At a shipping firm
(B) At a real estate agency
(C) At a financial company
(D) At a government facility

60. What is mentioned about recent transactions?
(A) They tend to be smaller in size.
(B) They are often from overseas.
(C) They can be canceled easily.
(D) They need to be individually reviewed.

61. According to the woman, how has the firm managed to stay profitable?
(A) By reducing its labor force
(B) By raising its transaction fees
(C) By closing its branch offices
(D) By using automated technology

Equipment Report

Device	Condition
X-ray Machine	Good
Patient Chair	Old but usable
Instrument Sterilizer	Glass cracked
Surgical Light	Needs cleaning

62. Where do the speakers work?
(A) At a pharmacy
(B) At a fitness center
(C) At a laboratory
(D) At a dental clinic

63. Look at the graphic. Which device are the speakers talking about?
(A) An X-ray machine
(B) A patient chair
(C) An instrument sterilizer
(D) A surgical light

64. What will the man do next?
(A) Pick up a shipment
(B) Choose a supplier
(C) Fill out a form
(D) Meet with a coworker

GO ON TO THE NEXT PAGE

Earl's Appointments	
Appointment	**Time**
Safety Inspection	8:00 A.M.
Factory Visit	10:00 A.M.
Distributor Meeting	12:00 P.M.
Welcome Luncheon	12:15 P.M.
Industry Seminar	2:00 P.M.

65. Where is the conversation occurring?

(A) At a restaurant
(B) At a distributor's office
(C) At an automobile factory
(D) At a convention center

66. What will be discussed by the speakers?

(A) A travel schedule
(B) A training program
(C) A company merger
(D) A policy update

67. Look at the graphic. Why does Earl need to leave early?

(A) He is performing a safety inspection.
(B) He is making a factory visit.
(C) He is meeting with a distributor.
(D) He is attending an industry seminar.

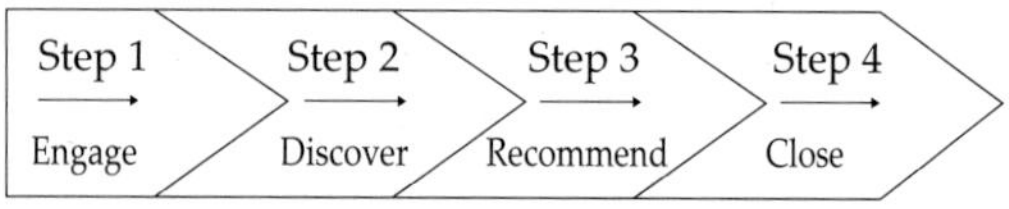

68. Where most likely are the speakers?

(A) At a board meeting
(B) At a performance review
(C) At a book signing
(D) At a career fair

69. Look at the graphic. Which step does the man say is most difficult?

(A) Engaging
(B) Discovering
(C) Recommending
(D) Closing

70. What does the woman say she will do if she is hired?

(A) Subscribe to a magazine
(B) Enroll in a class
(C) Contact a representative
(D) Write a thank-you note

PART 4

Directions: You will hear some talks given by a single speaker. You will be asked to answer three questions about what the speaker says in each talk. Select the best response to each question and mark the letter (A), (B), (C), or (D) on your answer sheet. The talks will not be printed in your test book and will be spoken only one time.

71. What does the speaker thank the listeners for?
(A) Making some recommendations
(B) Presenting some sales figures
(C) Attending an event
(D) Submitting some documents

72. What is the speaker excited about?
(A) A dinner party
(B) A musical performance
(C) An awards ceremony
(D) A renovation project

73. What will happen this weekend?
(A) An expansion will be completed.
(B) A new product will be released.
(C) A holiday sale will begin.
(D) A site will be inspected.

74. Who are the listeners?
(A) Administrative assistants
(B) Temporary employees
(C) Development trainers
(D) Team leaders

75. Why does the speaker say, "your employees will be understanding"?
(A) To acknowledge an update
(B) To give encouragement
(C) To compliment a staff
(D) To explain a procedure

76. What does the speaker remind the listeners to do?
(A) Request additional budget
(B) Show some appreciation
(C) Provide detailed information
(D) Distribute an evaluation survey

77. What is being advertised?
(A) Some cooking appliances
(B) Some athletic clothing
(C) An exercise program
(D) An energy bar

78. What does the speaker say is surprising about the product?
(A) Its accessibility
(B) Its affordability
(C) Its ease of use
(D) Its personalization

79. What can the listeners do on a Web site?
(A) Sign up for a newsletter
(B) Find store locations
(C) Chat with famous celebrities
(D) Purchase some items

80. Where was the listener last week?
(A) At a construction site
(B) At an exhibition
(C) On personal leave
(D) On a factory tour

81. What business does the speaker most likely work for?
(A) An engineering company
(B) An automobile manufacturer
(C) A consulting agency
(D) A magazine publisher

82. What does the speaker ask the listener to do?
(A) Attend an on-site meeting
(B) Revise a work schedule
(C) Examine his designs
(D) Return his phone call

GO ON TO THE NEXT PAGE

83. What is the broadcast mainly about?
(A) A library renovation
(B) A subway extension
(C) An artifact restoration
(D) An architecture conference

84. Why was Soodi and Partners selected for the project?
(A) It is a local firm.
(B) It has worked with City Hall before.
(C) It presented the most cost-effective proposal.
(D) It uses a contemporary approach.

85. According to the speaker, what can be found on a Web site?
(A) A company profile
(B) A virtual model
(C) A release timeline
(D) A list of sponsors

---

86. What type of event is taking place?
(A) An anniversary party
(B) A product launch
(C) An awards show
(D) A fundraising dinner

87. What product does the speaker highlight?
(A) A technologically advanced car
(B) A multipurpose home appliance
(C) An environmentally friendly smartphone
(D) An interactive entertainment system

88. Who is Tiffany Fant?
(A) An executive officer
(B) A product designer
(C) A reporter
(D) A software developer

89. Why does the speaker say, "we just moved to a new location"?
(A) To extend an invitation
(B) To provide an explanation
(C) To make an announcement
(D) To show excitement

90. What does the speaker show the listeners?
(A) A corporate manual
(B) A list of communities
(C) An organizational chart
(D) A sample advertisement

91. What are the listeners expected to do by next Monday?
(A) Purchase some items
(B) Create a survey
(C) Participate in a study
(D) Visit some clients

---

92. What is Kendrick Herro's area of expertise?
(A) Business consulting
(B) Corporate accounting
(C) Software development
(D) Public relations

93. What is HelloList?
(A) A voice recording device
(B) A social networking site
(C) A mobile app
(D) A news service

94. Why does the speaker say, "The app uploads user information to its private server without prior consent"?
(A) To describe why a product is not functioning correctly
(B) To give a reason why some critics do not approve of a product
(C) To ask listeners to provide some personal information
(D) To demonstrate how a product performs

Neighborhoods in Franklin County

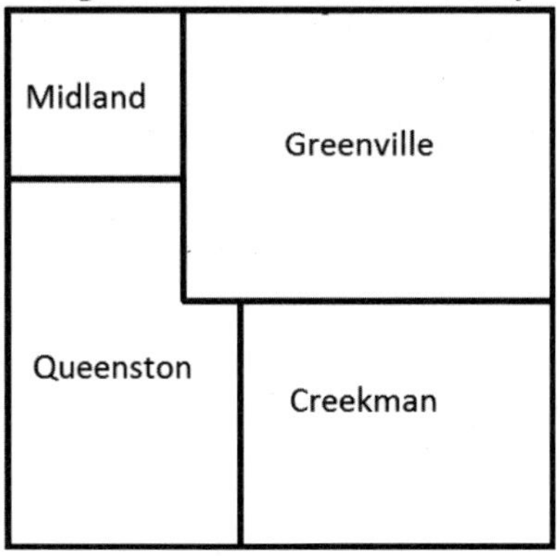

95. What type of business does the speaker own?

(A) A rideshare service
(B) A boutique shop
(C) A supermarket chain
(D) A deli franchise

96. Look at the graphic. In which neighborhood does the speaker want to offer a new service?

(A) Midland
(B) Greenville
(C) Queenston
(D) Creekman

97. What does the speaker want to discuss next?

(A) A relocation process
(B) A reimbursement policy
(C) Marketing strategies
(D) Business hours

Proposal Presentation Schedule for September 9

Company	Time
Plyold Co.	9 A.M.
Brical Inc.	11 A.M.
Marbon Corp.	2 P.M.
Sanite Firm	4 P.M.

98. Why is the speaker unable to participate in one of the interviews?

(A) He will be visiting a clinic.
(B) He missed his train.
(C) He has an urgent deadline.
(D) He is going on a work trip.

99. Look at the graphic. Who is the listener asked to interview?

(A) Plyold Co.
(B) Brical Inc.
(C) Marbon Corp.
(D) Sanite Firm

100. What does the speaker say he will do?

(A) Send some information
(B) Arrange for transportation
(C) Update a schedule
(D) Book a meeting room

This is the end of the Listening test. Turn to Part 5 in your test book.

GO ON TO THE NEXT PAGE

READING TEST

In the Reading test, you will read a variety of texts and answer several different types of reading comprehension questions. The entire Reading test will last 75 minutes. There are three parts, and directions are given for each part. You are encouraged to answer as many questions as possible within the time allowed.

You must mark your answers on the separate answer sheet. Do not write your answers in your test book.

PART 5

Directions: A word or phrase is missing in each of the sentences below. Four answer choices are given below each sentence. Select the best answer to complete the sentence. Then mark the letter (A), (B), (C), or (D) on your answer sheet.

101. The Altamont Inn is conveniently located and has ------- own café.

(A) every
(B) its
(C) one
(D) other

102. Passengers should anticipate ------- delays in bus service caused by the unusually hot weather.

(A) connected
(B) accessible
(C) frequent
(D) distant

103. The legal assistants who earned ------- last year will be assigned to specific attorneys starting next month.

(A) promotions
(B) promotes
(C) promoted
(D) promote

104. HH Clinic stops accepting patients at 6 P.M., ------- those already on the list will be treated.

(A) who
(B) but
(C) even
(D) or

105. Self-employed tax accountants should have a ------- location to store financial information for many years.

(A) secure
(B) securing
(C) security
(D) securely

106. To apply for the photographer position, interested parties are asked to ------- samples of their images.

(A) propose
(B) counsel
(C) sustain
(D) submit

107. A Ranger Investment broker will work ------- with you to make sure that your portfolio is profitable.

(A) closed
(B) close
(C) closeness
(D) closely

108. Rethark Corp.'s administrative assistants are expected to ensure regular ------- of the notebook computers issued for their use.

(A) record
(B) safety
(C) maintenance
(D) acquisition

109. Dunfield Acres sets its rental rates so that residents can feel ------- that they are living in the best condos in the city.

(A) confidentially
(B) confident
(C) confidential
(D) confiding

110. An outline is distributed to shareholders ------- before all financial report meetings.

(A) economically
(B) meticulously
(C) electronically
(D) eventually

111. Remember to ------- the story about the anniversary until some photographs can be added without taking up more pages.

(A) shorten
(B) shortest
(C) short
(D) shortly

112. Employees will greet the new doctors at an informal brunch with refreshments provided ------- a local bakery.

(A) as
(B) by
(C) with
(D) from

113. Stop by our exhibition space at this year's Audio Visual Convention, ------- our newest line of WiFi integrated products will be demonstrated.

(A) each
(B) regarding
(C) where
(D) instead

114. ------- interest in the seminar series did not meet expectations, it was quickly cancelled.

(A) When
(B) Even though
(C) Why
(D) Other than

115. Guests are recommended to read the activity liability agreement thoroughly before ------- it.

(A) signs
(B) sign
(C) signing
(D) signed

116. Before it can form a partnership with PC Peri Products, Cobalt Computers must complete a ------- analysis of its assets.

(A) careful
(B) supplied
(C) tractable
(D) previous

117. Only senior technicians at Galbraith Labs have ------- to enter the clean rooms.

(A) permitted
(B) permissive
(C) permit
(D) permission

118. Palimpsest, Inc. meets all your document needs ------- expert composition and printing.

(A) bringing
(B) including
(C) dealing
(D) causing

119. The sales associate knows very ------- about automotive parts, so she will contact a coworker with more experience.

(A) little
(B) many
(C) none
(D) any

120. This year, a lack of demand for apartments resulted in a ------- in overall property prices.

(A) reduction
(B) shortage
(C) collection
(D) purchase

GO ON TO THE NEXT PAGE

121. Mercury Athletics recently announced the opening of a chain of outlet stores, making its clothing ------- to a wider customer base.

(A) afford
(B) afforded
(C) affording
(D) affordable

122. Passengers are required to have their vehicles weighed ------- boarding the ferry for the mainland.

(A) before
(B) beyond
(C) about
(D) within

123. The technician advised us to progress ------- as we upgrade our operating systems.

(A) cautions
(B) caution
(C) cautiously
(D) cautious

124. The ------- volume of packages has created the need for more truck drivers.

(A) enticing
(B) light
(C) noisy
(D) rising

125. Mr. Watson is permitted to accept the produce shipment, when it -------.

(A) is delivered
(B) delivers
(C) deliveries
(D) will deliver

126. Of all the resorts on Grandiose Isle, Frontenac Hotel is regarded as ------- luxurious.

(A) successfully
(B) assuredly
(C) particularly
(D) repeatedly

127. The value of Norcroft shares increased by about 50 percent in May, ------- amazed even the most optimistic board members.

(A) what
(B) therefore
(C) it
(D) which

128. Due to a ------- vote, Ms. Phair and Mr. Schmidt both received the Innovator of the Year Prize at the Annual Technology Conference.

(A) tie
(B) pair
(C) large
(D) similar

129. In January, the city orchestra will perform many new musical -------.

(A) arrangers
(B) arrange
(C) arranging
(D) arrangements

130. After five years of working in advertising, Ms. Carter chose to ------- a degree in graphic design.

(A) adapt
(B) support
(C) graduate
(D) pursue

PART 6

Directions: Read the texts that follow. A word, phrase, or sentence is missing in parts of each text. Four answer choices for each question are given below the text. Select the best answer to complete the text. Then mark the letter (A), (B), (C), or (D) on your answer sheet.

Questions 131-134 refer to the following e-mail.

To: All Staff
From: Donna Biederman
Date: November 29
Subject: Site Updates

This is a reminder that the time has come for the Cybersecurity team to ------- **131.** regular software updates. -------. **132.** The site will be down from Tuesday at 8 P.M. until 8 A.M. Wednesday. Note that access to the app will also be affected. Because of this, several services will be temporarily unavailable. ------- **133.** this routine update, you will not be able to post on the site or use the company messenger system. In anticipation of this, staff members should arrange their schedules to make sure to get critical tasks done beforehand. We ------- **134.** any trouble resulting from this.

131. (A) perform
(B) improve
(C) submit
(D) remove

132. (A) Please include information on the times when you will be available.
(B) If you would like an upgraded version, notify your department head.
(C) IT will send an e-mail out the night before.
(D) The process will get underway tomorrow night.

133. (A) Until
(B) Completely
(C) Throughout
(D) Once

134. (A) regrettably
(B) regretting
(C) regretted
(D) regret

GO ON TO THE NEXT PAGE

Questions 135-138 refer to the following letter.

July 17
Ronald Beringer
90 North Road
Salford
M5 6WT
United Kingdom

Dear Mr. Beringer,

Congratulations on your exceptional ------- (135.) in Salford, Blackpool, and Sheffield. The Northwest region has increased its manufacturing output for three consecutive years. ------- (136.).

I'd like you to be our new Vice President of National Operations. The position ------- (137.) in London. I understand that moving across the country brings with it difficulties. ------- (138.), I think this could be a huge opportunity for your career and major promotion. In any case, take some time to consider it. When you have some time, call me so we can talk about this in more detail.

As always, thank you for your valuable contributions.

Best,
Mary Timony, CEO

135. (A) clients
(B) comments
(C) trips
(D) efforts

136. (A) I'm planning to be in Salford in a few weeks.
(B) Such performance should be rewarded.
(C) Please call a meeting to address this.
(D) Our records show it was produced in Sheffield.

137. (A) was based
(B) bases
(C) is based
(D) basing

138. (A) Still
(B) Besides
(C) Likewise
(D) For example

Questions 139-142 refer to the following memo.

To: All
From: Simon VanderVleet
Date: January 21
Subject: Wendy Garland

Hello everyone,

As I'm sure you already know, Wendy Garland, the firm's longest-serving member and managing partner, ------- (**139.**) on January 31. Three decades ago, when she and Mr. Williams founded the firm, Ms. Garland had ambitions of establishing a prestigious practice with a strong local reputation. -------. (**140.**) Williams and Garland now represent some of the biggest companies in the country and has won landmark cases for its clients time after time.

Ms. Garland will be ------- (**141.**) by Rachel McDuff, her protégé, who has become one of our star litigators over her 8 years with Williams and Garland.

A party will be held on the evening of January 25 to celebrate Ms. Garland's ------- (**142.**) career. More details about this celebration will be made available once the arrangements are finalized.

Best,

Simon VanderVleet

139. (A) was to retire
(B) would retire
(C) will be retiring
(D) retired

140. (A) The results exceeded all expectations.
(B) She got her degree in Economics there.
(C) Everyone is invited to the ceremony.
(D) The event will be held on the 8th floor.

141. (A) attained
(B) accomplished
(C) concluded
(D) succeeded

142. (A) potential
(B) illustrious
(C) studious
(D) leading

GO ON TO THE NEXT PAGE

Questions 143-146 refer to the following memo.

To: All
From: Foster McCluster
Date: March 15
Re: Client Entertainment

In order to reduce -------, the board has decided to revise our guidelines on client entertainment. (143.) The new rules will be ------- (144.) on April 2. Starting on that date, employees who plan on using up to $50 on dining out or otherwise entertaining clients must file a written request with their department head at least 48 hours in advance of doing so. -------. (145.)

------- (146.) questions or concerns about these new guidelines should be directed to the HR Department.

143. (A) spends
(B) spender
(C) spending
(D) spend

144. (A) discussed
(B) reversed
(C) evaluated
(D) implemented

145. (A) It has come to the board's attention that the policy has not been sufficient.
(B) Dining out together is an effective way of building a strong relationship with potential clients.
(C) Requests exceeding this amount require a confirmation from the Director of Accounting.
(D) The guidelines will be announced before the next board meeting in April.

146. (A) Other
(B) Any
(C) Former
(D) Those

PART 7

Directions: In this part, you will read a selection of texts, such as magazine and newspaper articles, e-mails, and instant messages. Each text or set of texts is followed by several questions. Select the best answer for each question and mark the letter (A), (B), (C), or (D) on your answer sheet.

Questions 147-148 refer to the following postcard.

Segale Ristorante

Get 40 percent off your total for orders exceeding $40 at any one of our branches until 1 December. Hand this postcard to your server when ordering to qualify for your discount.

It may not be eligible for use during lunch hours in some stores.

For a complete menu and nutritional information, visit www.segalefoods.com.

147. Why did Segale Ristorante send the postcard?

(A) To promote a lunch menu
(B) To advertise a Web site
(C) To invite diners to a new restaurant
(D) To provide a discount

148. What is indicated about Segale Ristorante?

(A) It no longer provides delivery.
(B) It offers healthy dining options.
(C) It sends postcards to members.
(D) It has multiple stores.

GO ON TO THE NEXT PAGE

Questions 149-150 refer to the following memo.

To: All staff
From: Kristen Jensen
Date: October 12
Subject: Notice

The photocopier will be out of commission in the morning on Tuesday from 9 until noon. The IT team will be putting in a new unit, which will require some set-up and assembly. They will dispose of the old one after this is completed.

Accordingly, I would like to remind everyone to plan ahead and copy, print, or scan anything they need beforehand or save it for after lunch. If absolutely necessary, the Maple Street Office, located only three blocks away, may be able to help.

Please contact me right away if you have any questions or concerns.

Best,

Kristen

149. What does Ms. Jensen indicate in the memo?

(A) A business is going to be closed on Tuesday.
(B) A photocopier will be replaced.
(C) A new Internet network is being set up.
(D) Someone has been misusing some equipment.

150. What does the memo suggest?

(A) Ms. Jensen needs some documents scanned.
(B) Ms. Jensen works at the Maple Street Office.
(C) There is only one printer in the office.
(D) A security system requires assembly.

Questions 151-153 refer to the following advertisement.

You're Already On Your Way With Australian Air

Sign up for our Frequent Flyer Rewards Program and start enjoying exclusive rewards today! Being a part of the program will entitle you to benefits including:

* Discounted seat upgrades
* Bonus Frequent Flyer Club Miles
* Charges waived on up to three checked suitcases
* Complimentary shuttle service to participating hotels
* Admittance to the Aussie Club at any of the nation's ten busiest airports

Club Amenities

* Fresh, free snacks and beverages 24/7
* Business Center, with private workspaces and personal desktop computers
* Charging points for mobile devices and high-speed Internet access
* Shower and sauna areas

Register online or in-person at any Australian Air boarding gate (up to 30 minutes prior to departure). Your perks will go into effect right away.

151. Who would most likely benefit from joining the Frequent Flyer Rewards Program?
(A) Passengers who fly with multiple pieces of luggage
(B) People who purchase first-class tickets
(C) Passengers who are health-conscious
(D) People who live close to a busy airport

152. Where are the clubs located?
(A) In well-trafficked airports
(B) At regional transportation centers
(C) On several continents
(D) In Australia's international airports

153. What is one feature the clubs do NOT offer?
(A) Shower facilities
(B) Boarding pass printing
(C) Device charging stations
(D) Complimentary refreshments

GO ON TO THE NEXT PAGE

Questions 154-155 refer to the following text message chain.

Manuel Acevedo 9:02 A.M.
Are you at your desk, Brion?

Brion Warden 9:05 A.M.
Just got out of a quick meeting. What do you need?

Manuel Acevedo 9:09 A.M.
I had some car trouble, and I'm running behind schedule. I don't think I'll make it in until 10, so I would really appreciate it if you could set up the projector in Conference Room B.

Brion Warden 9:11 A.M.
Sure thing. Do you know where it is at the moment?

Manuel Acevedo 9:12 A.M.
I know the marketing team was using it for a presentation yesterday. I'll message the clients about moving the start time back to 11.

154. What is Mr. Warden asked to do?

(A) Send an e-mail
(B) Prepare some equipment
(C) Analyze some data
(D) Reschedule a presentation

155. At 9:11 A.M., what does Mr. Warden most likely mean when he writes, "Sure thing"?

(A) He thinks Mr. Acevedo should complete a task.
(B) He agrees with Mr. Acevedo's idea.
(C) He has the same issue as Mr. Acevedo.
(D) He will be able to assist Mr. Acevedo.

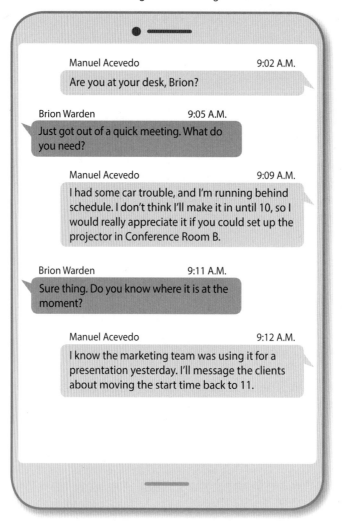

Questions 156-157 refer to the following announcement.

City of Cleveland
Department of Urban Development

Invitation For Bids
Apartment Building Roofing Repairs

The Department of Urban Development (DUD) needs experienced roofing specialists to submit competitive bids for an extensive series of roofing repairs at buildings in the Adams Housing Complex at 189 31st Street.

The bid documents can be found online at www.cityofcleveland.gov/dud or picked up from the County-City Building at 12 Euclid Avenue.

Bidders should include their state roofing certificate along with the necessary forms. Bids need to be addressed to Secretary Henry Schrader and clearly labeled "Roofing Bid." Send your bid via certified mail or deliver it in person in a sealed envelope at the above address. Submissions received after July 1 will not be considered.

156. What is stated about the bid documents?

(A) They must be submitted in a hard copy.
(B) They can be delivered electronically.
(C) They can be purchased at 189 31st Street.
(D) They need to be submitted in person.

157. Who is Mr. Schrader?

(A) A certified roofer
(B) An interested bidder
(C) A DUD employee
(D) A postal officer

GO ON TO THE NEXT PAGE

Questions 158-160 refer to the following Web page.

http://www.wayfarer.com/background

Wayfarer's co-founders, Erin Segroves and Angela Ivanovic became fast friends when they were undergraduates studying chemistry at Midlands University. While on a hiking trip to Chile, they were introduced to handmade bags that were made by local craftspeople from thin and lightweight materials. — [1] —.

During the rest of their trip, they had conversations about producing stylish urban backpacks made of the same fabrics. — [2] —. This seemed unrealistic, as neither had any business experience. But, in a stroke of good luck, William Porton, Ms. Segroves' uncle and a veteran entrepreneur, overheard their idea and encouraged them to carry it out. — [3] —.

With an initial investment and guidance from Porton, Segroves and Ivanovic began selling Wayfarer backpacks online eight years ago. — [4] —. Thanks to their creative team, Wayfarer Bags have become a must-have item for many consumers. Why not try one yourself?

158. According to the Web page, what is true about the company's founders?
(A) They thought of their business while traveling.
(B) Their products are a popular choice for campers.
(C) They have been in business for more than a decade.
(D) They first met while they were in Chile.

159. What is suggested about Mr. Porton?
(A) He has a background in chemistry.
(B) He has traveled to various countries.
(C) He has experience starting a business.
(D) He operates a fashion company.

160. In which of the positions marked [1], [2], [3], and [4] does the following sentence best belong?

"Since then, they have opened stores across the country."

(A) [1]
(B) [2]
(C) [3]
(D) [4]

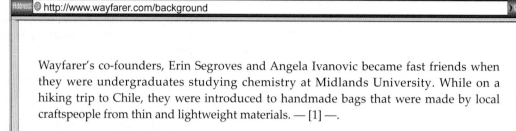

Questions 161-164 refer to the following e-mail.

To:	DKwon@TorranceFinancials
From:	Lloyd@StayAtTheStanley.com
Date:	November 4
Subject:	RE: Convention Inquiry

Dear Mr. Kwon,

I appreciate you reaching out about booking a block of rooms at The Stanley Hotel during the upcoming sales convention. Our 5-star hotel is located in a beautiful, newly renovated building overlooking the Overton Convention Center.

At The Stanley, we are proud to provide personalized experiences. If your group chooses The Stanley, I will serve as your concierge throughout your stay, looking after your group so that your visit is as seamless as possible. We offer a range of group rates during convention season. These prices vary based on the season, how far in advance the booking is made, the number of rooms required, and your dining and/or transportation needs.

Each room is a full suite with a gorgeous view and is equipped with a cutting-edge digital voice assistant. Each guest will also get discounts at the restaurant buffet and complimentary refreshments in the lounge each afternoon throughout their stay. Groups also will have the option of renting a conference room.

I understand that the sales convention is in the first week of March, but I need to know the exact dates to give you accurate information on availability. I know we were fully booked for the same event last year, so let me know right away.

Have a great afternoon.

Lloyd Nichols
The Stanley Hotel

161. Who is Mr. Nichols?
(A) A salesperson
(B) A hotel employee
(C) An event planner
(D) A travel agent

162. The word "block" in paragraph 1, line 1, is closest in meaning to
(A) area
(B) obstruction
(C) group
(D) housing

163. What is indicated about the group rates?
(A) They must be paid for in advance.
(B) They cannot be combined with other discounts.
(C) They depend on several factors.
(D) They are only available to members.

164. What is a feature of the guest rooms?
(A) They have a personal concierge service.
(B) They include access to a meeting room.
(C) They have state-of-the-art technology.
(D) They include a complimentary breakfast buffet.

GO ON TO THE NEXT PAGE

Questions 165-167 refer to the following notice.

Changes Coming This Spring

A number of improvements will soon get underway to enhance your experience at Gutfield Express Bus Terminal in Steelton. —[1]—. Keep in mind that from May 15 to June 3, the terminal will be closed, and buses will be temporarily rerouted.

During this period, workers will extend terminal B and build a new garage, making it possible for the terminal to offer improved interstate route coverage. A new route will connect Steelton to Capitol City. —[2]—. In addition, more dining options will also be available after the renovation.

For your convenience, the city will increase the number of subway trains from Gutfield Terminal to downtown Steelton until the work is completed. —[3]—. Commuters with valid bus passes will be able to use them to ride the metro throughout this period. For more on the construction schedule, check out www.steeltonta.gov. —[4]—.

165. What is scheduled to begin in May?

(A) Construction of a new terminal
(B) Changes to a booking system
(C) Additions to a structure
(D) Upgrades to public buses

166. What is NOT indicated about Gutfield Express Bus Terminal?

(A) It is located in downtown Steelton.
(B) It includes several restaurants.
(C) It is connected to the subway system.
(D) It will shut down for a limited time.

167. In which of the positions marked [1], [2], [3], and [4] does the following sentence best belong?

"This is scheduled to be in service by the end of the summer."

(A) [1]
(B) [2]
(C) [3]
(D) [4]

Questions 168-171 refer to the following article.

Local Store Has a Long Reach

KANSAS CITY—A casual shopper visiting DK & Associates could be forgiven for thinking it was just another store. Its humble size and its location on a quiet residential street don't do anything to reveal the company's growing popularity. DK & Associates is already the Midwest region's top custom-made furniture and interior decoration business, but it is increasingly becoming a national player, too.

The key to DK's appeal is that it offers much more than furniture. Like its competitors, it makes wood furniture to order. But what sets DK & Associates apart is the method for matching its furniture to its clients' spaces, a process which includes consultations with designers about the dimensions of the room, lighting and decoration options, and more.

"Each piece is meant to be in perfect harmony with every aspect of the room where it sits," says founder David Knight. "If a customer has a room with ivory walls, we recommend they choose furniture in complementary green or blue shades so they fit in perfectly."

DK has even commissioned the mixing of custom paints so that the pieces can exactly match each client's room décor. Mr. Knight has been known to work closely with contractors to make sure its customers and designers get the exact shades they have envisioned.

One sign of DK & Associates' success is Mr. Knight's recent trip to New York. Mr. Knight had talks with major retailers about bringing DK's full range of services to its department store nationwide.

"This is in its early stages at the moment," says Knight. "Still, it's an honor to know that the craft we're passionate about has a wider appeal."

---

168. The word "reveal" in paragraph 1, line 6, is closest in meaning to

(A) concede
(B) divulge
(C) indicate
(D) declare

169. According to the article, why are customers drawn to DK & Associates?

(A) It provides furniture at affordable prices.
(B) It offers personalized interior design.
(C) It sells antique home furnishings.
(D) It is located in a trendy area.

170. According to the article, why does DK & Associates employ contractors?

(A) To deliver furniture nationally
(B) To repair damaged items
(C) To make custom paints
(D) To market its products online

171. What did Mr. Knight do in New York?

(A) Attend an industry trade show
(B) Consult with a supplier
(C) Furnish a retailer's new headquarters
(D) Meet with potential business partners

GO ON TO THE NEXT PAGE

Questions 172-175 refer to the following text message chain.

Meyers Iosua **[8:31 A.M.]**

Hi, everyone. I'm here, and I'm ready for the meeting, but I don't see any of you guys.

Doug Christman **[8:32 A.M.]**

Yeah? We're inside, right next to the entrance.

Priscilla Russilo **[8:33 A.M.]**

I wasn't going to take my car, but they're doing construction on the subway. Now I'm stuck in traffic. Could someone text me the exact address of the diner?

Meyers Iosua **[8:34 A.M.]**

Diner? Did you end up going to Rico's Diner? Didn't we agree to meet up at the coffee shop next to the client's office?

Doug Christman **[8:35 A.M.]**

I changed my mind because the coffee shop is a little overpriced. I called everyone last night. You must not have heard my voice message.

Meyers Iosua **[8:36 A.M.]**

I understand. But I thought we were going to discuss my proposal first.

Doug Christman **[8:38 A.M.]**

So... Another group took our booth. We'll have to wait for a few minutes. Just sent you the location, Priscilla.

Priscilla Russilo **[8:39 A.M.]**

I see it. Be there in 10.

Meyers Iosua **[8:39 A.M.]**

What a relief!

Doug Christman **[8:42 A.M.]**

Meyers, I'd like to order now so we can get started right away. Do you know what you want?

Meyers Iosua **[8:42 A.M.]**

A ham and cheese panini would be nice. See you soon.

SEND

172. What is indicated about Ms. Russilo?

(A) She was delayed by construction.
(B) She forgot a meeting's start time.
(C) She got lost on her way to a diner.
(D) She is driving to the meeting.

173. Why did Mr. Christman choose Rico's Diner over the coffee shop?

(A) The diner has better menu options.
(B) The diner is closer to a client's office.
(C) The diner is more reasonably priced.
(D) The diner has more space for meetings.

174. At 8:39 A.M., what does Mr. Iosua most likely mean when he writes, "What a relief"?

(A) He is thankful to meet at the diner.
(B) He feels better about a delay.
(C) He is glad Ms. Russilo can come.
(D) He wants to make his proposal first.

175. What does Mr. Christman offer to do?

(A) Get a table at a restaurant
(B) Change a meeting agenda
(C) Order some food
(D) Send a location

GO ON TO THE NEXT PAGE

Questions 176-180 refer to the following brochure and article.

Crestside Office Agency
Workspace Rentals

Crestside Office Agency (COA) has two co-working locations in the city of Trenton.

DELL PLACE
91 Inverness Dr.
Amenities:

* Two spacious lounge areas
* Private offices for up to 500 employees
* Ten meeting rooms
* Large terrace on the roof overlooking the city
* Receipt and delivery of letters and packages
* Private phone booth
* Thirty minutes from the airport

REMINGTON CENTER
1532 Jesper Way
Amenities:

* Three floors of co-working space
* Conference rooms and phone booths
* Kitchenette with complimentary refreshments
* On-site community manager
* One hour from the airport
* Cleaning services

For more information on pricing plans or to book a tour of the premises, call us at 555-9472. Our representatives are available Monday through Friday from 10 A.M. to 8 P.M. and on Saturday and Sunday from 11 A.M. to 6 P.M.

COA Continues to Grow

TRENTON (22 August) – Crestside Office Agency, in union with the Trenton city government, will be purchasing the 15-story Aronium Apex Building.

The sale is expected to be finalized by the end of the month, and the office space will be available for companies in the first week of November. COA will cover 75 percent of the cost, with the city government putting up the rest.

COA has redefined the modern workplace by offering office spaces that are flexible and dynamic. With locations at Dell Place and the Remington Center, the company has found that businesses, particularly startups, are lining up to sign a lease with them.

COA founder Casey Heinisch noted that the Aronium Apex Building is a 15-minute drive away from the airport. He continued by saying, "The Aronium Apex Building will be perfect for business travelers who need a place to work while they are away from their home office."

176. What is stated about Crestside Office Agency?

(A) Its main office is in Trenton.
(B) It leases short-term residential spaces.
(C) It holds private tours every hour.
(D) Its representatives are available daily.

177. What is NOT listed as an amenity of the spaces at Dell Place?

(A) Lounge areas
(B) Exercise facilities
(C) Mail services
(D) Rooftop terrace

178. What does the article suggest about the spaces at Dell Place and Remington Center?

(A) Many businesses want to move there.
(B) Many businesses have started there.
(C) They will be available in November.
(D) They were built for startup companies.

179. What does the article mention about Aronium Apex Building?

(A) Its purchase was aided by the government.
(B) It will house 15 different organizations.
(C) Its maintenance supervisor will be Mr. Heinisch.
(D) It is restricted to business travelers only.

180. How will Aronium Apex Building differ from the other two properties?

(A) It will give discounts to business travelers.
(B) It will provide complimentary refreshments.
(C) It will be closer to the airport.
(D) It will hold social gatherings for its renters.

GO ON TO THE NEXT PAGE

Questions 181-185 refer to the following e-mails.

To	: Jasmine Massoud <jmassoud@g-h.com>
From	: Ted August <taugust@g-h.com>
Date	: Wednesday, 6 February, 11:43
Subject	: Recruitment

Jasmine,

The directors at Design and Engineering have selected the final candidates for the open positions in their respective departments here at Grayson-Hillis. Rhett Vernon has requested that Yvette Jones and Julio Rivers be informed of their third interview for the design position. Amy Sandberg would like Peter O'Brien to return for the last interview for the automotive engineering position.

I need you to contact the candidates and set up a day that they can come in, and you should also make the necessary lunch arrangements for them. Don't forget that Rhett will be on a business trip to Germany to speak with some clients next week.

I appreciate everything you did during this entire recruitment process. I know that it all happened very quickly in regard to finding candidates and scheduling the first round of interviews. You've been a big help.

Sincerely,
Ted August
HR Manager

To	: Ted August <taugust@g-h.com>
From	: Jasmine Massoud <jmassoud@g-h.com>
Date	: Wednesday, 6 February, 16:19
Subject	: RE: Recruitment

Ted,

I got in touch with the three candidates. Peter O'Brien accepted a position with our rival automaker Horchreder. I already spoke with Amy to let her know about the situation, and she believes that she will be able to find another qualified applicant.

Julio Rivers has agreed to come in on Monday, 18 February. Lunch has also been arranged for this day from our usual catering provider. Sadly, Ms. Jones has returned to Australia for a while to deal with some family issues. I was not sure how to proceed, so I'll await your further instructions.

Jasmine Massoud
HR Assistant

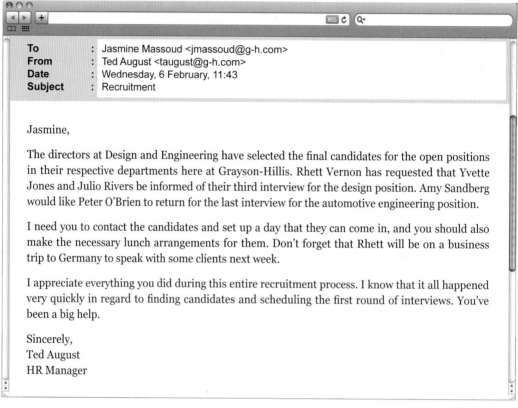

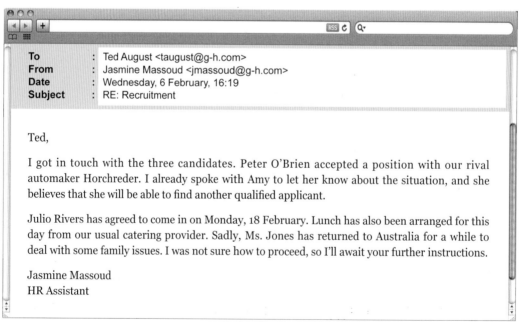

181. What is one purpose of the first e-mail?

(A) To announce some new hires
(B) To request that candidates be contacted
(C) To verify an applicant's résumé
(D) To offer a position to a job candidate

182. What type of company most likely is Grayson-Hillis?

(A) An express delivery business
(B) An automobile manufacturer
(C) A catering company
(D) A car rental agency

183. What is suggested about Ms. Jones?

(A) She will be interviewed by Mr. August.
(B) She currently works for Horchreder.
(C) She applied for the engineering position.
(D) She has been to Grayson-Hillis before.

184. What will Ms. Sandberg most likely do?

(A) Reserve a table at a restaurant
(B) Contact Ms. Jones
(C) Select another job candidate
(D) Visit some clients

185. What was Ms. Massoud NOT able to do?

(A) Assist Mr. August with organizing initial interviews
(B) Get in touch with Mr. O'Brien
(C) Make a lunch order
(D) Coordinate the appointments within a specific period of time

GO ON TO THE NEXT PAGE

Questions 186-190 refer to the following e-mails and form.

To	: All employees <all@allen.com>
From	: Garret Plescia <gplescia@allen.com>
Date	: August 7
Subject	: Tonya Malkin

Dear staff,

It is with great pleasure that we announce that our very own Tonya Malkin has just been named Salesperson of the Year by the International Association of Sales Professionals. This is the first time this award has been received by an Allen, Inc. employee in the 15 years it has been bestowed. Ms. Malkin only joined us three years ago, but she has already made a significant impact. Ever since her first day at Allen, Inc., Ms. Malkin's drive and optimism have been evident. Since her hiring, we have been able to double our client base in Europe and Asia. We look forward to seeing even greater accomplishments in the upcoming years!

To celebrate, we will be holding a dinner party on Thursday, August 22, at 6 P.M. in Jameson Ballroom at Brown Hotel. If you plan on attending, please RSVP to Alberto Mazetti, our event coordinator. For those who wish to assist with the party planning, please contact Mr. Mazetti by e-mail or stop by his office on the 20th floor of our main branch.

We are excited for Ms. Malkin, and we hope that you can join us in celebrating her achievement.

Garret Plescia
Director of Sales

To	: Winnie Calderon <wcalderon@allen.com>
From	: Alberto Mazetti <amazetti@allen.com>
Date	: August 8
Subject	: Malkin dinner assistance

Hi Winnie,

I have arranged for the R&D team to sit at the same table during Ms. Malkin's celebration dinner. I want to thank you and your team for your generous gesture of purchasing a gift.

I also appreciate your willingness to help out with the dinner. The majority of the preparations have been made. However, we are still in need of some supplies. I placed an order a few days ago, but it was only partially filled. Please come by my office when you have the time. I am in C2014, one floor down from your office. I will inform you of what items we need and provide the company credit card at that time.

Regards,

Alberto Mazetti

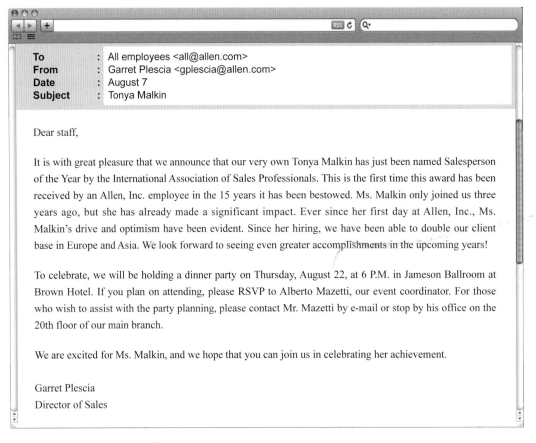

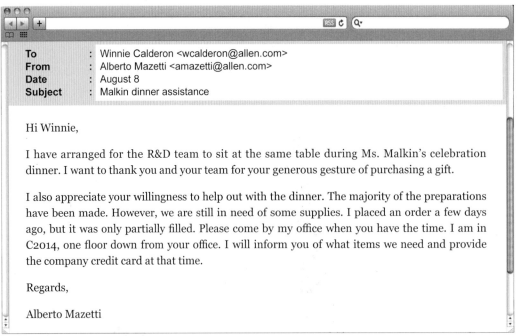

Delilah's Banquet Furnishings
Order Completion Form

Name: Allen, Inc.
Order No.: 12490

Product Code	Product	Quantity	Completed
D502	Purple cocktail napkins	200	√
D9185	Gold dinner napkins	200	√
D242	Cutlery set (forks and knives) in gold	150	√
D7493	Purple plastic tablecloths	50	√
D881	12 oz. white paper cups	200	Sold Out
D645	Gold dinner plates	125	Shipment delayed

186. Why is Ms. Malkin receiving recognition?
(A) For a product she invented
(B) For her years of commitment to Allen, Inc.
(C) For an award she received
(D) For her monetary donation to Allen, Inc.

187. What is indicated about Allen, Inc.?
(A) It produces high-tech gadgets.
(B) It was established 15 years ago.
(C) It does business overseas.
(D) It offers attractive benefits.

188. What is suggested about Ms. Calderon?
(A) Her office is at the main branch.
(B) Her team works closely with Ms. Malkin.
(C) She is organizing a dinner party.
(D) She was recently promoted to a department head.

189. What will Mr. Mazetti most likely ask Ms. Calderon to do?
(A) Exchange some napkins
(B) Contact a caterer
(C) Purchase some cups
(D) Pick up some decorations

190. What can be assumed based on the form?
(A) Allen, Inc. supplied its own cutlery.
(B) Allen, Inc. purchased too many paper napkins.
(C) The size of the tablecloth is incorrect.
(D) The dinner has a gold and purple color scheme.

GO ON TO THE NEXT PAGE

Questions 191-195 refer to the following e-mail, schedule and article.

To	: Lorenzo Dwelly <info@ldwelly.com>
From	: Usain Brown <ubrown@realnessprod.org>
Date	: 18 March
Subject	: Videographer
Attachment	: timetable

Hello, Mr. Dwelly!

We are excited to have you here at Realness Productions as our in-house videographer. The short film that you produced with our former in-house videographer, Courtney Berger, about healthy eating for Oasis Point school district was entertaining and informative.

Your primary responsibility as our in-house videographer will be to create videos highlighting the key aspects of several cities in our state. You will be working closely with city residents and city officials, as well as William Falk, our government liaison. After you collect pictures and create a storyboard, the local residents will record video clips and submit them to you. Your job will be to edit the videos as you best see fit. The completed video will then be aired throughout the state. You will spend about a month in each city during your one-year contract.

The first location for this project will be Logan Square in Provo. I have attached a calendar detailing the timeline.

Best,

Usain Brown
Executive Administrator, Realness Productions

Project Timetable for Provo Video Shoot with Realness Productions

Week 1

May 1-2: Meet with city officials and local residents to describe the project
May 3-6: Tour the area and begin creating a storyboard for the film

Week 2 and 3

May 10-20: Collect, watch, and select videos

Week 4

May 22-27: Edit and finalize
May 29: First broadcast of video

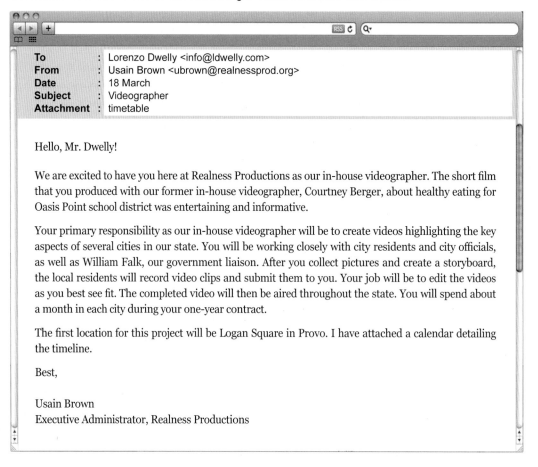

Provo Daily
Around Town

When Lorenzo Dwelly watched the prior welcome video depicting Provo, he could not believe his eyes. Not only was the film outdated and missing some of the best new features of Provo, it also failed to capture the essence of the community. It was his assignment to create a new video that properly represented the city.

After four short weeks, Mr. Dwelly and the residents of Provo created a video promoting the diverse cultural elements in the city by featuring places like Chinatown and Little Italy.

Even though Mr. Dwelly was raised in Provo, this was the first time he'd shot a video here. "I didn't know all the different aspects the city had until the residents showed me," Mr. Dwelly said. The video will be broadcast on May 31 on Channel 4.

191. What is suggested about Mr. Dwelly in the e-mail?

(A) He will edit multiple videos at a time.
(B) He has worked with a prior in-house videographer.
(C) He has personally chosen a location for a movie.
(D) He has submitted his work to Channel 4 before.

192. According to the e-mail, who will record the videos of Provo?

(A) Mr. Falk
(B) Mr. Brown
(C) Government officials
(D) City residents

193. What is indicated about Realness Productions?

(A) It will create a video for Oasis Point.
(B) It relocated its offices to Logan Square.
(C) It hired a native of Provo to be its in-house videographer.
(D) It released a new movie about healthy eating.

194. What is the topic of Provo's video?

(A) The surrounding landscape
(B) The investment opportunities
(C) The cultural diversity
(D) The historic buildings

195. According to the article, what change was made to the project after the schedule was sent?

(A) Its length
(B) Its release date
(C) Its filming location
(D) Its production team

GO ON TO THE NEXT PAGE

Questions 196-200 refer to the following Web page information and e-mails.

JML Support Center Schedule
Robbie Nunoz's team
December 3–9

Sunday–Wednesday

Yunus Lynn 7:00 A.M.–3:00 P.M.
Yunheng Lao 12:00 P.M.–8:00 P.M.
Collette Dalby 6:00 A.M.–1:00 P.M.

Thursday and Friday

Braden Page 7:00 A.M.–3:00 P.M.
Kimberly Ray 12:00 P.M.–8:00 P.M.

Saturday

Aisha Case 7:00 A.M.–1:00 P.M.
Max Curtis 11:00 A.M.–8:00 P.M.

To:	Max Curtis
From:	Kimberly Ray
Date:	Saturday, 2 December, 2:27 P.M.
Subject:	RE: Shift coverage

Hi Max,

I got your e-mail and looked at my schedule, and I'm glad to say that I'll be able to take your shift. Have you mentioned it to our team manager yet? I can go ahead and inform Mr. Nunoz of our plan to make sure he approves if you haven't.

I know you'll have a good time at the seminar. I was able to attend one of the previous yearly seminars right after I was hired, and it was a great experience. Be sure to take plenty of notes. That year, the main focus was on how to effectively troubleshoot software issues. However, I thought one workshop on effectively communicating with unhappy customers was the most helpful. I use many of the techniques I learned there now.

Regards,

Kimberly

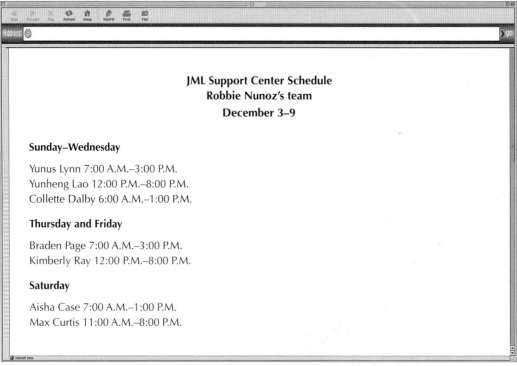

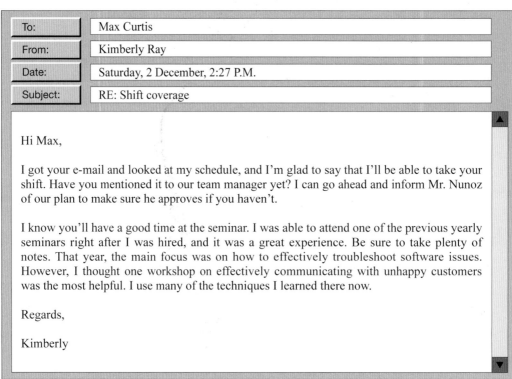

To:	JML Support Center
From:	Jason Cooper
Date:	Wednesday, 6 December, 2:00 P.M.
Subject:	Computer program problems

Greetings,

I am having issues with the company's messenger program. I tried to call Mr. Lynn (since he helped with my hard drive problem a few months ago), but his voice mail says that he will be unavailable for the rest of the day.

I have deleted the program and then put it back onto my computer to see if that would fix the problem, but the trouble persists. For now, I have been communicating with my colleagues through text messages on my phone. Is there someone you can send down to take a look at my computer? There is some information that I have to access from one of my previous messages, and I need it by the end of the day.

Jason Cooper

196. What is true about Ms. Ray?
(A) She assisted Mr. Curtis with a technical issue.
(B) She was recently hired by JML.
(C) She normally works on weekends.
(D) She attended an industry seminar.

197. When will Ms. Ray cover a coworker's shift?
(A) On Monday
(B) On Wednesday
(C) On Friday
(D) On Saturday

198. Who most likely is Mr. Nunoz?
(A) A team supervisor
(B) A seminar organizer
(C) A sales agent
(D) A computer programmer

199. Who will most likely respond to Mr. Cooper's e-mail?
(A) Mr. Lao
(B) Ms. Case
(C) Mr. Page
(D) Ms. Dalby

200. What did Mr. Cooper do when he tried to fix a program?
(A) He contacted a development company.
(B) He downloaded an updated version of it.
(C) He restarted his computer.
(D) He made an attempt to install it again.

Stop! This is the end of the test. If you finish before time is called, you may go back to Part 5, 6, and 7 and check your work.

실전 모의고사 3

MP3 바로 듣기

해설서 바로 가기

• **준비물:** OMR 카드, 연필, 지우개, 시계
• **시험시간:** LC 약 45분 RC 75분

나의 점수		
	LC	**RC**
맞은 개수		
환산 점수		
총점: _______________ 점		

점수 환산표			
LC		**RC**	
맞은 개수	환산 점수	맞은 개수	환산 점수
96-100	475-495	96-100	460-495
91-95	435-495	91-95	425-490
86-90	405-475	86-90	395-465
81-85	370-450	81-85	370-440
76-80	345-420	76-80	335-415
71-75	320-390	71-75	310-390
66-70	290-360	66-70	280-365
61-65	265-335	61-65	250-335
56-60	235-310	56-60	220-305
51-55	210-280	51-55	195-270
46-50	180-255	46-50	165-240
41-45	155-230	41-45	140-215
36-40	125-205	36-40	115-180
31-35	105-175	31-35	95-145
26-30	85-145	26-30	75-120
21-25	60-115	21-25	60-95
16-20	30-90	16-20	45-75
11-15	5-70	11-15	30-55
6-10	5-60	6-10	10-40
1-5	5-60	1-5	5-30
0	5-35	0	5-15

TEST 3

Actual Test_3.mp3

LISTENING TEST

In the Listening test, you will be asked to demonstrate how well you understand spoken English. The entire listening test will last approximately 45 minutes. There are four parts, and directions are given for each part. You must mark your answers on the separate answer sheet. Do not write your answers in your test book.

PART 1

Directions: For each question in this part, you will hear four statements about a picture in your test book. When you hear the statements, you must select the one statement that best describes what you see in the picture. Then find the number of the question on your answer sheet and mark your answer. The statements will not be printed in your test book and will be spoken only one time.

Statement (B), "A man is pointing at a document," is the best description of the picture, so you should select answer (B) and mark it on your answer sheet.

1.

2.

GO ON TO THE NEXT PAGE

3.

4.

5.

6.

GO ON TO THE NEXT PAGE

PART 2

Directions: You will hear a question or statement and three responses spoken in English. They will not be printed in your test book and will be spoken only one time. Select the best response to the question or statement and mark the letter (A), (B), or (C) on your answer sheet.

7. Mark your answer on your answer sheet.
8. Mark your answer on your answer sheet.
9. Mark your answer on your answer sheet.
10. Mark your answer on your answer sheet.
11. Mark your answer on your answer sheet.
12. Mark your answer on your answer sheet.
13. Mark your answer on your answer sheet.
14. Mark your answer on your answer sheet.
15. Mark your answer on your answer sheet.
16. Mark your answer on your answer sheet.
17. Mark your answer on your answer sheet.
18. Mark your answer on your answer sheet.
19. Mark your answer on your answer sheet.
20. Mark your answer on your answer sheet.
21. Mark your answer on your answer sheet.
22. Mark your answer on your answer sheet.
23. Mark your answer on your answer sheet.
24. Mark your answer on your answer sheet.
25. Mark your answer on your answer sheet.
26. Mark your answer on your answer sheet.
27. Mark your answer on your answer sheet.
28. Mark your answer on your answer sheet.
29. Mark your answer on your answer sheet.
30. Mark your answer on your answer sheet.
31. Mark your answer on your answer sheet.

PART 3

Directions: You will hear some conversations between two or more people. You will be asked to answer three questions about what the speakers say in each conversation. Select the best response to each question and mark the letter (A), (B), (C), or (D) on your answer sheet. The conversations will not be printed in your test book and will be spoken only one time.

32. Who is Ms. Chen?
(A) A business consultant
(B) A chef
(C) An interior designer
(D) A customer

33. Why did Ms. Chen send an e-mail?
(A) To complain about some work
(B) To order a product
(C) To inquire about a service
(D) To follow up on a job interview

34. What does the man say he will do?
(A) Refund some money
(B) Perform some repairs
(C) Make a phone call
(D) Visit a client

---

35. What will happen this afternoon?
(A) An employee orientation
(B) A membership event
(C) A sports competition
(D) An exercise class

36. What does the man think will happen?
(A) Staff performance will improve.
(B) Enrollments will increase.
(C) An additional location will open.
(D) Some new equipment will be purchased.

37. What will the woman do next?
(A) Stock some counters
(B) Contact a vendor
(C) Distribute some brochures
(D) Set up some machines

38. According to the speakers, what happened last week?
(A) An employee was absent.
(B) A factory was opened.
(C) A site was inspected.
(D) A schedule was revised.

39. What industry do the speakers work in?
(A) Finance
(B) Transportation
(C) Technology
(D) Agriculture

40. What will the woman do tomorrow?
(A) Visit another country
(B) Complete some paperwork
(C) Meet some officials
(D) Give a speech

---

41. Where do the speakers work?
(A) At a car rental agency
(B) At a driver's license office
(C) At a shipping company
(D) At an auto repair shop

42. Why is the man worried?
(A) A delivery has not been made.
(B) A computer system is too slow.
(C) Some customers have complained.
(D) Some files cannot be located.

43. What does the woman imply when she says, "I used to work for a technical support firm"?
(A) She can train a new employee.
(B) She is interested in a job opening.
(C) She is experienced in customer care.
(D) She may be able to fix a problem.

GO ON TO THE NEXT PAGE

44. What product are the speakers discussing?
(A) A computer
(B) A radio
(C) A vehicle
(D) A smartphone

45. What problem does the man mention?
(A) A device does not work properly.
(B) The color he wants is not offered.
(C) A promotional code is not valid.
(D) An advertised price is not reflected.

46. What does the branch manager suggest the man do?
(A) Come back the following day
(B) Purchase an extended plan
(C) Refer potential customers
(D) Pay with a credit card

---

47. Where does the conversation most likely take place?
(A) At a sporting goods store
(B) At a doctor's office
(C) At a manufacturing plant
(D) At a travel agency

48. What does the woman give to the man?
(A) A user's manual
(B) A parking permit
(C) A Web address
(D) A guidebook

49. What does the woman ask the man to do?
(A) Pay a fee
(B) Wait in a lobby
(C) Update some contact information
(D) Schedule an appointment

50. Where does the man work?
(A) At a financial firm
(B) At a technology company
(C) At an airline company
(D) At a relocation agency

51. What does the man mean when he says, "Management wants to find someone within the week"?
(A) He will go on vacation next week.
(B) An applicant must make a quick decision.
(C) He requires additional documentation.
(D) An applicant should contact a manager directly.

52. According to the man, what will the company pay for?
(A) Accommodations
(B) Transportation
(C) Meals
(D) Entertainment

---

53. What are the speakers mainly talking about?
(A) A charity dinner
(B) A recruitment fair
(C) An executive luncheon
(D) A sports competition

54. What does Steve say he will do this weekend?
(A) Book a flight
(B) Attend a board meeting
(C) Speak with some coworkers
(D) Interview some candidates

55. Why will the woman be in Singapore?
(A) To participate in a trade show
(B) To lead a training session
(C) To introduce a new product
(D) To sign a partnership agreement

56. Where do the speakers most likely work?
(A) At a museum gift shop
(B) At an office supply store
(C) At a clothing shop
(D) At a grocery store

57. Why does the woman decline the man's request at first?
(A) She is leaving for the day.
(B) She is working on a window display.
(C) She is not familiar with the merchandise.
(D) She is helping another client.

58. What does the woman say about an item?
(A) It is currently being discounted.
(B) It may have to be delivered.
(C) It is no longer being manufactured.
(D) It may be available in a different color.

---

59. What is the purpose of the call?
(A) To recommend a product
(B) To request some company information
(C) To inquire about renting some space
(D) To confirm an appointment

60. What does the man say he wants to do?
(A) Increase sales
(B) Retain staff
(C) Improve security
(D) Reduce expenses

61. What does the man ask for?
(A) A cost estimate
(B) A sample
(C) A customer reference
(D) A directory

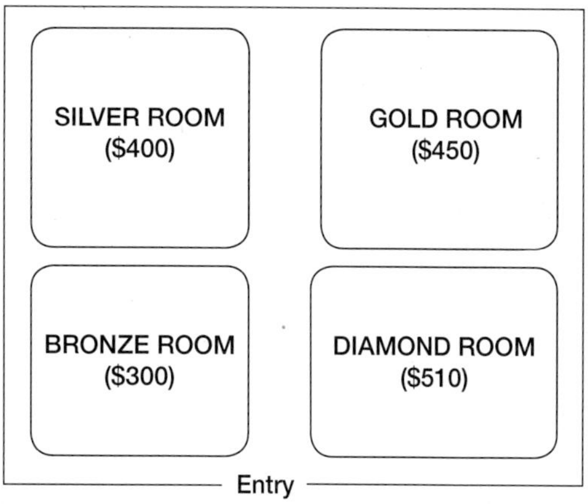

62. What is the woman planning?
(A) A product launch
(B) A farewell party
(C) An investor conference
(D) An anniversary dinner

63. Look at the graphic. How much will the woman's reservation cost?
(A) $300
(B) $400
(C) $450
(D) $510

64. Why does the man say a caterer is popular?
(A) It uses organic ingredients.
(B) It employs a well-known chef.
(C) It offers the most affordable prices.
(D) It has many dessert options.

GO ON TO THE NEXT PAGE

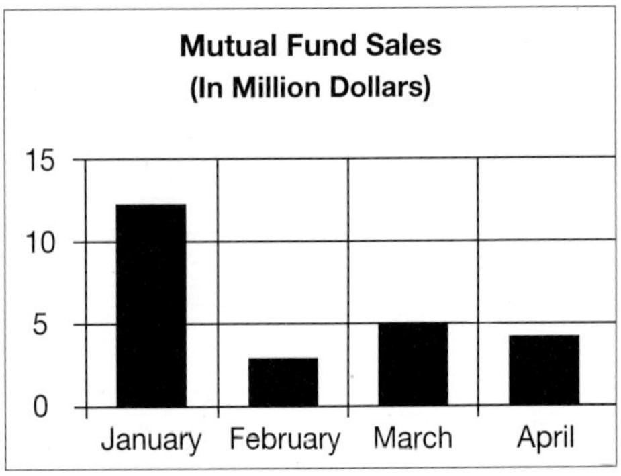

65. What will the woman do today?
(A) Give a presentation
(B) Invest some money
(C) Write an article
(D) Make some sales calls

66. Look at the graphic. Which month do the speakers want to focus on?
(A) January
(B) February
(C) March
(D) April

67. What does the man recommend?
(A) Reducing a budget projection
(B) Adding a new product line
(C) Delaying a staff meeting
(D) Revising an advertisement

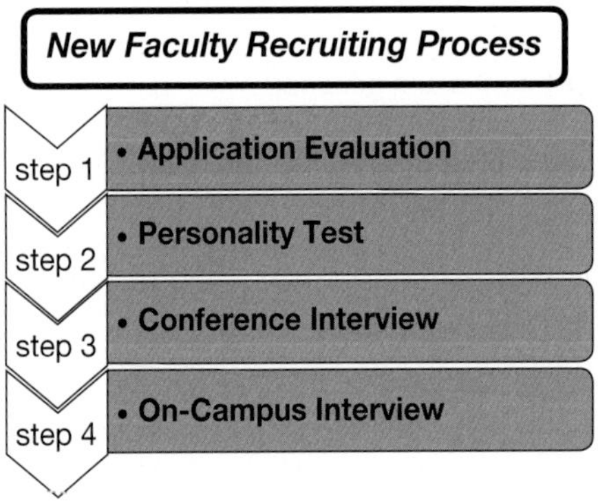

68. According to the man, what is the benefit of changing a process?
(A) It will increase the number of applicants.
(B) It will reduce student complaints.
(C) It will help you spend less time.
(D) It will bring in the most competent staff.

69. Look at the graphic. Which step will most likely be eliminated?
(A) Step 1
(B) Step 2
(C) Step 3
(D) Step 4

70. What will the speakers do next?
(A) Read some cover letters
(B) Prepare a proposal
(C) Create a survey
(D) Calculate some figures

PART 4

Directions: You will hear some talks given by a single speaker. You will be asked to answer three questions about what the speaker says in each talk. Select the best response to each question and mark the letter (A), (B), (C), or (D) on your answer sheet. The talks will not be printed in your test book and will be spoken only one time.

71. What event is the speaker mainly talking about?
(A) A theatrical performance
(B) An industry exposition
(C) A neighborhood festival
(D) An opening ceremony

72. What are the listeners encouraged to do during the event?
(A) Complete a questionnaire
(B) Watch a presentation
(C) Buy some concessions
(D) Take some photos

73. What can the listeners find on a Web site?
(A) An event timetable
(B) Some giveaway winners
(C) Some discount coupons
(D) Directions to a location

---

74. Where most likely does this announcement take place?
(A) At a car rental service
(B) At a bus terminal
(C) At a subway station
(D) At an airport

75. According to the speaker, what can some listeners receive for free?
(A) A seat upgrade
(B) A meal voucher
(C) Accommodations
(D) Beverages

76. What does the speaker ask some listeners to do?
(A) Sign up for membership
(B) Talk to an employee
(C) Provide photo identification
(D) Check their belongings

77. Who most likely is the speaker?
(A) A city official
(B) A restaurant owner
(C) A tourist guide
(D) A building architect

78. According to the speaker, what is special about Georgetown's Municipal Building?
(A) Its design
(B) Its materials
(C) Its age
(D) Its height

79. Why does the speaker say, "we have a dinner reservation at 5"?
(A) She wants the listeners to be on time.
(B) She thinks the listeners should eat later.
(C) She is concerned about a time change.
(D) She cannot attend an event.

---

80. What is the purpose of the meeting?
(A) To present questionnaire results
(B) To assign jobs
(C) To welcome a client
(D) To prepare for a conference

81. What is the main complaint about a phone application?
(A) It is difficult to use.
(B) It is outdated.
(C) It has too many advertisements.
(D) It runs too slowly.

82. What will happen next?
(A) Lunch will be catered.
(B) Employees will demonstrate a product.
(C) A phone application will be installed.
(D) An advisor will present some solutions.

GO ON TO THE NEXT PAGE →

83. Where do the listeners work?
(A) At a café
(B) At a hotel
(C) At a department store
(D) At a law firm

84. What does the speaker imply when he says, "our business is growing"?
(A) Additional staff members will be hired.
(B) The population of a town has increased.
(C) A store will be expanded.
(D) An advertisement has been profitable.

85. What does the speaker offer the listeners?
(A) A pay raise
(B) Extra vacation days
(C) On-the-job training
(D) A gift card

---

86. What does the speaker's company mainly sell?
(A) Consumer electronics
(B) Office furniture
(C) Fashion accessories
(D) Automotive parts

87. How has the company addressed a problem?
(A) By revising a product line
(B) By improving its customer service
(C) By redesigning a Web site
(D) By reducing prices

88. What does the speaker ask the listeners to do?
(A) Review some data
(B) Train some employees
(C) Set up a press conference
(D) Write a news article

89. What is the main purpose of the message?
(A) To confirm a schedule
(B) To announce a new project
(C) To postpone a deadline
(D) To accept a proposal

90. What problem does the speaker mention?
(A) A parking lot is for employees only.
(B) A building is under construction.
(C) A team member is unavailable.
(D) A street is inaccessible.

91. What does the speaker say the listener can do during lunch?
(A) Get an employee badge
(B) Set up a work area
(C) Watch an instructional video
(D) Ask some questions

---

92. Where do the listeners most likely work?
(A) At an employment agency
(B) At a design studio
(C) At an accounting firm
(D) At a shopping complex

93. What will the company do?
(A) Pay for some course fees
(B) Hire additional employees
(C) Expand its client base
(D) Update its logo

94. Why does the speaker say, "it has received a lot of accolades"?
(A) To accept a job offer
(B) To congratulate a team
(C) To agree with a decision
(D) To provide a suggestion

Greenville Cinema

Eight Brothers	10:45 A.M.	Theater 1
White Tree	12:00 P.M.	Theater 2
The Unmistakable Truth	1:20 P.M.	Theater 3
Nothing but Luck	2:35 P.M.	Theater 4

95. Why is the speaker calling?

(A) To complain about some employees
(B) To learn about a promotion
(C) To check some showing times
(D) To inquire about a missing item

96. Look at the graphic. Which auditorium was the speaker in yesterday?

(A) Theater 1
(B) Theater 2
(C) Theater 3
(D) Theater 4

97. What does the speaker request?

(A) An electronic ticket
(B) A sales receipt
(C) A return call
(D) A program guide

OptiTech Campus Map

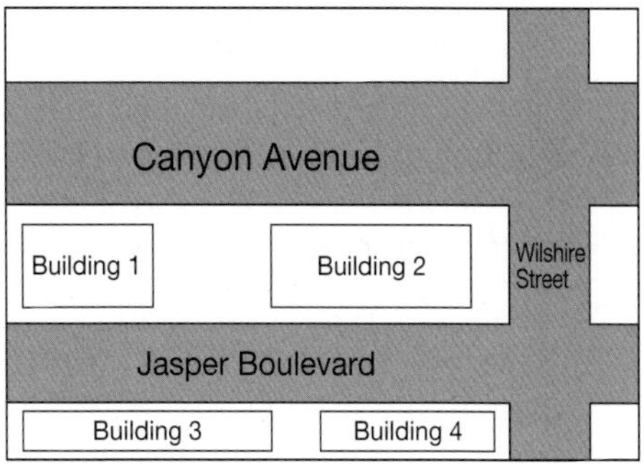

98. Who most likely are the listeners?

(A) University professors
(B) Security officers
(C) Technicians
(D) Cleaners

99. Look at the graphic. Which building does the speaker talk about?

(A) Building 1
(B) Building 2
(C) Building 3
(D) Building 4

100. What will the listeners most likely do next?

(A) Visit a work location
(B) Purchase some equipment
(C) Eat some lunch
(D) Fill out some documents

This is the end of the Listening test. Turn to Part 5 in your test book.

GO ON TO THE NEXT PAGE

READING TEST

In the Reading test, you will read a variety of texts and answer several different types of reading comprehension questions. The entire Reading test will last 75 minutes. There are three parts, and directions are given for each part. You are encouraged to answer as many questions as possible within the time allowed.

You must mark your answers on the separate answer sheet. Do not write your answers in your test book.

PART 5

Directions: A word or phrase is missing in each of the sentences below. Four answer choices are given below each sentence. Select the best answer to complete the sentence. Then mark the letter (A), (B), (C), or (D) on your answer sheet.

101. The cleaning crew members have been quite mindful of ------- safety regulations.

(A) ours
(B) our
(C) theirs
(D) them

102. Of all the lectures given at the Australian Dentistry Seminar, the presentation made by Dr. Toledo was the most -------.

(A) economic
(B) informative
(C) primary
(D) possible

103. Ms. Carter described the ------- of the extended hours of operation to the evening servers.

(A) benefiting
(B) beneficiary
(C) benefits
(D) beneficial

104. Flights leaving the international airport were grounded by windy conditions ------- the runway.

(A) except
(B) within
(C) from
(D) on

105. If you have recently ------- an insurance policy and want to learn about your coverage, this Web site is for you.

(A) to purchase
(B) purchases
(C) purchased
(D) purchase

106. The upcoming ------- of Trenton Train Station will add new platforms and increase the number of restaurants.

(A) supplement
(B) deadline
(C) renovation
(D) achievement

107. The survey showed that university students returned books to the library late ------- than visitors in any other groups.

(A) frequently
(B) frequency
(C) frequented
(D) more frequently

108. Applicants need to ------- 2 letters of reference before their interview can be scheduled.

(A) submit
(B) reject
(C) request
(D) confirm

109. The convention center's ------- transit cards allow guests to use the subway free of charge.

(A) complimentary
(B) complimented
(C) complimenting
(D) compliment

110. ------- weeks of talks to complete the contract, the representatives finally arrived at an agreement this morning.

(A) For
(B) From
(C) After
(D) Only

111. The chefs will evaluate all of the produce suppliers' bids and select ------- that suits their menu.

(A) another
(B) some
(C) rest
(D) one

112. The graphic designer made ------- to the company's logo for the ad campaign.

(A) duplications
(B) guidelines
(C) predictions
(D) revisions

113. Please be advised ------- we were unable to fill your order because of a shortage of the necessary materials.

(A) whether
(B) that
(C) of
(D) until

114. Albert Heijn Inc. ------- that its heaters are the most energy-efficient in the industry.

(A) competes
(B) claims
(C) collects
(D) convenes

115. Granite Ltd. will extend its business ------- with Tarner Insurance if a contract with some alterations is drawn up.

(A) agreement
(B) agree
(C) agreeing
(D) agreed

116. ------- signing up for the leadership seminar is not mandatory, HR advises attending it to all supervisors.

(A) Irrespective
(B) Although
(C) Already
(D) With

117. Readers can easily ------- to the students in the popular comic strip *Dunwich High*.

(A) relative
(B) relate
(C) related
(D) relatable

118. Tolliver College offers a full ------- of business courses to local residents in its Financial Outreach Program.

(A) balance
(B) means
(C) type
(D) range

119. The main entrance of the parking garage will be closed for repainting and not be ------- this weekend.

(A) accessing
(B) accessible
(C) accesses
(D) access

120. Ms. Kazama hopes to see Kazama sports goods -------, even in isolated parts of the world.

(A) everywhere
(B) fairly
(C) certainly
(D) furthermore

GO ON TO THE NEXT PAGE

121. We may order office ------- such as chairs and monitors from any of the suppliers on this list.

(A) equips
(B) equipment
(C) equipped
(D) equipping

122. When requesting a travel reimbursement, employees must complete this form and provide receipts for the ------- purchases.

(A) listed
(B) obtained
(C) projected
(D) addressed

123. The lounge area of the building will be cleaned ------- the workers remove the furniture.

(A) following
(B) once
(C) enough
(D) by

124. In a firm display of determination, the company's executives ------- approved the expansion budget.

(A) periodically
(B) inattentively
(C) unanimously
(D) splendidly

125. When recently -------, assembly workers at Shrankhaus Furnishings said that break time is the issue that needs to be resolved.

(A) poller
(B) polled
(C) poll
(D) polls

126. Mr. Park agreed to lead the intern orientation ------- Ms. Kowalski could speak at the convention.

(A) concerning
(B) rather
(C) as though
(D) so that

127. The security team visits each vendor twice a day and takes their cash to the safe -------.

(A) too far
(B) upstairs
(C) all along
(D) though

128. Please notify Ms. Koike of any problems ------- those already addressed in yesterday's meeting.

(A) against
(B) among
(C) since
(D) beyond

129. The Amstel Artists Association is a prominent group with very ------- members.

(A) accomplish
(B) accomplished
(C) accomplishes
(D) accomplishing

130. As Ms. Fontana's personal secretary, Mr. Tombach is responsible for ------- her on the daily meeting schedule.

(A) relying
(B) narrating
(C) briefing
(D) reviewing

PART 6

Directions: Read the texts that follow. A word, phrase, or sentence is missing in parts of each text. Four answer choices for each question are given below the text. Select the best answer to complete the text. Then mark the letter (A), (B), (C), or (D) on your answer sheet.

Questions 131-134 refer to the following article.

TORONTO (February 9) – Representatives from Red Line Studios have confirmed that its newest fantasy series will be uploaded to streaming services at the beginning of March. An episode of the show ------- (131.) an interview with its lead actor will be released to social media sites tomorrow night at midnight. To this point, very few details have emerged about the series. Many fans are already ------- (132.) that it will be a continuation of the popular fantasy drama Eternal Equinox. That show, which first debuted a decade ago, was an ------- (133.) success for the studio, drawing over 3 million viewers per episode in Canada. ------- (134.).

131. (A) however
(B) as well as
(C) even if
(D) accordingly

132. (A) speculating
(B) encouraging
(C) considering
(D) demanding

133. (A) impress
(B) impression
(C) impressing
(D) impressive

134. (A) The studio's CEO plans to hire a new creative team.
(B) It was watched by ten times that many people overseas as well.
(C) It will be aired for the first time tomorrow night.
(D) Red Line Studios was unable to attract its target audience.

GO ON TO THE NEXT PAGE

Questions 135-138 refer to the following letter.

May 28

Ms. Francesca Thomas,

Thank you for meeting with me the other day regarding the opening in the Human Resources Department at Turner Engineering. -------. (135.) With my previous background, I believe I will excel in this -------. (136.) Excellent communication skills, quick decision-making, and engineering experience ------- (137.) at my previous employer. In addition, I am very proficient at data analysis using the latest software.

Thanks for taking time out of your busy schedule to ------- (138.) me. I am eager to hear your final decision.

Best,

Michelle Harris

135. (A) Keep in mind that I will be sending my résumé to other companies as well.
(B) I have heard about your firm's excellent reputation.
(C) Please let me know which date works the best for you.
(D) I think my qualities make me the ideal candidate for the position.

136. (A) role
(B) performance
(C) event
(D) meeting

137. (A) were all required
(B) have all required
(C) all requirements
(D) all require

138. (A) interview
(B) alert
(C) treat
(D) suggest

Questions 139-142 refer to the following article.

Preservation Efforts

The Carlos Morales Historical Library (CMHL) makes sure the collection will be available for future generations to enjoy by carefully ------- (139.) the amount of light in the building. All paper documents are vulnerable to light damage over time. ------- (140.), the library does not allow its oldest books to be removed from a special windowless climate-controlled section. Nor does it keep any of its collection in spaces with direct exposure to ------- (141.), potentially damaging sunlight. ------- (142.). By using such precautions, CMHL will be able to pass down these invaluable records of our history for centuries.

139. (A) protecting
(B) utilizing
(C) monitoring
(D) displaying

140. (A) For example
(B) Nonetheless
(C) Accordingly
(D) By contrast

141. (A) brightly
(B) bright
(C) brightness
(D) brighten

142. (A) Therefore, we ask that you refrain from making loud noises.
(B) Restoring books damaged in this way requires specialized tools and expertise.
(C) Regrettably, it can be hard to tell which books were affected already.
(D) In addition, all lamps in the library are fitted with filters to block the most harmful rays.

GO ON TO THE NEXT PAGE

Questions 143-146 refer to the following memo.

To: All sales staff
From: Melissa Montgomery
Date: May 25
Subject: Awards Dinner

Hi Everyone,

With only a week left in May, it's time to make arrangements for the first awards dinner of the year. As most of you are aware, this ------- (143.) gathering gives management a chance to show our appreciation for your most outstanding contributions in the first six months. Also, it gives everyone on the sales team a chance ------- (144.) time with their coworkers in a casual environment.

I understand that the lack of public transportation options to the last awards dinner created issues for some of you. In order to make the event accessible to more people, we need to find a ------- (145.) that is located on a subway line. ------- (146.).

143. (A) launch
(B) semiannual
(C) preliminary
(D) occasional

144. (A) having spent
(B) will spend
(C) to spend
(D) spending

145. (A) venue
(B) condition
(C) function
(D) transit

146. (A) A shuttle service from the office will be made available.
(B) You will find detailed directions in the attachment below.
(C) I am sorry for any delay this may have caused.
(D) Please email me if you have a recommendation.

PART 7

Directions: In this part, you will read a selection of texts, such as magazine and newspaper articles, e-mails, and instant messages. Each text or set of texts is followed by several questions. Select the best answer for each question and mark the letter (A), (B), (C), or (D) on your answer sheet.

Questions 147-148 refer to the following ticket.

Fleck County Transportation Commission
General Admission Weekday Pass

Possessing this ticket allows you unlimited crossing on the date of purchase.

Save your ticket until you disembark, as a crew member may need to check it at any point.

- General Admission Passes are valid from Monday to Friday, 6:00 A.M. to 9:30 P.M.
- Those who need to travel with us at other times will need to purchase a special Night Time Pass for an additional $2.50.

Fultz Bay to Port Hoover
Wayne Ferry Terminal to Bauza Island

147. What is true about the ticket?

(A) It may be returned for a refund.
(B) It is good for multiple trips.
(C) It was purchased for $2.50.
(D) It is valid for 24 hours.

148. For what mode of transportation is the ticket?

(A) A ship
(B) A tram
(C) A train
(D) A bus

GO ON TO THE NEXT PAGE

Questions 149-150 refer to the following advertisement.

Social Media Manager Wanted

The Lorry-Irwin Museum of Natural History (LIMNH) has an opening for a talented and dedicated individual. The position involves promoting LIMNH on social network sites, organizing live events, and producing promotional media. To qualify, you must demonstrate a familiarity with video editing software and have at least three years of marketing experience at a past company. To apply, visit www.limnh.org/opportunities and post your CV and samples of your work along with your application form. Submissions will be accepted until December 16. For more information, visit the museum during our regular opening hours and speak with one of our tour guides.

149. What is a requirement of the job?

(A) A degree in business marketing
(B) Previous employment at a non-profit institution
(C) Proficiency with video editing programs
(D) A background in science education

150. How can job applicants get more information?

(A) By accessing a Web site
(B) By sending an e-mail
(C) By booking a tour
(D) By visiting a museum

Questions 151-152 refer to the following memo.

MEMO

To: All Staff
From: Kjrsten Klobach
Date: May 25
Subject: SupporTech K9000

SupporTech Furniture is offering an opportunity to try out ten of their new ergonomic chairs during the month of June. Ergonomic chairs give users the back support they need when working long hours in front of a computer. We will use the latest SupporTech K9000, a model that comes with six full adjustable dimensions, making it easy to tilt or swivel the chair to the exact angle you need. The proper back support can mitigate much of the risk of repetitive stress injury. It can have a positive effect on workplace morale as well. Those interested in the trial should let me know ASAP. If we have more demand than chairs, those who contacted me first will be rewarded. At the end of the month, those who have used the new chairs will fill out a questionnaire reviewing their benefits to evaluate if we should replace our current chairs.

151. What is the primary purpose of the memo?
(A) To ask workers to fill out a questionnaire about office furniture
(B) To explain a new employee wellness program
(C) To request help in setting up some chairs
(D) To give staff a chance to sample new furniture

152. What is indicated about the SupporTech K9000?
(A) It will improve the overall health of the employees.
(B) It is SupporTech's best-selling model.
(C) It requires some time for adjustment.
(D) It can be set to different angles.

GO ON TO THE NEXT PAGE

Questions 153-154 refer to the following text message chain.

Antonio Snell 10:11 A.M.
Hi, again. Glen Ronson is saying he misplaced his smartphone. Is it possible it's still in the third-floor conference room?

Nora Grimwald 10:14 A.M.
Is it a silver CyberCorp CC-7 Max?

Antonio Snell 10:15 A.M.
That's exactly right. He's headed over to fetch it.

Nora Grimwald 10:16 A.M.
Looks like he left his sunglasses as well. All the overtime work is making him forgetful!

Antonio Snell 10:17 A.M.
Do you know that they're his?

Nora Grimwald 10:18 A.M.
I think so. They're sitting right beside the phone.

153. What will Mr. Ronson most likely do next?

(A) Make a call with Mr. Snell's phone
(B) Find some replacement accessories
(C) Speak with Ms. Grimwald's assistant
(D) Claim his belongings from the third floor

154. At 10:18 A.M., what does Ms. Grimwald most likely mean when she writes, "I think so"?

(A) She believes Mr. Ronson's schedule is too busy.
(B) She is confident the sunglasses are Mr. Ronson's.
(C) She wonders if the sunglasses are Mr. Snell's.
(D) She thinks Mr. Snell may have forgotten something.

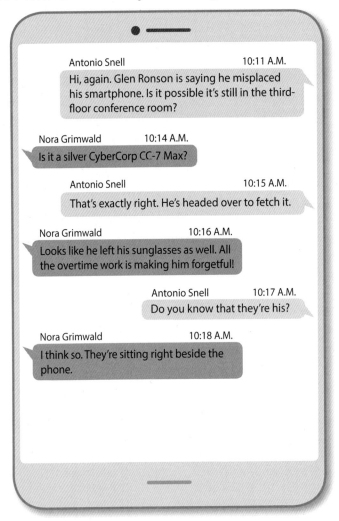

Questions 155-157 refer to the following property listing.

Luxury living with breathtaking views! This sumptuous unit, which was renovated late last year, has over 3,500 square feet of floor space split across two stories, a stunning 1,500-square-foot rooftop terrace, and 24-hour access to a state-of-the-art 2,500-square-foot gymnasium. —[1]—. The property is located right across the street from Emerald Shopping Mall and less than 1,000 feet from the beach. —[2]—. The unit is fully furnished, with everything from designer couches to high-end end tables. —[3]—. Renting the unit requires a security deposit and a minimum 24-month lease. —[4]—. To inquire about the property, email Marcus Murray at mmurray@zdparadise.ag.

155. How large is the workout facility?

(A) 1,000 square feet
(B) 1,500 square feet
(C) 2,500 square feet
(D) 3,500 square feet

156. What is NOT mentioned as an advantage of the property?

(A) It comes with furniture.
(B) It has been remodeled recently.
(C) It is located near a shopping center.
(D) It is within walking distance of a school.

157. In which of the positions marked [1], [2], [3], and [4] does the following sentence best belong?

"Subject to availability, shorter-term leases may be available on request."

(A) [1]
(B) [2]
(C) [3]
(D) [4]

GO ON TO THE NEXT PAGE

Questions 158-160 refer to the following e-mail.

Date	: March 23
Subject	: Update
To	: Brittany Douglas
From	: Victoria Clarkson

Dear Brittany,

The grand opening of the new downtown location has been moved to April 7. I did not anticipate that the event would conflict with building inspections the same weekend. My apologies for any confusion this causes.

I will have more details for you soon, along with the new invitations for the opening. I'm still expecting a strong turnout, including a group from company headquarters.

As we have discussed, we will mark this special occasion with discounts on room rates. We have also put together a deal with Kaiser Rent-a-Car so that customers can bundle their hotel and car rentals. As a result, we hope to attract more family travelers in addition to our usual corporate clientele.

See you soon,

Victoria Clarkson

158. The word "conflict" in paragraph 1, line 2, is closest in meaning to

(A) contend
(B) oppose
(C) compete
(D) overlap

159. What does Ms. Clarkson suggest in her e-mail?

(A) She has rescheduled a conference.
(B) She has corrected an error.
(C) She is in charge of a product launch.
(D) She will visit her company's main office.

160. What will open on April 7?

(A) A catering business
(B) A car rental office
(C) A hotel chain location
(D) A travel agency

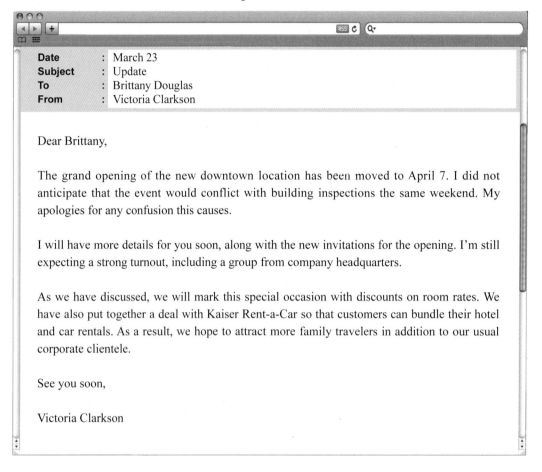

Questions 161-163 refer to the following letter.

Midgard Airways

34 Frederiksberg,
Adalen,
Region Sjaelland 1879

August 29

A message to our Frequent Fliers Club members:

Midgard Airways appreciates your continued loyalty. In our 20 years in business, we have provided innovative services to customers all over Scandinavia with some of the best perks on the market. Despite industry-wide challenges, we have kept track of what makes our brand special—customer satisfaction. In that spirit, I am proud to announce that we will be undergoing a merger with Tangerine Airlines.

How will this change the airline you have come to trust? In only one respect. Starting from January 1, we will be known as Tangerine Airlines North. You will still retain your rewards mileage, have access to members' lounges at the same airports, and receive the same seat upgrades. However, you will now have the entire network of Tangerine Airlines at your fingertips, including its access to a greater range of exciting destinations. Tangerine Airlines is Europe's fastest-growing airline, with a track record of award-winning passenger service and timeliness.

To learn more about Tangerine Airlines, download the Tangerine Airlines app or call 1-800-555-8284. If you need to book a flight, please continue to use www.midgardairways.dk/bookings.

We are always happy to have you aboard.

Best,

Sven Svenson
Midgard Airlines President

161. What is the purpose of the letter?
(A) To notify members about a corporate partnership
(B) To show appreciation to long-term members
(C) To let customers know about a new flight route
(D) To announce changes to its online booking system

162. What is suggested about Tangerine Airlines?
(A) It has operated for two decades.
(B) It does not offer admissions to airport lounges.
(C) It has more available flights than Midgard.
(D) It will be revising its mileage system.

163. According to the letter, what should the recipients do to book a flight?
(A) Download the Tangerine Airlines mobile application
(B) Log on to the same Web site as before
(C) Call Tangerine Airlines' toll-free number
(D) Send a message to Midgard customer service

GO ON TO THE NEXT PAGE

Questions 164-167 refer to the following online chat discussion.

Judy Custer **[11:08 A.M.]**

Are the trainers who are coming by to demonstrate the new metal fabrication tools ready for Thursday morning's workshop?

George Holiday **[11:10 A.M.]**

They are. The plan is that they will arrive at 9 on Thursday. Will someone be at the front gate to greet them and lead them to where the demonstration is taking place?

Judy Custer **[11:11 A.M.]**

My secretary will take care of that.

George Holiday **[11:12 A.M.]**

Will the rooms be equipped with projectors and have USB connections?

Fred Milch **[11:13 A.M.]**

As Judy mentioned, I'll greet the trainers and get them temporary security badges.

Judy Custer **[11:14 A.M.]**

The meeting rooms will be set up with everything that was requested.

Fred Milch **[11:15 A.M.]**

The shift ends at 9:30, so the machine operators will arrive a few minutes after that. I plan to be there and pass out refreshments.

George Holiday **[11:16 A.M.]**

Sounds good. The workshops will wrap up around 11:30. Will either of you be around? Will the trainers need to tidy things up after?

Judy Custer **[11:18 A.M.]**

I'll be there to take care of that.

George Holiday **[11:19 A.M.]**

Got it. We're all set.

Judy Custer **[11:20 A.M.]**

I will be on-site until noon. Let me know if you need my assistance.

SEND

164. Why did Ms. Custer contact Mr. Holiday?

(A) To request some technical information
(B) To go over some arrangements
(C) To order new security badges
(D) To confirm a scheduling change

165. When will Mr. Milch be at the front gate?

(A) At 9:00 A.M.
(B) At 9:30 A.M.
(C) At 11:30 A.M.
(D) At 12:00 P.M.

166. What is indicated about the machine operators?

(A) They are supervised by Mr. Holiday.
(B) They will break for lunch at 11:30 A.M.
(C) They will attend a post-work seminar.
(D) They are newly hired employees.

167. At 11:19 A.M., what does Mr. Holiday mean when he writes, "We're all set"?

(A) He has already arranged a meeting room.
(B) He agrees to Ms. Custer's plan.
(C) He does not have any other questions.
(D) He received the requested equipment.

GO ON TO THE NEXT PAGE

Questions 168-171 refer to the following e-mail.

To	: Monica Beahan
From	: Ahmad Simpson
Date	: 5 October
Subject	: Re: Monday Meeting

Monica,

I appreciated your honesty concerning your current assignments. — [1] —. We can certainly do a better job assigning tasks so that they can be completed within normal business hours. — [2] —. As you now need to add analyzing financial statements on top of your list of other duties, the department has arranged to bring in an intern to assist you—a graduate student at a local university named Cynthia Jung. — [3] —. You will be in charge of supervising her work, which will include processing payroll, compiling financial data, and logging expense reports.

When Ms. Jung arrives on the first of November, we would like you to brief her on the department's procedures and show her how to perform routine tasks. Make sure to inform her about our confidentiality and cyber security policies.

Feel free to contact me with any questions. — [4] —.

Sincerely,
Ahmad Simpson

168. Who most likely is Ms. Beahan?

(A) A graphic designer
(B) A salesperson
(C) An accountant
(D) An IT professional

169. What problem did Ms. Beahan report?

(A) Excessive workload
(B) Security weaknesses
(C) Long commutes
(D) Unscheduled meetings

170. What is Ms. Beahan asked to do next month?

(A) Review some job applications
(B) Present a report
(C) Meet with her supervisors
(D) Train an intern

171. In which of the positions marked [1], [2], [3], and [4] does the following sentence best belong?

"This should help you with certain tasks."

(A) [1]
(B) [2]
(C) [3]
(D) [4]

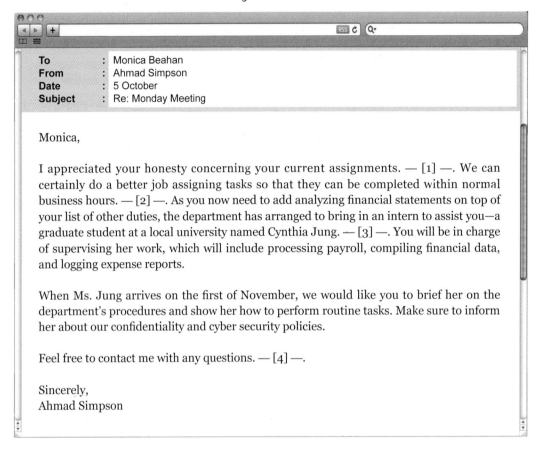

Questions 172-175 refer to the following Web article.

The Signal Monthly
December Edition

A View From the Top

If you want to find Harold Rossi, you are going to have to look up—specifically, in the mountains. That's where he is filming rare birds, as he did masterfully in last year's documentary *The Final Flock*.

Rossi discovered his love for films when he started borrowing his brother's camcorder at the age of 13. Though he attended the occasional lecture on cinematography in university, his English major led to a successful career in editing for print publications.

After graduation, Rossi joined the staff of *The Signal* and had little time to film, as he shaped successful stories issue after issue. But that ended after he took a rock-climbing course in Bolivia. The footage he shot of local endangered birds during the course encouraged him to pursue film on a full-time basis.

Though he started out using a simple camcorder, Mr. Rossi now uses cameras that record at an ultra-fast frame rate. "To film something fast, you need to think fast," he says. And he is always looking for models that better capture slow motion, which leads to frequent equipment upgrades.

After a decade of looking for rare birds, Rossi is not slowing down. His work has made him a seasoned climber, and he has become an expert on many avian species. He says, "This is my passion; I'll do anything for it."

The majority of his work, including his award-winning documentary, has been in the Andes. Next month, though, he will travel to Namibia to film swifts for a forthcoming nature series for CBV TV.

172. What is the purpose of the article?
(A) To advertise a new documentary film
(B) To describe a former magazine employee
(C) To give advice on slow-motion filming
(D) To promote a magazine story

173. What inspired Mr. Rossi to film rare birds?
(A) A cinematography lecture
(B) An assignment in Bolivia
(C) A brother's encouragement
(D) A climbing course

174. The word "seasoned" in paragraph 5, line 2 is closest in meaning to
(A) weathered
(B) prepared
(C) accomplished
(D) considered

175. What is indicated about Mr. Rossi?
(A) He has taken photographs in Namibia.
(B) He films with an older model of camera.
(C) He is an experienced climber.
(D) He will soon release a debut film.

GO ON TO THE NEXT PAGE

Questions 176-180 refer to the following Web page and e-mail.

http://newdelhitexglobe.co.in

About | News | Calendar | Media | Information | Contact | Sign Up

New Delhi Texglobe: The International Textile Conference
September 27-29 Dwarka Expo Centre, India

New Delhi Texglobe, the top textile convention in the world, welcomes you again this September as we anticipate our biggest event to date. Join us to get a firsthand look at the latest and greatest in textile innovation.

Participants who register by August 27 will be given an early bird discount. Register on our Web site by clicking on the "Sign Up" tab. Those who sign up online between August 28 and September 23 will be charged the original fee. Guests may also register for entry passes on any day of the event by visiting the conference center's ticketing office.

If you intend to set up a booth featuring your company's items, you must make an advance booking. These booths will be available for pick up at the venue's West Auditorium, next to conference rooms 1 and 2. Click on the "Information" tab for more details. Please be advised that the circulation of marketing materials (e.g., brochures, product samples, etc.) by non-exhibitors is strictly prohibited.

To:	eholmes@CNWinc.com
From:	ctissera@kandylions.lk
Date:	September 25
Subject:	New Delhi Texglobe Conference

Dear Mr. Holmes,

I am the director of the Technology Management Department for the Kandy Lions Sportswear in Sri Lanka. We manufacture various sporting apparel, but mainly uniforms for professional sports teams. I wanted to talk to you about the new electronic textile that you will be demonstrating at Texglobe in New Delhi. We are always looking to provide a competitive edge for our customers. With your product, I believe we will be able to incorporate wearable technology and provide our end users with the ability to analyze and monitor their athletes for optimal performance. Because customers will be using our product during practices and competitions, we need a fabric like yours that can tolerate sweat and wet weather conditions while withstanding repeated rapid movements.

I will be able to travel to the conference this weekend to meet you on the day that suits you the best. I'm sure that you and your team have a full schedule as it is, but please inform me when you will be free to talk about your product. Thank you for your time.

Best,

Chathuri Tissera

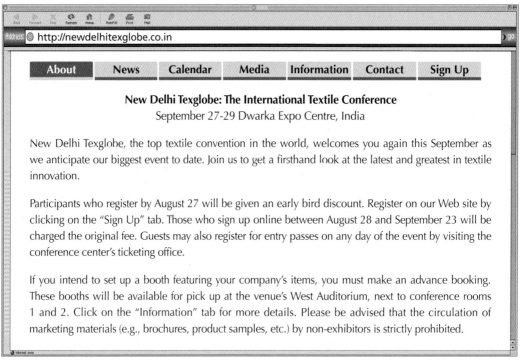

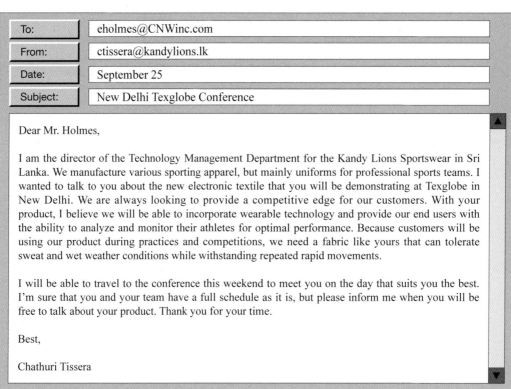

176. Who most likely are the attendees at the New Delhi Texglobe Conference?

(A) Fashion retailers
(B) Sports engineers
(C) Journalists
(D) Manufacturers

177. What is indicated about the event?

(A) It only allows exhibitors to distribute marketing materials.
(B) It is held multiple times a year.
(C) It is the first time New Delhi is hosting it.
(D) It offers a discount to prior participants.

178. Why is Ms. Tissera interested in Mr. Holmes' product?

(A) It is comfortable.
(B) It is affordable.
(C) It is customizable.
(D) It is durable.

179. What does Ms. Tissera ask Mr. Holmes to provide?

(A) Information regarding his availability
(B) Technical specifications
(C) A product sample
(D) A catalog

180. How will Ms. Tissera most likely register for the conference?

(A) Online
(B) On-site
(C) By phone
(D) By fax

GO ON TO THE NEXT PAGE

Questions 181-185 refer to the following memo and membership card.

NOTICE

To: Employees at Empower
From: Fraser Hong, HR Department
Date: 12 February
Subject: Pinnacle Career School

Pinnacle Career School provides employees with Empower Energy instruction at reduced tuition fees. When enrolling at Pinnacle, confirm your employment status by providing a letter from Human Resources or your previous month's payslip, which can be obtained from Accounting.

Pinnacle Career School offers a wide range of courses. In addition, top local business leaders share their insights as guest lecturers. Register for more than one course and receive a courtesy sweatshirt with Pinnacle's emblem.

Courses recommended for Empower employees are as follows:

Course	Tuition	Reduced Tuition
Public Speaking	$1,200	$950
Spreadsheet Basics	$875	$625
Leadership Skills	$1,350	$1,100

Pinnacle Career School
www.pinnaclecs.com

Name: Regina Miller
Place of Employment: Empower Energy
Registered Course: Public Speaking
Start Date: 2 March

This is your temporary ID card. You should receive your official ID card by mail within five business days. If you do not receive it by then, please contact the Campus Service Center at 555-4128 or email us at campussc@pinnaclecs.com. For more information on the functions of the card, visit www.pinnaclecs.com/studentid.

181. What is the purpose of the memo?

(A) To describe an employee benefit
(B) To announce an accounting error
(C) To advertise a local business
(D) To explain a new corporate policy

182. In the memo, the word "courtesy" in paragraph 2, line 3, is closest in meaning to

(A) ceremonial
(B) considerate
(C) complimentary
(D) personalized

183. What will be Ms. Miller's tuition fee?

(A) $1,350
(B) $1,200
(C) $950
(D) $625

184. What is implied about Ms. Miller?

(A) Her previous month's payslip is unavailable.
(B) Her official identification card should be delivered in less than a week.
(C) She will receive a sweatshirt from Pinnacle Career School.
(D) She is the Human Resources manager at Empower Energy.

185. According to the card, how can Ms. Miller learn more about how the card can be used?

(A) By visiting the Pinnacle Career School campus
(B) By going to the institution's Web site
(C) By reading the information on the back of the card
(D) By contacting the Campus Service Center

GO ON TO THE NEXT PAGE

Questions 186-190 refer to the following article, advertisement, and e-mail.

El Dorado (23 November) — Nucleus Tech released a statement yesterday afternoon introducing its newest microprocessor, Lyra. After four years of trial-and-error testing, the Lyra has been able to achieve significantly faster performance than any other models available.

In addition to its quickness, Nucleus Tech's microprocessor will easily match its competitors when it comes to multitasking, graphics, and the ability to support the latest technology. And the firm states that the Lyra is twice as fast as microprocessors that are currently on the market. The Lyra will arrive at retailers in two months' time.

Nucleus has already begun tests on its successor to the Lyra, which is expected to be much more energy-efficient than competing microprocessors.

JOIN OUR TEAM

Nucleus is looking for qualified candidates to join our Engineering, Sales, and R&D Departments to help in the advancement of Taurus-X, the successor to our industry-leading microprocessor, the Lyra.

Applicants must have a degree relevant to the positions they are applying for. Candidates for the sales position must be business proficient in Arabic or French. Those interested in the R&D Department will be required to travel to our facilities across the country. Applicants must have five years of experience in the industry, with at least one year in a managerial role.

Nucleus provides various incentives, including monthly bonuses for reaching performance goals.

For more information about the company or the listed positions, visit our online page at www.nucleustech.com/jobs.

To	:	bgrant@tcu.edu
From	:	pnewton@wiremail.com
Date	:	15 March
Subject	:	Recommendation

Dear Professor Grant,

Thank you for writing a recommendation letter to Nucleus Tech in regard to my proficiency in the Arabic language. Because of your help, I was able to land the job, and I am excited to start my first day on 22 March. I am grateful for your support and appreciate everything that you have done for me.

Best,

Pamela Newton

186. What makes the Lyra microprocessor unique?

(A) Its graphics
(B) Its complexity
(C) Its compatibility
(D) Its speed

187. According to the article, when will the Lyra be available?

(A) In one month
(B) In two months
(C) In one year
(D) In two years

188. How will Taurus-X differ from its competitors?

(A) It will consume less power.
(B) It will be smaller.
(C) It will have faster memory.
(D) It will cost more.

189. What is true of all applicants who get hired?

(A) They all receive monthly bonuses.
(B) They all travel for their work.
(C) They must have at least a year of experience.
(D) They must have relevant degrees.

190. What department has hired Ms. Newton?

(A) Engineering
(B) Sales
(C) R&D
(D) Human Resources

GO ON TO THE NEXT PAGE

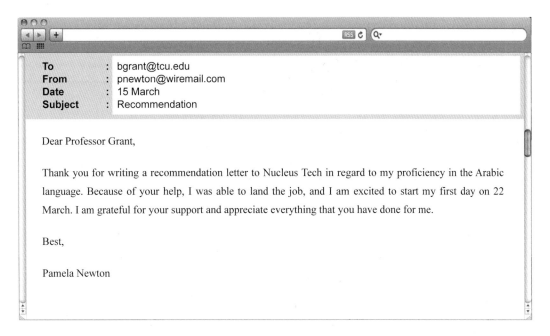

Questions 191-195 refer to the following Web page, e-mail, and form.

http://www.qualiprint.co.uk/home

-QUALIPRINT-

Qualiprint is a virtual shopping Web site providing you with solutions to all your business card needs.

- Choose from 100 different styles
- Upload your own graphics or work with one of our designers
- Orders for 500 cards or more receive free shipping
- Made from eco-friendly materials
- Square and rounded corner shapes available
- Premium and Ultra Thick paper stock
- Varnish and foil stamping finishes

Additional style options are available for return clients. After you have selected your desired paper and finished it, please fill out and attach the Card Order Form(s) at the Purchase page and press "Upload". The Card Order Form can be found on our Selections page.

All inquiries will be answered by our customer service agents at (491) 555-8104 or service@qualiprint.co.uk.

To	:	Employees
From	:	Lamar Snead
Date	:	Wednesday, September 13
Subject	:	Business cards
Attachment	:	Card Order Form.doc Template.doc

Dear Employees,

Starting October 1, our company will be rebranded as Sintal Beverages. Our logo will also change on this day. In preparation, all employees will be issued new business cards. As a reminder, the card costs will be handled by your respective teams.

Human Resources has already chosen the style and the finish. I have attached a template of the new business card as well as an order form. Please fill it out and send it back to me by Wednesday, September 20. Qualiprint, our usual supplier, has guaranteed delivery before October 1 if we are able to submit our order by Thursday, September 21.

Best,

Lamar Snead
Purchasing Manager

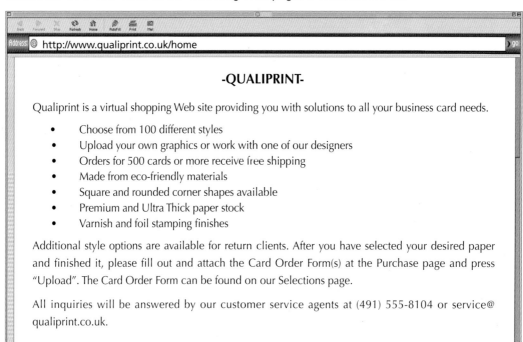

-QUALIPRINT-
Card Order Form

Date: September 14
Name: Ava Bremby
Team: Finance
Quantity of Cards Needed: ☐ 100 ☐ 250 ☐ 500 ☐ 750 ☐ 1,000 ☑ Other 1,500

Please write the information you wish to appear on your business card below.

Position: Director of Finance
Phone Number: ____________
Mobile Number: (471) 555-5930
E-mail: abremby@sintalbev.co.uk

191. What information does the Web page provide?
(A) A list of product options
(B) A location of an offline store
(C) A seasonal discount offer
(D) A set of instructions about payment

192. What does Mr. Snead suggest about his company's current business cards?
(A) They do not have the updated Web site address.
(B) They are missing the company motto.
(C) They will soon be outdated.
(D) They are too expensive.

193. According to the e-mail, what do the staff need to do by September 20?
(A) Renew their employment contracts
(B) Vote for a new company logo
(C) Make a payment to Qualiprint
(D) Turn in a form to Mr. Snead

194. What is implied about the new business cards?
(A) Their style was selected from more than 100 choices.
(B) They will include the former name of the company.
(C) The company logo will not be on them.
(D) They will be made from premium paper.

195. What is suggested about Ms. Bremby?
(A) She is a first-time customer of Qualiprint.
(B) She will collect the order forms for her team.
(C) She has contacted a Qualiprint customer service agent.
(D) She will receive free shipping of her business cards.

GO ON TO THE NEXT PAGE

Questions 196-200 refer to the following instructions, e-mail, and notice.

Fasbert Research Institute

Standard Operating Procedure (Revised 5 June)

Sanitation

— Hands must be cleaned before entering the lab. Please use the hand sanitizer located next to the door after washing your hands. Only washing with soap is not sufficient as it does not kill all the bacteria on your hands. Do not touch your hair or face after application.

— Hair must be pulled back and secured while in the medical laboratory. Germs and other microbes may reside in your hair, which can contaminate the cell cultures we work with.

Safety Gear

All technicians must wear the appropriate safety gear when in the laboratory.

— Goggles and latex gloves are essential to the practice of safe science. Goggles must be disinfected after every use without exception. Latex gloves must be discarded in the designated bins located by the exit. Do not wear them out of the lab, as there is a high potential for cross-contamination.

— Shoe covers must also be worn when working in the laboratory. They can be found at the entrance of all medical laboratories. Please dispose of them when you go out to the receiving area, and put new ones on before you bring a sample delivery into the lab.

To:	Kelsey Richards
From:	Ji-hoon Kim
Date:	June 6
Subject:	Updated Standard Operating Procedure

Dear Kelsey,

Thank you for revising our standard operating procedures. The new outline is less complicated, and now there should no longer be any confusion regarding the procedure. With that being said, please edit out the segment on shoe cover disposal. It no longer applies, as Ressling Corp. has now agreed to handle that portion of the process.

Since there is still a lot of material to take in from the procedure list, it would be helpful to put up signs in each designated area to caution employees on what needs to be done. Please send me the final version with the above changes so I can pass it along to Logan Pasternak. He will hand out copies and upload it to our intranet site.

Ji-hoon Kim
Laboratory and Safety Manager

WARNING!

Dispose of gloves in the green bin before advancing.

We appreciate your cooperation!

Fasbert Research Institute

196. For whom are the instructions most likely intended?

(A) Employees in a restaurant
(B) Medical lab technicians
(C) Doctors in a hospital
(D) Sales representatives

197. According to the instructions, what is an advantage of using hand sanitizer?

(A) It makes a process more effective.
(B) It is less expensive than other conventional methods.
(C) It dries quickly.
(D) It is easy to use.

198. Why does Mr. Kim thank Ms. Richards in his e-mail?

(A) She simplified a document.
(B) She introduced a new client.
(C) She met a project deadline.
(D) She purchased some new equipment.

199. What does the e-mail imply about Ressling Corp.?

(A) It produces safety gear.
(B) It has updated its sanitation policy.
(C) It operates a clinical trials center.
(D) It delivers samples to Fasbert.

200. Where is the notice most likely posted?

(A) On the door of a restroom
(B) On the wall of a mailroom
(C) At the entrance of a hospital
(D) At the exit of a work area

Stop! This is the end of the test. If you finish before time is called, you may go back to Part 5, 6, and 7 and check your work.

NO TEST MATERIAL ON THIS PAGE

MEMO

MEMO

1타 강사의 속성 과외!

토익 950+ 벼락치기

최신 경향 완벽 반영

최신 시험 분석 · 반영은 물론,
효과적인 대비 전략 수록

고득점을 위한 비법 공개

950점 이상 목표달성을 위한
1타 강사만의 필수 학습 내용 공개

동영상 강의 무료 제공

책과 함께 보면
실력 200% 상승

950점 플러스 전략

가장 넘기 힘든 950점!
950+를 위한 개념만 집약!

해 설 서

PAGODA Books

1타 강사의 속성 과외!

토익 950+ 벼락치기

해설서

PAGODA Books

1 인물 사진

미국

(A) A man is descending a staircase.
…› 동작 묘사 오류, descend가 아니라 올라가는 ascend가 되어야 한다.
(B) A man is closing a laptop.
…› 동작 묘사 오류
(C) A woman is grasping a handrail.
(D) A woman is sweeping the steps.
…› 동작 묘사 오류

남자가 계단을 내려오고 있다.
남자가 노트북을 닫고 있다.
여자가 난간을 잡고 있다.
여자가 계단을 쓸고 있다.

어휘 descend 내려가다 | staircase 계단 | grasp 쥐다 | handrail 난간 | sweep 쓸다

2 인물 사진

호주

(A) A woman is standing next to a man.
…› 동작 묘사 오류, 서로 마주 보고 있으므로 face each other로 표현하면 된다.
(B) Clothes are being arranged on a rack.
…› 상태 묘사 오류, 이미 진열된 상태이다.
(C) A purchase is being made at a counter.
(D) Several customers are waiting in line.
…› 사진에 없는 내용(several customers)

여자가 남자 옆에 서 있다.
옷이 선반에 진열되고 있다.
계산대에서 물건이 구매되고 있다.
몇몇 고객들이 줄 서서 기다리고 있다.

어휘 rack 선반 | wait in line 줄을 서서 기다리다

3 인물 사진

영국

(A) A woman is waiting on customers.
…› wait for '기다리다'와 착각하지 않도록 하자. wait on은 '시중들다'로 쓰인다.
(B) Some people are taking their seats.
…› 동작 묘사 오류, take a seat은 자리에 앉으려고 하는 동작이고, 사진은 앉아 있는 상태이므로 be seated라고 쓴다.
(C) A table is being set up.
…› 상태 묘사 오류
(D) Food is being served on the table.
…› 상태 묘사 오류

여자가 고객을 응대하고 있다.
몇몇 사람들이 좌석에 앉고 있다.
테이블이 준비되고 있다.
음식이 테이블에 제공되고 있다.

어휘 wait on 시중들다

4 인물 사진

미국

(A) A ladder is being placed on the floor.
…› 상태 묘사 오류, 사다리는 놓여 있는 상태이므로, has been placed로 써야 한다.
(B) A man is wheeling cargo up a ramp.
(C) Some furniture is being assembled.
…› 상태 묘사 오류
(D) A man is repairing a vehicle.
…› 동작 묘사 오류

사다리가 바닥에 놓이고 있다.
남자가 경사로 위에서 물건을 끌고 있다.
몇몇 가구가 조립되고 있다.
남자가 차량을 수리하고 있다.

어휘 ladder 사다리 | wheel (바퀴 달린 것을) 밀다, 끌다 | cargo 화물 | ramp 경사로 | assemble 조립하다

5 인물 사진 영국

(A) Travelers are putting their bags in the overhead compartment.
···› 사진에 없는 내용(overhead compartment)

(B) An airplane is about to take off.
···› 상태 묘사 오류, 사진에서는 비행기가 이미 착륙(land)한 상태이다.

(C) Passengers are disembarking from an aircraft.

(D) Luggage is being moved to a vehicle.
···› 상태 묘사 오류

여행객들이 머리 위 짐칸에 가방을 놓고 있다.
비행기가 이륙하려고 하고 있다.
승객들이 비행기에서 내리고 있다.
짐이 차량으로 옮겨지고 있다.

어휘 overhead compartment 머리 위 짐칸 | take off 이륙하다 | disembark 내리다

6 인물 사진 미국

(A) Some people are setting up a table.
···› 상태 묘사 오류

(B) Some people are facing the presenter.

(C) A whiteboard is being installed on a wall.
···› 상태 묘사 오류

(D) Some chairs are unoccupied.
···› 상태 묘사 오류, 사람들이 앉아 있기 때문에 unoccupied가 아니라 occupied로 해야 정답이다.

몇몇 사람들이 테이블을 설치하고 있다.
몇몇 사람들이 발표자를 보고 있다.
화이트보드가 벽에 설치되고 있다.
몇 개의 의자가 비어있다.

어휘 presenter 발표자 | unoccupied 비어있는

7 인물 사진 호주

(A) Some workers are mowing the lawn.
···› 사진에 없는 내용(some workers), 사진에는 한 사람만 등장하므로 some workers는 오답이다.

(B) A vehicle is being filled with logs.
···› 상태 묘사 오류, 나무가 가득 차 있는 상태이므로 진행 수동은 오답

(C) A wheelbarrow is being pushed in a work area.

(D) A man is leaning against a pole.
···› 동작 묘사 오류

몇몇 작업자들이 잔디를 깎고 있다.
운송 수단이 나무로 채워지고 있다.
작업장에서 외부 수레를 밀고 있다.
남자가 기둥에 기대어 있다.

어휘 mow the lawn 잔디를 깎다 | be filled with 채워져 있다 | log 통나무 | wheelbarrow 외바퀴 수레 | lean against ~에 기대다

8 사물 / 배경 사진 미국

(A) Some fruits are being delivered to a store.
···› 사물 사진 be being p.p.

(B) Display racks have been cleared of items.
···› 상태 묘사 오류, 물건이 꽉 차 있다.

(C) Some produce has been stacked in a basket.

(D) Some people are shopping outdoors.
···› 사진에 없는 내용(some people)

몇 개의 과일이 가게로 배송되고 있다.
진열대에 물건이 치워져 있다.
몇 개의 농산물이 바구니에 쌓여 있다.
몇몇 사람들이 야외에서 쇼핑하고 있다.

어휘 rack 선반 | produce 농산물 | stack 쌓다

9 사물 / 배경 사진

미국

(A) People are swimming in the water.
···› 사진에 없는 내용(people)

(B) A bridge spans a body of water.

(C) Branches are scattered on the ground.
···› 상태 묘사 오류

(D) A pathway is being repaved.
···› 사물 사진 be being p.p.

사람들이 물에서 수영하고 있다.
다리가 물을 가로질러 놓여 있다.
나뭇가지가 땅에 흩어져 있다.
길이 포장되어 지고 있다.

어휘 span 걸쳐 이어지다 | branch 나뭇가지 | scatter 흩어지다 | pathway 길

10 사물 / 배경 사진

영국

(A) Trees are casting shadows on the rooftop.
···› 상태 묘사 오류

(B) Some curtains have been left open.
···› 상태 묘사 오류, 커튼이 닫혀 있는 상태이므로 open이 아니라 closed로 표현해야 한다.

(C) Some people are swimming on the beach.
···› 사진에 없는 내용(some people)

(D) Balconies overlook a swimming pool.

옥상에 나무 그림자가 생기고 있다.
몇 개의 커튼이 활짝 열려 있다.
몇몇 사람들이 바닷가에서 수영을 하고 있다.
발코니에서 수영장이 내려다보인다.

어휘 cast a shadow 그림자를 드리우다 | rooftop 옥상 | overlook 내려다보다

11 사물 / 배경 사진

영국

(A) Cars are parked in a garage.
···› 사진에 없는 내용(cars)

(B) A mechanic is repairing a car.
···› 사진에 없는 내용(mechanic)

(C) Tires are being displayed outside.
···› 사람이 없는 사진이라도 display는 be being p.p.를 쓸 수 있는 예외 단어이다.

(D) Vehicles have been advertised for sale.
···› 사진에 없는 내용(vehicles)

자동차들이 주차장에 주차되어 있다.
정비사가 차를 수리하고 있다.
타이어가 밖에 진열되어 있다.
차들이 판매를 위해 광고되고 있다.

어휘 mechanic 정비사

12 사물 / 배경 사진

호주

(A) Some windows are being cleaned.
···› 사물 사진 be being p.p.

(B) Paint is being applied to the wall.
···› 사물 사진 be being p.p.

(C) A ladder is propped against a building.
···› be propped against는 '~에 기대어 놓여있다'라는 의미이다.

(D) A roof is being repaired.
···› 사물 사진 be being p.p.

몇 개의 창문들이 청소되고 있다.
페인트가 벽에 칠해지고 있다.
사다리가 건물에 기대어져 있다.
지붕이 수리되고 있다.

어휘 be propped against ~에 기대어 놓여있다 / 받쳐져 있다

13 사물 / 배경 사진

미국

(A) Some lamps are being put on the table.
···› 사물 사진 be being p.p.

(B) A mirror has been mounted on a wall.
···› be mounted on은 '~에 고정 / 설치되어 있다'라는 의미이다.

(C) Some pillows are being arranged on the bed.
···› 사물 사진 be being p.p.

(D) A light fixture is hanging from the ceiling.
···› 상태 묘사 오류

몇 개의 등이 테이블에 놓이고 있다.
거울이 벽에 설치되어 있다.
몇 개의 베개가 침대 위에 배열되고 있다.
조명이 천장에 매달려 있다.

어휘 mirror 거울 | be mounted on ~에 고정되어 있다 | pillow 베개 | light fixture 조명 | ceiling 천장

14 인물 사진

호주

(A) A man is standing in front of a camera.
···› 상태 묘사 오류, 카메라 앞이 아니라 뒤(behind)에 서 있으므로 오답

(B) Poles are leaning against a wall.
···› 상태 묘사 오류

(C) A man is taking a picture out of the frame.
···› 동작 묘사 오류, take a picture만 보고 '사진 찍다'라는 개념으로 생각하면 안 된다. take out of라고 해서 '꺼내다'의 의미가 적합하므로 오답이다.

(D) Photographic equipment has been set up.
···› 요즘에는 집합적 개념으로 카메라를 photographic equipment로 통칭해서 사용하기도 한다.

남자가 카메라 앞에 서 있다.
기둥이 벽에 기대어 있다.
남자가 사진을 액자에서 꺼내고 있다.
카메라가 설치되어 있다.

어휘 lean against 기대어 있다

15 사물 / 배경 사진

미국

(A) Chairs have been stacked on top of each other.
···› 상태 묘사 오류

(B) Partitions are being set up on a table.
···› 사물 사진 be being p.p.

(C) Workstations are unoccupied.

(D) Computers are being used.
···› 사물 사진 be being p.p.

의자가 차곡차곡 쌓여 있다.
칸막이가 테이블에 설치되고 있다.
사무실이 비어있다.
컴퓨터가 사용되고 있다.

어휘 partition 칸막이

1 Where 의문문 미국 - 미국

Where's the performance review meeting taking place?
(A) Monday morning. ···› When에 대한 대답
(B) I didn't know you were interested in coming.
(C) The CEO led them. ···› meeting의 연상 어휘

업무 평가 미팅이 어디에서 개최되나요?
월요일 아침에요.
참석하시는 것에 관심 있으신 줄 몰랐네요.
CEO가 주관합니다.

어휘 performance 업무

2 When 의문문 미국 - 영국

When will the updated budget be completed?
(A) Financial information. ···› budget의 연상 어휘: financial
(B) I'm on my last page. 고난도 - 우회적인 표현
(C) Yes, it was completed on the third floor.
···› 의문사 의문문에 Yes로 대답

업데이트된 예산이 언제 완성될까요?
재무 정보요.
저는 마지막 페이지를 하고 있습니다.
네, 3층에서 완성되었어요.

어휘 budget 예산

3 일반 의문문 영국 - 호주

Do you know which room the Finance Department office is in?
(A) It's in the top drawer. ···› 장소 오류
(B) Don't forget to submit the budget today.
···› finance의 연상 어휘: budget
(C) I just started working here. 고난도 - 우회적인 표현

어디가 재무팀 사무실이 있는 곳인지 아시나요?
제일 위 서랍에요.
오늘 예산을 제출하는 것을 잊지 마세요.
여기서 일한 지 얼마 안 되었어요.

어휘 Finance Department 재무팀 | top drawer 위 서랍

4 일반 의문문 미국 - 호주

Would you be able to visit us this Thursday?
(A) Okay, I'm not busy this weekend.
···› 이번 주 목요일을 물어봤는데 이번 주말을 이야기하므로 오답
(B) It would have to be later in the afternoon.
(C) Sure, I can help you with that. ···› sure는 맞지만 동문서답

이번 주 목요일에 저희를 방문하실 수 있으세요?
좋아요, 이번 주말에 안 바빠요.
오후 늦게나 되어야 합니다.
물론이죠, 제가 그것에 대해 도와드릴 수 있어요.

어휘 later in the afternoon 오후 늦게

5 Who 의문문 미국 - 미국

Who can I contact for a cost estimate on office renovations?
(A) It should say on the flyer.
(B) A three-year contract. ···› contact의 유사 발음: contract
(C) It was very costly. ···› cost의 유사 발음: costly

사무실 보수공사의 가격 견적서에 관해 누구에게 이야기할 수 있을까요?
책자에 나와 있어요.
3년 계약서예요.
매우 비쌌어요.

어휘 cost estimate 가격 견적서 | flyer 책자 | contract 계약서 | costly 값비싼

6 기타 의문문(평서문) 미국 - 호주

The front entrance of the building is locked.
(A) Yes, in my locker. ···› lock의 유사 발음: locker
(B) Someone from the maintenance department can help you soon. 고난도 - 평서문에 대한 자세한 설명
(C) I requested the rear entrance.
···› front entrance의 연상 어휘, 유사 발음: rear entrance

건물 입구가 잠겼어요.
네, 제 사물함 안에요.
유지보수팀에서 누군가가 곧 도와드릴 거예요.
저는 뒷문을 요청했어요.

어휘 front entrance 입구 | locker 사물함 | maintenance department 유지보수팀 | rear entrance 뒷문

7 Why 의문문 미국 - 영국

Why was the IT workshop moved to next Wednesday?
(A) I moved to New York last weekend. ···› move 어휘 반복
(B) I can reschedule it for tomorrow.
(C) No, it was held in Berlin. ···› 의문사 의문문에 No로 대답

IT 워크숍 일정이 왜 다음 주 수요일로 변경되었나요?
지난 주말에 뉴욕으로 이사 왔어요.
내일로 다시 변경할게요.
아니요, 그것은 베를린에서 개최되었습니다.

어휘 reschedule 일정을 변경하다

8 선택 의문문 영국 - 호주

Do you want to take the subway or drive to the museum?
(A) I'm OK, thank you. ···› 동문서답
(B) Over 70 paintings are on display. ···› museum의 연상 어휘
(C) It's right by the subway exit. 고난도 - 우회적인 표현

박물관까지 지하철을 타고 가시고 싶으세요? 운전해서 가시고 싶으세요?
저는 괜찮아요. 감사합니다.
70개가 넘는 그림 전시요.
박물관이 지하철 바로 옆에 있어요.

어휘 take the subway 지하철을 타다 | on display 전시된

9 How long 의문문 미국 - 미국

How long does the presentation for new staff last?
(A) It is very informative. ···› presentation의 연상 어휘
(B) There are only five slides. ···› 얼마 걸리지 않는다는 우회적 표현
(C) Yes, a business marketing presentation.
···› 의문사 의문문에 Yes로 대답

신입직원들을 위한 프레젠테이션이 얼마나 오랫동안 지속될까요?
굉장히 유익해요.
슬라이드 5개만 있어요.
네, 비즈니스 마케팅 프레젠테이션요.

어휘 informative 유익한

10 When 의문문 미국 - 영국

When will the garden renovation be finished?
(A) About 800 dollars a month. ···› 가격에 대한 대답
(B) Not until next month.
(C) It was Samuel Landscaping.
···› renovation의 연상 어휘, who에 대한 정답

정원 보수공사는 언제 끝나나요?
한 달에 800달러요.
다음 달에요.
사무엘 조경이었어요.

어휘 renovation 보수공사

11 제안 의문문 　미국 - 미국

Why don't you add more pictures to the menu?
(A) I'm studying the menu. ···› menu 어휘 반복
(B) That's a really good idea.
(C) Because we don't have enough dishes. ···› Why에 대한 대답

메뉴에 사진을 더 추가하는 게 어때요?
메뉴를 보고 있어요.
정말 좋은 아이디어에요.
왜냐하면 충분한 음식이 없으니까요.

어휘 study the menu 메뉴를 살펴보다

12 부정 의문문 　호주 - 영국

Aren't you supposed to send the contract to Mr. Walker's assistant?
(A) Yes, she was a building contractor.
···› contract의 유사 발음: contractor
(B) I was asked to email it directly to him.
(C) Thank you for helping me. ···› assistant의 연상 어휘: helping

워커 씨의 비서에게 계약서를 보내기로 되어 있지 않나요?
네, 그녀는 건설업자였어요.
저는 그에게 바로 이메일을 보내 달라고 요청받았어요.
저를 도와주셔서 감사해요.

어휘 contractor 계약업자

13 일반 의문문 　호주 - 미국

Would you mind sending the documents with this new fax machine?
(A) Yes, put it next to the printer. ···› yes는 맞지만 동문서답
(B) No, I don't mind at all.
(C) To an important client. ···› 누구에게 보낼까에 대한 대답

새 팩스 기계로 서류를 보내주는 게 힘드실까요?
네, 프린터 옆에 두세요.
아니요, 전혀 그렇지 않아요.
중요한 고객에게요.

어휘 mind 꺼리다

14 부가 의문문 　미국 - 영국

The software convention was held in Moscow last year, wasn't it?
(A) No, I bought a laptop computer.
···› software의 연상 어휘: laptop computer
(B) Yes, we unveiled our new program there.
(C) Two software programmers. ···› software 어휘 반복

소프트웨어 컨벤션이 작년에 모스크바에서 열렸죠, 그렇죠?
아니요, 저는 노트북을 샀어요.
네, 거기서 우리는 새 프로그램을 출시했죠.
두 명의 소프트웨어 프로그래머요.

어휘 Moscow 모스크바 | unveil 출시하다

15 선택 의문문 　미국 - 미국

Would you like me to print the report or email it to you?
(A) Please print your company name here. ···› print 어휘 반복
(B) The Internet is not working now.
···› 고난도 - 우회적인 표현 (프린트로 해달라는 의미)
(C) She reports directly to the manager. ···› report 어휘 반복

보고서를 프린트해서 드릴까요? 이메일로 드릴까요?
여기에 회사 이름을 프린트하세요.
인터넷이 안 됩니다.
그녀는 매니저에게 직접 보고합니다.

어휘 work 작동하다

16 Where 의문문

영국 - 호주

Where's the exhibition center located?
(A) She has relocated to the Melbourne branch. ···› 주어 불일치
(B) Here is a map in this brochure.
(C) From Monday to Thursday. ···› When에 대한 대답

전시센터가 어디에 있죠?
그녀는 멜버른 지사로 옮겼습니다.
여기 이 책자에 지도가 있어요.
월요일부터 목요일까지요.

어휘 relocate to ~로 이전하다 | brochure 책자

17 How 의문문

호주 - 미국

How did your interview for senior marketing position go?
(A) I haven't had it yet.
(B) It was a great view. ···› interview의 유사 발음: view
(C) Three opening positions. ···› position 어휘 반복

시니어 마케팅 직책에 대한 인터뷰가 어떻게 되었나요?
아직 안 했습니다.
좋은 경치였어요.
세 개의 공석이요.

어휘 opening position 공석

18 부정 의문문

미국 - 미국

Isn't the microphone in Conference Room A broke?
(A) Conference B instead. ···› conference의 유사 어휘
(B) The Maintenance Department has an extra one in the storage room.
(C) Put it under the microscope. ···› microphone의 유사 발음: microscope

회의실 A의 마이크가 고장 났나요?
대신에 회의실 B에서요.
유지보수팀이 창고에 여분을 가지고 있어요.
현미경 아래에 두세요.

어휘 microphone 마이크 | storage room 창고 | microscope 현미경

19 부가 의문문

호주 - 영국

We're releasing the new home appliances next Wednesday, right?
(A) Yes, it was held in Las Vegas. ···› 시제 불일치, Where에 대한 대답
(B) There have been some delays.
(C) I bought a TV. ···› home appliance의 연상 어휘

우리는 다음 주 수요일에 새로운 가전제품을 출시하죠, 그렇죠?
네, 라스베이거스에서 열렸어요.
지연이 있었어요.
저는 TV를 샀어요.

어휘 release 출시하다 | home appliance 가전제품

20 Who 의문문

미국 - 미국

Who's leading the management committee?
(A) Almost 25 members. ···› how many의 대답, committee의 연상 어휘
(B) I'm not on the committee this year.
(C) It leads to the building. ···› lead의 유사 발음

경영 회의를 누가 이끄나요?
거의 25명의 멤버들이요.
올해 저는 회의에 참석 안 합니다.
건물로 연결되어 있어요.

어휘 committee 위원회 | lead to ~로 이어지다

21 기타 의문문(평서문)

미국 - 호주

I'm afraid I won't be able to attend the workshop this afternoon.
(A) Sure, you can join it. ···› attend의 연상 어휘: join
(B) OK, thanks for letting me know.
(C) In three hours. ···› 동문서답

오늘 오후에 워크숍에 참석 못 할 것 같아요.
물론이죠, 참석하실 수 있어요.
알겠습니다, 알려주셔서 감사해요.
3시간 후에요.

어휘 let me know 나에게 알려주다

22 Why 의문문 영국 - 호주

Why is the Gallop theater so busy today?
(A) Have you checked today's event schedule? 되묻기 / 반문
(B) No, I have some time. ···› 의문사 의문문에 No로 대답
(C) On Park Avenue. ···› Where에 대한 대답

오늘 갤럽 극장이 왜 붐비나요?
오늘 이벤트 스케줄 확인하셨어요?
아니요, 시간 있습니다.
파크 애비뉴에서요.

어휘 I have some time 시간이 됩니다

23 Who 의문문 미국 - 미국

Who got the promotion to department head?
(A) Put it in the overhead compartment.
···› department의 유사 발음: compartment
(B) It hasn't been decided yet.
(C) Okay, I'll think about it. ···› 의문사 의문문에 Okay로 대답

부서장으로 누가 승진했나요?
머리 위 짐칸에 두세요.
아직 결정되지 않았어요.
좋아요, 생각해 볼게요.

어휘 department head 부서장 | overhead compartment 머리 위 짐칸 | It hasn't been decided yet. 아직 결정되지 않았어요.

24 How 의문문 호주 - 미국

How do I log in the new system?
(A) Sorry, we can't change. ···› 의문사 의문문에 Sorry로 대답
(B) It's written in the manual.
(C) Every five minutes. ···› How often에 대한 대답

새로운 시스템에서 어떻게 로그인할까요?
미안하지만, 변경할 수가 없어요.
매뉴얼에 적혀있어요.
5분마다요.

어휘 log (일지에) 기록하다

25 부정 의문문 영국 - 미국

Shouldn't we change our company logo?
(A) It is conveniently located. ···› 동문서답
(B) No, we need the CEO's approval first.
(C) It charged more. ···› change의 유사 발음: charge

회사 로고를 변경해야 하지 않을까요?
편리하게 위치되어 있어요.
아니요, CEO의 승인이 먼저 필요합니다.
더 청구되었어요.

어휘 conveniently 편리하게 | approval 승인

26 기타 의문문(평서문) 호주 - 영국

Ms. Yamamoto can't go to the training session today.
(A) The train was late. ···› training의 유사 발음: train
(B) Conference room C. ···› training session의 연상 어휘
(C) Oh, then I'll take notes. ···› 해결책 제시

야마모토 씨는 오늘 교육에 갈 수 없습니다.
열차가 늦었어요.
회의실 C요.
오, 그러면 제가 필기할게요.

어휘 training session 교육 | take notes 필기하다

27 What 의문문 미국 - 미국

What session do you want to deliver a speech?
(A) He was an excellent speaker, wasn't he?
···› 주어 불일치, speech의 연상 어휘: speaker
(B) The award ceremony isn't until the 5th.
(C) Expedited delivery service. ···› deliver의 유사 발음: delivery

어느 세션에서 연설하시기를 원하세요?
그는 훌륭한 발표자였어요, 그렇죠?
시상식은 5일이에요.
빠른 배송 서비스요.

어휘 deliver a speech 연설하다 | award ceremony 시상식 | expedited delivery service 빠른 배송 서비스

1 참고 / 참조 미국 - 미국

Where is the Payroll Department located?
(A) That seems high. ···› locate의 연상 어휘: high
(B) Here's the building directory.
···› 참고 / 참조를 나타내는 표현이 빈출 정답
(C) Monthly payment. ···› payroll의 연상 어휘

급여 담당 부서가 어디에 있나요?
높아 보입니다.
여기 건물 안내도가 있어요.
월급이요.

어휘 Payroll Department 급여 담당 부서 | building directory 건물 안내도 | monthly payment 월급

2 우회적 표현 호주 - 미국

When are the new office supplies going to be shipped?
(A) I already ordered office supplies. ···› office supplies 어휘 반복
(B) He is downstairs. ···› 주어 불일치
(C) Our packaging machine has just broken. ···› 우회적 표현

새 사무용품은 언제 배송될까요?
제가 이미 새 사무용품을 주문했어요.
그는 아래층에 있어요.
포장 기계가 방금 고장 났어요.

어휘 office supplies 사무용품 | downstairs 아래층에 있는 | packaging machine 포장 기계

3 제3자 / 책임 전가 미국 - 영국

Have you reviewed the slides before the meeting?
(A) It is a nice view. ···› review의 유사 발음: view
(B) Walter is delivering a presentation.
(C) No, it was on the third floor. ···› No는 맞지만 동문서답

회의 전에 슬라이드를 검토해 보셨어요?
좋은 경치에요.
월터가 프레젠테이션을 합니다.
아니요, 3층이었어요.

어휘 deliver a presentation 프레젠테이션하다

4 되묻기 / 반문 / 확인 미국 - 호주

Why was the interview postponed for later in the day?
(A) Because the deadline was yesterday.
···› why에 대한 because 대답 함정
(B) Haven't you checked the memo yet?
···› 대답 대신 되묻기 / 반문 그리고 check가 나오는 빈출 정답 유형
(C) 4 P.M. this afternoon. ···› When에 대한 대답

왜 면접이 오후 늦게로 연기되었나요?
왜냐하면 어제가 마감 날짜였어요.
아직 메모 확인 안 해보셨어요?
오늘 오후 4시에요.

어휘 postpone 연기하다

5 평서문에 대한 대답 – 동조 / 공감 영국 - 호주

I'm not sure how to change the password on the new system.
(A) I haven't used the new system yet, either.
···› 평서문에 대한 정답 유형 중 동조 / 공감
(B) A monthly pass. ···› password의 유사 발음: pass
(C) Sorry, it is on my desk. ···› 동문서답

새로운 시스템에서 패스워드를 어떻게 바꾸는지 잘 모르겠어요.
저도 새로운 시스템을 사용 안 해봤어요.
월 통행권이요.
미안합니다, 제 책상 위에 있어요.

어휘 a monthly pass 월 통행권

6 제3자 / 책임 전가 영국 - 호주

Why don't we fly to Chicago instead of taking a train?
(A) A frequent flyer program. ···› fly의 유사 발음: flyer
(B) Two seats on the aisle. ···› fly, train의 연상 어휘
(C) Elizabeth is in charge of organizing it.
···› 제3자 / 책임 전가 빈출 정답 유형

열차 대신에 비행기를 타고 시카고로 가는 게 어떨까요?
상용 고객 우대 프로그램이요.
복도에 두 좌석이요.
엘리자베스가 그것을 준비하는 데 책임지고 있어요.

어휘 frequent flyer program 상용 고객 우대 프로그램

7 우회적 표현 미국 - 미국

How did you like the social media seminar?
(A) I registered for a different session. ···› 우회적 표현
(B) By signing up the Web site.
···› How에 대한 대답, 질문은 의견을 물어보는 how did you like ~
(C) Yes, it was held in Boston. ···› 의문사 의문문에 Yes로 대답

소셜미디어 세미나는 어땠나요?
저는 다른 세션을 등록했어요.
웹사이트에 등록함으로써요.
네, 보스턴에서 개최되었어요.

어휘 social media seminar 소셜미디어 세미나

8 우회적 표현 / still 미국 - 영국

Wasn't the CEO supposed to review the feedback on our proposal?
(A) He is still away on a business trip.
···› 우회적 표현, still이 들어가는 빈출 정답 유형
(B) It was supposed to be open. ···› supposed 어휘 반복
(C) I would like to propose a toast to the CEO.
···› proposal 유사 발음: propose

CEO께서 우리 제안서에 대해 피드백을 검토하시기로 하지 않았나요?
그는 여전히 출장 중입니다.
열려있어야 했는데요.
CEO에게 건배를 제안하고 싶습니다.

어휘 be supposed to ~하기로 되어 있다 | be away on a business trip 출장 중이다 | propose a toast 건배를 제안하다

9 참고 / 참조 미국 - 호주

Who will be leading the next monthly meeting?
(A) A talk about business trends
···› What에 대한 대답
(B) No, 9 A.M. this morning. ···› 의문사 의문문에 No로 대답
(C) It's on the meeting agenda.
···› 참고 / 참조를 나타내는 빈출 정답 유형

다음 달 월례 미팅을 누가 주최하나요?
비즈니스 트렌드에 관한 이야기예요.
아니요, 오늘 오전 9시에요.
미팅 안건에 있어요.

어휘 meeting agenda 미팅 안건

10 actually / already 미국 - 영국

The deadline for the Mcallister project was extended, wasn't it?
(A) Actually, I've already finished.
···› actually, already 빈출 정답 유형
(B) The projector was fixed. ···› project의 유사 발음: projector
(C) Yes, she met the deadline.
···› 주어 불일치, deadline 어휘 반복

맥알리스터 프로젝트에 대한 마감일이 연장되었죠, 그렇죠?
실은 저는 벌써 끝났어요.
프로젝터가 수리되었어요.
네, 그녀는 마감 날짜를 맞췄어요.

어휘 meet the deadline 마감 날짜를 맞추다

11 되묻기 / 반문

미국 - 미국

What are we publishing on the weekly magazine's front cover?
(A) Yes, I already submitted an article.
···› 의문사 의문문에 Yes로 대답
(B) Why don't we discuss it after lunch?
···› 대답 대신 되묻기 / 반문 빈출 정답 유형
(C) Put it in the front desk on the first floor. ···› magazine의 연상 어휘

주간 잡지책 표지에 어떤 것을 출간할까요?
네, 벌써 기사를 제출했습니다.
점심 먹고 이야기하는 것은 어떨까요?
그것을 1층 프런트에 두세요.

어휘 weekly magazine 주간 잡지책

12 우회적 표현

영국 - 호주

How long does it take you to finish entering the data?
(A) Only one page left. ···› 우회적 표현
(B) In the database system. ···› data의 유사 발음: database
(C) No, I already finished.
···› 의문사 의문문에 no로 대답, finish의 유사 발음

데이터 입력을 완료하는 데 얼마나 오래 걸리나요?
한 페이지 남았어요.
데이터베이스 시스템에요.
아니요, 벌써 끝냈어요.

어휘 enter the data 데이터를 입력하다

13 되묻기 / 반문

호주 - 영국

Ashley and Mike are going to attend the product launch tomorrow, right?
(A) That lunch was delicious. ···› launch의 유사 발음: lunch
(B) Sure, it was quite informative. ···› product launch의 연상 어휘
(C) Aren't you going? ···› 되묻기 / 반문 빈출 정답 유형

애슐리와 마이크가 내일 제품 출시에 참석할 거죠, 그렇죠?
점심 맛있었어요.
물론이죠, 굉장히 유익했어요.
당신은 안 가시나요?

어휘 launch 출시하다 | informative 유익한

14 우회적 표현

미국 - 영국

Would you mind removing the items from the display shelf?
(A) I moved to a new branch last week. ···› remove의 유사 발음: move
(B) Actually, I'm on my break.
···› 휴식 중이라 못한다는 우회적 표현
(C) Yes, it is mine. ···› mind의 유사 발음: mine

진열대 선반에서 물건을 제거해 주시겠어요?
지난주에 새 지사로 옮겼어요.
실은, 휴식 중이에요.
네, 그것은 제 거예요.

어휘 branch 지점 | break 휴식

15 제3자

호주 - 미국

Do you want to take the subway or rent a car?
(A) Richard can pick us up. ···› 제3자 언급
(B) $50 a day. ···› rent의 연상 어휘
(C) It doesn't stop at this station. ···› subway의 연상 어휘

지하철을 타시겠어요? 차를 렌트하시겠어요?
리처드가 데리러 올 수 있어요.
하루에 50달러예요.
이 역에서 정차 안 합니다.

어휘 pick up 데리러 가다

16 되묻기 / 반문

영국 - 미국

How do I install the video conference equipment?
(A) Sorry, it's already been sold out. ···› 동문서답
(B) Didn't you read the instruction manual?
···› 되묻기 / 반문 빈출 정답 유형
(C) Monthly installments. ···› install의 유사 발음: installment

어떻게 화상회의 장비를 설치하나요?
미안합니다. 벌써 매진입니다.
설명서 안 읽어보셨어요?
매달 할부요.

어휘 be sold out 매진되다 | installment 할부

17 우회적 표현

미국 - 미국

Which training sessions are you planning to go to?
(A) It depends on when they start.
(B) Only for two hours. ···› how long에 대한 대답
(C) My train is late. ···› training의 유사 발음: train

어느 교육 과정을 가실 계획이세요?
그 과정이 언제 시작하느냐에 따라 다릅니다.
2시간 동안만이에요.
열차가 늦네요.

어휘 depend on ~에 달려 있다

18 우회적 표현

영국 - 호주

Can't we use a different venue for the company celebration?
(A) It was held in Renoir Hotel. ···› venue의 연상 어휘
(B) To celebrate the 10th anniversary. ···› celebration의 유사 발음: celebrate
(C) The event is this weekend.
···› 이벤트가 이번 주라 다른 데 이용할 수 없다는 우회적 표현

회사 기념식을 위해 다른 장소를 사용할 수 없나요?
르누아 호텔에서 개최되었어요.
10주년을 기념하기 위해서요.
이벤트가 이번 주입니다.

어휘 venue 장소

19 우회적 표현

호주 - 영국

When is the technician from the Maintenance Department coming to repair the copy machine?
(A) I need to use it, too.
···› 나도 사용해야 하므로 궁금하다는 우회적 표현
(B) Sure, I can help you. ···› 의문사 의문문에 sure로 대답
(C) There is a coffee maker in the break room.
···› copy의 유사 발음: coffee

유지 보수팀의 기술자가 복사기를 고치러 언제 오시나요?
나도 그것을 사용해야 해요.
물론이죠. 도와드릴게요.
휴게실에 커피 기계가 있어요.

어휘 coffee maker 커피 기계

20 우회적 표현

미국 - 미국

Would you like me to book a conference room for interviews?
(A) We haven't selected any candidates yet.
···› 예약할 준비가 되지 않았다는 우회적 표현
(B) On the 10th floor. ···› conference room의 연상 어휘
(C) It was a great view. ···› interview의 유사 발음: view

면접을 위해서 제가 회의실을 예약하기를 원하세요?
아직 지원자를 간추리지도 않았습니다.
10층에서요.
경치가 굉장히 좋았어요.

어휘 candidate 지원자

21 우회적 표현

미국 - 영국

Who should pay for lunch for the clients?
(A) There's a company budget for that.
(B) The official launch date is tomorrow. ···› lunch의 유사 발음: launch
(C) No, I am full. ···› 의문사 의문문에 No로 대답, lunch의 연상 어휘

누가 고객들을 위한 점심을 사나요?
회사 예산에 있어요.
공식적인 출시 날짜는 내일입니다.
아니요, 배부릅니다.

어휘 launch date 출시 날짜

22 우회적 표현

영국 - 호주

Mr. Joe arrived at 5 today, didn't he?
(A) No, departures are on the first floor.
···› arrive의 연상 어휘: departure
(B) Actually, it was 50 dollars. ···› 5의 연상 어휘: 50
(C) All flights were delayed. ···› 도착하지 않았다는 우회적 표현

조 씨는 오늘 5시에 도착했습니다, 그렇죠?
아니요, 출발은 1층입니다.
실은, 50달러였어요.
모든 비행기가 연착되었어요.

어휘 departure 출발

23 제3자

호주 - 미국

How do I join the company picnic for next week?
(A) Amy is organizing that. ···› 제3자 언급 빈출 정답 유형
(B) Snacks and beverages will be served.
···› picnic의 연상 어휘: snack, beverage
(C) No, it was last week. ···› 의문사 의문문에 No로 대답

다음 주에 있는 회사 피크닉에 어떻게 등록하나요?
에이미가 준비하고 있어요.
스낵과 음료수는 제공될 것입니다.
아니요, 지난주에요.

어휘 beverage 음료수

24 되묻기 / 반문

미국 - 미국

I would like to send this package to Seattle.
(A) Of course, here's the menu.
···› of course는 맞지만 동문서답
(B) When does it have to arrive? ···› 되묻기 / 반문 빈출 정답 유형
(C) At the post office. ···› package의 연상 어휘

이 소포를 시애틀에 보내고 싶습니다.
물론이지요, 여기에 메뉴가 있어요.
언제 도착하면 되나요?
우체국에서요.

어휘 post office 우체국

25 우회적 표현

영국 - 호주

There is a parking garage near the building, right?
(A) I take public transportation. ···› 잘 모른다는 우회적 표현
(B) There is a park near the beach. ···› parking의 유사 발음: park
(C) Would you like the receipt? ···› parking garage의 연상 어휘

건물 근처에 주차장이 있지요, 그렇죠?
저는 대중교통을 이용합니다.
바닷가 옆에 공원이 있어요.
영수증 필요하세요?

어휘 parking garage 주차장 | public transportation 대중교통

26 우회적 표현

미국 - 영국

Haven't you checked the travel expenses report?
(A) No, I didn't finish it yet. ···› no는 맞지만 동문서답
(B) I've been out of the office.
···› 체크 못 했다는 우회적 표현
(C) You can check it whenever you want. ···› check 어휘 반복

여행경비 보고서를 확인 안 해보셨어요?
아니요, 아직 안 끝냈습니다.
사무실에 없었어요.
원하실 때마다 확인하실 수 있어요.

어휘 travel expense 여행경비

27 제3자

호주 - 미국

Isn't the printer on the second floor broken?
(A) The Technology Department should have an extra one.
(B) Print in color, please. ···› printer의 유사 발음: print
(C) How many copies? ···› printer의 연상 어휘

2층에 있는 프린터가 고장 나지 않았나요?
기술팀이 여분을 갖고 있어요.
컬러로 프린트해 주세요.
몇 부나요?

어휘 Technology Department 기술팀

호주 - 미국 - 미국

Questions 1-3 refer to the following conversation with three speakers.

M2: Hello, Shirley. I'd like to welcome you to the MXB Publishing family. My name is Maxwell, and I work in Personnel.

M1: And I'm Gerard. ❶❷ We are in charge of coordinating three-day orientations for incoming editors. Starting tomorrow, you'll be spending a lot time with us and other new editing employees.

W: Hello, Maxwell. Hello, Gerard. Thank you for the warm greeting. ❶ I'm excited to work on the editing team.

M1: Do you have any questions before you return to your desk?

W: Actually, I do. ❸ I noticed there was a cafeteria on the first floor. Is that where MXB staff members usually eat lunch?

M2: Yes, that's right. You can actually sign up for a company meal program there. But we'll give you more information about that tomorrow.

1-3번은 다음 세 화자의 대화에 관한 문제입니다.

남2: 안녕하세요, 셜리. 앰액스비 출판의 가족이 되신 걸 환영합니다. 제 이름은 맥스웰이고 인사부에서 일해요.

남1: 그리고 저는 제럴드예요. **우리는 새로 들어오는 편집자들을 위한 3일간의 오리엔테이션을 조직하는 일을 맡고 있어요.** 내일부터 저희와 다른 신입 편집 직원들과 많은 시간을 보내게 되실 겁니다.

여: 안녕하세요, 맥스웰. 안녕하세요, 제럴드. 반갑게 맞아주셔서 감사합니다. **편집팀에서 일하게 되어 기대됩니다.**

남1: 자리로 돌아가시기 전 질문 있으신가요?

여: 사실 있습니다. **1층에 카페테리아가 있는 걸 봤는데요. 앰액스비 직원들이 보통 그곳에서 점심을 먹나요?**

남2: 네, 맞습니다. 거기서 사실 회사 식사 프로그램 신청을 하실 수 있어요. 하지만 그에 대한 정보는 내일 알려드리겠습니다.

어휘 publishing 출판 | personnel 인사부 | in charge of ~를 맡고 있는 | coordinate 편성하다, 조정하다 | incoming 들어오는, 도착하는 | editor 편집자 | notice 알아차리다

1 주제 / 목적

What most likely is the woman's job?
(A) Graphic designer
(B) Editor
(C) Bookkeeper
(D) Sales representative

여자의 직업은 무엇이겠는가?
그래픽 디자이너
편집자
경리
외판원

해설 대화 초반에서 남자가 여자의 직업과 관련된 단어를 말하고(We are in charge of coordinating three-day orientations for incoming editors.) 여자가 편집팀에서 일하게 되어 기대된다고 했으므로(I'm excited to work on the editing team.) 정답은 (B)가 된다.

2 직업 / 업종

What do the men do at their company?
(A) They coordinate orientation sessions.
(B) They manage client accounts.
(C) They make travel arrangements.
(D) They review departmental budgets.

남자들은 회사에서 무슨 일을 하는가?
오리엔테이션을 조직한다.
고객 계정을 관리한다.
여행 관련 주선을 한다.
부서 예산을 검토한다.

해설 대화 초반에서 남자들이 신규 입사 편집자를 위한 3일간의 오리엔테이션을 조직한다고 했으므로(We are in charge of coordinating three-day orientations for incoming editors.) 정답은 (A)가 된다.

3 미래

What does the woman inquire about?
(A) A computer password
(B) A salary figure
(C) A parking permit
(D) A dining area

여자는 무엇에 대해 묻는가?
컴퓨터 패스워드
연봉
주차 허가증
식사 구역

해설 여자의 대사에서 1층에 카페테리아가 있는 것을 보았고 그곳에서 점심을 먹는지 묻고 있으므로(I noticed there was a cafeteria on the first floor. Is that where MXB staff members usually eat lunch?) 정답은 (D)가 된다.

Questions 4-6 refer to the following conversation.

W: Hey, Stuart. ❹ The news reporter and her camera crew will be here next Wednesday. ❺ Will you be able to give them a brief presentation about our product line?
M: Umm… I'm leading a training seminar all day Wednesday.
W: Oh, I see. Do you know if Naoko would be available?
M: She should be. I could ask her for you.
W: Please do. Let her know that she can reach out to me if she has any questions.
M: Sure thing. I see that our company has been getting a lot of media attention lately. That sure is a good sign.
W: Yeah, and who knows? After going on television next week, ❻ we might even be able to export our products internationally by the end of the year.

4-6번은 다음 대화에 관한 문제입니다.

여: 안녕하세요, 스튜어트. **뉴스 기자와 카메라맨이 다음 주 수요일에 여기에 올 것입니다. 우리 제품 라인에 대해서 그들에게 간략하게 프레젠테이션을 해주시겠어요?**
남: 음… **다음 주 수요일 내내 교육세미나를 주최합니다.**
여: 아, 그렇군요. 나오코가 혹시 시간이 되는지 아세요?
남: 시간이 될 거예요. 제가 물어볼 수 있어요.
여: 그렇게 해주세요. 질문이 있으면 언제든지 저에게 연락할 수 있다고 말해주세요.
남: 물론이죠. 최근에 우리 회사가 언론의 관심을 많이 받고 있어요. 좋은 징조에요.
여: 네, 그리고 누가 아나요? 다음 주에 TV에 방송되고 나면, **올 연말까지 해외로 우리 제품을 수출할 수도 있어요.**

어휘 reach out to 연락하다 | get a lot of attention 관심을 많이 받다 | overseas 해외의 | fulfill a request 요청을 이행하다 | look forward to ~을 학수고대하다 | kick off 시작하다 | expand into ~로 확장하다

4 직업 / 업종

Who will be visiting the company?
(A) A CEO
(B) A TV reporter
(C) An overseas client
(D) A local politician

누가 회사를 방문할 것인가?
CEO
TV 기자
해외 고객
지역 정치인

해설 뉴스 기자와 카메라맨이 온다고(The news reporter and her camera crew will be here next Wednesday.) 했으므로 정답은 (B)가 된다.

5 화자의 의도 파악

Why does the man say, "I'm leading a training seminar all day Wednesday"?
(A) He requests a list of seminar attendees.
(B) He is unable to fulfill a request.
(C) He needs help preparing for an event.
(D) He is looking forward to completing a task.

남자가 "다음 주 수요일 내내 교육세미나를 주최합니다"라고 말한 이유는 무엇인가?
그는 세미나 참석자 명단을 요청한다.
그는 요청을 이행할 수 없다.
그는 이벤트를 준비하는 데 도움이 필요하다.
그는 일을 끝내는 데 학수고대한다.

해설 앞에서 제품에 관해 간략하게 프레젠테이션을 해 줄 수 있냐는(Will you be able to give them a brief presentation about our product line?) 요청사항을 이행할 수 없다고 하므로 정답은 (B)가 된다.

6 미래

According to the woman, what does the company hope to do by the end of the year?
(A) Kick off a marketing campaign
(B) Launch a new product line
(C) Expand into a foreign market
(D) Open a new location

여자에 따르면, 회사가 올 연말까지 하기를 바라는 것은 무엇인가?
마케팅 캠페인을 시작한다
신제품을 출시한다
해외 시장으로 진출한다
새로운 장소에 오픈한다

해설 연말에 해외로 제품을 수출할 수도 있다는 내용이 나오므로(we might even be able to export our products internationally by the end of the year) 정답은 (C)가 된다.

Questions 7-9 refer to the following conversation.

W: Good afternoon, Mr. Jeon. ❼❽ I'm Rosemary calling from Woodrow Health Clinic. You have an annual checkup scheduled with Dr. Elliott at 4 P.M. on August 9. Would you be open to moving up your appointment to 11 instead?

M: Umm... I have an early morning marketing presentation that day, but I should be able to get there by then.

W: Thank you for your understanding. Dr. Elliott has a family matter to tend to that afternoon.

M: I see. That shouldn't be a problem. ❾ I'll make a note of the change in my calendar right away.

7-9번은 다음 대화에 관한 문제입니다.

여: 안녕하세요, 전 씨. **저는 우드로 건강 클리닉의 로즈메리입니다. 8월 9일 오후 4시에 엘리엇 박사와 연례 건강검진이 있으신데요. 11시로 옮기실 수 있을까요?**

남: 음… 그날 오전 일찍 마케팅 프레젠테이션이 있는데, 그때까지는 갈 수 있을 거예요.

여: 이해해주셔서 감사합니다. 엘리엇 박사가 그날 오후에 집에 일이 있어서요.

남: 아 그렇군요. 아무 문제 없어요. **당장 달력에 변경사항을 적어 놓을게요.**

어휘 make a note of 필기하다 | receptionist 접수 담당자 | insurance agent 보험회사 직원 | payment 급여 | medical records 의료기록

7 직업 / 업종

What most likely is the woman's job?

(A) Receptionist
(B) Doctor
(C) Lab researcher
(D) Insurance agent

여자의 직업은 무엇일 것 같은가?

접수 담당자
의사
실험실 연구원
보험회사 직원

해설 병원에서 연락하는 사람으로 예약 변경에 대해 이야기하고 있으므로(I'm Rosemary calling from Woodrow Health Clinic. You have an annual checkup scheduled with Dr. Elliott at 4 P.M. on August 9. Would you be open to moving up your appointment to 11 instead?) 예약을 담당하는 정답은 (A)가 된다. 병원이라고 해서 (B)를 하지 않도록 주의하자.

8 세부정보 - 언급

What does the woman want to change?

(A) Payment information
(B) The time of an appointment
(C) The location of a hospital
(D) A marketing strategy

여자가 변경하고 싶은 것은 무엇인가?

급여 정보
예약 시간
병원 위치
마케팅 전략

해설 4시 예약을 11시로 변경하고 싶다는 내용이므로(I'm Rosemary calling from Woodrow Health Clinic. You have an annual checkup scheduled with Dr. Elliott at 4 P.M. on August 9. Would you be open to moving up your appointment to 11 instead?) 정답은 (B)가 된다.

9 미래

What will the man do next?

(A) Look for his medical records
(B) Update a calendar
(C) Call a credit card company
(D) Complete a patient information form

남자가 다음으로 할 일은 무엇인가?

의료 기록을 찾는다
달력에 업데이트한다
신용카드 회사에 전화한다
환자 정보 서류를 완성한다

해설 변경사항을 적겠다고 했으므로(I'll make a note of the change in my calendar right away.) 정답은 (B)가 된다. 패러프레이징에 자주 쓰이는 change / revise / update 단어를 잘 익혀두자.

Questions 10-12 refer to the following broadcast.

W: ⑩ This is Clover Radio 92 with this week's news. If you're a movie fan, head to the theater this week to catch Marcella Richard's newest drama flick. ⑪ If that name sounds familiar, it's because she is the latest recipient of the Film of the Year award. Her latest movie, *Paper Planes*, will be showing at all cinemas this weekend. ⑫ We'll be back with the traffic report right after a quick commercial break.

10-12번은 다음 방송에 관한 문제입니다.

여: **저는 이번 주 뉴스를 알려드리는 클로버 라디오 92입니다. 만약 영화 애호가시라면, 이번 주 영화관으로 가셔서 마르셀라 리처드의 새 드라마 영화를 보세요. 이름이 익숙하시다면, 최근에 올해의 영화상을 받은 분이라서 그렇습니다.** 그녀의 최근 영화 〈페이퍼 플레인즈〉는 이번 주말에 모든 영화관에서 상영될 예정입니다. **잠시 광고 바로 듣고 교통 정보로 돌아오겠습니다.**

어휘 drama flick 드라마 좋아하는 사람 | recipient 수령자 | commercial 광고 | election 선거 | movie release 영화 개봉 | prestigious 일류의 | traffic report 교통 정보

10 주제 / 목적

What is the broadcast about?
(A) The city's election results
(B) A performance review
(C) A new movie release
(D) A famous drama

무엇에 관한 방송인가?
시 선거 결과
공연 후기
새 영화 개봉
유명한 드라마

해설 영화 애호가라면 극장에서 새로 나온 영화를 보라는 내용이 나오므로(This is Clover Radio 92 with this week's news. If you're a movie fan, head to the theater this week to catch Marcella Richard's newest drama flick.) 정답은 (C)가 된다.

11 세부정보 – 언급

According to the speaker, what did Marcella Richard do recently?
(A) She won a prestigious prize.
(B) She created a new organization.
(C) She returned from overseas.
(D) She participated in a play.

화자에 따르면, 마르셀라 리처드는 최근에 무엇을 했는가?
그녀는 명망 있는 상을 받았다.
그녀는 새 조직을 만들었다.
그녀는 해외에서 돌아왔다.
그녀는 연극에 참석했다.

해설 올해의 영화상을 받았다고 나와 있으므로(If that name sounds familiar, it's because she is the latest recipient of the Film of the Year award.) 정답은 (A)가 된다.

12 세부정보 – 언급

What will listeners most likely hear next?
(A) An advertisement
(B) An interview
(C) A traffic update
(D) A weather report

청자가 다음으로 들을 것은 무엇인가?
광고
인터뷰
교통 정보
일기 예보

해설 광고를 듣고 교통 정보를 듣는 것이므로(We'll be back with the traffic report right after a quick commercial break.) 다음에 들을 것은 (A)가 된다. (C)랑 헷갈리지 않도록 조심하자.

Questions 13-15 refer to the following introduction.

W: ⑬ Thank you again for coming to this year's shareholder meeting. ⑭ Now we will unveil something we have been working on for two years. It is a new computer that can disrupt the industry. Some of the features that we want to highlight include an incredibly long battery life and the fastest, most powerful processor we've used yet. Did I mention the best part? It only weighs in at two kilograms. Our new product eclipses anything our competitors have on the market right now. ⑮ I want to invite Molly Underwood, President of Pennington, to the stage. She will explain our marketing strategy for this offering.

13-15번은 다음 소개에 관한 문제입니다.

여: 올해 주주 회의에 오신 것에 대해 다시 한번 감사드립니다. 이제 저희가 2년 동안 착수해온 것을 발표할 예정입니다. 산업에 영향을 줄 새 컴퓨터입니다. 우리가 강조하고 싶은 특징 중에 몇 개는 놀라울 정도의 긴 밧데리 수명과 우리가 여태까지 사용하지 못했던 아주 빠른 프로세스입니다. 제가 최고인 부분에 대해 언급했었나요? 그것은 이것이 고작 2kg 밖에 무게가 나가지 않는다는 것입니다. 우리 신제품은 지금 시장에 현존하는 경쟁업체의 어떠한 것도 무색하게 만듭니다. **페닝턴의 회장인 몰리 언더우드를 무대로 모시고 싶습니다.** 그녀는 저희 마케팅 전략에 대해서 설명해 주실 겁니다.

어휘 shareholder 주주 | disrupt 방해하다 | highlight 강조하다 | incredibly 믿을 수 없을 정도로 | eclipse 무색하게 만들다 | competitor 경쟁자 | retirement party 은퇴식 | awards ceremony 시상식 | innovative 혁신적인 | eco-friendly 친환경적인 | adjustable 조절 가능한 | wireless 무선의 | corporate executive 임원

13 직업 / 업종

What type of event is taking place?
(A) A software convention
(B) A shareholder meeting
(C) A retirement party
(D) An awards ceremony

어떤 종류의 이벤트가 개최되고 있는가?
소프트웨어 컨벤션
주주회의
은퇴식
시상식

해설 주주회의에 오신 것을 환영한다고 했으므로(Thank you again for coming to this year's shareholder meeting.) 정답은 (B)가 된다.

14 주제

What product does the speaker highlight?
(A) An innovative device
(B) An eco-friendly automobile
(C) An adjustable desk
(D) A wireless keyboard

화자가 강조하는 것은 어떤 제품인가?
혁신적인 장치
친환경적인 자동차
조절 가능한 책상
무선 키보드

해설 산업 분야에 지장을 줄 새 컴퓨터라고 했으므로(Now we will unveil something we have been working on for two years. It is a new computer that can disrupt the industry.) 정답은 (A)가 된다.

15 직업 / 업종

Who is Molly Underwood?
(A) A marketing director
(B) A human resources worker
(C) A corporate executive
(D) A product designer

몰리 언더우드는 누구인가?
마케팅부장
인사부 직원
임원
제품 디자이너

해설 페닝턴의 회장을 무대로 모시고 싶다고 했으므로(I want to invite Molly Underwood, President of Pennington, to the stage.) 정답은 (C)가 된다.

Questions 16-18 refer to the following excerpt from a meeting.

M: I want to shift our attention to this year's expansion strategy. As you know, we opened up three stores in the Northeastern area. ⑯What we've heard from the store managers is that sales have been slow. Of course, it's only been two months. However, our reputation alone should have created more of a presence. ⑰I'm putting up a list of our main competitors on the screen now. As you can see, the area is heavily contested. ⑱What I want us to do is to go to these stores and find out what products they have in stock. Let's reconvene on Friday to discuss our findings.

16 – 18번은 다음 회의 발췌록에 관한 문제입니다.

남: 다음은 올해의 확장 전략에 관한 것입니다. 아시다시피, 북동 지역에 세 개의 점포를 오픈했습니다. **가게 매니저들에게 들은 바로는 판매가 저조하다고 합니다.** 물론, **2개월밖에 되지 않았습니다.** 하지만, 우리 평판만 두고 봤을 때 더 좋은 결과를 낼 수 있어야 합니다. **지금 제가 화면에 주요 경쟁업체들 목록을 올려드리겠습니다.** 보시다시피, 이 지역이 굉장히 치열합니다. **우리가 해야 할 것은 이들 점포에 가서 어떤 제품이 재고가 있는지 확인하는 것입니다.** 우리가 조사한 것을 논의하기 위해 금요일에 다시 모이도록 하겠습니다.

어휘 shift 바꾸다 | expansion 확장 | reputation 명성, 평판 | presence 존재, 참석 | put up a list 명단을 작성하다 | competitor 경쟁자 | heavily contested 굉장히 치열한 | in stock 재고 있는 | reconvene 다시 모이다 | findings 조사 결과들 | highlight 강조하다 | study on ~에 대한 연구 | set up a meeting 회의를 잡다

16 화자의 의도 파악

Why does the speaker say, "it's only been two months"?
(A) To give an explanation
(B) To highlight a peculiarity
(C) To agree with an opinion
(D) To make a suggestion

화자가 "2개월밖에 되지 않았습니다"라고 말한 이유는 무엇인가?
설명하기 위해서
특이한 점을 강조하기 위해서
의견에 동의하기 위해서
조언을 하기 위해서

해설 판매는 저조하지만 2개월밖에 되지 않았다는 상황을 설명하기 위해서로(What we've heard from the store managers is that sales have been slow.) 정답은 (A)가 된다.

17 세부정보 – 언급

What does the speaker show the listeners?
(A) A graph of monthly sales
(B) A study of some products
(C) A report on a new trend
(D) A list of some stores

화자가 청자들에게 보여주는 것은 무엇인가?
매월 판매 그래프
몇몇 제품에 대한 연구
새로운 트렌드에 대한 보고서
몇몇 가게 목록

해설 화면에 경쟁업체들의 목록을 올린다고 했으므로(I'm putting up a list of our main competitors on the screen now.) 정답은 (D)가 된다.

18 미래

What are the listeners expected to do by Friday?
(A) Sign up for a service
(B) Prepare a presentation
(C) Visit some stores
(D) Set up a meeting

청자들이 금요일까지 무엇을 할 거라고 예상하는가?
서비스를 신청한다
프레젠테이션을 준비한다
가게를 방문한다
회의를 잡는다

해설 가게에 가서 어떤 제품이 재고가 있는지를 확인해 보자고 했으므로(What I want us to do is to go to these stores and find out what products they have in stock) 정답은 (C)가 된다.

본서 090페이지

미국 - 미국

Questions 1-3 refer to the following conversation and map.

M: Hey, Joanna. What a coincidence!
W: Oh, hey, Leon!
M: I'm so glad I ran into you. I'm headed to the airport, ❶ but I'm not sure which subway line I should take. I'm hoping to take one of the nonstop lines, but they don't run on weekends.
W: Let's look at the subway map. Hmm... ❷ Why don't you take this route? The train stops at Airport Interchange, but it's the fastest option.
M: Thanks! I can't afford to be late for my flight to Philadelphia.
W: Are you going on a vacation?
M: No, for work. ❸ I'll be meeting the representatives at MJ Incorporated to close a deal. We've been working hard for that account. I'll let you know how it goes when I get back next week.
W: Sounds good.

1-3번은 다음 대화와 지도에 관한 문제입니다.

남: 안녕하세요, 조안나. 이게 무슨 우연이에요!
여: 오, 안녕하세요, 레온.
남: 당신을 마주쳐서 너무 기뻐요. 제가 공항으로 가는 길인데, **어떤 지하철 노선을 타야 할지 모르겠어요.** 직행을 타고 싶은데, 주말에는 운행을 안 하네요.
여: 지하철 노선도를 같이 보죠. 흠… **이 노선은 어떤가요? 열차가 공항 인터체인지에 서지만, 가장 빠른 선택이네요.**
남: 고마워요! 필라델피아로 가는 비행기에 늦을 수는 없어요.
여: 휴가 가는 건가요?
남: 아니에요, 일 때문에 갑니다. **계약을 마무리 짓기 위해 엠제이 사 직원을 만나러 갑니다.** 그 계약 건을 위해서 열심히 해왔어요. 다음 주에 돌아와서 어떻게 되었는지 말씀드릴게요.
여: 좋습니다.

어휘 coincidence 우연 | run into 우연히 마주치다 | head to ~를 향하다 | nonstop 직행의 | representative 직원 | close a deal 계약을 체결하다

1 장소

Where does the conversation take place?
(A) At an airport
(B) At a conference center
(C) At a subway station
(D) At a bus terminal

대화가 일어나는 장소는 어디인가요?
공항에서
콘퍼런스 센터에서
지하철역에서
버스 터미널에서

해설 둘이 우연히 만났고 어느 지하철 노선을 타야 하냐고 물어봤기 때문에(but I'm not sure which subway line I should take) 정답은 (C)가 된다.

2 시각 정보 연계

Look at the graphic. Which line does the woman suggest the man take?
(A) Line Blue
(B) Line Red
(C) Line Green
(D) Line Yellow

시각 정보를 보시오. 여자가 남자에게 제안하는 노선은 어느 것인가?
블루 노선
레드 노선
그린 노선
옐로우 노선

해설 공항 인터체인지에 서는 노선이라고 말했으므로(Why don't you take this route? The train stops at Airport Interchange, but it's the fastest option.) 정답은 (C)가 된다.

3 이유 / 원인

Why is the man going to Philadelphia?
(A) To attend a conference
(B) To meet a client
(C) To examine a facility
(D) To interview a candidate

남자가 필라델피아에 가는 이유는 무엇인가?
회의에 참석하기 위해서
고객을 만나기 위해서
시설을 점검하기 위해서
지원자를 인터뷰하기 위해서

해설 계약을 마무리 짓기 위해 엠제이 사 직원을 만나러 간다고 했으므로(I'll be meeting the representatives at MJ Incorporated to close a deal.) 정답은 (B)가 된다.

Questions 4-6 refer to the following conversation and map.

W: Dumpling Palace. Can I take your order?
M: Hey, Melanie. It's Nelson. I'm at the City Hall on Campbell Road right now. ❹ I have one more place to deliver to, but ❺ the address is wrong. I'm sure there is no Carr Street in our city.
W: Hmm... Do you know the customer's name?
M: Let's see... It says Bernie Martinez.
W: Alright. I'll check the database. The Martinez order should be delivered to Newman Building, Unit 302.
M: Oh, ❻ that's the one on Jackson Road, right across from the bank. Thanks a lot!

4-6번은 다음 대화와 지도에 관한 문제입니다.

여: 덤플링 팰리스입니다. 주문하시겠어요?
남: 안녕하세요, 멜라니. 넬슨이에요. 지금 캠벨 로의 시청에 있는데요. **배송 한 건이 남았는데, 주소가 잘못된 것 같아요.** 우리 도시에는 카르 가가 없어요.
여: 음… 고객 이름을 아시나요?
남: 찾아볼게요… 베니 마르티네스네요.
여: 좋아요. 데이터베이스를 확인해 볼게요. 마르티네스의 주문 건은 뉴맨 빌딩 302호로 배송되어야 해요.
남: 오, **은행 바로 건너편 잭슨 로에 있는 거네요.** 감사합니다!

어휘 take an order 주문받다 | postal worker 우체부 | city official 공무원 | malfunctioning (기계 따위가) 제대로 움직이지 않는 | under construction 공사 중인

4 직업 / 업종

Who most likely is the man?
(A) A building manager
(B) A postal worker
(C) A delivery person
(D) A city official

남자가 누구일 것 같은가?
건물 담당자
우체부
배달부
공무원

해설 배송할 곳이 하나 남았다고 했으므로(I have one more place to deliver to) 정답은 (C)가 된다.

5 문제점

What problem does the man mention?
(A) Some information is incorrect.
(B) Some equipment is malfunctioning.
(C) A road is under construction.
(D) A product has been damaged.

남자가 언급하는 문제는 무엇인가?
정보가 틀리다.
장비가 고장이다.
도로가 공사 중이다.
제품이 손상됐다.

해설 배송할 곳의 주소가 다르다고 나와있으므로(the address is wrong) 정답은 (A)가 된다.

6 시각 정보 연계

Look at the graphic. Where will the man go next?
(A) To Building A
(B) To Building B
(C) To Building C
(D) To Building D

시각 정보를 보시오. 남자가 다음으로 어디에 가겠는가?
빌딩 A로
빌딩 B로
빌딩 C로
빌딩 D로

해설 은행 바로 건너편이라고 했으므로(that's the one on Jackson Road, right across from the bank) 정답은 (D)가 된다.

Questions 7-9 refer to the following conversation and pie chart.

W: ⑦ The final item on today's agenda is the hiring plan for the upcoming year. Until recently, we were able to find many talented new employees at university jobs fairs, but this time, ⑦ I want to do something different.

M: Really? Why?

W: Well, our department spends a lot of time and resources traveling to different universities across the country. It's put quite a dent in our budget.

M: That's a good point. ⑧ Maybe we should concentrate our efforts on the second-most effective recruitment strategy. According to our data, around a quarter of our staff were hired that way.

W: That's what I was thinking as well. ⑨ Can you work with Lorraine in Public Relations and talk about how we can go about this?

7-9번은 다음 대화와 파이 그래프에 관한 문제입니다.

여: **오늘의 마지막 안건은 다음 해의 고용 계획입니다.** 현재까지는, 대학교 채용 박람회에서 많은 재능 있는 신입 직원들을 찾을 수 있었지만, 이번에는 **조금 다르게 하고 싶습니다.**

남: 정말요? 왜요?

여: 음, 우리 부서는 전국의 여러 대학을 돌아다니면서 많은 시간과 자원을 씁니다. 우리 예산이 꽤 듭니다.

남: 좋은 지적이에요. **두 번째로 효과적인 채용 전략에 초점을 둬야 합니다.** 우리 데이터에 따르면, 우리 직원의 1/4이 그 방식으로 고용되었습니다.

여: 저도 또한 같은 생각입니다. **홍보부의 로렌과 같이 작업하셔서 우리가 어떻게 할 수 있을지 논의하시겠어요?**

어휘 job fair 채용박람회 | put a dent in 타격을 주다 | edit 편집하다 | job posting 채용공고 | modify 바꾸다 | tactic 전략 | travel itinerary 여행 일정표 | finalize 마무리하다 | referral 추천 | personnel evaluation form 인사 평가서 | collaborate with ~와 협력하다 | revise 수정하다 | employment contract 고용계약서

7 주제

What would the woman like to do?
(A) Edit an online job posting
(B) Modify a recruitment tactic
(C) Confirm a travel itinerary
(D) Finalize a department budget

여자는 무엇을 하고 싶어 하는가?
온라인 채용 공고를 편집한다
채용 전략을 바꾼다
여행 일정표를 확인한다
부서 예산을 마무리한다

해설 다가올 채용 계획에 대해서 다른 방식으로 하고 싶다고 했으므로(The final item on today's agenda is the hiring plan for the upcoming year., I want to do something different.) 정답은 (B)가 된다.

8 시각 정보 연계

Look at the graphic. Which method does the man suggest using?
(A) University Job Fairs
(B) Social Media Posts
(C) Company Web site
(D) Staff Referrals

시각 정보를 보시오. 남자는 어떤 방식을 사용하는 것을 제안하는가?
대학교 채용 박람회
소셜 미디어 공지
회사 웹사이트
직원 추천

해설 파이 그래프에서 두 번째로 높은 것에 집중하자고 했으므로 26%를 나타내는(Maybe we should concentrate our efforts on the second-most effective recruitment strategy.) 정답은 (B)가 된다.

9 제안 / 요청

What does the woman ask the man to do?
(A) Design a personnel evaluation form
(B) Collaborate with a colleague
(C) Interview some potential candidates
(D) Revise an employment contract

여자가 남자에게 무엇을 하라고 요청하는가?
인사 평가서를 디자인한다
회사 동료와 협업해서 일한다
잠재적 후보자와 면접 본다
고용계약서를 수정한다

해설 홍보부의 로렌을 만나서 같이 일하라고 했으므로(Can you work with Lorraine in Public Relations and talk about how we can go about this?) 정답은 (B)가 된다.

Questions 10-12 refer to the following telephone message and the reimbursement form.

W: Good morning, Mr. Smit. This is Ginger Purvis from the Finance Department. ⑩ I'm just calling to let you know about the travel expenses report you provided for your trip to the trade show last week. I compared your information with the receipts, and it looks like there's a discrepancy. ⑪ The restaurant receipts add up to 30 dollars less than what you listed on your travel expenditure sheet. Please check this and send it back to me so that I can process it. ⑫ Also, we have revised the reimbursement form. All employees have been emailed the new one. Please use it for future expenditure. Thanks!

10-12번은 다음 전화 메시지와 환급 양식에 관한 문제입니다.

여: 슈미트 씨, 좋은 아침입니다. 재무팀의 진저 퍼비스입니다. **지난주에 무역 박람회에 가셨을 때 제출하신 여행경비 보고서에 관해서 연락드립니다.** 영수증에 나와 있는 정보와 비교를 해봤는데, 불일치되는 부분이 있어서요. **레스토랑 영수증이 여행경비 보고서에 목록화되어 있는 것보다 30달러 적습니다.** 점검하시고 제가 처리할 수 있도록 다시 보내주세요. **또한, 환급 양식을 수정했습니다. 모든 직원들이 새로운 양식을 이메일로 받았습니다.** 다음 경비 환급 때에는 이것을 사용해 주세요. 감사합니다!

어휘 Finance Department 재무부 | travel expense 여행경비 | discrepancy 불일치 | expenditure 지출 | reimbursement form 환급 양식 | function 행사

10 세부정보 - 과거 사실

What did the listener do last week?
(A) He attended a function.
(B) He toured an office building.
(C) He trained a new staff member.
(D) He purchased some equipment.

청자는 지난주에 무엇을 했는가?
행사에 참여했다.
사무실 건물 탐방을 했다.
신입 직원을 교육했다.
장비를 구매했다.

해설 지난주에 무역 박람회에 참석해서 제출한 여행경비 보고서에 관해 이야기하므로(I'm just calling to let you know about the travel expenses report you provided for your trip to the trade show last week.) 정답은 (A)가 된다.

11 시각 정보 연계

Look at the graphic. Which amount needs to be checked?
(A) $235
(B) $675
(C) $410
(D) $750

시각 정보를 보시오. 어느 금액이 확인되어야 하는가?
235 달러
675 달러
410 달러
750 달러

해설 레스토랑 비용이 차이가 난다고 했으므로(The restaurant receipts add up to 30 dollars less than what you listed on your travel expenditure sheet.) 정답은 (C)가 된다.

12 세부정보 - 언급

What does the speaker say was sent to the staff?
(A) An updated form
(B) A discount code
(C) A software manual
(D) Some contacts

화자는 직원들에게 무엇이 보내졌다고 말하는가?
수정된 양식
할인 코드
소프트웨어 설명서
몇몇 연락처

해설 수정된 환급 양식이 이메일로 보내졌다고 말했으므로(Also, we have revised the reimbursement form. All employees have been emailed the new one.) 정답은 (A)가 된다.

Questions 13-15 refer to the following talk and map.

W: Welcome to our annual Nature Trail Walk sponsored by Lubbock City Council. There are four trails we can go on today. [13] However, the lake is beautiful this time of year, so I highly recommend going out to Lake Land. I hope you brought some food and drinks because we'll also be having a picnic by the lake. [14] At 3 P.M., there will be a bus that will take us back to the Town Hall, so make sure you don't go too far. The trail will take around 3 hours, so let's get started now. [15] I'm going to hand out some maps now so that you know where we are. If you're ready, grab your water bottles and let's make a start.

13–15번은 다음 담화와 지도에 관한 문제입니다.

여: 러벅 시의회에서 주관하는 연례 자연 트레일 걷기에 오신 것을 환영합니다. 오늘 갈 수 있는 곳은 4개의 트레일입니다. **하지만 매년 이맘때쯤 호수가 아름다워서 레이크 랜드에 있는 트레일로 가는 것을 추천드립니다.** 호수 옆에서 피크닉을 할 것이기 때문에 음식과 음료수를 가지고 왔기를 바랍니다. **오후 3시에는, 시청으로 다시 데리고 가 줄 버스가 있을 것이니, 너무 멀리 가지 마세요.** 트레일은 약 3시간 진행될 예정이니, 지금 출발해 봅시다. **우리가 어디 있는지를 알 수 있도록 지도를 나눠드리도록 하겠습니다.** 만약 준비되셨다면, 물병을 들고 출발해 봅시다.

어휘 trail 길 | highly recommend 매우 추천하다 | hand out 나눠주다 | grab 잡다 | distribute 나눠주다 | assign 할당하다

13 시각 정보 연계

Look at the graphic. Which path does the speaker recommend?
(A) Taurus
(B) Scorpio
(C) Pisces
(D) Aries

시각 정보를 보시오. 화자는 어느 경로를 추천하는가?
토저스
스콜피오
파이시스
에리즈

해설 Lake Land로 가는 트레일을 추천한다는 내용이 나오므로(However, the lake is beautiful this time of year, so I highly recommend going out to Lake Land.) 정답은 (B)가 된다.

14 세부정보 – 예정

According to the speaker, what will happen at 3 P.M.?
(A) A bus will arrive.
(B) A competition will begin.
(C) A group photo will be taken.
(D) A picnic will take place.

화자에 따르면, 3시에 무엇이 일어나는가?
버스가 도착할 것이다.
대회가 시작될 것이다.
단체 사진을 찍을 것이다.
소풍이 열릴 것이다.

해설 3시에 시청으로 다시 데리고 가줄 버스가 온다고 했으므로(At 3 P.M., there will be a bus that will take us back to the Town Hall, so make sure you don't go too far.) 정답은 (A)가 된다.

15 미래 행동 추측

What does the speaker say she will do next?
(A) Distribute some maps
(B) Take a water bottle
(C) Call for help
(D) Assign a group leader

화자는 그녀가 다음으로 무엇을 할 거라고 이야기하는가?
지도를 나눠준다
물병을 가져간다
도움을 요청한다
그룹 대표자를 배정한다

해설 지도를 나눠준다고 나와 있으므로(I'm going to hand out some maps now so that you know where we are.) 정답은 (A)가 된다. hand out이 distribute로 패러프레이징 되었다.

미국

Questions 16-18 refer to the following telephone message and list of services.

M: Hi, John. ⑯ I'm calling to let you know that I just stopped by the renovated building we were considering. I think it's the perfect place to start our bistro. ⑰ I saw the other businesses in the area, and I was really pleased with how good the place looked. There are lots of established companies that look like they can benefit from our services. We'll be able to attract lots of customers by being situated here. Also, I sent over a list of the companies that can supply us with services. I narrowed it down to four companies. Price is a very big concern, but ⑱ I think it is important to be flexible with our range of food and expand what we can offer. Therefore, I suggest going for the company that has the most products for us to choose from.

16-18번은 다음 전화 메시지와 서비스 목록에 관한 문제입니다.

남: 안녕하세요, 존. **우리가 고려했었던 보수된 건물을 방문했다고 알려 드리려고 연락드립니다. 식당을 하기에 완벽한 장소라고 생각합니다. 지역의 다른 업체들도 봤고 장소가 매우 좋아 보여서 정말 기뻤습니다. 우리 서비스의 혜택을 받을 수 있어 보이는 훌륭한 업체들이 많습니다.** 이곳으로 이동함으로써 많은 고객들을 만날 수 있을 것 같습니다. 또한, 서비스를 우리에게 공급해 줄 수 있는 회사들 목록을 보냈습니다. 제가 4개의 회사로 간추렸습니다. 가격이 큰 문제이긴 합니다만, **제 생각에 여러 가지 음식과 우리가 제공할 수 있는 것을 확장하는 것이 중요하다고 생각합니다. 그래서 가장 많은 제품을 선택할 수 있는 회사를 제안합니다.**

어휘 stop by 들리다 | bistro 식당 | established company 훌륭한 업체 | benefit from 혜택을 받다 | narrow down 좁히다, 줄이다 | flexible 유연성 있는, 유연한 | real estate agency 부동산 중개소 | dining establishment 식당 | shared facility 공유 시설 | neighboring building 주변 건물

16 직업 / 업종

What type of business is being launched?
(A) A fitness center
(B) A real estate agency
(C) A remodeling firm
(D) A dining establishment

어떤 종류의 사업을 시작하려고 하는가?
휘트니스 센터
부동산 중개소
리모델링 회사
식당

해설 화자가 생각하고 있는 식당을 열려고 하는 곳을 방문했다는 내용이 나오므로(I'm calling to let you know that I just stopped by the renovated building we were considering. I think it's the perfect place to start our bistro.) 정답은 (D)가 된다.

17 세부정보 – 언급

What does the speaker say he is pleased about?
(A) Some employee applications
(B) Some shared facilities
(C) The neighboring buildings
(D) The price of some services

화자는 무엇이 기쁘다고 말하는가?
직원 신청서
공유 시설
주변 건물
서비스 가격

해설 그 지역의 다른 업체를 봤는데 도움이 많이 될 것 같다는 내용이 나오므로(I saw the other businesses in the area, and I was really pleased with how good the place looked. There are lots of established companies that look like they can benefit from our services.) 정답은 (C)가 된다.

18 시각 정보 연계

Look at the graphic. Which company does the speaker want to use?
(A) TPP
(B) Grissom
(C) Kovar
(D) L-Train

시각 정보를 보시오. 화자는 어떤 회사를 이용하고 싶어 하는가?
TPP
그리섬
코바르
L-트레인

해설 여러 가지 제품을 제공할 수 있는 곳이 좋다고 했으므로(I think it is important to be flexible with our range of food and expand what we can offer. Therefore, I suggest going for the company that has the most products for us to choose from.) 정답은 (C)가 된다.

미국 - 미국

Questions 1-3 refer to the following conversation.

M: Hello, Carol. Thanks for taking the time out of your busy schedule to meet with me. ❶ I'm sure you're aware that we need to start planning this year's team building day for our employees, and I wanted to discuss some ideas with you.

W: Of course. But we could just do what we did in the previous years. Everyone had fun going to the baseball stadium.

M: You're right, but we've been doing that for the last five years.

W: That's a good point. ❷ What did you have in mind then?

M: How about going on a hike as a group?

W: Hmm… that's not a bad idea. ❸ But what if someone ends up getting injured during the hike? We should probably explore more options.

1-3번은 다음 대화에 관한 문제입니다.

남: 캐럴, 안녕하세요. 바쁜 일정 속에 시간을 내어 만나주셔서 감사합니다. **알고 계시다시피 직원들을 위한 올해 단합 대회 날 계획을 시작할 필요가 있어서,** 당신과 이것에 대해 논의하고 싶습니다.

여: 물론이지요. 하지만 그냥 작년에 우리가 했던 것처럼 할 수도 있습니다. 모든 사람들이 야구 경기장에서 즐거운 시간을 보냈습니다.

남: 맞아요, 하지만 **우리는 그것을 지난 5년 동안 해왔습니다.**

여: 좋은 지적이에요. **그러면 혹시 생각하고 계신 것이 있나요?**

남: 그룹별로 하이킹은 어떨까요?

여: 음… 나쁜 생각은 아니에요. **하지만 하이킹하는 동안에 누군가가 다치면 어떻게 하나요?** 다른 옵션들도 생각할 필요가 있습니다.

어휘 be aware that ~를 알다 | team building 단합의 | end up -ing 결국 ~하게 되다 | explore 탐구 / 분석하다 | charity fundraiser 자선 기금 모금 | repeat 반복하다 | well-being 건강, 웰빙 | tight deadline 빡빡한 마감일

1 주제 / 목적

What are the speakers planning?
(A) A team building day
(B) A company picnic
(C) An anniversary celebration
(D) A charity fundraiser

화자들이 계획하고 있는 것은 무엇인가?
단합 대회 날
회사 야유회
기념 축하
자선기금 모금

해설 단합 대회 날에 대해서 계획하자고 했으므로(I'm sure you're aware that we need to start planning this year's team building day for our employees,) 정답은 (A)가 된다.

2 화자 의도 파악

What does the man mean when he says, "we've been doing that for the last five years"?
(A) He does not enjoy watching sporting events.
(B) He does not want to repeat an activity.
(C) He believes an event was successful.
(D) He is unsure how to complete a procedure.

남자가 "우리는 그것을 지난 5년 동안 해왔습니다"라고 말한 의미는 무엇인가?
그는 스포츠 경기 보는 것을 좋아하지 않는다.
그는 같은 액티비티를 반복하고 싶지 않다.
그는 이벤트가 성공적이었다고 생각한다.
그는 절차를 끝내는 방법을 모른다.

해설 지난 5년 동안 해왔다고 하고 다음 문장에서 다른 생각이 있냐고 물어봤으므로, 같은 액티비티를 다시 하고 싶지 않다는 의미를 나타낸다(What did you have in mind then?). 따라서, 정답은 (B)가 된다.

3 문제점

What is the woman worried about?
(A) Low registration numbers
(B) Employee well-being
(C) The department budget
(D) The tight deadline

여자가 우려하는 바는 무엇인가?
낮은 등록 숫자
직원들의 건강
부서 예산
빡빡한 마감일

해설 만약 하이킹하는 도중에 다치기라도 하면 어떻게 하냐고 물어봤으므로(But what if someone ends up getting injured during the hike?) 정답은 (B)가 된다.

Questions 4-6 refer to the following conversation.

M: Mara, ❹ I want to speak with you about the remodeling work your team will be doing on this mansion today. Let me guide you to the living room.
W: Wow, ❺ look at the carpeting. It looks at least 60 years old. I doubt it would go well with the new interior design.
M: Yeah, the wallpaper is in horrible shape as well. It is way too faded, and it'll look out of place after the redesign. That's why we'll be stripping the wallpaper and the carpeting today.
W: Umm... This room is quite big. ❻ Do you still want us to retile the bathrooms today?
M: No, that won't be necessary. As soon as I saw the size of this living room, I rescheduled that job to tomorrow.

4-6번은 다음 대화에 관한 문제입니다.

남: 마라, **오늘 당신 팀이 이 맨션에 할 리모델링 작업에 관해서 이야기하고 싶습니다.** 거실로 제가 안내할게요.
여: 와우. **카펫 좀 보세요. 적어도 60년은 되어 보입니다.** 새 인테리어 디자인과 잘 어울릴지 모르겠네요.
남: 네, 벽지 또한 안 좋은 상태입니다. 너무 바랬고, 리모델링 이후에 어울리지도 않아 보일 거예요. 그래서 오늘 벽지와 카펫을 뜯어낼 거예요.
여: 음… **이 공간은 꽤 큽니다. 오늘 욕실 타일도 다시 교체하기를 원하세요?**
남: 아니에요. 그것은 필요 없습니다. 거실 크기를 보자마자, 그 작업은 내일 하기로 조정했습니다.

어휘 go with 어울리다 | wallpaper 벽지 | faded 빛깔이 바랜 | strip 뜯어내다 | retile 타일을 다시 깔다 | blueprint 청사진 | cost estimate 가격 견적서 | recycled material 재활용 재료 | outdated 구식의 | heavily stained 얼룩이 많은 | property 건물, 자산

4 주제 / 목적

What are the speakers mainly discussing?
(A) A building blueprint
(B) A construction material
(C) A cost estimate
(D) A renovation project

화자들이 주로 이야기하는 것은 무엇인가?
건물 청사진
건축 자재
가격 견적서
보수 공사 프로젝트

해설 리모델링 작업에 관해서 이야기하고 싶다고 했으므로(I want to speak with you about the remodeling work your team will be doing on this mansion today.) remodeling을 renovation으로 패러프레이징한 정답은 (D)가 된다.

5 세부정보 - 언급

What does the woman say about the carpeting?
(A) It is made from recycled materials.
(B) It looks outdated.
(C) It is heavily stained.
(D) It will be delivered today.

여자는 카펫에 대해서 뭐라고 말하는가?
재활용 재료로 만들어졌다.
오래되었다.
얼룩이 많다.
오늘 배송될 것이다.

해설 카펫이 60년 정도 되어 보인다고 했으므로(look at the carpeting. It looks at least 60 years old.) 오래되었다라는 정답은 (B)가 된다.

6 화자 의도 파악

What does the woman imply when she says, "This room is quite big"?
(A) The property has a good value.
(B) A job will take a long time to finish.
(C) More furniture should be purchased.
(D) She would like to hire more workers.

여자가 "이 공간은 꽤 큽니다"라고 말할 때 의미하는 것은 무엇인가?
건물의 가치가 훌륭하다.
일이 끝마치는 데 시간이 걸릴 것이다.
가구를 더 구매해야 한다.
더 많은 직원을 고용하고 싶다.

해설 꽤 크다고 말하면서 욕실도 작업해야 하냐고 물어봤으므로(Do you still want us to retile the bathrooms today?) 시간이 오래 걸린다는 내용을 내포하고 있으므로 정답은 (B)가 된다.

Questions 7-9 refer to the following conversation.	7-9번은 다음 대화에 관한 문제입니다.
M: ❼Welcome to Rick's Body Shop. We service your vehicle regardless of its make or model. We're now offering a free consultation for our customers interested in preparing for the cold weather.	**남: 릭 바디 샵에 오신 것을 환영합니다. 만든 회사 혹은 모델명에 상관없이 당신의 차량을 점검해 드립니다.** 우리는 지금 추운 날씨를 대비하는 데 관심 있으신 고객들에게 무료 컨설팅을 제공하고 있습니다.
W: I see. Could you tell me more?	**여:** 아 그렇군요. 좀 더 자세히 설명해 주시겠어요?
M: ❽If you make an appointment with one of our specialists, they will thoroughly inspect your car and make sure it's well-prepared.	**남: 만약 우리 전문가들 중에 한 명과 예약을 잡으시면, 당신의 자동차를 철저하게 점검해 드리고 잘 준비될 수 있도록 해 드릴 것입니다.**
W: Hmm... It's almost winter. But I'm leading a major project at work, and ❽I won't have the time to come back for a consultation.	**여:** 음… **거의 겨울이네요.** 하지만 제가 지금 직장에서 주요 프로젝트를 맡아서요. **컨설팅을 위해 다시 올 시간이 없을 것 같은데요.**
M: Well, we're open on the weekends, too.	**남:** 음, 주말에도 이용 가능하세요.
W: Let me think about it first.	**여:** 일단 생각 좀 해보겠습니다.
M: OK. ❾Here's a brochure outlining the various services we offer. My number's on it, so feel free to call me any time.	**남:** 알겠습니다. **여기에 우리가 제공하는 여러 가지 서비스를 간략하게 적은 브로슈어가 있습니다.** 제 번호가 있으니, 언제든지 편하실 때 연락 부탁드립니다.

어휘 regardless of ~의 상관없이 | thoroughly 철저하게 | well-prepared 잘 준비된 | outline 개요를 서술하다 | sporting goods store 스포츠용품 가게 | auto repair shop 자동차 정비소 | hardware store 철물점 | stress 강조하다 | express interest in ~에 관심을 표현하다 | business card 명함

7 장소

Where does the conversation take place?	대화가 일어나고 있는 장소는 어디인가?
(A) At a factory	공장에서
(B) At a sporting goods store	스포츠용품 가게에서
(C) At an auto repair shop	**자동차 정비소에서**
(D) At a hardware store	철물점에서

해설 Body Shop, vehicle이라는 단어를 통해서 자동차 정비소라는 것을 알 수 있으므로(Welcome to Rick's Body Shop. We service your vehicle regardless of its make or model.) 정답은 (C)가 된다.

8 화자 의도 파악

Why does the woman say, "It's almost winter"?	여자가 "거의 겨울이네요"라고 말한 이유는 무엇인가?
(A) To purchase some new supplies	새로운 장비를 구매하기 위해서
(B) To show excitement about traveling	여행에 신남을 표현하기 위해서
(C) To stress an upcoming work deadline	다가오는 마감 날짜를 강조하기 위해서
(D) To express interest in a service	**서비스에 관해 관심을 표현하기 위해서**

해설 앞에서 겨울을 대비해서 무료 컨설팅을 제공한다고 했으며, 그 이후에 컨설팅 받을 시간이 안 된다고 설명했으므로(If you make an appointment with one of our specialists, they will thoroughly inspect your car and make sure it's well-prepared., I won't have the time to come back for a consultation.) 여자는 서비스를 받는데 관심을 두고 있다는 것을 알 수 있으므로 정답은 (D)가 된다.

9 세부정보 - 언급

What does the man give to the woman?	남자가 여자에게 무엇을 주는가?
(A) A brochure	**브로슈어**
(B) A receipt	영수증
(C) A work schedule	일정
(D) A business card	명함

해설 여러 가지 서비스가 적혀있는 브로슈어가 여기 있다고 말했으므로(Here's a brochure outlining the various services we offer.) 정답은 (A)가 된다.

Questions 10-12 refer to the following telephone message.

W: Hello, Bobby. ⑩ This is Courtney from Product Development. ⑪ I'm calling because I would like to get your approval for the purchase of eight new laptops for our engineers. They've been working from their desktops, but they need to travel back and forth from the research lab to the manufacturing plant. For now, they're using notepads to record their findings, and they transfer those notes to their computers when they return to the lab. This is time-consuming and leaves much room for error. Ideally, ⑫ I'd like to make the order soon. The budget is due on Wednesday, isn't it? ⑫ Let me know what you think before then. Thanks.

10-12번은 다음 전화 메시지에 관한 문제입니다.

여: 안녕하세요, 바비. **저는 생산 개발팀의 코트니입니다. 우리 엔지니어들을 위한 8개의 새 노트북을 구매하기 위해서 당신의 승인을 받고자 전화드렸습니다.** 그들은 책상에 있는 데스크톱에서 일했습니다만, 연구 실험실에서 공장까지 왔다 갔다 해야 합니다. 현재는, 조사 결과를 기록하기 위해 노트패드를 이용하고 있는데, 실험실에 돌아와서는 컴퓨터에 그 노트를 옮겨야 합니다. 이것은 시간 낭비인 데다가 실수를 할 여지가 많습니다. 이상적으로 **바로 주문하고 싶습니다. 예산이 수요일까지죠, 맞죠? 그전에 어떻게 생각하는지 알려주세요.** 감사합니다.

어휘 approval 승인 | back and forth 왔다 갔다 | time-consuming 시간 낭비의 | Public Relations 홍보부 | stationery 문구류 | business trip 출장

10 직업 / 업종

What department does the speaker most likely work in?
(A) Public Relations
(B) Information Technology
(C) Product Development
(D) Human Resources

화자는 어느 부서에서 일할 것 같은가?
홍보부
정보 기술부
제품 개발부
인사부

해설 자기를 소개하는 과정에서 생산 개발팀이라고 이야기했으므로(This is Courtney from Product Development.) 정답은 (C)가 된다.

11 세부정보 - 언급

What does the speaker want to purchase?
(A) Stationery
(B) Vehicles
(C) Furniture
(D) Electronics

화자가 구매하고 싶은 것은 무엇인가?
문구류
차량
가구
전자 장비

해설 엔지니어들을 위한 노트북을 사고 싶다고 했으므로(I'm calling because I would like to get your approval for the purchase of eight new laptops for our engineers.) 정답은 (D)가 된다. 이처럼 토익에서는 단어를 그대로 나오는 경우도 있지만 통칭해서 종류 군이 답이 되는 경우가 대부분이다.

12 화자 의도 파악

What does the speaker imply when she says, "The budget is due on Wednesday, isn't it"?
(A) She will have to adjust the deadline.
(B) She would like to confirm the listener's availability.
(C) She is going on a business trip on Wednesday.
(D) She wants the approval to be processed quickly.

여자가 "예산이 수요일까지죠, 맞죠?"라고 말할 때 무엇을 의미하는가?
그녀는 마감 날짜를 조정해야 할 것이다.
그녀는 청자가 가능한지 확인하고 싶어 한다.
그녀는 수요일에 출장을 갈 것이다.
그녀는 승인을 빨리 받고 싶어 한다.

해설 앞 문장에서 바로 주문하고 싶다고 했고(I'd like to make the order soon.), 그 뒤에는 청자의 승인을 받아야 한다고 했으므로(Let me know what you think before then.) 정답은 승인을 빨리 받고 싶어 한다는 (D)가 된다.

Questions 13-15 refer to the following talk.

M: Good afternoon. ⑬ Welcome to the training seminar for all department managers. The first item on today's agenda is employee evaluations. Some managers struggle with giving negative feedback to their staff, but constructive criticism will help them reach their full potential. ⑭ Some of you may be concerned about hurting your staff's feelings. But remember, your staff is very professional. And one more thing—⑮ don't forget to express your gratitude for all the work they do. Giving your staff compliments will motivate them to work harder.

13-15번은 다음 담화에 관한 문제입니다.

남: 안녕하세요. **모든 부서장들을 위한 교육 세미나에 오신 것을 환영합니다.** 오늘 안건의 제일 첫 번째는 직원 평가입니다. 몇몇 매니저들은 직원들에게 부정적인 평가를 주는 데 굉장히 힘들어하시지만, 건설적인 평가는 그들이 최대의 잠재력에 도달하는 데 도움을 줄 수 있습니다. **몇몇 분들은 직원들에게 상처를 줄까 봐 걱정하실 수 있습니다.** 하지만 기억하세요, **여러분들의 직원들은 매우 전문적입니다.** 그리고 한 가지 더. **그들이 일한 것에 대해 감사를 표시하는 것을 잊지 마시기 바랍니다.** 직원들에게 칭찬하는 것은 그들에게 일을 더 열심히 할 수 있도록 동기부여를 줄 것입니다.

어휘 department manager 부서장 | employee evaluation 직원 평가 | struggle 고군분투하다 | negative 부정적인 | criticism 비평 | full potential 최대 잠재력 | gratitude 감사 | compliment 칭찬 | motivate 동기부여를 주다 | professional recruiter 전문 채용가 | board members 이사진 | department head 부서장 | reassure 안심시키다 | acknowledge 인지하다 | employee directory 직원 주소록 | appreciation 감사

13 직업 / 업종

Who are the listeners?
(A) Professional recruiters
(B) Board members
(C) Department heads
(D) Administrative assistants

청자들은 누구인가?
전문 채용가
이사진
부서장
사무보조

해설 모든 부서장을 위한 교육 세미나에 오신 걸 환영한다고 했으므로(Welcome to the training seminar for all department managers.) 청자는 (C)가 된다.

14 화자 의도 파악

Why does the speaker say, "your staff is very professional"?
(A) To congratulate an employee
(B) To reassure the listeners
(C) To acknowledge a problem
(D) To ask for a recommendation

화자는 왜 "여러분들의 직원들은 매우 전문적입니다"라고 말하는가?
직원을 축하해 주기 위해서
청자들을 안심시키기 위해서
문제를 인지하기 위해서
추천을 요청하기 위해서

해설 앞에서 걱정하지만이라고 하고 역접을 나타내는 but 뒤에 나와있으므로(Some of you may be concerned about hurting your staff's feelings.) 걱정하지 말고 안심시켜주는 정답은 (B)가 된다.

15 세부정보 - 언급

What does the speaker remind the listeners to do?
(A) Submit some evaluation forms
(B) Update an employee directory
(C) Ask a lot of questions
(D) Show some appreciation

화자가 청자들에게 무엇을 하라고 상기시켜주는가?
평가서를 제출한다
직원 주소록을 업데이트한다
질문을 많이 한다
감사를 표현한다

해설 직원들인 한 일에 대해서 감사를 표현하는 것을 잊지 말라고 했으므로(don't forget to express your gratitude for all the work they do.) gratitude의 패러프레이징 appreciation이 들어가는 정답은 (D)가 된다.

Questions 16-18 refer to the following talk.

W: Hi, everyone. ⑯ Let's start the weekly personnel meeting by talking about the London flagship store. You all know that our team started looking to fill the retail director job there back in the spring. ⑰ Unfortunately, none of the external candidates we've met is qualified to take on the role. And, well, it's the last week of June. ⑰ I'd like to invite our current staff members to apply for the position as well. ⑱ Let's aim to interview some candidates next month. Wilson, can you make the job posting available on the internal Web site?

16-18번은 다음 담화에 관한 문제입니다.

여: 안녕하세요, 여러분들. **런던 플래그십 스토어에 관해 논의함으로써 주간 인사부 회의를 시작하겠습니다.** 여러분도 아시다시피 우리 팀이 봄에 그쪽에 소매담당자 자리를 채울 사람을 물색하기 시작했습니다. **유감스럽게도, 외부 지원자들 중에 그 직책에 적합한 지원자를 찾을 수가 없었습니다.** 그리고 **6월 마지막 주에요.** **저는 현 직원들이 이 직책에 지원할 수 있도록 요청하고 싶습니다. 다음 달에 몇몇 지원자들을 면접을 보는 것을 목표로 하죠.** 윌슨 씨 내부 웹사이트에 공석 공고를 내주실 수 있나요?

어휘 weekly personnel meeting 주간 인사부 회의 | flagship store 플래그십 스토어 | external 외부의 | aim to ~을 목표로 하다 | job posting 취업 공고 | retail sales associate 소매영업 직원 | executive 임원 | alternative 대안의, 대체의 | colleague 회사 동료 | internal communication 내부 커뮤니케이션

16 직업 / 업종

Who most likely is the speaker?
(A) A retail sales associate
(B) An executive
(C) A human resources manager
(D) A customer service representative

화자는 누구일 것 같은가?
소매영업 직원
임원
인사부장
고객 서비스 담당자

해설 주간 인사부 미팅을 시작한다고 했으므로(Let's start the weekly personnel meeting by talking about the London flagship store.) 정답은 (C)가 된다.

17 화자 의도 파악

What does the speaker mean when she says, "it's the last week of June"?
(A) She must take an alternative approach.
(B) She is disappointed with her colleagues.
(C) She needs to submit an application soon.
(D) She has already completed a task.

화자가 "6월 마지막 주에요"라고 말할 때 무엇을 의미하는가?
그녀는 다른 대책을 강구해야 한다.
그녀는 회사 동료들에게 실망했다.
그녀는 곧 지원서를 제출할 필요가 있다.
그녀는 벌써 일을 끝냈다.

해설 앞에서 외부 지원자를 찾지 못해서 현직원들에게 부탁하는 내용이 나오므로(Unfortunately, none of the external candidates we've met is qualified to take on the role., I'd like to invite our current staff members to apply for the position as well.) 다른 대책을 이야기하는 정답은 (A)가 된다.

18 세부정보 - 예정

According to the speaker, what will happen next month?
(A) A proposal will be revised.
(B) Internal communication will improve.
(C) Interviews will be conducted.
(D) A Web site will be shut down for maintenance.

화자에 따르면, 다음 달에 무슨 일이 일어날 것인가?
제안서가 수정될 것이다.
내부 커뮤니케이션이 향상될 것이다.
인터뷰가 실행될 것이다.
웹사이트가 점검 때문에 폐쇄될 것이다.

해설 다음 달에 지원자들을 인터뷰하자고 했으므로(Let's aim to interview some candidates next month.) 정답은 (C)가 된다.

미국 - 미국

Questions 1-3 refer to the following conversation.

M: Hello, Lucy. ❶We successfully won the Sanders Inc. contract. We'll need to go down to their office on Rivermont Street to finalize some details. We should probably leave in an hour or so.

W: Wait a minute. ❷I usually take Rivermont to work every morning, but I had to take a detour because it was closed for maintenance today. The traffic in the area was horrible. That's why I was late to work.

M: Oh, no! Sorry to hear that. ❸I guess we should probably take the subway there then. Their office is a short walk from Rivermont Street Station.

1-3번은 다음 대화에 관한 문제입니다.

남: 루시, 안녕하세요. **우리가 성공적으로 샌더스 사의 계약을 따냈어요. 리버몬트 가에 있는 그들 사무실에 가서 몇 가지 세부사항을 마무리 지어야 해요.** 우리는 한 시간 이후쯤 출발할 거예요.

여: 잠깐만요. **매일 아침 리버몬트를 통해 출근하는데, 오늘은 보수 때문에 폐쇄되어 우회해야 했어요.** 그 지역의 교통이 심각했습니다. 그래서 제가 오늘 지각했습니다.

남: 오! 그랬군요. **그럼 지하철을 타야겠네요.** 그들 사무실이 리버몬트 가 역에서 조금만 걸어가면 되는 거리에 있어요.

어휘 win a contract 계약을 따내다 | take a detour 우회하다 | short walk 걸어서 짧은 거리 | fulfill an order 주문을 이행하다 | traffic sign 교통 표지판 | public transportation 대중교통 | postpone 연기하다

1 주제 / 목적

What are the speakers discussing?
(A) Purchasing a new vehicle
(B) Fulfilling an order
(C) Visiting a client
(D) Revising an agreement

화자들이 논의하고 있는 것은 무엇인가?
새 차량을 구입하는 것
주문을 이행하는 것
고객을 방문하는 것
계약을 수정하는 것

해설 리버몬트 가에 있는 사무실에 가서 세부적인 것을 마무리 짓는다고 했으므로(We successfully won the Sanders Inc. contract. We'll need to go down to their office on Rivermont Street to finalize some details.) 고객을 만나는 것에 대해 이야기하는 정답은 (C)가 된다.

2 세부정보 - 문제점

What does the woman say about Rivermont Street?
(A) Traffic signs are broken there.
(B) It connects to the city center.
(C) It is closed to traffic.
(D) A parking facility is being built nearby.

리버몬트 가에 대해서 여자는 무엇을 말하고 있는가?
그곳의 표지판이 부러졌다.
그곳은 시티센터로 연결된다.
그곳은 통행을 막았다.
근처에 주차장이 지어지고 있다.

해설 보수 공사 때문에 폐쇄되어 우회했다고 했으므로(I usually take Rivermont to work every morning, but I had to take a detour because it was closed for maintenance today.) 정답은 (C)가 된다.

3 제안 / 요구 / 요청

What does the man suggest doing?
(A) Checking the traffic report
(B) Using public transportation
(C) Leaving the office right away
(D) Postponing an appointment

남자가 제안하는 것은 무엇인가?
교통보고서를 확인하는 것
대중교통을 이용하는 것
사무실을 당장 떠나는 것
약속을 미루는 것

해설 지하철을 타고 거기에 가야 한다고 했으므로(I guess we should probably take the subway there then.) 정답은 (B)가 된다.

Questions 4-6 refer to the following conversation.

W: Hello, Mr. Wong. This is Claire from Commercial Appliances. I know you are expecting to receive your order of two refrigerators today. ❹ But I'm afraid that there has been an error. One of the appliances didn't make it on the truck. We just caught this problem, and I apologize for the inconvenience.

M: That's horrible. ❺ Some city officials are visiting my restaurant on Thursday for a final inspection. If the fridge is not installed on time, I'll fail the inspection, and the grand opening will be delayed.

W: Oh, no. That's not much time at all. ❻ Could you hold on? I'll put you through to my manager. I believe he'll be able to help you meet your deadline.

4-6번은 다음 대화에 관한 문제입니다.

여: 안녕하세요, 웡 씨. 상업용 기기의 클레어입니다. 주문하신 두 대의 냉장고를 오늘 받기로 되어있는 것으로 알고 있는데요. **유감스럽게도 문제가 생겼습니다. 냉장고 한 대를 트럭에 못 실었습니다.** 문제를 지금 막 발견했는데요, 불편을 끼쳐 죄송합니다.

남: 안 되는데요. **시 공무원이 마지막 점검을 위해 목요일에 우리 레스토랑에 방문하기로 했습니다.** 냉장고가 제시간에 설치가 안 된다면, 검사에 통과하지 못할 거고, 개업일도 미뤄질 거예요.

여: 오, 그러면 안 되는데. 시간이 별로 없네요. **잠깐 기다려 주시겠어요? 제가 매니저에게 연결해 드릴게요.** 제 생각에 그가 날짜를 맞추는 데 도와주실 수 있을 거예요.

어휘 apologize for the inconvenience 불편을 끼쳐드려 죄송합니다 | fridge 냉장고 | grand opening 개업식 | hold on 기다리다 | meet the deadline 마감 날짜를 맞추다 | oversight 실수, 간과 | be sold out 매진되다 | malfunctioning (기계 따위가) 제대로 움직이지 않는 | product launch 제품 출시 | transfer a call 전화를 연결해 주다 | inventory 재고 | extend a warranty 보증서를 연장하다

4 세부정보 - 문제점

What problem does the woman mention?
(A) There was a delivery oversight.
(B) A vehicle was in an accident.
(C) Some machinery is sold out.
(D) Some products are malfunctioning.

여자가 언급하는 문제는 무엇인가?
배송 실수가 있었다.
차량이 사고가 났다.
기계가 매진되었다.
몇몇 제품이 고장 났다.

해설 배송에 실수가 있었다고 했고, 원래는 두 대를 실어야 하는데 한 대만 실은 실수(oversight)를 이야기하고 있으므로(But I'm afraid that there has been an error. One of the appliances didn't make it on the truck.) 정답은 (A)가 된다.

5 세부정보 - 예정

What does the man say will take place on Thursday?
(A) A grand opening
(B) A cooking class
(C) A store inspection
(D) A product launch

남자가 목요일에 무엇이 일어날 것이라고 이야기하는가?
개업식
요리 수업
가게 점검
제품 출시

해설 목요일에 시 공무원들이 마지막 점검을 위해 방문한다고 했으므로(Some city officials are visiting my restaurant on Thursday for a final inspection.) 정답은 (C)가 된다.

6 미래 행동 추측

What does the woman say she will do?
(A) Contact a driver
(B) Transfer a call
(C) Check the inventory
(D) Extend a warranty

여자가 무엇을 할 것이라고 말하는가?
운전자에게 연락한다
전화를 연결해 준다
재고를 확인한다
보증서를 연장한다

해설 매니저를 바꿔준다고 했으므로(Could you hold on? I'll put you through to my manager.) 정답은 (B)가 된다.

Questions 7-9 refer to the following conversation and schedule.

W: Mike, did you check the e-mail about the employee development seminars?

M: Yes. ❼ I read that it's a part of a new personnel initiative to encourage professional growth. It looks like there will be a new topic every day.

W: Yeah, and ❽ we are required to sign up for at least one session each week. I heard they might be a part of our evaluations.

M: Right. The sessions do sound interesting, though. I'm curious about the two related to communications.

W: Will you be going to both of them?

M: No, ❾ I'll be out of the office until the 17th, so I can't go to the first one. I'll be at the second one.

7-9번은 다음 대화와 일정표에 관한 문제입니다.

여: 마이크, 직원 발전 세미나에 관한 이메일을 체크하셨나요?

남: 네. **전문적 성장을 장려하는 새로운 인사기획의 일부분이라고 읽었습니다. 날마다 새로운 주제가 있는 것처럼 보였습니다.**

여: 네. **매주 하나의 세션에 등록해야 합니다. 우리 평가 중에 일부가 될 수도 있다고 들었어요.**

남: 맞습니다. 그래도 세션들이 재미있어 보이더라고요. 저는 커뮤니케이션과 관련된 두 개에 관심이 있습니다.

여: 두 개 다 참석하실 거예요?

남: 아니요. **17일까지 사무실에 없어서, 첫 번째는 못 가요. 두 번째는 갈 것 같아요.**

어휘 initiative 기획 | scheduling conflict 스케줄 상충 | on a first-come, first-served basis 선착순의

7 세부정보 - 언급

According to the man, what has recently changed?
(A) An office layout
(B) An employee handbook
(C) A scheduling conflict
(D) A corporate policy

남자에 따르면, 최근에 무엇이 바뀌었는가?
사무실 레이아웃
직원 핸드북
스케줄 상충
회사 방침

해설 새로운 인사(직원) 기획의 일부라고 했으므로(I read that it's a part of a new personnel initiative to encourage professional growth.), initiative의 패러프레이징 단어인 policy가 들어가는 정답은 (D)가 된다.

8 세부정보 - 언급

What does the woman say about the seminars?
(A) Topics will change monthly.
(B) Attendance is mandatory.
(C) Seating is on a first-come, first-served basis.
(D) Sessions will be led by the personnel manager.

여자는 세미나에 대해서 뭐라고 이야기하는가?
주제가 매달 바뀔 것이다.
참석이 의무적이다.
좌석은 선착순이다.
세션은 인사부장이 이끌 것이다.

해설 매주 하나의 세션에 등록해야 하며 그것이 평가의 일부가 될 수 있다고 했기 때문에(we are required to sign up for at least one session each week. I heard they might be a part of our evaluations.) 정답은 (B)가 된다.

9 시각 정보 연계

Look at the graphic. What session will the man attend?
(A) Clear Communication
(B) Advanced Business Writing
(C) Effective Speaking
(D) Strategies for Customer Satisfaction

시각 정보를 보시오. 남자는 어떤 세션을 참석할 것인가?
명확한 의사소통
고급 비즈니스 라이팅
효과적인 말하기
고객 만족을 위한 전략들

해설 커뮤니케이션에 관심 있다고 했으며, 커뮤니케이션에 관한 것은 Clear Communication과 Effective Speaking이 있는데, 17일까지는 사무실에 없기 때문에 첫 번째 것은 참석을 못 한다고 했으므로(I'll be out of the office until the 17th, so I can't go to the first one. I'll be at the second one.) 정답은 (C)가 된다.

Questions 10-12 refer to the following recorded message.

W: Thank you for calling Columbus Convention Center. ⑩ We regret to inform you that our business center is currently closed for renovations until the end of September. Until then, the business center will be moved to room 202. ⑪ Since the temporary location only has a limited number of computers, you can reserve them ahead of time on our Web site. ⑫ We also offer free laptop rentals upon request. If you would like to borrow one, all you have to do is submit your credit card as a deposit. You can pick up your card when you return the laptop. For directions on how to get there, please check our Web site.

10-12번은 다음 녹음 메시지에 관한 문제입니다.

여: 콜럼버스 컨벤션 센터에 전화 주셔서 감사합니다. **유감스럽게도 우리 비즈니스 센터가 현재 보수 공사로 9월 말까지 문을 닫습니다. 그때까지, 비즈니스 센터는 202호로 옮겨질 것입니다. 옮겨간 임시 장소에는 제한된 수의 컴퓨터가 있는 관계로 저희 웹사이트에서 예약하실 수 있습니다. 또한 요청하시면 노트북 대여도 무료로 제공해 드립니다. 만약 대여를 원하시면 보증금으로 신용카드만 제출해 주시면 됩니다.** 노트북을 반납하실 때 신용카드를 가지고 가시면 됩니다. 그곳에 가는 방법은 저희 웹사이트를 확인해 주세요.

어휘 temporary location 임시 장소 | ahead of time 미리 | upon request 신청에 의해 | deposit 보증금 | direction 약도 | temporary move 임시 이전 | directory 주소록

10 주제 / 목적

What is the message mainly about?
(A) A temporary move
(B) A technology conference
(C) A business news center
(D) A laboratory renovation

메시지는 무엇에 관한 것인가?
임시 이전
기술 회의
비즈니스 뉴스 센터
실험실 보수공사

해설 현재 비즈니스 센터가 보수 공사로 인해 202호로 옮긴다는 내용이므로(We regret to inform you that our business center is currently closed for renovations until the end of September. Until then, the business center will be moved to room 202.) 정답은 (A)가 된다.

11 세부정보 - 언급

According to the speaker, what can be accessed on a Web site?
(A) A map
(B) A directory
(C) An events calendar
(D) A reservation form

화자에 따르면, 웹사이트에서 얻을 수 있는 것은 무엇인가?
지도
주소록
이벤트 달력
예약 양식

해설 컴퓨터가 한정적이어서 웹사이트에서 미리 예약을 할 수 있다고 했으므로(Since the temporary location only has a limited number of computers, you can reserve them ahead of time on our Web site.) 정답은 (D)가 된다.

12 세부정보 - 방법

How can the listeners borrow a laptop?
(A) By paying a fee in advance
(B) By submitting a credit card
(C) By showing an ID badge
(D) By subscribing to a service

청자들이 노트북을 어떻게 대여할 수 있는가?
미리 요금을 지불함으로써
신용카드를 제출함으로써
ID 배지를 보여줌으로써
서비스에 정기구독함으로써

해설 노트북 대여 시 신용카드를 제출하라고 했으므로(We also offer free laptop rentals upon request. If you would like to borrow one, all you have to do is submit your credit card as a deposit.) 정답은 (B)가 된다.

Questions 13-15 refer to the following radio broadcast.

W: Thank you for listening to Radio WXKB. Time for a traffic update. All motorists traveling on Route 61 to Chapel Hill should pay close attention. ⑬ Due to heavy rain from last night, two lanes of the highway had to be closed for maintenance. Traffic heading south to Chapel Hill has come to a complete halt. ⑭ Motorists are advised to adhere to the signs marking the detour. Clearing the debris and repairing the damage is expected to take more than a week. ⑮ The maintenance work is scheduled to end on October 15, but this date is subject to change. Please stay tuned for the latest updates.

13-15번은 다음 라디오 방송에 관한 문제입니다.

여: 라디오 WXKB를 청취해 주셔서 감사합니다. 교통 업데이트 시간입니다. 루트 61에서 채펄힐로 가는 운전자들은 모두 주의하세요. **지난밤에 내린 폭우로 인해, 고속도로 2차선이 공사로 폐쇄되었습니다.** 채펄힐로 가는 남쪽 방면은 교통이 완전히 중단되었습니다. **운전자들은 우회를 의미하는 표지판을 지켜주세요.** 잔해를 치우고 손상을 복구하는 것이 1주일 이상 걸릴 예정입니다. **보수 공사는 10월 15일에 끝날 예정이지만,** 이 날짜는 변경될 수 있습니다. 마지막 업데이트까지 채널 고정해 주세요.

어휘 motorists 운전자 | pay close attention 세심한 주의를 하다 | heavy rain 폭우 | come to a halt 중지시키다 | detour 우회(하다) | debris 잔해 | stay tuned 채널 고정하다 | road closure 도로 폐쇄 | inclement weather 악천후 | detour sign 우회 표지판 | carpool 함께 타다 | toll fee 톨 요금

13 주제 / 목적

What is the broadcast mainly about?
(A) Highway construction
(B) Road closure
(C) Inclement weather
(D) A vehicle accident

방송은 무엇에 관한 것인가?
고속도로 공사
도로 폐쇄
악천후
차량 사고

해설 지난밤 폭우로 인해 도로를 폐쇄한다는 내용이므로(Due to heavy rain from last night, two lanes of the highway had to be closed for maintenance.) 정답은 (B)가 된다.

14 제안 / 요구 / 요청

What are the motorists advised to do?
(A) Use public transportation
(B) Reduce their speed
(C) Follow detour signs
(D) Carpool with others to work

운전자들이 권고받은 것은 무엇인가?
대중교통을 이용한다
속도를 낮춘다
우회 표지판을 따른다
출근 시 다른 이들과 자동차 함께 타기를 하다

해설 우회를 표시하는 표지판을 잘 따르라고 했으므로(Motorists are advised to adhere to the signs marking the detour.) 정답은 (C)가 된다.

15 세부정보 – 예정

What will happen on October 15?
(A) Some roadwork will be finished.
(B) A new bus terminal will open.
(C) Some drivers will be stopped for a license check.
(D) A toll fee will be increased.

10월 15일에 무슨 일이 일어날 것인가?
도로공사가 끝날 것이다.
새로운 버스 터미널이 오픈될 것이다.
몇몇 운전자들은 면허증 확인을 위해 서야 한다.
톨 요금이 인상될 것이다.

해설 공사가 10월 15일에 끝날 것이라고 했으므로(The maintenance work is scheduled to end on October 15.) 정답은 (A)가 된다.

Questions 16-18 refer to the following radio broadcast.

W: You're listening to Gail Davidson with today's business news. [16] McBrayer Developers has announced that a new office complex will begin its construction in Leeds. **The project will commence next week after many months of negotiations with the city to obtain proper permits. According to the developers,** [17] the construction will take around a year to complete. [18] This news is welcomed by Leeds residents, as the complex is projected to boost the local economy, **which has steadily declined over the past few years due to a lack of infrastructure.**

16 – 18번은 다음 라디오 방송에 관한 문제입니다.

여: 오늘의 비즈니스 뉴스와 함께 개일 데이비슨을 듣고 계십니다. **맥브레이어 디벨로퍼즈에서 리즈에 새로운 사무실 단지 공사를 시작할 것이라고 공지했습니다.** 프로젝트는 적합한 허가증을 얻기 위해 시와의 수개월 동안 협상 끝에 다음 주에 시작될 것입니다. 개발업자에 따르면, **공사는 완공되는 데 1년 정도 걸릴 것입니다. 이 뉴스를 리즈 주민들은 환영합니다. 왜냐하면** 기반 시설이 부족해서 지난 몇 년 동안에 꾸준히 위축되었던 **지역 경기를 부양할 수 있을 것으로 예상되기 때문입니다.**

어휘 commence 시작하다 | proper 적합한 | project 예상(추정)하다 | boost 부양하다 | steadily 꾸준하게 | decline 감소하다, 거절하다 | infrastructure 기반 시설 | relocation 이전 | apartment complex 아파트 단지 | have yet to 아직 ~하지 못하고 있다 | outskirts 교외

16 주제 / 목적

What is the broadcast mainly about?
(A) The relocation of a local company
(B) The expansion of the apartment complex
(C) The construction of an office complex
(D) The remodeling of a shopping center

무엇에 관한 방송인가?
지역 회사 이전
아파트 단지 확장
사무실 단지 건설
쇼핑센터 리모델링

해설 새로운 사무실 단지 공사를 시작한다고 했으므로(McBrayer Developers has announced that a new office complex will begin its construction in Leeds.) 정답은 (C)가 된다.

17 세부정보 – 언급

What is mentioned about the project?
(A) It has yet to receive proper permits.
(B) It will commence this week.
(C) It will be finished in a year.
(D) It is located in the outskirts of the city.

프로젝트에 관해 언급된 것은 무엇인가?
적합한 허가서를 아직 받지 못했다.
이번 주에 시작할 것이다.
일 년 후에 끝날 것이다.
교외에 위치할 것이다.

해설 공사가 완공되는 데 1년 정도 걸린다고 했으므로(the construction will take around a year to complete) 정답은 (C)가 된다.

18 세부정보 – 특정 사실

What advantage of the project does the speaker mention?
(A) Business activity will increase.
(B) A city's population will grow.
(C) A city will receive more funding.
(D) More jobs will be created.

화자가 언급하는 프로젝트의 이점은 무엇인가?
비즈니스 활동이 증가할 것이다.
도시의 인구가 증가할 것이다.
시가 더 많은 예산을 받을 것이다.
더 많은 고용이 창출될 것이다.

해설 그 지역주민에게 희소식이 되는 이유는 프로젝트가 지역 경제를 향상시킬 것이라는 기대 때문이므로(This news is welcomed by Leeds residents, as the complex is projected to boost the local economy.) 정답은 (A)가 된다.

1 동사의 자리

The time needed to obtain all relevant skills ------- on numerous elements.

(A) depend **(B) depends**
(C) depending (D) to depend

모든 관련된 기술을 얻기 위해 필요한 시간은 여러 가지 요소에 달려있다.

해설 빈칸은 문장의 동사 자리로 주어는 The time 단수이므로 동사는 단수 동사인 (B)가 정답이다. needed는 앞에 나오는 The time을 수식하는 자리로 들어갔으므로 문장의 동사로 착각하지 않도록 조심하자.

어휘 relevant 관련된 | numerous 많은

2 명사의 자리

------- to William Street is expected to be limited to one lane when the road construction project starts next June.

(A) Access (B) Accessing
(C) Accesses (D) Accessible

도로 공사 프로젝트가 다음 6월에 시작되면 윌리엄 가로의 접근은 1차선으로 제한될 예정이다.

해설 빈칸은 주어 자리이자 명사 자리로 (A), (B), (C)가 답이 될 수 있다. is라는 단수 동사가 나오므로 (C)는 오답이 되며, (B)의 경우는 access가 타동사이므로 뒤에 to가 나오지 말아야 하므로 정답은 (A)가 된다.

어휘 road construction 도로 공사

3 어휘-동사

The international sales department has ------- valuable to our operations overseas since its foundation five years ago.

(A) proved (B) searched
(C) told (D) achieved

5년 전에 해외영업부가 설립된 이래로, 우리의 해외 사업이 가치 있음을 증명했다.

해설 빈칸은 동사 자리로 뒤에 valuable이라는 형용사를 취하는 2형식 동사를 찾는 자리로 정답은 (A)가 된다. (B)의 경우 search for '~를 찾다', (C), (D)의 경우는 타동사이므로 뒤에 목적어인 명사 형태가 와야 한다.

어휘 international sales department 해외영업부 | valuable 귀중한 | overseas 해외 | foundation 창립

4 어휘-부사

For safety reasons, a city official must inspect your newly built restaurant ------- before allowing you to open for business.

(A) powerfully (B) extremely
(C) solidly **(D) thoroughly**

안정상의 이유로, 시 공무원은 개업을 허가하기 이전에 새로 지은 레스토랑을 철저하게 검사해야 한다.

해설 부사 어휘 문제로 빈칸 앞까지는 완전한 문장이다. 완전한 문장 뒤에 부사는 가까운 동사인 inspect를 수식하므로 해석상 '철저하게 점검 / 검사하다'의 의미가 되어야 하므로 정답은 (D)가 된다. 자칫 해석에 의존해서 (B)를 하는 경우가 있는데, (B)는 형용사 / 부사만 수식하는 부사이다.

어휘 for safety reasons 안전상의 이유로 | city official 시 공무원 | newly built 새로 지은 | powerfully 강력하게 | extremely 극도로 | solidly 확고하게 | thoroughly 철저하게

5 명사의 자리

Due to urgent road repairs, drivers must use ------- when driving on Highway 25.

(A) cautious (B) cautiously
(C) cautioned **(D) caution**

긴급한 도로 공사 때문에, 운전자들은 고속도로 25를 운전할 때 조심해야 한다.

해설 빈칸은 use라는 타동사의 목적어 자리로 명사인 (D)가 적합하다. 동사 뒤라고 해서 (B)를 고르지 않도록 조심하자. use / exercise caution은 '조심하다'로 암기해두자.

어휘 urgent 긴급한 | use / exercise caution 조심하다

6 부사의 자리

The conversation with Mr. Davidson was ------- *Biznet Magazine*'s best interview of the year.

(A) easy (B) easiest

(C) easily (D) easing

데이빗슨 씨와의 대화는 분명히 올해 〈비즈넷 매거진〉에서 한 최고의 인터뷰였다.

해설 빈칸을 빼도 완전한 문장이므로 정답은 부사인 (C)가 된다. 자칫, 동사 was 뒤라고 해서 형용사를 고르지 않도록 조심한다. 이때 easily는 '쉽게'가 아닌, 「easily + 최상급」 '분명히, 최고의, 가장 좋은' 등으로 쓰이니 명심해두자.

어휘 easily + **최상급** 분명히, 최고의

7 어휘-부사

Even though his presentation is long and detailed, Travis Kim thinks viewers will ------- find it interesting.

(A) still (B) quite

(C) too (D) ever

트래비스 킴의 프레젠테이션이 길고 상세했음에도 불구하고, 그는 청중들이 여전히 재미있었을 거라고 생각한다.

해설 빈칸은 부사 자리로 해석상 '여전히'의 의미인 (A) still을 정답으로 고를 수 있지만, although, even though, in spite of, despite라는 양보를 나타내는 전치사 / 접속사의 경우 '~에도 불구하고 여전히 ~ 하다'의 의미로 잘 쓰이므로, 문장 앞에 even though를 보고 still을 정답으로 처리해도 좋다.

어휘 informative 유익한 | quite 꽤

8 어휘-동사

The conference organizers will ------- all attendees with complimentary lunch and refreshments.

(A) offer (B) donate

(C) provide (D) suggest

회의 주최 측에서 무료 점심과 다과를 모든 참석자들에게 제공할 것이다.

해설 빈칸은 동사 자리로 해석상 '제공하다'의 의미가 적합하므로 정답은 (A)와 (C)가 될 수 있다. 하지만, 이 문장은 provide somebody with something 구조이므로 정답은 (C)가 된다.

어휘 attendee 참석자 | complimentary 공짜의 | refreshment 다과

9 부사의 자리

According to the annual employee questionnaire, morale at the JTB Toy factory has become ------- better over the last three years.

(A) progresses (B) progressive

(C) progressing **(D) progressively**

매년 직원 설문조사에 따르면, JTB 장난감 공장 직원들의 사기가 지난 3년간에 걸쳐서 점진적으로 좋아졌다.

해설 become이라는 2형식 동사의 보어로 형용사가 온다고 해서 (B)를 고르지 않도록 조심하자. 빈칸 뒤에는 이미 형용사 good의 비교급인 better가 2형식 동사 become의 보어 자리에 왔으므로 뒤의 빈칸에는 형용사를 꾸미는 부사가 필요하다. 따라서, 정답은 (D)가 된다.

어휘 questionnaire 설문조사 | morale 사기 | progressively 점진적으로

10 어휘-명사

Ms. Adeel, HR director at Roxen Inc., considers punctuality an important ------- for all newly hired employees to have.

(A) device (B) type

(C) action **(D) trait**

락센 사의 인사부장인 아딜 씨는 시간 엄수를 신입 직원들이 가져야 하는 중요한 특성이라고 생각한다.

해설 빈칸은 명사 어휘 자리로 5형식 동사 consider의 목적격 보어 자리이다. 목적격 보어 자리의 명사는 앞의 목적어와 동격이 되어야 하므로 punctuality '시간 엄수'와 동격의 어휘를 찾으면 된다. 해석상 '특성'이라는 의미의 (D)가 답이다.

어휘 punctuality 시간 엄수 | device 장치 | trait 특성

11 동사-수 / 시제 / 태

Although only department managers were required to attend, Ms. Salito ------- all staff members to come to last week's meeting.

(A) to have urged **(B) had urged**
(C) will have urged (D) was urged

비록 부서장들만 참석할 의무가 있었지만, 살리토 씨는 모든 직원들에게 지난 주 미팅에 참석하라고 요구했다.

해설 빈칸은 동사 자리로 수, 시제, 태를 따져서 문제를 푼다. 일단 동사 자리에 들어가지 못하는 (A)는 오답이고, last week라는 명백한 과거가 나오므로 (C) 또한 오답이 된다. (D)의 경우는 빈칸 뒤에 목적어가 나와 있으므로 수동태가 올 수 없기 때문에 오답이다. 따라서, 정답은 (B)가 된다.

어휘 require 요구하다 | urge 촉구하다

12 어휘-동사

Before deciding to invest in the property market, Ms. Min ------- that Mr. Xian consider the potential risks more carefully.

(A) requested (B) announced
(C) reported (D) notified

부동산 시장에 투자하는 것을 결정하기 전에, 민 씨는 시안 씨에게 잠재적 위험요소를 더 신중히 고려하라고 요청했다.

해설 빈칸은 동사 어휘 문제로 자칫 잘못하면 (B)를 고를 수 있는데, that절의 Mr. Xian 다음에 동사원형인 consider가 온 것을 보고 should가 생략된 것임을 알 수 있다. 보기에서 주장 / 요구 / 명령 / 추천 / 제안 동사를 찾으면 되며, 정답은 (A)가 된다.

어휘 invest in ~에 투자하다 | property market 부동산 시장 | potential 잠재적인 | risk 위기

13 동사 시제

Our experienced accountants offer solutions to help companies like yours ------- issues that may affect a company's success.

(A) address (B) addressed
(C) can address (D) are addressing

우리의 경험이 풍부한 회계사들은 귀하의 회사처럼 회사의 성공에 영향을 미칠 수 있는 문제들을 해결할 수 있도록 도와줄 수 있는 해결책을 제공합니다.

해설 빈칸 뒤의 issues를 수식하는 형용사 자리로 착각해서 (B)를 고르지 않도록 조심하자. 빈칸은 앞에 나온 help라는 준사역동사에 걸리는 목적격 보어 자리로 「help + 목적어 + to부정사 / 동사원형」을 나타내는 to address 또는 address가 와야 하므로 정답은 (A)가 된다.

어휘 accountant 회계사 | solution 해결책 | address 다루다

14 어휘-형용사

The marketing manager was ------- of the team members' efforts to make the new advertising campaign a success.

(A) willing **(B) appreciative**
(C) fulfilled (D) decisive

마케팅 부장은 새 광고캠페인의 성공을 거둔 팀원들의 노력에 감사했다.

해설 빈칸에는 be동사의 보어인 형용사가 와야하는 자리로 해석상 '~에 감사하다'의 의미가 적합하므로 정답은 (B)가 된다.

어휘 be willing to 기꺼이 ~하다 | be appreciative of ~에 감사하다 | fulfill 이행하다 | decisive 결단력 있는

15 부사의 자리

The advertisement team's ideas were presented so ------- that the clients have already agreed to work with us.

(A) skill (B) skilled
(C) skillful **(D) skillfully**

광고팀의 아이디어가 너무 훌륭해서 고객들은 벌써 우리와 함께 일하기로 합의했다.

해설 「so + 형용사 / 부사 + that」으로 '너무 ~ 해서 ~ 하다'의 의미가 되어야 하므로 형용사 / 부사인 (B), (C), (D)가 답이 될 수 있다. 보기에서 형용사 / 부사를 빨리 구분하는 방법은 앞의 동사이다. 앞의 동사가 be동사이면 형용사, 일반동사이면 부사가 와야 한다. 앞의 동사가 were presented라는 일반동사가 나왔으므로 정답은 부사인 (D)가 된다.

어휘 present 제시하다 | skillfully 능숙하게, 솜씨있게

16 어휘 - 동사

The recent survey indicates that most people ------- Sweet Candy's cookies very appetizing.

(A) find (B) feel
(C) take (D) like

최근 설문조사에서 많은 사람들이 스윗 캔디의 쿠키가 매우 맛있다고 생각한다고 나타난다.

해설 빈칸은 동사 자리로 빈칸 뒤에 목적어 cookies가 나오고 형용사 appetizing이 나오는 5형식 동사를 찾는 문제이다. 정답은 (A) find가 된다.

어휘 appetizing 입맛 당기는

17 형용사의 자리

In order to advertise your brands, please contact Macmore Inc., which specializes in ------- promotional merchandise.

(A) personally **(B) personalized**
(C) personality (D) personalizes

귀하의 브랜드를 광고하기 위해서, 맞춤화된 홍보상품을 전문적으로 하는 맥모어 사에 연락해 보세요.

해설 빈칸은 promotional을 수식하는 부사 자리로 생각하기 쉽지만, 명사 merchandise를 수식하는 형용사 자리다. 따라서, 정답은 (B)가 된다.

어휘 specialize in ~를 전문적으로 하다 | promotional 홍보의 | personalized 맞춤형의

18 어휘 - 동사

It is my great pleasure to ------- you that the new vice president will be appointed by the board of directors.

(A) announce (B) mention
(C) inform (D) say

새 부사장이 이사진에 의해 선출되리라는 것을 알려드리게 되어 기쁩니다.

해설 동사 어휘 문제로 (A), (B), (D)는 목적어로 that을 취할 수 있지만, (C)는 사람 다음에 that을 취하는 4형식 동사이므로 정답은 (C)가 된다.

어휘 vice president 부사장 | appoint 임명하다 | the board of directors 이사진

19 어휘 - 부사

Applications from potential candidates remain active for ten years and ------- are kept in our filing system.

(A) thereafter (B) instead
(C) unless (D) rather

유력한 지원자들의 지원서는 10년간 유효하며 그 이후에 기록 시스템에 보관될 것입니다.

해설 빈칸을 빼고도 이미 완전한 문장이므로, 빈칸에는 부사가 와야 한다. 해석상 순접의 의미인 (A)가 정답이 된다.

어휘 filing system 기록 시스템 | thereafter 그 후에

20 부사의 자리

GDX Inc. will try to attract a lot of potential buyers by ------- advertising its Web site.

(A) effective **(B) effectively**
(C) more effective (D) most effective

GDX 사는 그 회사의 웹사이트를 효과적으로 광고함으로써 많은 잠재 고객들을 유치하려고 노력할 것이다.

해설 빈칸 뒤의 동명사 advertising을 수식하는 부사가 필요하므로 정답은 (B)가 된다.

어휘 potential buyer 잠재 고객 | effectively 효과적으로

1 명사의 자리

The excellent service and food are the ------- gourmets flock to this restaurant.

(A) reasonable (B) reasoning
(C) reasoned **(D) reason**

훌륭한 서비스와 음식이 미식가들이 이 식당으로 모여드는 이유이다.

해설 gourmets라는 명사를 수식한다고 형용사인 (A)를 고르지 않도록 조심하자. 빈칸은 the라는 한정사 뒤의 명사 자리이며, gourmets부터 restaurant까지는 앞의 빈칸을 수식하는 역할을 한다. the reason (why) gourmets flock~으로 중간에 why가 생략된 문장 구조로 이해하면 된다. 따라서, 정답은 (D)가 된다.

어휘 gourmet 미식가 | flock 떼; 모이다 | reasonable 합리적인 | reason 이유

2 동사-수 / 시제 / 태

For the past 10 years, Olive Tech. ------- approximately 3,000 books to the public libraries.

(A) will be donated (B) is donated
(C) was donated **(D) has donated**

지난 10년 동안에, 올리브 테크는 공공도서관에 대략 3,000권의 책을 기증해왔다.

해설 빈칸은 동사 자리로 수, 시제, 태를 고려한다. 문장 맨 앞의 for the past 10 years는 현재완료와 잘 사용되므로 정답은 (D)가 된다. 설사 현재완료와 잘 쓰이는 시간 어구를 모른다고 해도, 나머지 보기는 수동태 형태로 빈칸 뒤에 books라는 명사가 나오므로 들어갈 수가 없다.

어휘 approximately 대략 | donate 기부하다

3 전치사

------- recent system errors, the Finance Department completed the next year's budget ahead of schedule.

(A) Although (B) Whereas
(C) Notwithstanding (D) Moreover

최근의 시스템 오류에도 불구하고, 회계부서는 예상보다 빨리 내년 예산을 끝냈다.

해설 빈칸은 명사 앞에 들어가는 전치사 문제로, (A)와 (B)는 접속사이고, (D)는 접속부사이다. 굳이 해석하지 않더라도 나머지 보기는 탈락이 되어 정답은 (C)가 된다.

어휘 system error 시스템 오류 | ahead of schedule 예상보다 빨리 | notwithstanding ~에도 불구하고

4 동사-수 / 시제 / 태

After taking a vacation for two weeks, Ms. Apana ------- to her office on September 9.

(A) returning **(B) returned**
(C) was returned (D) to return

아파나 씨는 2주 동안의 휴가를 끝낸 후, 9월 9일에 사무실로 복귀했다.

해설 빈칸은 동사 자리로 동사 자리에 들어갈 수 없는 (A)와 (D)는 오답이다. 이때 조심해야 할 것이 빈칸 뒤에 전치사가 나오므로 보통은 수동태가 오지만, 전치사를 동반하는 자동사도 들어갈 수 있다. return의 경우 return to '돌아오다'의 의미인 자동사로도 쓰이며, return '반납하다'의 의미인 타동사로도 사용된다. 해석상 '복귀하다'라는 의미가 적합하므로 정답은 (B)가 된다.

어휘 take a vacation 휴가를 얻다 | return to ~에 돌아오다

5 부사절 접속사

------- Ms. Choi returns from her trip in Tokyo, the weekly department meeting will resume.

(A) That **(B) Once**
(C) As well (D) Then

일단 최 씨가 그녀의 도쿄 출장에서 돌아오면, 주간 부서 회의가 재개될 것이다.

해설 빈칸은 주어(Ms. Choi)와 동사(returns) 앞에 들어가는 접속사 자리이다. 주절의 시제가 will resume으로 미래 시제라고 할지라도 종속절의 시제는 returns로 현재 동사를 쓰는 시간 / 조건의 부사절 접속사가 필요하다. 해석상 '일단 ~하면'이 적합하므로 정답은 (B)가 된다.

어휘 weekly 매주의

6 어휘 - 동사

Mr. Carlton from Piwan Inc. will be using conference room C while he ------- the company's market research data.

(A) specializes (B) proceeds
(C) responds **(D) compiles**

피완 사의 칼턴 씨는 회사의 시장 조사 데이터를 취합하는 동안에 회의실 C를 사용할 것입니다.

해설 동사 어휘 문제로, 해석도 중요하지만 자동사인지 타동사인지를 고려해야 한다. 빈칸 뒤에 목적어가 나오는 타동사를 찾는 자리인데, specialize in, proceed to / with, respond to와 같이 (A), (B), (C)는 자동사이므로 탈락이 되어 정답은 (D)가 된다.

어휘 proceed 진행하다 | compile 모으다, 편집하다

7 대명사의 자리

The position of office manager at PCS Inc. is highly recommended by a former colleague of -------, Ms. Jenkins.

(A) my (B) me
(C) mine (D) myself

PCS 사의 매니저 직책은 제 예전 직장 동료 중의 한 명인 젠킨스 씨에 의해 추천되었다.

해설 전치사 of 뒤라고 해서 목적격인 (B)를 고르지 않도록 조심하자. 내 친구 중 한 명, a friend of my friends(mine)를 생각하면 쉽게 답을 찾을 수가 있다. 정답은 (C)가 된다.

어휘 a colleague of mine 직장 동료 중의 하나

8 접속사

------- KCX Supermarket was founded in 1993, its sales have increased dramatically.

(A) Instead (B) While
(C) However **(D) Since**

KCX 슈퍼마켓이 1993년에 창립된 이래로, 판매가 급격하게 증가했다.

해설 빈칸은 주어 KCX Supermarket과 동사 was founded 앞에 들어가는 접속사 자리로 과거 시제와 현재완료 시제를 연결해 주는 역할을 하는 것이 보기에는 since밖에 없으므로 정답은 (D)가 된다. (A)와 (C)는 접속부사라 오답이 되고, (B)의 경우는 해석상 '~ 이래로'라는 의미가 와야 하므로 오답이 된다.

어휘 found 창립하다 | sale 판매 | increase dramatically 급격하게 증가하다

9 동사 - 수 / 시제 / 태

Ms. Suharman from the accounting department ------- the updated policy for travel expenses at tomorrow's meeting.

(A) will be addressed (B) had addressed
(C) is addressing (D) address

회계부서의 슈할만 씨는 내일 회의에서 여행 경비에 대한 업데이트된 정책을 다룰 예정입니다.

해설 빈칸은 동사 자리로 수, 시제, 태를 고려한다. 주어는 단수이고 시제는 tomorrow라는 명백한 미래를 나타내므로 (A)를 고르지 않도록 주의하자. 빈칸 뒤에는 policy라는 목적어가 나오므로 수동태는 오답이 된다. 정답은 '가까운 미래'를 나타내는 현재진행이 필요하므로 정답은 (C)가 된다.

어휘 accounting department 회계부서 | travel expense 여행 경비

10 전치사

All application forms and references for the marketing manager position must be postmarked ------- May 5 to be eligible.

(A) until (B) within
(C) before (D) recently

마케팅 부장 직책의 모든 지원서와 추천서는 자격 요건이 되기 위해서는 5월 5일 전까지 소인이 찍혀야 합니다.

해설 빈칸은 전치사 자리로, 해석하면 '5월 5일까지'라고 해서 (A)를 고르기 쉽지만, until은 지속적인 의미임에 반해 postmark는 완료의 의미를 가지는 동사이므로 by와 잘 어울린다. (B)의 경우에는 뒤에 기간이 나와야 하는데 5월 5일이라는 시점이 나왔기 때문에 오답이 되고, 결국 정답은 (C)가 된다.

어휘 reference 추천서 | postmark 소인을 찍다 | eligible ~할 자격이 있는

11 동사-수 / 시제 / 태

Bellevue Cookware's promotional offer ------- from March 31 until June 30.

(A) extends (B) extending
(C) extensive (D) extensively

벨뷰 쿡웨어의 할인 혜택은 3월 31일부터 6월 30일까지로 연장된다.

해설 빈칸은 동사 자리로 보기에서 동사는 (A)밖에 없다. offer를 동사로 착각하지 않도록 하자. 설사 offer가 동사라고 하더라도 앞에 주어가 없으며, offer에 대한 목적어도 없으므로 offer는 동사가 아닌 주어로 사용되었음을 알 수 있다.

어휘 extend 연장하다 | extensively 널리, 광범위하게

12 형용사 / 분사의 자리

Given the comfortable seats, overnight travel on the West Connect bus is never -------.

(A) tired (B) tires
(C) tiring (D) tiredly

편안한 좌석을 고려하면, 웨스트 커넥트 버스의 야간 여행은 결코 피곤하지 않다.

해설 빈칸에는 be동사의 보어 자리에 들어갈 수 있는 형용사 / 분사가 와야 한다. tire는 사람의 감정 동사로 주어가 사람일 때는 tired가 되어야 하는데, 주어가 overnight travel로 사람이 아니므로 정답은 tiring인 (C)가 된다.

어휘 given ~를 고려하면 | comfortable 편안한 | overnight 하룻밤 동안의

13 전치사

------- a newly designed system, Brooks Inc.'s profits will increase by 15 percent next year.

(A) Even though (B) Since
(C) Due to (D) Besides

새롭게 디자인된 시스템 때문에, 브룩스 사의 수익은 내년에 15퍼센트 인상될 것이다.

해설 system이라는 명사 앞에 들어가는 전치사 문제로, 해석상 '~ 때문에'가 적합하므로 (C)가 정답이 된다. (B)의 경우도 '때문에'라는 의미가 될 수 있지만, since가 '때문에'라는 의미로 사용될 때는 접속사로 사용되므로 오답이 된다.

어휘 profit 수익 | besides 게다가

14 어휘-구동사

Please ------- from playing loud music after midnight so as not to disturb neighbors in residential areas.

(A) refrain (B) emerge
(C) prohibit (D) differ

거주 지역의 이웃들에게 방해되지 않기 위해, 자정 이후에는 시끄러운 음악을 틀어놓는 것을 금합니다.

해설 '~을 금하다 / 삼가하다'의 의미가 되어야 하므로 정답 (A)가 된다. (C)의 경우는 prohibit A from B의 형태가 되어야 하므로 오답이 된다.

어휘 refrain from ~를 삼가다 | midnight 자정 | so as to ~하기 위해서 | disturb 방해하다 | residential area 거주 지역 | emerge 드러나다

15 접속사

------- Mr. Fahad is ready to make another order, Brig Office Supplies will have provided a new pricing chart.

(A) By the time (B) In order for
(C) So that (D) Moreover

파해드 씨가 또 다른 주문을 준비할 때쯤에, 브리그 사무용품은 새 가격 차트를 제공했을 것이다.

해설 주어(Mr. Fahad)와 동사(is) 앞에 들어가는 접속사 문제로, 주절의 시제가 미래완료(will have provided)라고 할지라도 종속절에 is라는 현재를 쓰는 접속사 by the time이 적합하므로 정답은 (A)가 된다.

어휘 pricing chart 가격 차트 | so that ~할 수 있도록 하기 위해서

16 동사-수 / 시제 / 태

The enclosed brochure contains detailed information Mr. Corson -------.

(A) correct (B) has been corrected
(C) to correct **(D) will correct**

동봉된 책자에는 콜슨 씨가 수정할 상세화된 정보가 포함되어 있다.

해설 빈칸은 동사 자리로 동사 자리에 들어갈 수 없는 (C)는 오답이 되며, 수일치로 (A) 또한 오답이다. 빈칸 뒤에 목적어가 없기 때문에 (B)를 고를 수 있는데, 이 문장은 detailed information (that) Mr. Corson이라고 해서 목적격 관계대명사 that이 생략된 구조이다. 따라서 뒤에는 불완전한 문장이 나와야 하며, 해석상으로도 '고칠 정보'이지 '고쳐지는 것'은 아니므로 정답은 (D)가 된다.

어휘 enclosed 동봉된 | detailed information 상세한 정보

17 대명사의 자리

When registering for the upcoming Modiva Expo in Hong Kong, be sure to help ------- to a name tag and brochure.

(A) you (B) your
(C) yours **(D) yourself**

다가오는 홍콩에서 개최될 모디바 엑스포에 등록할 때, 이름표와 책자를 챙겨가세요.

해설 타동사 help의 목적어 자리로, 명령문 be sure to의 주체가 you가 되면 '네가 너 자신을 돕는다'라는 의미인 재귀대명사의 재귀 용법이 필요하므로 정답은 (D)가 된다. 관용적인 표현으로 help yourself를 기억해두자.

어휘 help yourself ~하셔도 돼요 | name tag 이름표

18 접속사

Employees interested in attending the company excursion are asked to register by next Monday ------- we can prepare sufficient refreshments for all attendees.

(A) unless (B) in order to
(C) in case **(D) so that**

회사 야유회에 참석하는 데 관심 있는 직원들은 모든 참석자들을 위한 충분한 다과를 준비할 수 있도록 하기 위해서 다음 주 월요일까지 등록하셔야 합니다.

해설 주어(we)와 동사(can prepare) 앞에 들어가는 접속사 문제로 can / could / may라는 조동사와 잘 쓰여 '~할 수 있도록 하기 위해서'의 의미가 되는 (D)가 정답이 된다.

어휘 excursion 여행 | sufficient 충분한 | refreshment 다과 | in case ~인 경우를 대비하여

19 전치사 / 부사절 접속사

A recent survey indicates that some employees check their work-related e-mails regularly ------- on vacation.

(A) so that (B) during
(C) whether **(D) while**

최근 설문조사에 따르면, 몇몇 직원들은 휴가 기간에도 회사 관련된 이메일을 정기적으로 체크하는 것으로 나타났다.

해설 '휴가 기간'에라는 표현으로 while on vacation이라고 쓴다. during을 고르지 않도록 조심하자. 이와 비슷한 표현으로는 while on duty '근무 기간에', while aboard the aircraft '비행기 탑승 동안에'라는 표현이 있다.

어휘 work-related 업무와 관련된 | while on vacation 휴가 기간에

20 동사-수 / 시제 / 태

Mr. Alfredo recently ------- Employee of the Year due to his outstanding achievements.

(A) named **(B) was named**
(C) is named (D) has named

알프레도 씨는 그의 훌륭한 성과로 인해 올해의 직원으로 명명되었다.

해설 빈칸은 동사 자리로 recently라는 부사는 과거 시제 또는 현재완료 시제와 잘 쓰인다. name은 5형식 동사로 수동태로 쓰여도 동사 뒤에 목적어인 명사가 올 수 있다. 또한, 해석상 '명명되다'라는 의미가 적합하므로 정답은 (B)가 된다. (D)의 경우는 has been named가 적합하다.

어휘 name 명명하다 | Employee of the year 올해의 직원 | outstanding 뛰어난

1 현재분사 / 과거분사

Monetary contributions ------- by Hartford Co. will be given to charities throughout the city.

(A) generating **(B) generated**
(C) have generated (D) are generating

하트퍼드 사의 기부는 도시 전역의 자선 단체에 주어질 것입니다.

해설 이미 will be given이라는 동사가 나와 있으므로 (C)와 (D)는 오답인다. 빈칸에는 앞의 contributions라는 명사를 수식하는 분사가 와야 하고 뒤에 by라는 전치사가 나오므로 정답은 (B)가 된다.

어휘 monetary 화폐의, 통화의 | contribution 공헌 | charity 자선 | generate 만들어내다

2 대명사의 자리

The customer service center called Mr. Schwartz yesterday to tell him that the camera ------- ordered is not available until next week.

(A) he (B) that
(C) were (D) until

고객서비스 센터에서 어제 슈바르츠 씨에게 전화를 걸어 그가 주문했던 카메라가 다음 주까지 없다고 말했다.

해설 이미 문장의 동사가 called와 is가 나와 있으므로 (C)의 경우는 오답이며, (B)의 경우는 빈칸 앞의 the camera를 수식할 수 있지만 그렇게 되면 수동의 의미가 들어가야 해서 the camera that were ordered가 되어야 한다. 정답은 the camera (that) he ordered라고 해서 목적격 관계대명사 뒤에 들어가는 주어가 들어가야 하므로 정답은 (A)가 된다.

어휘 customer service center 고객서비스 센터

3 관계대명사의 자리

A recent survey has shown that those ------- regularly check food ingredients on labels are likely to be healthy.

(A) what (B) where
(C) who (D) when

최근 설문조사에 따르면 라벨에 있는 음식 재료를 정기적으로 체크하는 사람들은 건강할 가능성이 크다고 나타났다.

해설 빈칸에는 those라는 선행사를 받으면서 check 동사 앞에 들어가는 주격 관계대명사가 필요하므로 정답은 (C)가 된다. 평소에 '~하는 사람들'이라고 해서 those who 이렇게 암기하면 좀 더 빨리 답을 찾을 수가 있다.

어휘 ingredient 재료 | be likely to ~할 것 같다 | healthy 건강한

4 형용사의 자리, 현재분사 / 과거분사

Due to its proximity to the highway, Dayton could be a very ------- location to build a plant.

(A) offering (B) proposing
(C) promising (D) identifying

고속도로의 접근성 때문에, 데이턴은 공장을 지을 매우 유망한 장소가 될 수 있다.

해설 location을 수식하는 형용사 / 분사 문제로 (A), (B), (D)가 들어갈 경우 수동의 개념이므로 p.p.형태로 들어가야 한다. 해석상 '유망한'이라는 의미가 적합하므로, 정답은 (C)가 된다.

어휘 proximity to ~에 대한 접근성 | promising location 유망한 지역

5 관계대명사의 자리

Mr. Rudriguez will send a copy of the presentation ------- the marketing manager gave at the meeting last week.

(A) then (B) what
(C) that (D) when

루드리구에즈 씨는 지난주 마케팅 부장이 했던 프레젠테이션 사본을 보낼 것이다.

해설 a copy of the presentation을 수식하는 관계대명사 문제로, 빈칸 뒤에 타동사 gave의 목적어가 없기 때문에 빈칸에는 목적격 관계대명사가 들어가야 하므로 정답은 (C)가 된다.

어휘 send a copy 사본을 보내다

6 현재분사 / 과거분사

When ------- prospective candidates, the interviewers need to ask as many questions as possible.
(A) interviewing (B) interviews
(C) interviewed (D) interview

전도유망한 지원자를 인터뷰할 때, 면접관은 가능한 한 많은 질문을 해볼 필요가 있다.

해설 접속사 When 뒤에 주어와 동사가 나와야 하지만, 없으면 분사 구문인 -ing나 p.p. 형태를 고른다. 빈칸 뒤에 prospective candidates라는 명사가 나와 있으므로 정답은 (A)가 되며, when -ing '~할 때'로 암기해두면 다음에 좀 더 쉽게 답을 찾을 수가 있다.

어휘 prospective 전도유망한 | interviewer 면접관

7 관계대명사의 자리

Mr. Parkston, ------- donations have helped build the new community center, will deliver a speech at the opening ceremony.
(A) who (B) whom
(C) whoever **(D) whose**

새 커뮤니티 센터를 건립하는 데 기부를 했던 파크스턴 씨가 개회식에서 연설할 것이다.

해설 빈칸은 앞에 Mr. Parkston이라는 선행사를 수식하면서 뒤에 donations라는 명사를 받는 소유격 관계대명사가 필요하므로 정답은 (D)가 된다.

어휘 donation 기부 | deliver a speech 연설하다 | opening ceremony 개회식

8 형용사의 자리, 현재분사 / 과거분사

The Hartford Photography Contest will provide an ------- deadline for candidates who were not able to submit their entries.
(A) extensive (B) extends
(C) extension **(D) extended**

하트퍼드 포토그래피 대회는 출품작을 제출할 수 없었던 지원자들을 위해 연장된 마감 시간을 제공할 것이다.

해설 빈칸은 deadline이라는 명사를 수식하는 형용사 / 분사 자리로 (A) 또는 (D)가 답이 될 수 있다. 보통 형용사가 답이 되는 경우가 많으나 해석상 '광범위한 마감 시간'이 아니라 '연장된 마감 시간'이라는 말이 적합하므로 정답은 (D)가 된다.

어휘 extensive 광범위한 | extended 연장된

9 관계대명사의 자리

We had a series of workshops with five speakers yesterday, most of ------- are renowned in the field.
(A) who (B) them
(C) that **(D) whom**

우리는 어제 다섯 명의 연사들과 일련의 워크숍을 가졌고, 그 연사들의 대부분은 그 분야에서 유명한 사람들이다.

해설 문장에서 had와 are라는 두 개의 동사가 나오므로 접속사 역할을 하는 (A)와 (D)가 가능하다. (C)의 경우는 전치사 다음에 나올 수가 없으므로 오답이 된다. of라는 전치사의 목적어인 목적격이 들어가야 하므로 정답은 (D)가 된다.

어휘 a series of 일련의 | renowned 유명한

10 분사 자리

Any staff members ------- in joining the fitness program should complete an enrollment form by next Friday.
(A) interest (B) interests
(C) interesting **(D) interested**

헬스장에 등록하시는 데 관심 있으신 직원들은 다음 주 금요일까지 등록서를 작성하셔야 합니다.

해설 빈칸은 앞에 Any staff members라는 명사를 수식하는 분사 자리로 뒤에 전치사 in이 나와 있으므로 p.p. 형태인 (D)가 답이 된다.

어휘 enrollment form 등록서

11 부사

Technicians at BYF Inc. take ongoing safety training sessions, ------- fulfilling the company's requirements.

(A) throughout (B) between
(C) thereby (D) such as

BYF 사의 기술자들은 정기적으로 진행 중인 안전 교육을 듣고, 그렇게 함으로써 회사의 요구사항을 이행한다.

해설 「주어 + 동사, thereby -ing」 형태의 '~함으로, ~하면서'라는 의미를 나타내는 (C)가 정답이다.

어휘 ongoing 진행 중인 | safety training session 안전 교육 | fulfill 이행하다 | thereby 그렇게 함으로써

12 어휘 - 관용 표현

Unless instructed -------, all employees should turn off electronic devices like computers and fax machines at the end of each workday.

(A) indeed (B) meanwhile
(C) accordingly **(D) otherwise**

별다른 지시사항이 없으면, 모든 직원들은 매일 모든 일이 끝나고 나서 모든 컴퓨터와 팩스기 같은 전자 장치를 다 꺼야 한다.

해설 분사 구문의 관용 표현으로 '별다른 지시사항이 없으면'이라는 의미를 나타내는 unless instructed otherwise가 적합하므로 정답은 (D)가 된다.

어휘 unless instructed otherwise 별다른 지시 사항이 없으면 | turn off 끄다 | meanwhile 그동안에 | accordingly 따라서

13 명사절 접속사

When applying for a managerial position, make sure that you understand ------- the job involves.

(A) which **(B) what**
(C) how (D) when

관리직에 지원할 때, 그 직책이 어떤 것을 포함하고 있는지 잘 알아야 한다.

해설 빈칸은 understand라는 타동사의 목적어 자리로 뒤에 the job involves라는 주어, 동사를 가지는 명사절 접속사가 들어가야 한다. 타동사 involve의 목적어가 없는 불완전한 문장이 나오고 해석상 '~것'이라는 명사절은 보기에서 what밖에 없으므로 정답은 (B)가 된다.

어휘 managerial position 관리직

14 분사 구문

------- met this week's sales goals, all sales associates in PCA Publishing received a $100 gift certificate.

(A) Being (B) To have
(C) Having (D) To be

이번 주 판매 목표를 달성했기에, 모든 PCA 출판사 영업 직원들은 100달러 상품권을 받았다.

해설 빈칸 뒤에 sales goals라는 목적어가 나오므로 수동 형태인 be p.p.가 들어가면 안 되기 때문에 (A)와 (D)는 오답이 되며, 해석상 '~하기 위해서'라는 의미가 아니므로 (B) 또한 오답이 된다. 주절의 상품권을 받은 것과 판매 목표에 도달한 것의 시제 차이가 나므로 having p.p.가 정답이 된다.

어휘 sales goal 판매 목표 | sales associate 판매 직원 | gift certificate 상품권

15 관계부사

Mrs. Robinson chose the place ------- the company will hold its 20th anniversary.

(A) where (B) which
(C) until (D) during

로빈슨 씨는 회사가 20주년 기념식을 할 장소를 선택했다.

해설 chose와 will hold라는 2개의 동사가 나오므로 빈칸에는 접속사가 와야 한다. 빈칸 앞의 the place를 수식하고 뒤에 완전한 문장이 나오는 관계부사가 적합하므로 정답은 (A)가 된다.

어휘 hold 개최하다

16 형용사의 자리, 현재분사 / 과거분사

The founder of Rocco Services, Mr. Lester, always stresses that the primary goal of the company is to keep customers -------.

(A) satisfied (B) satisfyingly
(C) satisfaction (D) satisfying

로코 서비스의 창립자인 레스터 씨는 항상 고객들이 만족되는 것이 회사의 주목적이라고 강조한다.

해설 빈칸은 5형식 동사 keep의 목적격 보어 자리로 형용사 / 분사가 들어가야 하며 해석상 '고객들이 만족되는 것'이 되어야 하므로 정답은 (A)가 된다.

어휘 founder 창립자 | stress 강조하다 | primary goal 주목적

17 분사 구문

According to the recently released survey, most customers respond to the questions regarding their shopping habits, ------- to spend more money online.

(A) prefer **(B) preferring**
(C) preferred (D) preference

최근에 나온 설문조사에 따르면, 대부분의 고객들은 쇼핑 습관에 관한 질문에 대한 응답으로, 온라인상에서 돈을 더 소비하는 것을 선호하는 것으로 나타났다.

해설 「주어 + 동사, -ing / p.p.」의 구조로 빈칸에는 분사 구문이 와야 한다. 빈칸 뒤의 to는 전치사가 아닌 to부정사의 to이고, prefer의 주체는 most customers이므로 능동의 형태인 (B)가 정답이 된다.

어휘 shopping habit 쇼핑 습관

18 관계대명사

Fifteen buildings on Flamingo Road, five of ------- were over 100 years old, were recently remodeled.

(A) what **(B) which**
(C) them (D) these

플라밍고 로의 15개의 건물은 최근에 리모델링되었고, 그중 5개는 100년 정도 되었다.

해설 문장의 동사로 were가 두 번 나오므로 접속사가 필요하기 때문에 (C)와 (D)는 오답이 된다. 선행사로 Fifteen buildings가 나와 있으므로 (A) 역시 오답으로 정답은 (B)가 된다.

어휘 recently remodeled 최근에 리모델링된

19 형용사 / 분사의 자리

KG Consulting helps ------- retail owners to have a competitive advantage over other companies by offering business strategies.

(A) emerged **(B) emerging**
(C) emerge (D) emerges

KG 컨설팅은 최근에 사업을 시작한 소매상들에게 사업 전략을 제공함으로써 다른 회사보다 경쟁적 우위를 얻는 데 도움을 준다.

해설 명사 retail owners를 수식하는 형용사 / 분사 문제로 (A)와 (B)가 가능한데, emerge는 자동사로 p.p. 형태를 쓰지 못하므로 정답은 (B)가 된다. emerging을 하나의 형용사로 생각한다면 빠르게 답을 찾을 수 있다.

어휘 competitive advantage over ~보다 경쟁적 우위 | emerge 드러나다

20 형용사의 자리, 현재분사 / 과거분사

The building manager will explain the ------- paper recycling policy at the monthly meeting.

(A) revising (B) revision
(C) revised (D) revise

빌딩 관리자는 월례 미팅에서 수정된 종이 재활용 정책을 설명할 것이다.

해설 빈칸에는 명사 policy를 수식하는 형용사 / 분사가 들어가야 하므로 (A)와 (C)가 답이 될 수 있는데, 해석상 '수정된'이라는 수동의 개념이 들어가야 하므로 정답은 (C)가 된다.

어휘 paper recycling 종이 재활용 | revise 수정하다

1 동사-수 / 시제 / 태

Taking pictures during musical performances is strictly prohibited, so audiences ------- to turn off their cameras or mobile phones.

(A) had urged (B) will be urging
(C) were urging **(D) are urged**

뮤지컬 공연 중에 사진을 찍는 것은 엄격히 금하므로 청중들은 카메라 혹은 휴대폰을 꺼야 한다.

해설 빈칸은 동사 자리로 수, 시제, 태를 고려한다. urge는 대표적인 5형식 동사로 목적격 보어로 to부정사를 취하는데 목적어 없이 to부정사가 바로 나왔다는 것은 수동태 형태를 찾는 문제이므로 정답은 (D)가 된다.

어휘 strictly prohibit 엄격하게 금하다 | audience 청중 | urge 촉구하다

2 명사절 접속사

A recent poll indicates ------- the popularity of Mr. Han's latest film has been decreasing since the harsh reviews were revealed in the local newspaper.

(A) that (B) which
(C) what (D) those

최근 여론조사에서 한 씨의 최근 영화의 인기는 지역 신문에서 혹평이 나온 이래로 감소했다고 나타난다.

해설 빈칸은 뒤에 주어 동사가 나오므로 빈칸에는 접속사 역할을 하면서 타동사 indicate의 목적어가 될 수 있는 명사절 접속사가 와야 한다. 빈칸 뒤에 완전한 문장이 나오므로 완전한 문장을 이끄는 명사절 접속사 (A)가 답이 된다.

어휘 popularity 인기 | harsh review 혹평 | reveal 드러내다

3 비교급 강조 부사

Despite the inclement weather conditions, the shipment we ordered last week will arrive ------- earlier than expected.

(A) much (B) more
(C) as (D) like

악천후에도 불구하고, 지난주에 우리가 주문했던 수송품이 예상했던 것보다 매우 일찍 도착할 것이다.

해설 빈칸 뒤에 than이 나온다고 해서 (B)를 고르지 않도록 조심하자. 이미 earlier라는 비교급이 나와 있으므로 more를 쓰지 않는다. 빈칸은 비교급 earlier를 강조하는 부사인 much가 들어가야 하므로 정답은 (A)가 된다.

어휘 inclement weather condition 악천후

4 명사절 접속사

The department supervisor should explicitly state ------- is in charge of assigning a new task.

(A) when (B) everything
(C) who (D) some

부서장은 새 업무를 분장하는 일을 누가 책임질 것인지를 명료하게 명시해야 한다.

해설 should state와 is라는 두 개의 동사가 나왔으므로 접속사인 (A)와 (C)가 가능하며, 타동사 state의 목적어 자리에 오는 명사절 접속사를 찾는 문제이다. when의 경우는 뒤에 완전한 문장이 나와야 하는데, is로 시작하는 불완전한 문장이므로 (C)가 정답이다.

어휘 department supervisor 부서장 | explicitly 명쾌하게 | state 명시하다 | assign 배정하다

5 명사절 접속사

------- Carlton's newly released song will be as enthusiastically received as his previous one remains to be seen.

(A) As though **(B) Whether**
(C) Regarding (D) Moreover

칼튼의 새롭게 발표된 노래가 이전의 노래만큼 열렬한 반응을 얻을지는 두고 봐야 한다.

해설 문장의 동사는 will be received와 remains to be seen으로 접속사가 필요해서 전치사인 (C)와 접속부사 (D)는 오답이 된다. 동사 remains to be seen의 주어 자리에 들어가는 명사절 접속사를 찾는 문제이므로 정답은 (B)가 된다.

어휘 whether ~ remains to be seen ~인지 아닌지 두고 봐야 한다 | enthusiastically 열광적으로

6 to부정사

Sales representatives should remind customers ------- the device cautiously before purchasing it.

(A) handling (B) handled
(C) to handle (D) handles

영업 직원들은 고객들에게 장치를 구매하기 전에 조심스럽게 다룰 것을 상기시켜줘야 한다.

해설 remind는 목적어 다음에 to부정사 / of / that을 가지는 동사이므로 정답은 (C)가 된다.
어휘 sales representative 영업 직원 | cautiously 조심스럽게

7 명사절 접속사

KJ International Arts Festival will award the prize to ------- submission gets the most votes from the judges.

(A) some **(B) whichever**
(C) these (D) whoever

KJ 국제 미술 축제는 어느 출품작이든 심사위원으로부터 가장 득표를 많이 받은 출품작에 상을 줄 것이다.

해설 will award와 gets라는 두 개의 동사가 나오므로 접속사인 (B)와 (D)가 정답이 될 수 있다. whoever의 경우는 anyone who와 같아서 whoever 뒤에 동사가 들어가야 하는데 submission이라는 명사가 왔으므로 오답이 된다. 따라서, (B)가 답이 된다. 또 다른 방법으로는 to라는 전치사의 목적어 자리에 들어가는 명사절 접속사로 뒤에 명사 submission을 받은 'whichever + 명사' 형태가 들어가야 하므로 정답이 (B)가 된다.
어휘 award a prize 상을 주다 | submission 출품작 | vote 투표(하다) | judge 심사위원

8 비교급과 최상급의 기본 형태

Sakamoto Footwear produces its ------- handmade leather boots of any manufacturer in Italy.

(A) finely **(B) finest**
(C) finer (D) fine

사카모토 신발은 이탈리아에서 다른 어떤 제조업체들 중에서도 최고의 핸드메이드 가죽 부츠를 생산한다.

해설 빈칸 뒤에 명사가 나와서 빈칸에는 형용사가 들어가야 하며, 앞에 its라는 소유격이 있으므로 뒤에는 최상급이 들어가야 하기 때문에 (B)가 정답이 된다. 최상급 앞에 들어갈 수 있는 the / 소유격 / 's를 잘 기억해 두자.
어휘 leather 가죽

9 접속사

------- is interested in joining this year's Christmas party should speak to Mr. Chen in the marketing department.

(A) Whoever (B) Anyone
(C) Them (D) Some

올해 크리스마스 파티에 참석하는 데 관심 있는 누구라도 마케팅 부서의 첸 씨에게 이야기하셔야 합니다.

해설 문장에 is interested와 should speak라는 두 개의 동사가 나오므로 접속사가 필요하고, 보기에서 접속사는 (A)밖에 없다. 또한, whoever는 anyone who와 같은데 해석상으로도 자연스러우므로 정답은 (A)가 된다.
어휘 whoever 누구든지

10 명사절 접속사

The safety manual explains ------- new technicians need to know about handling hazardous materials.

(A) which (B) where
(C) how **(D) what**

안전 설명서는 새로운 기술자들이 위험한 물질을 다루는 데 있어서 알아야 할 필요가 있는 것을 설명한다.

해설 타동사 explain의 목적어 자리에 들어가는 명사절 접속사를 찾는 문제인데, know라는 타동사의 목적어가 나와 있지 않으므로 불완전한 문장이다. 뒤에 불완전한 문장이 나오고 '~것'이라고 해석이 되는 정답은 (D)가 된다.
어휘 safety manual 안전 설명서 | technician 기술자 | hazardous 위험한

11 어휘-구동사

Please note that a special request for an ocean view room is ------- to availability at the time of check-in.

(A) current (B) likely

(C) subject (D) standard

바다 전망 방에 대한 특별 요청은 체크인할 당시의 이용 가능성에 따라 달라짐을 알아두세요.

해설 해석상 '~에 영향을 받기 쉽다'가 되어야 하므로 정답은 (C)가 된다.

어휘 be subject to ~에 영향을 받기 쉽다

12 전치사

Additional information ------- to the upcoming workshop next week was emailed to those who had expressed interest in participating.

(A) granted **(B) pertaining**

(C) receiving (D) similar

다음 주에 있을 다가오는 워크숍에 관한 추가적인 정보는 참석에 관심을 표현하신 분들에게 이메일로 보내드렸습니다.

해설 빈칸은 명사 upcoming workshop 앞에 들어가는 전치사 문제로 해석상 '~에 관한'이란 의미가 적합하므로 정답은 (B)가 된다.

어휘 pertaining to ~에 관하여 | express interest in ~에 관심을 표현하다 | grant 주다

13 명사절 접속사

Of all the bids submitted by various contractors, it can be difficult to choose ------- would best meet the company's budget.

(A) when (B) why

(C) which (D) where

여러 명의 계약업자들이 제출한 모든 입찰 중에서 회사의 예산에 가장 충족할 수 있는 것이 어느 것인지를 선택하는 것은 어려울 수 있다.

해설 타동사 choose의 목적어 자리에 들어가는 명사절 접속사로 뒤에 불완전한 문장을 가지는 것은 (C)밖에 없다. (A), (B), (D)의 경우는 뒤에 완전한 문장이 나오므로 오답이 된다.

어휘 bid 입찰 | various 많은 | contractor 계약업자

14 동명사

In addition to ------- residential complexes, Harim Construction also builds commercial buildings.

(A) construct **(B) constructing**

(C) construction (D) constructed

하림 건설은 주거 단지를 건설하는 것 이외에도, 상가 단지도 짓는다.

해설 in addition to에 to는 전치사의 to이므로 뒤에 명사 혹은 동명사 -ing가 온다. 빈칸 뒤의 residential complex를 목적어를 취하므로 동명사인 (B)가 답이 된다.

어휘 in addition to ~에 더하여 | residential complex 주거 단지 | commercial 상업의

15 명사절 접속사

The fact ------- the local farmers expanded their land area by 10 percent last year was surprising.

(A) because **(B) that**

(C) which (D) unless

그 지역 농부들이 작년에 땅을 10퍼센트 확장했다는 사실은 놀라웠다.

해설 '~라는 사실'이라는 the fact that을 기억하자. 이때 that은 명사절 동격의 that이므로 정답은 (B)가 된다.

어휘 the fact that ~라는 사실 | expand 확장하다

16 동사-수 / 시제 / 태

The primary goal of the customer service center ------- all customer inquiries and complaints in a timely manner.

(A) had addressed **(B) is to address**
(C) is addressed (D) address

고객 서비스 센터의 중요한 주목적은 모든 고객들의 요구와 불만을 시기적절하게 다루는 것이다.

해설 문장의 주어로 goal이 나왔을 때는 동사는 be to 구문을 사용하므로 정답은 (B)가 된다. goal / purpose / job / aim / objective / mission ~ be to로 암기를 해두면 쉽게 풀 수 있다.

어휘 primary goal 주목적 | inquiry 질문 | in a timely manner 시기적절하게

17 동명사

Profits increased after the acquisition, so the board of directors will consider ------- another factory.

(A) build (B) to build
(C) building (D) built

인수 후에 수익이 증가했으므로, 이사진에서 다른 공장을 지을 것을 고려할 것이다.

해설 동사 consider는 동명사를 목적어로 취하는 대표적인 동사이므로 정답은 (C)가 된다.

어휘 profit 수익 | board of directors 이사진

18 동사-수 / 시제 / 태

If the hotel reservation ------- sooner, it must have been possible to accommodate all participants at one hotel.

(A) had made (B) was made
(C) had been made (D) made

만약 호텔 예약이 좀 더 빨리 되었더라면, 한 호텔에 모든 참석자들을 수용할 수 있었음에 틀림없다.

해설 뒤에 must have p.p.가 들어가는 가정법 과거 완료 시제 구문으로 if절에는 had p.p.가 들어가야 하기 때문에 (A)와 (C)가 정답이 될 수 있는데, 뒤에 목적어가 없으므로, 정답은 수동태 형태인 (C)가 된다.

어휘 accommodate 수용하다

19 의문형용사

Once the renovation projects have been reviewed by the management, the accounting team will determine ------- proposal will be chosen.

(A) whatever **(B) which**
(C) why (D) who

보수공사 프로젝트가 경영진에 의해 검토되면, 회계 팀은 어떤 제안을 선택할지를 결정해야 할 것이다.

해설 빈칸은 타동사 determine의 목적어 자리로, 뒤에 주어와 동사가 들어가는 명사절로 명사 proposal을 수식하는 의문형용사가 들어가야 하므로 정답은 (B)가 된다. 「choose / decide / determine + which + 명사」 형태로 '어떤 ~를 선택 / 결정하다'로 암기해두면 쉽게 문제를 풀 수 있다.

어휘 management 경영진 | determine + which + **명사** 어떤 ~를 결정하다

20 어휘-동사

We at O'Neil Law Firm ------- to make our legal services available to as many clients as possible.

(A) encourage **(B) strive**
(C) disregard (D) recognize

우리 오닐 로펌은 최대한 많은 고객들에게 이용 가능한 법률 서비스를 제공하기 위해 고군분투하고 있습니다.

해설 '고군분투하다'의 의미로 strive to가 들어가야 하므로 정답은 (B)가 된다.

어휘 strive to 고군분투하다 | legal service 법률 서비스 | disregard 무시하다 | recognize 인정하다

1 어휘 - 부사

According to the new data, MG Automobile's latest vehicle in the European market will be only ------- successful.

(A) suspiciously (B) regrettably
(C) marginally (D) permanently

새 데이터에 따르면, MG 자동차의 유럽 시장에 선보인 최신 차량은 단지 미미하게 성공했다.

해설 부사 어휘 문제로 빈칸 앞의 only라는 제약을 나타내는 어휘가 나오고 크게 성공한 것이 아닌 '단지 미미하게 성공했다'는 의미가 적합하므로 정답은 (C)가 된다.
어휘 marginally 미미하게 | suspiciously 수상쩍게 | regrettably 유감스럽게도 | permanently 영구히

2 어휘 - 형용사

Savers Supplies provides a ------- selection of personalized partitions to organize office areas for its customers.

(A) diverse (B) prolonged
(C) several (D) various

세이버스 서플라이스는 고객들에게 사무실 공간을 정리할 다양한 종류의 맞춤화된 칸막이를 제공한다.

해설 '폭넓게 다양한'이라는 의미를 가진 a diverse range / selection of라는 정답은 (A)가 된다. (D)의 경우는 뒤에 복수 명사가 나와야 해서 오답이 된다.
어휘 a diverse selection of 폭넓게 다양한 | personalized 맞춤화의 | partition 칸막이 | prolong 연장하다 | various 수많은

3 어휘 - 형용사

Due to additional tourist attractions, the city of Milford drew much larger groups of visitors in ------- years.

(A) subsequent (B) next
(C) followed (D) late

추가적인 관광명소들 때문에, 밀퍼드 시는 연이은 해 동안에 더 많은 관광객들을 유치했다.

해설 '연이은 해에'라는 의미의 정답은 in subsequent years라는 (A)가 된다.
어휘 tourist attraction 관광명소 | draw 유치하다, 끌다 | in subsequent years 연이은 해에

4 어휘 - 형용사

The lawyers working at the Fitz and Gerald Law Firm are reminded that they cannot comment on any ------- cases.

(A) dependent (B) attentive
(C) practical **(D) pending**

피츠 앤 제럴드 로펌에서 근무하는 변호사들은 미해결된 소송에 관해 언급할 수 없다는 것을 알아야 한다.

해설 해석상 '미해결된, 임박한'이란 의미를 가진 pending이 정답이다.
어휘 comment on ~에 언급하다 | pending 미해결된, 임박한 | dependent ~에 의지하는 | attentive 배려하는, 신경을 쓰는

5 어휘 - 동사

Regardless of the size of purchases, Peer Store customers ------- the same high quality of service.

(A) satisfy **(B) deserve**
(C) complete (D) produce

구매한 물건의 크기에 상관없이, 피어 상점의 고객들은 똑같은 높은 품질의 서비스를 받을 자격이 된다.

해설 해석상 '~할 자격이 되다'라는 의미인 (B) deserve가 답이 된다. (A)의 경우 주어가 사람일 때 be p.p. 형태로 사용해야 한다.
어휘 regardless of ~에 상관없이 | deserve 받을 만하다

6 어휘 - 명사

Please keep in mind that all employees in the sales department should avoid ------- of customers' personal information.

(A) permission (B) confession
(C) allowance **(D) disclosure**

모든 영업부 직원들은 고객의 개인정보를 유출하지 않도록 명심해야 한다.

해설 해석상 '폭로'라는 의미가 적합하므로 정답은 (D)가 된다.

어휘 keep in mind 명심하다 | avoid 피하다 | disclosure 폭로 | permission 허가, 허락 | confession 자백 | allowance 용돈, 수당

7 어휘 - 형용사

All new technicians should complete a ------- safety training course before dispatching.

(A) various **(B) rigorous**
(C) prosperous (D) spacious

모든 신입 기술자들은 파견되기 전에 엄격한 안전 교육 코스를 이수해야 한다.

해설 (A)의 경우는 뒤에 복수 명사가 나와야 하므로 (A)를 고르지 않도록 주의하자. 해석상 '엄격한, 철저한'의 의미를 가진 (B)가 정답이다.

어휘 rigorous 철저한, 엄격한 | prosperous 번영한 | spacious 공간이 넓은

8 어휘 - 동사

Renowned novelist Anton Hales ------- the plot for his recent detective story, *Into The Mirror*, during his travel to London last winter.

(A) lectured **(B) conceived**
(C) resemble (D) motivated

유명한 소설가인 앤톤 헤일은 지난 겨울 런던을 여행하는 동안에 최근 그의 탐정문 〈거울 속으로〉의 줄거리를 생각해 냈다.

해설 '~를 생각해 내다, 구상해 내다'로 conceive the plot이 들어가야 하는 정답은 (B)가 된다.

어휘 renowned 유명한 | novelist 소설가 | conceive the plot 줄거리를 구상하다 | detective 탐정 | lecture 강연(하다) | resemble 닮다 | motivate 동기부여하다

9 어휘 - 명사

Starting next Monday, there will be a brief ------- in the electronic service in A Building for regular maintenance.

(A) statement (B) outline
(C) interruption (D) production

다음 주 월요일부터 시작하여, 정기적인 점검을 위해 A 건물의 전기 서비스가 잠시 중단될 것입니다.

해설 brief만 보고 (A)나 (B)를 고르지 않도록 조심하자. 해석상 '잠시 중단'이라는 의미가 적합하므로 정답은 (C)가 된다.

어휘 starting ~에 시작하여 | brief interruption 잠시 중단 | electronic 전자의 | regular maintenance 정기 점검 | statement 성명, 진술 | outline 개요

10 어휘 - 형용사

Mr. Lanner was finally chosen for a senior analyst position because his research was very -------.

(A) qualified (B) knowledgeable
(C) pleased **(D) impressive**

래너 씨는 그의 연구가 너무 인상적이라서 마침내 고위 분석가 직책에 선택되었다.

해설 해석상 (A)가 적합한 것 같지만, (A)의 경우는 사람 주어와 잘 쓰인다. 해석상 '인상적인'이라는 말이 적합하므로 (D)가 정답이다.

어휘 analyst 분석가 | qualified 자격을 갖춘 | knowledgeable 아는 것이 많은

11 어휘-명사

In order to promote the company's products and services, ------- from satisfied regular customers are very helpful.

(A) intervals **(B) testimonials**
(C) technology (D) solidity

회사 제품과 서비스를 홍보하기 위해서, 만족된 단골 고객들로부터 나온 상품평이 매우 도움이 된다.

해설 해석상 '상품평, 추천글, 후기'라는 의미가 적합하므로 정답은 (B)가 된다.
어휘 regular customer 단골 고객 | helpful 도움이 되는 | solidity 견고함

12 어휘-동사

Ms. Maseratti, the chief marketing officer, is recruiting a focus group to ------- consumers' needs.

(A) gauge (B) administer
(C) settle (D) comply

마케팅 총괄 담당자인 마세라티 씨는 고객의 요구를 알아내기 위해서 포커스 그룹을 모집한다.

해설 해석상 '알아내다, 측정하다'의 의미가 적합하므로 정답은 (A)가 된다.
어휘 gauge 측정하다 | administer 관리하다

13 어휘-동사

Even though the parts may be purchased online, the production of the printer has been -------.

(A) notified **(B) suspended**
(C) deducted (D) expired

부품이 온라인상에서 구매 가능함에도 불구하고, 프린터 생산은 중단되었다.

해설 해석상 '만료되다'라고 해서 (D)도 답이 될 수 있는 것 같지만, expire는 자동사로 수동태가 불가능하며 오답이다. production과 잘 어울리는 동사는 suspend이므로 정답은 (B)가 된다.
어휘 suspend 중단하다 | deduct 공제하다 | expire 만료하다

14 어휘-부사 문제

Based on a recent survey, consumers reacted ------- to the newly released software program, Whiz 3.2.

(A) unfavorably (B) probably
(C) potentially (D) unlikely

최근 조사를 바탕으로, 소비자들은 새롭게 출시된 소프트웨어 프로그램 위즈 3.2에 대해 부정적으로 반응했다.

해설 react와 궁합이 맞는 부사로 '안 좋게'라고 생각해서 (D)를 고를 수가 있는데, (D)는 '안 좋게'가 아니라 '~할 것 같지 않은'이라는 의미이므로 정답은 '부정적으로, 불리하게'라는 의미의 (A)가 답이 된다.
어휘 react to 반응하다 | unfavorably 불리하게 | potentially 잠재적으로 | unlikely ~할 것 같지 않은

15 어휘-명사

A retired executive who has a ------- of expertise across a wide range of industries decided to deliver a speech for our employees next week.

(A) wealth (B) height
(C) labor (D) fame

다양한 분야에 걸쳐 높은 전문성을 가진 은퇴한 임직원들은 다음 주에 우리 직원들에게 연설하기로 결정했다.

해설 해석상 '전문성이 높다'라는 의미가 적합하므로 '풍부함'이란 의미를 가진 (A)가 답이다.
어휘 retired 은퇴한 | wealth 부, 다량 | expertise 전문성 | a wide range of 폭넓게 다양한 | deliver a speech 연설하다 | height 높이 | labor 노동 | fame 명성

16 어휘-명사

The City Transportation Official announced yesterday that a ten-kilometer ------- between Park Avenue and Queens Road will be widened in September.

(A) journey **(B) stretch**
(C) duration (D) instance

시 교통국에서 어제 파크 가와 퀸스 로 사이에 10km 쭉 뻗은 도로가 9월에 확장될 것이라고 발표했다.

해설 해석상 '쭉 뻗은 거리 / 도로'를 나타내는 (B) stretch가 정답이다. (D)의 경우 거리(distance)라고 착각해서 고르지 않도록 조심하자.

어휘 stretch 쭉 뻗은 구간 | widen 확장하다 | journey 여행, 여정 | duration 지속 | instance 사례, 경우

17 어휘-전치사

The red dots ------- Watanabe's book are helpful for readers to understand the important information described in it.

(A) among **(B) throughout**
(C) during (D) toward

와타나베의 책 곳곳에 있는 빨간색 점들은 독자들이 책 안에 묘사된 중요한 정보를 이해하는 데 도움을 준다.

해설 해석상 '책 사이'라고 해서 (A)를 고르지 않도록 조심하자. (A)의 경우는 셋 이상의 사이라고 해서 뒤에 복수 명사가 와야 한다. 정답은 '곳곳에'라는 의미의 (B)가 된다.

어휘 dot 점 | throughout 곳곳에 | helpful 도움이 되는 | describe 묘사하다

18 어휘-형용사

Valentino Restaurant will remodel the interior and an ------- courtyard for an outdoor terrace.

(A) entertained (B) assessed
(C) enclosed (D) accidental

발렌티노 레스토랑은 야외 테라스를 위해 인테리어와 에워싸여진 마당을 리모델링할 것이다.

해설 해석상 '에워싸여진'이라는 의미의 (C)가 답이다. 흔히 enclosed는 '동봉된'의 의미로 쓰이지만 다른 의미도 있으니 반드시 암기하자.

어휘 enclosed 동봉된, 에워싸여진 | entertain 즐겁게 해주다 | assess 평가하다 | accidental 우연한

19 어휘-구동사

Despite harsh reviews from customers, SC Electronics' remote control is ------- with most television brands.

(A) reportable (B) reflective
(C) compatible (D) conclusive

고객들 사이에 혹평에도 불구하고, SC 전자의 리모컨은 대부분의 텔레비전 브랜드와 호환 가능하다.

해설 '~로 호환 가능한'의 의미로 be compatible with를 사용하므로 정답은 (C)가 된다.

어휘 harsh review 혹평 | compatible 호환 가능한 | reportable 보고할 수 있는 | reflective ~을 반영하는 | conclusive 결정적인, 확실한

20 어휘-명사

Barnum Co.'s increased profits resulted from the recent ------- to use environmentally friendly materials.

(A) restrictions (B) inquiries
(C) explanation **(D) initiatives**

바넘 사의 증가한 수익은 친환경 재료에 대한 최근 계획의 결과이다.

해설 해석상 '기획, 계획'의 의미로 정답은 (D)가 된다.

어휘 result from ~이 원인이다 | initiative 기획, 계획 | environmentally friendly 친환경적인 | restriction 제한, 규제

Questions 1-4 refer to the following e-mail.

To: Triton Jackson <tjackson@strategiescomn.org>
From: Amy Torres <atorres@torresmanufacturing.com>
Date: May 7
Subject: April 30 Workshop

Dear Mr. Jackson,

I would like to share our ❶ appreciation for the workshop Anita Huxley led at our headquarters on April 30. Several employees ❷ had expressed their concerns about the usefulness of the workshop. However, they participated actively throughout the day and even asked about whether there will be follow-up sessions. We requested that participants fill out our firm's evaluation form ❸ afterwards in order to better evaluate the effectiveness of the workshop. Mostly, the results are very positive, with 89 percent of participants reporting that their communication skills have become stronger. ❹ A few participants mentioned the workshop would have been more useful with practices included. Please contact me if you would like to talk about the workshop in more detail.

Best regards,

Amy Torres

1-4번은 다음 이메일에 관한 문제입니다.

수신: 트리톤 잭슨 〈tjackson@strategiescomn.org〉
발신: 에이미 토레스 〈atorres@torresmanufacturing.com〉
날짜: 5월 7일
제목: 4월 30일 워크숍

잭슨 씨에게

4월 30일에 아니타 헉슬리가 본사에서 진행했던 워크숍에 **감사**드리고 싶습니다. 몇몇 직원들은 워크숍의 유용성에 대해 우려를 **표명했었습니다**. 하지만, 그들은 종일 활동적으로 참여했으며, 심지어 그 이후의 세션에 대해서도 문의했습니다. 우리는 워크숍의 효율성에 대해 좀 더 평가하기 위해서 참석자들에게 **이후에** 평가서를 작성하도록 요청했습니다. 일반적으로, 그 결과는 매우 긍정적이었습니다. 89%의 참석자들이 커뮤니케이션 실력이 좋아졌다고 보고했습니다. **몇몇 참석자들은 좀 더 실습이 포함되었으면 더 유용했을 거라고 언급했습니다.** 만약 워크숍에 대해 좀 더 자세히 이야기하고 싶으시다면 저에게 연락을 주세요.

진심을 담아,

에이미 토레스

어휘 appreciation 감사 | headquarters 본사 | usefulness 유용성 | evaluate 평가하다

해설 ❶ 명사의 자리
소유격 our 다음에 나오는 빈칸이므로 명사가 들어가야 하기 때문에 정답은 (D) appreciation이 된다.

❷ 동사-수 / 시제 / 태
워크숍은 4월 30일로 글 쓴 날짜를(5월 7일) 기준으로 과거인데, 우려를 표명한 것은 워크숍 전이다. 즉, 과거 이전의 시제가 필요하므로 had p.p. 형태인 (D) had expressed가 정답이 된다.

❸ 어휘-부사
빈칸은 부사 자리로 해석상 '그 후에'라는 의미가 적합하므로 정답은 (A)가 된다.

❹ 문장 삽입
빈칸을 중심으로 앞 문장과 뒤 문장은 워크숍 평가에 관한 것이다. 좀 더 알고 싶으면 연락을 달라고 했으므로, 평가에 관한 이야기가 들어가는 (B)가 정답이 된다.

Questions 5-8 refer to the following letter.	5-8번은 다음 편지에 관한 문제입니다.
Morrison Bakery 12 Main Street Broadway, New York 31034	몬리슨 베이커리 12 메인 가 브로드웨이, 뉴욕 31034
Dear Customers,	고객님들께,
Over the last two years, we have offered our baked goods, including cakes, pies, cookies, and brownies, at low prices. We regret to inform you that soaring costs for ingredients, such as yeast and sugar, have compelled us to increase our prices by 7 percent, ❺ effective July 1. We have made all possible efforts not to increase our prices so far. ❻ However, we never want to compromise on the quality of our baked goods. Using the best ingredients available on the market will enable us to offer delicious desserts that meet your expectations. ❼ We think you will find that our products are still of great value. We appreciate your ❽ support and look forward to serving you the best quality products.	지난 2년간, 케이크, 파이, 쿠키, 브라우니를 포함한 제과 종류를 저렴한 가격에 제공해왔습니다. 유감스럽게도 이스트(효모균), 설탕과 같은 재료 가격의 급격한 상승으로 인해, 불가피하게 7% 가격 인상을 7월 1일부터 **시행할 수밖에** 없습니다. 여태까지 가격 인상을 하지 않으려고 온갖 노력을 다했습니다. **하지만**, 저희 제과 제품의 품질을 결코 양보하고 싶지는 않습니다. 시장에서 최고의 엄선된 재료를 사용함으로써 고객님들의 기대를 충족시킬 수 있는 맛있는 디저트를 제공할 것입니다. **아마 여전히 최고의 제품을 보시게 될 것입니다. 성원**에 감사드리며 최고의 제품을 제공할 수 있기를 학수고대합니다.
Sincerely,	진심을 담아,
Tony Corelli, Owner	토니 코렐리, 주인

어휘 baked good 제과 | ingredient 재료 | yeast 효모균 | compel 강요하다 | effective + 날짜 효력이 발생하는 | compromise 타협하다 | meet expectations 기대를 충족시키다 | look forward to ~을 학수고대하다

해설 ❺ 어휘 - 형용사

날짜 앞에 들어가는 '~에 시작하여, 시행하여'라는 의미의 표현으로, beginning, starting, as of, effective가 있다. 그러므로 정답은 (D)가 된다.

❻ 어휘 - 부사

앞 문장과 뒤 문장을 연결하는 접속부사 문제로, '온갖 노력을 다했지만 어쩔 수 없이 가격을 올려야 한다'는 내용이 적합하므로 역접을 나타내는 (C) However가 정답이 된다.

❼ 문장 삽입

전반적인 흐름이 가격을 올리고 싶지 않지만, 올려야 하는 상황임을 보여준다. 최고 품질의 제품을 제공한다는 내용에 일맥상통한 (A)가 정답이 된다.

❽ 명사의 자리

해석상 '성원, 지지'의 의미가 들어가는 명사 자리로 (B), (D)가 들어갈 수 있는데, 이때 support는 불가산 명사이므로 a / an, s / es를 붙이지 않는다. 그러므로 정답은 (B)가 된다.

Questions 9-12 refer to the following excerpt from a manual. This manual contains procedures for quality control at Tuckman Inc. Our up-to-date manufacturing system relies on ⑨ precise quality control. Only by keeping an accurate monitoring system ⑩ are we able to minimize unnecessary costs and meet customer satisfaction. To achieve this goal, we must avoid defects. When items are delivered in good condition, we can reduce costs for returns and exchanges. ⑪ However, this might not be possible if unexpected defects occur. Therefore, all the processes need to be correctly ⑫ implemented.	9-12번은 다음 매뉴얼 발췌문에 관한 문제입니다. 이 매뉴얼은 터크만 사의 품질관리에 관한 절차를 포함하고 있습니다. 우리 최신 제조 시스템은 **정확한** 품질 관리에 의존하고 있습니다. 정확한 관리 시스템을 유지함으로써 불필요한 비용을 최소화하고 고객 만족을 충족시킬 수 **있습니다.** 이러한 목표를 달성하기 위해서, 하자는 피해야 합니다. 물건이 좋은 상태로 배송될 때, 반품이나 교환에 관한 비용을 줄일 수 있습니다. **하지만 만약 예상치 못한 하자가 발생한다면 이것은 불가능 할 수도 있습니다.** 그러므로 모든 절차는 올바르게 **시행될** 필요가 있습니다.

어휘 quality control 품질관리 | up-to-date 최신의 | rely on ~에 의지 / 의존하다 | precise 정확한 | accurate 정확한 | minimize 최소화하다 | unnecessary 불필요한 | customer satisfaction 고객만족 | defect 하자, 결함 | implement 실행 / 시행하다

해설 **⑨ 어휘-형용사**

빈칸은 형용사 어휘 문제로, 해석상 '정확한'이란 의미가 들어가야 하므로 정답은 (A)가 된다. 영어를 잘하는 사람은 같은 어휘를 반복해서 쓰기보다는 동의어를 사용한다. 빈칸 뒤의 문장에 accurate이라는 단어가 나오므로 그 단어와 유사한 (A)로 답을 고를 수도 있다.

⑩ 도치

보통 정답을 (A)로 고르는 경우가 종종 있는데, by -ing는 주어로 나올 수가 없다. 이 문장은 Only by keeping ~ 부분을 강조하기 위해 앞으로 나왔기 때문에 도치 구문으로 '주어 + 동사'가 아닌 '동사 + 주어'가 와야 한다. 원래는 We are able to minimize ~ only by keeping ~. 나오는 문장을 도치시킨 문장이다.

⑪ 문장 삽입

전체 문장의 논리가 앞에서는 정확하게 해야 함을 강조하고 뒤에서는 다시 한번 절차의 중요성에 대해 강조한다. 그러기 위해선 역접의 상황이 나와서 다시 한번 강조로 마무리 짓는 것이 필요하므로 however가 들어가는 정답은 (C)가 된다.

⑫ 어휘-동사

수동태는(be p.p.) 주어와의 관계를 따진다. 주어가 plan, policy, process, system, procedure 등일 때 잘 어울리는 동사는 implement이므로 정답은 (A)가 된다.

Questions 13-16 refer to the following letter.

1 April
Ricky Howe
3519 Patrick Rd.
Toronto, ON 4877

The Jessop Community Association(JCA) is pleased to ⓭announce that its annual Spring Festival will be held at Central Park on April 30 from 3 P.M. to 9 P.M. This event will feature a variety of exciting activities and a tasty barbecue dinner that will be offered at 6 P.M. Visitors must pay a $10 entrance fee. The proceeds from the event will ⓮primarily go towards a park renovation project. This project will include hiring a construction company to remodel the park, and the remaining funds will be used for a city cleaning campaign.

This special event ⓯promises to be a lot of fun. ⓰We hope you will be able to join us.

Regards,

Justin Charles
Director, The Jessop Community Association(JCA)

13 – 16번은 다음 편지에 관한 문제입니다.

4월 1일
라키 하우
3519 패트릭 로
토론토, 온타리오 4877

제솝 공동체 협회(JCA)는 매년 개최되는 봄 축제가 4월 30일 중앙 공원에서 오후 3시부터 9시까지 열릴 것을 **공지하게** 되어 기쁩니다. 이 이벤트에는 여러 가지 흥미로운 활동과 오후 6시에 제공될 바비큐 저녁이 특별히 포함될 것입니다. 방문객들은 입장료 10달러를 내셔야 합니다. 이벤트에서 나온 수익금은 **주로** 공원 보수공사 작업에 쓰일 것입니다. 이 프로젝트는 공원 리모델링 작업을 해줄 건설회사를 고용하는 것을 포함할 것이며, 나머지 돈은 도시 정화 캠페인에 사용될 것입니다.

이 특별한 이벤트는 많은 즐거움을 **줄 것입니다. 우리는 여러분들의 많은 참여 부탁드립니다.**

진심을 담아,

저트틴 카를로스
책임자, 제솝 공동체 협회(JCA)

어휘 tasty 맛있는 | entrance fee 입장료 | proceeds 수익금 | primarily 주로 | remaining 남아있는

해설 ⓭ 어휘 – 동사

빈칸은 동사 어휘 문제로 해석상 '공지하다'의 의미가 적합하므로 (A) announce가 정답이다.

⓮ 어휘 – 부사

빈칸은 부사 어휘 문제로 (A)와 (C)가 답이 될 수 있는데, 뒤에 the remaining funds라고 해서 '남은 금액으로는 다른 곳에 쓰인다'고 하니 다 쓰는 게 아닌 '주로'라는 의미의 (C)가 정답이 된다.

⓯ 동사의 자리

빈칸은 동사 자리로, 아직 개최되지 않아 미래의 일을 나타내는 데 보기에 미래가 없을 때는 현재가 미래를 대신할 수도 있다. 사실을 이야기하는 현재로 (B)가 정답이 된다.

⓰ 문장 삽입

마지막 문장의 문장 삽입으로 '이러한 행사가 있으니 오라'고 하는 (C)가 정답이 된다.

Questions 1-3 refer to the following advertisement.

LUNCHEON AT RYERSON MUSEUM

❶We, Ryerson Museum, invite residents of Harrington to attend a luncheon on May 8. The museum houses a large collection of artwork from the 18th and 19th centuries as well as a wide range of paintings produced by innovative artists here in Harrington. ❸One of the special features is the private sculpture collection donated by the late ❷❸Arthur Fleury, who used to live in this elegant building with his family before it was renovated in 1938.

Advance registration is needed. Tickets for the luncheon are priced at $50, and the reservation can be made by calling 555-2598. ❶All proceeds from this event will go toward the upcoming renovation of the west wing of the museum. After the luncheon, ❸attendees can enjoy live music by the famous local band The Gravey. Moreover, ❸most exhibitions will be open to every attendee for viewing, including Mr. Fleury's special private collection. ❸The event is scheduled to begin at 12 P.M. and last approximately one hour. There will be plenty of time for attendees to enjoy the luncheon and view the artwork.

1-3은 다음 광고에 관한 문제입니다.

라이어슨 박물관에서 오찬

라이어슨 박물관에서 해링턴 주민들을 5월 8일 오찬에 초대합니다. 박물관은 18세기와 19세기의 여러 가지 예술 작품을 소장할 뿐만 아니라 해링턴의 혁신적인 예술가들이 만든 다양한 그림을 소장하고 있습니다. **특별한 특징 중에 하나는 1938년에 보수공사 전에 가족과 함께 이 우아한 건물에서 살았던 고인인 아서 플레리가 기부한 조각품입니다.**

사전 등록이 필요합니다. 오찬 가격은 $50이며, 예약은 555-2598을 통해서 할 수 있습니다. **이 행사의 모든 수익금은 박물관의 서쪽 별관을 보수 공사하는 데 쓰일 것입니다.** 오찬 이후에 **참석자들은 지역의 유명한 밴드인 그레이비가 연주하는 라이브 음악을 즐기실 수 있습니다.** 게다가, **대부분의 전시회는 모든 참석자들에게 공개되며, 플레리 씨의 특별 개인 소장품도 포함됩니다. 오찬은 12시에 시작해서 약 한 시간 진행될 예정입니다.** 참석자들이 오찬과 전시를 즐길 수 있는 충분한 시간이 될 것입니다.

어휘 luncheon 오찬 | artwork 예술 작품 | a wide range of 폭넓은, 다양한 | sculpture 조각품 | donate 기부하다 | used to ~하곤 했다 | elegant 우아한 | advance registration 사전 등록 | proceeds 수익금 | fundraiser 모금 행사 | sculptor 조각가 | an array of 다수의 | under construction 공사 중인 | residence 거주지 | contemporary 현대의 | entertainment 오락, 여흥

1 주제 / 목적

What is the advertisement about?
(A) A museum opening
(B) A local fundraiser
(C) A speech by a sculptor
(D) An artwork workshop

무엇에 관한 광고인가?
박물관 개관
지역 모금 행사
조각가의 연설
예술 워크숍

해설 지문 전반적으로 박물관이 나온다고 해서 (A)를 고르지 않도록 하자. 첫 번째 줄에 해링턴 주민들을 초대하고(We, Ryerson Museum, invite residents of Harrington to attend a luncheon on May 8.), 두 번째 단락에서 오찬 수익금으로 박물관 보수공사에 쓴다고 했기 때문에(All proceeds from this event will go toward the upcoming renovation of the west wing of the museum.), 모금 행사인 정답은 (B)가 된다.

2 세부정보 - 언급

What is indicated about Ryerson Museum?
(A) It provides an array of art classes to local people.
(B) It is currently under construction.
(C) It was once used as a residence.
(D) It mainly displays contemporary art.

라이어슨 박물관에 관해 맞는 것은?
지역 주민들에게 여러 가지 예술 수업을 제공한다.
현재 공사 중이다.
한때 거주지로 사용되었다.
현대 예술작품을 주로 전시한다.

해설 첫 번째 단락의 마지막 부분에서 플레리 씨가 한때 이 건물에서 살았던 적이 있다고 했으므로(Arthur Fleury, who used to live in this elegant building with his family before it was renovated in 1938.), 정답은 (C)가 된다.

3 일치 / 불일치

What is NOT scheduled to happen at the May 8 event?
(A) A speech will be held one hour before the luncheon.
(B) A meal will finish around 1 P.M.
(C) A sculpture collection will be on display.
(D) Guests can enjoy the entertainment.

5월 8일 행사에서 일어날 일이 아닌 것은?
오찬 전에 한 시간 연설이 있을 예정이다.
식사는 오후 1시에 끝날 것이다.
조각 컬렉션이 전시될 것이다.
손님들은 엔터테인먼트를 즐길 수 있다.

해설 오찬이 12시에 시작해서 한 시간 정도 진행된다고 했으므로(The event is scheduled to begin at 12 P.M. and last approximately one hour.) (B)는 나와 있고, 두 번째 단락에서 플레리 씨의 개인 소장품이 전시된다고 했고(most exhibitions will be open to every attendee for viewing, including Mr. Fleury's special private collection.), 첫 번째 단락에서 플레리 씨가 조각품을 기증했다고 나와 있으므로(One of the special features is the private sculpture collection donated by the late Arthur Fleury, who used to live in this elegant building with his family before it was renovated in 1938.) (C)도 맞다. live music을 entertainment로 패러프레이징한(attendees can enjoy live music by the famous local band The Gravey.) (D)도 나와 있으므로 정답은 (A)가 된다.

Questions 4-6 refer to the following online chat discussion.

Ana Cruz [2:13 P.M.]
Today, we need to talk about the annual skills workshop, which will be held on April 10.

Dylan Reynolds [2:14 P.M.]
Janet, ❹ you were working at the Carlton branch last April during this event, weren't you?

Janet Lee [2:17 P.M.]
Right, I was. ❹ I'm so excited to see how to handle the professional development event here at the Dayton branch.

dylan reynolds [2:18 P.M.]
Please remember that you'd better register in advance. ❺ The main conference can only accommodate 80 people.

Ana Cruz [2:19 P.M.]
Oh, okay. That's a good reminder. Now, let's move on to the next item on the agenda. Kate Erickson has finally selected the topic for the small group session, right?

Janet Lee [2:19 P.M.]
Yes. I got her e-mail. The title of the topic is "How to Save Your Time by Using E-mail Tools". It will be added to the schedule now.

Ana Cruz [2:21 P.M.]
Elizabeth Wilson, who is scheduled to speak in the morning session, called me this morning. She can't make it in the morning, but she can come to the afternoon session. I think I need to change her time rather than cancel her presentation. What do you think?

Dylan Reynolds [2:22 P.M.]
Hmm. Why don't we just have Grace McLean switch times with her? If so, the problem will be solved.

Janet Lee [2:23 P.M.]
That's a good idea. That will work. I know Grace will be present in both the morning and afternoon sessions.

Ana Cruz [2:24 P.M.]
❻ Then we're all in agreement. I'll ask Grace about changing times.

4-6번은 다음 온라인 채팅에 관한 문제입니다.

아나 크루즈 [2:13 P.M.]
오늘, 4월 10일에 있을 연례 스킬 워크숍에 관해 이야기할 필요가 있어요.

딜런 레이놀즈 [2:14 P.M.]
자넷, **이 행사가 열린 작년 4월에 칼튼 지점에 일하고 있었죠**, 그렇죠?

자넷 리 [2:17 P.M.]
네, 맞아요. **저는 데이턴 지점에서 어떻게 이러한 전문적인 기술 개발 행사를 다룰지에 대해서 기대하고 있어요.**

딜런 레이놀즈 [2:18 P.M.]
미리 등록하시는 것을 잊지 마세요. **주요 회의는 80명밖에 수용할 수 없답니다.**

아나 크루즈 [2:19 P.M.]
아, 알겠습니다. 잘 기억할게요. 이제 다음 안건으로 넘어가겠습니다. 케이트 에릭슨이 마침내 소규모 세션의 주제를 선택했습니다. 맞죠?

자넷 리 [2:19 P.M.]
네. 그의 이메일을 받았습니다. 제목은 "어떻게 하면 이메일 도구를 사용함으로 시간을 절약하는가"입니다. 지금 스케줄에 추가될 것입니다.

아나 크루즈 [2:21 P.M.]
아침 세션에 말하기로 예정되었던 엘리자베스 윌슨이 오늘 아침에 저에게 연락했습니다. 그녀는 아침에는 힘들고, 오후 세션에만 가능하다고 했습니다. 제가 생각하기에 그녀의 프레젠테이션을 취소하기보다는 시간을 바꾸는 게 좋아 보여요. 어떻게 생각하세요?

딜런 레이놀즈 [2:22 P.M.]
음, 그레이스 매클레인과 바꾸는 것은 어떤가요? 그러면 문제가 해결될 것 같은데요.

자넷 리 [2:23 P.M.]
좋은 생각이에요. 그러면 되겠네요. 그렇게 되면 그레이스가 아침과 오후 세션 둘 다 참석할 거예요.

아나 크루즈 [2:24 P.M.]
그럼 우리 다 동의된 거네요. 그레이스에게 시간을 바꿀 수 있는지에 대해 요청해 볼게요.

어휘 branch 지점 | in advance 미리 | accommodate 수용하다 | reminder 상기시키는 것 | agenda 안건 | make it 해내다, 성공하다 | switch 바꾸다 | present 참석하다 | around the world 전 세계에 | seating capacity 좌석 수용능력 | trade 바꾸다

4 암시 / 추론

What can be inferred about Ms. Lee?
(A) She has not received the updated schedule.
(B) She has invited Ms. McLean to an event.
(C) She asked for advice on the workshop.
(D) She has worked at this branch for less than a year.

리 씨에 대해 유추할 수 있는 것은?
그녀는 바뀐 스케줄을 받지 못했다.
그녀는 매클레인 씨를 이벤트에 초대했다.
그녀는 워크숍에 관한 충고를 요청했다.
그녀는 이 지점에서 1년이 채 안 되게 근무했다.

해설 연례행사가 4월 10일에 있을 예정이고, 작년 행사 때 리 씨는 칼톤 지점에서 있었다(you were working at the Carlton branch last April during this event). 이번 데이턴 지점에서의 행사를 기대한다고 했으므로(I'm so excited to see how to handle the professional development event here at the Dayton branch.) 아직 그 연례행사 이전이다. 이 지점에서 1년 미만으로 근무했다는 (D)가 정답이 된다.

5 세부정보 - 언급

What is suggested about the workshop?
(A) It will be open to people around the world.
(B) There is a deadline to be filled.
(C) It has a limited seating capacity.
(D) It will be hosted at a convention center.

워크숍에 관해 맞는 것은?
전 세계 사람들에게 열려있다.
맞춰야 할 마감이 있다.
제한된 좌석 수용능력이 있다.
컨벤션 센터에서 개최될 예정이다.

해설 2:18 P.M.에서 '주요 회의는 80명밖에 수용할 수 없다'고 했으므로(The main conference can only accommodate 80 people.), 패러프레이징하면 '제한된 좌석 수용 능력'이라는 정답은 (C)가 된다.

6 화자 의도 파악

At 2:24 P. M., what does Ms. Cruz mean when she writes, "Then we're all in agreement"?
(A) She thinks all problems have been solved.
(B) She will hire another speaker.
(C) She supports trading two speaking times.
(D) She confirms the cancellation of Wilson's workshop.

2:24 P.M.에서 크루즈 씨가 쓴 "그럼 우리 다 동의된 거네요"는 무엇을 의미하는가?
그녀가 생각하기에 모든 문제가 해결되었다.
그녀는 또 다른 연사를 고용할 것이다.
그녀는 두 개의 연설 시간을 바꾸는 데 동의한다.
윌슨의 워크숍 취소를 확인한다.

해설 2:22 P.M.에서 모든 문제가 해결될 것 같다고 해서 (A)를 하지 않도록 조심하자. 문제가 해결된 것이 아니라 시간을 바꾸는 것에 동의를 한 것이고, 뒤 문장에서 그레이스에게 의견을 요청해 본다고 했으므로(Then we're all in agreement. I'll ask Grace about changing times.) 문제가 해결되었는지는 알 수 없다.

Questions 7-10 refer to the following article.

Boden Clothing to open Asian stores

October 8 - ❶At a today's press conference, Gale Banks, CEO of Boden Clothing, announced his plan to expand the thriving local clothing business into international markets by opening flagship retail stores in Hong Kong, Korea, and Japan. Construction for a new manufacturing plant has already begun. ❸The distribution warehouses in China and Indonesia are scheduled to begin operations in early March, just one month before the opening of the flagship stores. –[1]–.

7-10번은 다음 기사에 관한 문제입니다.

보덴 의류가 아시아 가게를 오픈할 예정

10월 8일 – **오늘 기자회견에서, 보덴 의류의 사장인 게일 뱅크스는 국내 성장하는 의류 사업을 홍콩, 한국, 일본에 대표 매장을 오픈함으로써 해외 시장으로 확장할 계획을 발표했습니다.** 새 제조공장에 대한 공사가 벌써 시작되었습니다. **중국과 인도네시아의 유통 창고는 대표 매장이 오픈하기 한 달 전인 3월 초에 운영될 예정입니다.** –[1]–.

PART 6

For Boden Clothing, this year was a successful year, and ❾ Mr. Banks attended the grand opening of the company's largest retail location in Melbourne. "Thanks to the employees' hard work and dedication, we've seen unprecedented growth over the last five years", he told journalists at the press conference today. –[2]–. ❿ "Our company aims to establish itself as one of the world's leading clothing companies by expanding operations into foreign markets for the first time." –[3]–.

Financial analysts predict that today's announcement will make Boden Clothing's share price increase. This will undoubtedly bring more attention to the company, and its sales will continue to soar over the coming year. –[4]–.

보덴 의류에 있어서 올해는 성공적인 한 해였고, **뱅크스 씨는 멜버른에 있는 가장 큰 매장의 개업에 참석했습니다.** "직원들의 헌신과 노력에 감사합니다. 우리 회사는 지난 5년간 전례가 없는 성장을 해왔습니다"라고 오늘 기자 회견에서 기자들에게 말했습니다. –[2]–. **"우리 회사의 목표는 처음으로 해외 시장에 운영을 확장함으로써 세계적인 일류 의류 회사 중에 하나가 되는 것입니다."** –[3]–.

재정분석가들은 오늘의 발표가 보덴 의류의 주가를 오르게 만들 것이라고 예상합니다. 이것은 의심의 여지 없이 더 많은 관심을 불러일으킬 것이며, 향후에 판매가 계속해서 증가하게 될 것입니다. –[4]–.

어휘 press conference 기자회견 | thriving 번성하는, 성대한 | flagship store 대표 매장 | manufacturing plant 공장 | distribution warehouse 유통 창고 | grand opening 개회식 | dedication 헌신 | unprecedented 전례가 없는 | journalist 기자 | aim to ~를 목표로 하고 있다 | foreign market 해외시장 | undoubtedly 의심의 여지없이 | bring attention 관심을 끌다 | soar 급등하다 | considerably 상당히 | previously 이전에 | focus on 집중하다 | domestic sales 국내 판매 | world-famous 세계적으로 유명한 | foreign company 외국회사 | rival 경쟁의

7 세부정보 - 특정 사실

What is indicated about Boden Clothing?
(A) Its international sales have increased considerably.
(B) It was founded in Hong Kong.
(C) It has previously focused on domestic sales.
(D) It considers opening a factory in Melbourne.

보덴 의류에 대해서 맞는 것은?
해외 판매가 상당히 증가했다.
홍콩에서 창립되었다.
이전에 국내 판매에만 집중했다.
멜버른에 공장 오픈을 고려하고 있다.

해설 (A)를 고르지 않도록 조심하자. 아직 해외 시장에 진출하기 전이고 판매가 증가할 것이라고 예상하는 미래 표현을 썼는데 증가했다고 하면 시제가 불일치하므로 오답이다. 해외 시장으로 처음 확장한다는 말이 언급되어 있으므로(At a today's press conference, Gale Banks, CEO of Boden Clothing, announced his plan to expand the thriving local clothing business into international markets by opening flagship retail stores in Hong Kong, Korea and Japan.), 국내 시장에만 집중했음을 알 수 있는 정답은 (C)가 된다.

8 세부정보 - 언급

What is suggested about Boden Clothing's Asian stores?
(A) They are scheduled to open for business next April.
(B) They have recently been visited by Gale Banks.
(C) They will be the largest location of the company.
(D) They will only sell world-famous clothing brands.

보덴 의류의 아시아 가게들에 대해 맞는 것은?
내년 4월에 오픈할 예정이다.
게일 뱅크스가 최근 방문했다.
회사에서 가장 큰 곳이 될 것이다.
세계적으로 유명한 옷 브랜드만 판매할 것이다.

해설 첫 번째 단락, 제일 마지막에 3월에 유통 창고가 오픈하는데, 그 시기는 아시아 가게들이 오픈하기 한 달 전이므로(The distribution warehouses in China and Indonesia are scheduled to begin operations in early March, just one month before the opening of the flagship stores.), 4월에 가게를 오픈함을 유추할 수 있으므로 정답은 (A)가 된다.

9 세부정보 - 특정 사실

According to the article, what has Boden Clothing accomplished this year?
(A) It launched a new line of clothing.
(B) It opened its new fashion retail store.
(C) It made a business contract with a foreign company.
(D) It achieved more sales than its rival companies.

기사에 따르면, 보덴 의류가 올해 성취한 것은 무엇인가?
새로운 의류를 출시했다.
새 패션 소매상을 오픈했다.
외국 회사와 계약을 맺었다.
경쟁 회사보다 더 많은 판매를 얻었다.

해설 두 번째 단락에서 게일 뱅크스가 멜버른의 개업에 참석했다고 했으므로(Mr. Banks attended the grand opening of the company's largest retail location in Melbourne.) 새 가게를 오픈했음을 알 수 있다. 정답은 (B)가 된다.

10 문장 삽입

In which of the positions marked [1], [2], [3], and [4] does the following sentence best belong?

"If Boden Clothing continues to expand so quickly, Mr. Banks' goal may become a reality."

(A) [1]
(B) [2]
(C) [3]
(D) [4]

[1], [2], [3] 그리고 [4]로 표시된 곳 중에, 아래 문장이 들어가기에 가장 적절한 곳은?

"만약 보덴 의류가 빠르게 확장을 계속한다면, 뱅크스 씨의 목표가 현실이 될 것입니다."

해설 뱅크스 씨의 목표가 현실이 된다고 하면 그 목표가 무엇인지를 알아야 하는데, [3]번 앞에 goal과 유사한 단어인 aim to가 들어가는 표현을 사용해서 일류 의류회사 중에 하나가 되고 싶다고 언급했으므로("Our company aims to establish itself as one of the world's leading clothing companies by expanding operations into foreign markets for the first time.") 정답은 (C)가 된다.

Questions 11-15 refer to the following e-mails.

To: Julia Soto <jsoto@jcreviews.net>
From: Oliver Ventura <oventura@kokomagazine.com>
Subject: More work
Date: April 30

Dear Ms. Soto

After receiving your review of *The Guideline for Successful Home-Cooking*, I was so impressed with your evaluation of the book. So, I have requested a personal interview with the author for future books.

We always try to find which books will attract more interest among our readers even though we publish all kinds of reviews. ⑫ I think most *Koko Magazine*'s readers are likely to read about nutrition and health.

In the June issue, we will feature a story about healthy lifestyles. Norman Bright, the well-known nutritionist, has coincidentally written a book called *The Importance of Nutrition*. So, I would like to highlight this book alongside.

⑬ We would also like to cover a review of Jackson Barham's *Successful Gardening*, which is a practical handbook for gardening enthusiasts.

⑪ As a keen reader of books, we were hoping that you would have time to review both books by May 15 for our June edition. Please respond to confirm as soon as possible whether you would be available. If you would consider writing one rather than both, please let me know your preference for which one you would be able to review by the above deadline.

Regards,

Oliver Ventura, Editor-In-Chief
Koko Magazine

11-15번은 다음 이메일들에 관한 문제입니다.

수신: 줄리아 소토 〈jsoto@jcreviews.net〉
발신: 올리버 벤투라 〈oventura@kokomagazine.com〉
제목: 추가 작업
날짜: 4월 30일

소토 씨에게

〈성공적인 가정 요리를 위한 지침서〉의 비평을 받고 나서, 당신의 책 평가에 너무 감동하였습니다. 그래서 앞으로의 책에 관한 작가와의 개인 인터뷰를 요청했습니다.

우리는 여러 종류의 비평을 출간하지만, 우리 독자들 사이에서 더 많은 관심을 불러일으킬 수 있는 책이 어떤 책인지를 찾는 데 노력하고 있습니다. **제가 생각하기에 〈코코 잡지〉의 독자들이 영양과 건강에 관해 읽는 것으로 알고 있습니다.**

6월호에서, 건강한 생활 양식에 관한 이야기를 특집으로 실을 예정입니다. 유명한 영양학자인 노먼 브라이트는 우연하게도 〈영양의 중요성〉이라는 책을 저술했습니다. 그래서 그 이야기와 함께 강조하고 싶습니다.

원예를 좋아하시는 분들을 위한 실용서인 **잭슨 바럼의 〈성공적인 정원 만들기〉 비평 또한 포함할 것입니다.**

애독가로서, 6월호를 위해 5월 15일까지 두 권의 책을 비평해주셨으면 좋겠습니다. 시간이 되시는지 가능한 한 빨리 확인 답변 부탁드립니다. 만약 두 권보다 한 권을 고려하고 계신다면, 마감 날짜까지 비평하실 수 있는 책이 어떤 것인지를 말씀해주시기 바랍니다.

안부를 전하며,

올리버 벤투라, 편집장
〈코코 잡지〉

To: Oliver Ventura <oventura@kokomagazine.com>
From: Julia Soto <jsoto@jcreviews.net>
Subject: RE: More work
⑮ Date: May 1

Dear Mr. Oliver Ventura

Based on my previous reviews on a variety of books, I would enjoy reviewing the books you mentioned. ⑬ However, regarding the second book you listed, I have doubts. Actually, I have already reviewed the author's previous books. Honestly, I am simply not a fan of his writing style. Therefore, I might not be able to evaluate his book.

I am still interested in reviewing two books. ⑭ If possible, I would like to propose a different book for my second submission: *From Garden to Table* by Rowan Charles.

And lastly, regarding the May 15 deadline, due to the tight schedule, would it be possible to extend this by a week? As far as I know, ⑮ the magazine will hit shelves on the last day of the month. So I would really appreciate it if you could extend my deadline to May 22.

Regards

Julia Soto, JC Reviews

수신: 올리버 벤투라 〈oventura@kokomagazine.com〉
발신: 줄리아 소토 〈jsoto@jcreviews.net〉
제목: RE: 추가 작업
날짜: 5월 1일

올리버 벤투라 씨에게

여러 가지 책에 대한 제 이전의 비평을 고려해 볼 때 언급하신 책들을 즐겁게 비평했습니다. **하지만, 말씀하신 두 번째 책에 관해서는 그렇지 않습니다. 사실, 그 작가의 이전 책들을 벌써 비평한 적이 있습니다. 솔직히 말씀드리면, 그 작가의 문체 스타일이 제가 좋아하는 것이 아닙니다.** 그래서 비평은 어려울 것 같습니다.

책 두 권을 비평하는 것이 관심이 있긴 합니다. **가능하면, 로완 카블로스의 제목이 〈정원에서 테이블까지〉라는 다른 책을 제안하고 싶습니다.**

마지막으로, 5월 15일 마감에 관해서는, 빡빡한 일정 때문에 일주일 정도 연장이 가능할까요? 제가 아는 한, **잡지가 이달 말일에 출간되는 것으로 알고 있습니다.** 5월 22일로 마감을 연장해주시면 감사하겠습니다.

안부를 전하며,

줄리아 소토, JC 리뷰

어휘 impressed 감동받은 | evaluation 평가 | author 작가 | be likely to ~할 것 같은 | nutrition 영양 | issue (잡지의) ~호 | well-known 잘 알려진 | nutritionist 영양사 | coincidentally 우연하게도 | highlight 강조하다 | alongside ~와 함께 | cover 다루다, 포함하다 | enthusiast 열렬한 지지자 | keen 열정적인 | preference for ~에 대한 선호 | regarding ~에 관하여 | simply 단순히 | evaluate 평가하다 | propose 제안하다 | submission 출품작, 제출 | tight schedule 빡빡한 일정 | hit shelves 발매되다 | promote 홍보하다 | focus on ~에 중점을 두다 | audience 독자, 청중 | dominate 지배하다 | award 상 | critique 비평하다 | critically acclaimed 비평가들의 극찬을 받은 | revise 수정하다

11 주제 / 목적

Why did Mr. Ventura write the first e-mail?
(A) To propose that Ms. Soto write new book reviews
(B) To promote Ms. Soto's new novel
(C) To give Ms. Soto a magazine
(D) To ask Ms. Soto for a job interview

벤투라 씨가 첫 이메일을 쓴 목적은?
새로운 글 작업을 소토 씨에게 제안하기 위해서
소토 씨의 새로 나온 소설을 홍보하기 위해서
소토 씨에게 잡지를 주기 위해서
소토 씨에게 면접을 요청하기 위해서

해설 글의 목적은 주로 초반에 있으나, 이 글의 목적은 제일 마지막 단락에서 비평해달라고 하고 있으므로(As a keen reader of books, we were hoping that you would have time to review both books by May 15 for our June edition.) 정답은 (A)가 된다.

12 일치 / 불일치

What is true about *Koko Magazine*?
(A) It mainly focuses on home improvement.
(B) Much of its audience seems to be influenced by nutrition and health.
(C) It has won several awards for its book review.
(D) One of its well-read articles was about history.

〈코코 잡지〉에 관해 맞는 것은?
주로 집수리하기에 중점을 두고 있다.
독자들의 대부분은 영양과 건강에 영향을 받는 것처럼 보인다.
비평에 관해 몇 개의 상을 받았다.
많이 읽힌 기사들 중의 하나는 역사에 관한 것이었다.

해설 첫 번째 이메일, 두 번째 단락에서 독자들이 영양과 건강에 관해 읽는 경향이 있다고 나와 있으므로(I think most *Koko Magazine's* readers are likely to read about nutrition and health.) 정답은 (B)가 된다.

13 이중지문 - 연계

What can be inferred about Jackson Barham?
(A) He has worked on a writing project with Ms. Soto.
(B) His reviews were covered in *Koko Magazine*.
(C) His previous work was critiqued by Ms. Soto.
(D) His new book has been critically acclaimed.

잭슨 바럼에 관해 맞는 것은?
소토 씨와 함께 글쓰기 작업을 해 왔다.
그의 비평은 〈코코 잡지〉에 실렸다.
소토 씨는 그녀의 이전 작업을 비평했다.
그의 신간 책은 찬사를 받았다.

해설 두 번째 이메일, 첫 번째 단락에서 소토 씨가 두 번째 책, 즉 잭슨 바럼의 책을 비평한 적이 있지만 자기가 좋아하는 스타일이 아니라고 했으므로(However, regarding the second book you listed, I have doubts. Actually, I have already reviewed the author's previous books. Honestly, I am simply not a fan of his writing style.) 정답은 (C)가 된다.

14 세부정보 - 권고 / 요구 / 요청

What does Ms. Soto suggest Mr. Ventura do?
(A) Ask for a personal interview with Rowan Charles
(B) Allow her to review a different book
(C) Revise her latest reviews
(D) Arrange a meeting with Norman Bright

소토 씨가 벤투라 씨에게 제안하는 것은 무엇인가?
로완 카를로스와 개인적인 인터뷰 요청한다
다른 책을 비평하도록 허용한다
최근 비평을 수정한다
노먼 브라이트와 미팅을 정한다

해설 두 번째 이메일, 두 번째 단락에서 다른 책을 비평하면 안 되겠냐고 했으므로(If possible, I would like to propose a different book for my second submission: *From Garden to Table* by Rowan Charles.) 정답은 (B)가 된다.

15 세부정보 - 예정

When is the June issue of the magazine likely to be published?
(A) May 19
(B) May 22
(C) May 30
(D) June 1

잡지의 6월호는 언제 출간될 예정인가?
5월 19일
5월 22일
5월 30일
6월 1일

해설 두 번째 이메일, 세 번째 단락에서 이달 말 일에 출간된다고 나와 있으며(the magazine will hit shelves on the last day of the month), 이메일을 쓴 날짜가 5월 1일이므로(Date: May 1) 정답은 5월 30일인 (C)가 정답이다.

Questions 16-20 refer to the following notice, letter, and Web site.

Renew your TBA membership!

As a reminder, it is time for you to renew your membership with TBA Broadcasting. As a membership holder, you are aware that we have provided incredible benefits that come with membership fees.

- ⑯ A three-month free trial subscription to our magazine about the broadcast
- Weekly e-mail updates about upcoming events and exclusive offers for our members
- Provide an opportunity to join "First Listens" to new programs

Recently, we have added new membership categories listed below. You can renew at the same level or choose to change to another.

16-20번은 다음 공지사항, 편지, 웹사이트에 관한 문제입니다.

TBA 멤버십을 갱신하세요!

TBA 방송의 귀하의 멤버십을 갱신할 때입니다. 멤버십 소지자로서 멤버십 비와 함께 훌륭한 혜택들이 있다는 것을 알아주세요.

- **방송에 관한 3개월 무료 잡지 구독권**
- 회원들을 위한 곧 있을 행사와 독점적으로 제공하는 혜택에 관한 매주 이메일 업데이트
- 신규 프로그램의 "첫 청취"에 가입할 기회 제공

최근에, 아래와 같은 멤버십 카테고리를 추가했습니다. 똑같은 레벨 혹은 다른 것으로 변경해서 갱신하실 수 있습니다.

PART 7

Annual Membership Category	
Blue Level-$55	**Crown Level-$150**
All the membership benefits listed above	All the benefits listed above for up to five guests
⑰ Red Level-$85	**Diamond Level-$250**
Blue Level benefits plus two guest passes to any TBA event	Crown Level benefits plus four guest passes and ⑯ a 15% discount on our online products

연간 멤버십 카테고리	
블루 레벨 – 55달러	크라운 레벨 – 150달러
위에 언급된 모든 멤버십 혜택	위에 언급된 모든 멤버십 혜택과 다섯 명 게스트까지 제공
레드 레벨 – 85달러	다이아몬드 레벨 – 250달러
블루 레벨 혜택과 더불어 TBA 행사에 2명의 게스트 패스 제공	크라운 레벨 혜택과 더불어 4명의 게스트 패스와 15% 온라인 제품 할인

Ms. Caroline Clark
365 Ridgeway Road
Cincinnati, OH 45201

Dear Ms. Clark,

We really appreciate that you decided to renew your TBA membership. As a ⑱ network, one of the biggest networks in the country, we are not able to continue providing high-quality programming to our listeners without supporters like yourself. ⑳ Also, you will find your new membership card and guest passes enclosed with this letter.

Moreover, in order for members to provide feedback easily, you can find the comment section for each of our programs on our Web site at www.feedbacktbabroadcasting.org. We have also created a survey form to evaluate our membership program. We would greatly appreciate if you would take five minutes to fill it out.

Best Wishes,

James Clear, TBA Broadcasting

캐롤라인 클라크
365 리즈웨이 로
신시내티, 오하이오 45201

클라크 씨에게

TBA 멤버십을 갱신을 결정해주셔서 정말로 감사드립니다. 우리나라에서 가장 큰 **방송국** 중에 하나로서 귀하의 성원이 없었더라면 시청자들을 위해서 고품질 프로그램을 계속해서 제공할 수 없었을 것입니다. **또한, 이 편지와 함께 동봉된 새 멤버십 카드와 게스트 패스를 보실 수 있을 것입니다.**

게다가, 회원들이 피드백을 쉽게 제공하실 수 있도록 하기 위해서, 웹사이트 www.feedbacktbabroadcasting.org에 가시면 프로그램마다 피드백을 남기실 수 있는 공간을 보실 수 있습니다. 저희는 또한 멤버십 프로그램을 평가할 수 있도록 설문조사 양식을 만들었습니다. 만약 5분 정도의 시간을 내어 작성해주시면 정말 감사하겠습니다.

행운을 빌며,

제임스 클리어, TBA 방송

TBA Membership Survey Form

Name: Caroline Clark

Do you think the membership fee is reasonable?

> ⑰ I think $85 is a little high But, the main reason why I decided to choose that membership is to support the broadcasting you provide rather receive the benefits.

What is the most important benefit of membership?

> ⑲ Broadcasting magazine is quite interesting, and it contains useful information. So I really enjoy reading it.

Do you have any other comments?

> I recently renewed my membership, but ⑳ I only got free passes. I would really appreciate it if you check one more time and send me the item that I am still missing.

TBA 멤버십 설문조사 양식

이름: 캐롤라인 클라크

회비가 합리적이라고 생각하시나요?

> **제 생각에는 85달러는 저에게 조금 비싸다고 생각합니다.** 하지만, 제가 선택한 이유는 혜택보다는 제공해 주는 방송을 지원할 수 있어서입니다.

멤버십의 가장 중요한 혜택은 무엇입니까?

> **방송에 관한 잡지가 꽤 흥미롭고 유용한 정보가 담겨 있습니다.** 그래서 정말 잘 읽고 있습니다.

다른 하실 말씀이 있으신가요?

> 멤버십을 최근에 갱신했지만, **무료 패스만 받았습니다. 만약 제가 아직 못 받은 물건이 있다면 한 번 더 확인하고 보내주시면 감사하겠습니다.**

어휘 renew 갱신하다 | reminder 상기시키는 것 | be aware that 알다 | incredible 믿기 힘든 | trial 재판, 시험 | subscription 정기구독 | exclusive offer 독점 제공 | benefit 혜택 | supporter 지지자 | enclosed 동봉된 | reasonable 합리적인 | Web-based 온라인의 | structure 구조 | community 공동체 | station 역, 방송국 | reasonably priced 합리적으로 가격이 매겨진 | complimentary 무료의 | educational 교육적인 | voucher 쿠폰

16 세부정보 – 특정 사실

What is indicated about TBA Broadcasting?
(A) It has a Web-based store.
(B) It sends out monthly e-mails.
(C) It hosts four events annually.
(D) Its membership can be canceled at any time.

TBA 방송으로 맞는 것은?
온라인 상점이 있다.
매달마다 이메일을 보낸다.
매년 4개의 이벤트를 개최한다.
언제든지 멤버십을 취소할 수 있다.

해설 첫 번째 지문, 다이아몬드 레벨에 보면 온라인 상품 구매 시 15% 할인이 나오므로(a 15% discount on our online products) 온라인에서 상품을 구매할 수 있는 상점이 있다는 이야기이다. 정답은 (A)가 된다.

17 삼중지문 – 연계

What is Ms. Clark's membership level?
(A) Blue Level
(B) Red Level
(C) Crown Level
(D) Diamond Level

클라크 씨의 멤버십 레벨은 무엇인가?
블루 레벨
레드 레벨
크라운 레벨
다이아몬드 레벨

해설 세 번째 지문에서 $85이라는 말이 나오므로(I think $85 is a little high.) 정답은 첫 번째 지문에서 언급한 레드 레벨(Red Level–$85) (B)가 답이 된다.

18 동의어

In the letter, the word "network" in paragraph 1, line 1, is closest in meaning to
(A) structure
(B) community
(C) station
(D) connection

편지에서 첫 번째 단락 첫 번째 줄에, network와 가장 가까운 의미는?
구조
공동체
방송국
접속

해설 '가장 큰 network로서 우리는'이라고 하는데 이 글을 쓴 사람은 TBA 방송, 즉 TBA 방송국이므로 정답은 방송국을 나타내는 (C)가 정답이 된다.

19 삼중지문 – 연계

What does Ms. Clark suggest about the TBA Broadcasting membership?
(A) It could upgrade another membership level.
(B) Its fee is reasonably priced.
(C) Its complimentary publication is educational.
(D) It may remove the comment section from its Web site.

클라크 씨가 TBA 방송 멤버십에 관해서 언급한 것으로 맞는 것은?
또 다른 멤버십 레벨로 업그레이드 할 수 있다.
가격이 합리적이다.
무료 출간물이 교육적이다.
웹사이트에서 피드백 섹션을 제거할지도 모른다.

해설 세 번째 지문에서 잡지에 굉장히 유용한 정보가 담겨있다고 했고(Broadcasting magazine is quite interesting, and it contains useful information.), 제일 첫 번째 지문에서 매달 무료 잡지 구독권을 준다고 했으므로(A three-month free trial subscription to our magazine about the broadcast) 정답은 (C)가 된다.

20 삼중지문 - 연계

What item did Ms. Clark ask to be sent?
(A) A free guest pass
(B) A membership card
(C) A discount voucher
(D) A program calendar

클라크 씨는 어떤 물건을 받기를 요청하는가?
무료 게스트 패스
멤버십 카드
할인 쿠폰
프로그램 달력

해설 두 번째 지문, 첫 번째 단락에 게스트 패스와 멤버십 카드를 동봉한다고 했는데(Also, you will find your new membership card and guest passes enclosed with this letter.), 세 번째 지문에서 게스트 패스만 받았다고 했다(I only got free passes. I would really appreciate it if you check one more time and send me the item that I am still missing.). 멤버십 카드를 받지 못해서 요청했으므로 정답은 (B)가 된다.

MEMO

MEMO

1타 강사의 속성 과외!

토익 950+ 벼락치기

10일 완성

LC+RC